Including Students
with Severe Disabilities

Including Students with Severe Disabilities

Craig H. Kennedy

Vanderbilt University

Eva M. Horn

University of Kansas

Boston • New York • San Francisco
Mexico City • Montreal • Toronto • London • Madrid • Paris
Hong Kong • Tokyo • Cape Town • Sydney

Executive Editor: *Virginia Lanigan*
Series Editorial Assistant: *Robert Champagne*
Executive Marketing Manager: *Amy Cronin Jordan*
Senior Production Editor: *Annette Pagliaro*
Editorial Production Service: *Walsh & Associates, Inc.*
Composition Buyer: *Linda Cox*
Manufacturing Buyer: *Andrew Turso*
Cover Administrator: *Joel Gendron*
Electronic Composition: *Publishers' Design and Production Services, Inc.*

For related titles and support materials, visit our online catalog at www.ablongman.com.

Between the time Website information is gathered and then published, it is not unusual for some sites to have closed. Also, the transcription of URLs can result in unintended typographical errors. The publisher would appreciate notification where these occur so that they may be corrected in subsequent editions.

Library of Congress Cataloging-in-Publication Data

Including students with severe disabilities / [edited by] Craig H. Kennedy, Eva M. Horn.
    p. cm.
  Includes bibliographical references and index.
  ISBN 0-205-34394-5
    1. Children with disabilities—Education. 2. Inclusive education. I. Kennedy, Craig H.
II. Horn, Eva M.

  LC4015.I45   2003
  371.9′046–dc21

                                           2003056335

Printed in the United States of America

10 9 8 7 6 5 4 3 2 1 07 06 05 04 03

CONTENTS

10 Directing Paraprofessional Work   185

Michael F. Giangreco and Mary Beth Doyle

P A R T   T W O   Inclusive Education at Different Ages   205

11 Preschool   207

Eva Horn, Barbara Thompson, Susan Palmer, Ronda Jenson, and Vicki Turbiville

12 Elementary School   222

Christine Salisbury and Toni Strieker

PREFACE

The emergence of inclusion as the predominant approach for educating students with severe disabilities has required the rethinking of a number of fundamental issues. The most immediate change has been the location where students receive their education. However, this change also has required a reconsideration of who is involved in a student's education, how they work together, who has responsibility for specific learning outcomes, and how these various individuals will coordinate their efforts. It has also placed family members and the student with severe disabilities at the center of educational planning. In addition, the issue of how to align the curriculum of students with severe disabilities so that it is consistent with their peers without disabilities has emerged.

The result has been a significant evolution in educational practices over the past decade in special education, general education, and related services. Normalization has evolved into inclusion. A functionally oriented curriculum has evolved into accessing the general education curriculum. Behavior management has evolved into positive behavior supports. The special education teacher as primary support provider has evolved into interdisciplinary collaboration. Related services have evolved from pullout therapy to embedded, functional instruction. Social development has evolved into a curricular domain of equal importance to academic development.

Because of the changes in how we conceptualize and practice the education of students with severe disabilities, there has been a growing need to change how we prepare the next generation of professionals to work in inclusive settings. This book has grown out of our own classroom experiences involving students with severe disabilities and how best to meet their needs. Those classroom experiences include directly working with students in educational settings, as well as personnel preparation in institutions of higher education. As university instructors, we realized that a new approach to textbook design was required to meet the needs of preparing people to work in inclusive settings. We believed that what was needed was a textbook that provides the reader with expertise in critical content areas and demonstrates the implementation of this knowledge into actual inclusive settings. The result is this book.

The book has two general sections: Part One, essential issues in inclusive education, and Part Two, inclusive education at different ages. The first part is composed of a series of chapters by distinguished researchers that focus on particular issues key to the effective inclusion of students with severe disabilities. The second part is composed of chapters by equally distinguished researchers who discuss the "look" of quality inclusive programs in different educational contexts and how they function to support the learning and development of students with severe disabilities.

Chapter 1, by Craig H. Kennedy, provides an overview of the characteristics of students with severe disabilities. This chapter emphasizes curricular goals and support requirements that maximize the effectiveness of inclusive education.

The foundation of inclusive educational practices is collaboration among a range of people. Chapter 2, written by Eva Horn, Barbara Thompson, and Chelie Nelson, provides the reader with a definition of collaboration, various models for making this process work, and a discussion of the many benefits that result from coordinating support efforts among a range of individuals.

Chapter 3 discusses what has emerged as a central issue for effective inclusion: what to teach students with severe disabilities in general education settings. Diane L. Ryndak and Felix Billingsley discuss how to align the curriculum of students with severe disabilities with that of their peers without disabilities to facilitate access to the general education curriculum.

The next chapter, written by James W. Halle, Janis Chadsey, Suzanne Lee, and Adelle Renzaglia, looks at instructional procedures. These authors review the essential components of using systematic instruction to facilitate skill acquisition. They review specific procedures for teaching, as well as how to make decisions about whether particular teaching practices are effective.

One of the most important changes in special education over the last decade has been the emergence of family-centered practices. In Chapter 5 Amy Childre discusses how to embed the needs of a student and his or her family into educational practices and how educational plans change as a result of this shift in perspective.

Next, Craig H. Kennedy discusses social development. In Chapter 6 he reviews what social relationships are and how to use peer support strategies to facilitate the development and maintenance of friendships among students with and without disabilities.

In Chapter 7, Ann N. Garfinkle and Ann P. Kaiser discuss an essential part of all human interactions: communication. The authors define what communication is, the different forms it can take, how to teach new communication skills effectively, and how to embed opportunities for communication throughout the school day.

Chapter 8, written by Robert E. O'Neill, focuses on positive behavior supports. This approach to understanding challenging behavior relies on identifying the underlying causes of the behaviors of concern and how a comprehensive approach to support plan development can reduce a student's problem behavior and improve positive interactions.

Another support issue that often needs to be addressed for students with severe disabilities are sensory and motor needs. Sally Roberts, in Chapter 9, discusses how to assess these needs in a range of students and how to adjust instructional strategies to appropriately address a student's learning needs.

The final chapter in the first section is by Michael F. Giangreco and Mary Beth Doyle. These authors discuss a critical but often overlooked topic: paraprofessionals. They review the roles that paraprofessionals can serve in inclusive settings and how special education teachers can effectively manage staffing issues, thus maximizing the benefit of this important resource for students with severe disabilities.

The focus of the book changes in Chapters 11 through 15. The last five chapters are designed to synthesize the particular curriculum and instruction issues discussed in previous chapters within the context of different school settings. Our goal is to provide future educators with a sense of how inclusion differs from one age level to the next and how educational practices need to be adjusted across the age range.

The second section begins with a discussion of inclusive practices at the preschool level (3- to 5-year-olds) by Eva Horn, Barbara Thompson, Susan Palmer, Ronda Jenson, and Vicki Turbiville. In Chapter 12, Christine Salisbury and Toni Strieker discuss inclusive practices at the elementary school level, focusing on grades K through 4. Douglas Fisher, Nancy Frey, and Craig H. Kennedy continue this discussion in Chapter 13 with a description of inclusive practices at the middle school level (grades 5 through 8).

Inclusion at the secondary level and beyond is the focus of Chapters 14 and 15. Michael Wehmeyer and Wayne Sailor provide a review of educational issues at the high school level (Chapter 14), while Mary Morningstar and Dana L. Lattin discuss critical issues in transition to community living and employment (Chapter 15).

Acknowledgments

On a more personal note, many people assisted us in the development of this book. We are deeply indebted to the very able editorial staff at Allyn and Bacon, particularly Virginia Lanigan (Executive Editor) and Robert Champagne (Editorial Assistant). We would also like to thank our assistants Brenda McSurley and Melissa Rogers — for their help in processing manuscripts and coordinating correspondence. Lisa Cushing and Nitasha Clark provided important feedback on an earlier version of the book. We deeply appreciate the effort and feedback generated by the Allyn and Bacon reviewers: Rhoda Cummings, University of Nevada, Reno; Joseph W. George, Columbus State University; Donna Lehr, Boston University; Craig Miner, Southern Illinois University-Carbondale; Rosanne K. Silberman, Hunter College of CUNY; and Teresa A. Taber, Purdue University. Finally, we would like to thank our spouses, Tiina Hyvönen and Steven Warren, who provided us with advice and support throughout the process of creating this book.

Craig H. Kennedy
Nashville, TN

Eva Horn
Lawrence, KS

PART ONE

Essential Issues in Inclusive Education

1 Students with Severe Disabilities

CRAIG H. KENNEDY
Vanderbilt University

Cali

Cali is twelve years old and attends middle school in a suburban city located anywhere in North America. Her school days are unremarkable for someone her age, comprising a routine that changes little from day to day or week to week.

Her parents have to remind her several times to get up from bed when the alarm goes off in the morning. She waits for the school bus down the street with her friends (except for school holidays and the occasional snow storm!). She arrives at school at 8 A.M. and goes to homeroom, where she and her class take attendance and say the Pledge of Allegiance. From there she is off to science, then math, followed by social studies. During these classes the usual routines are followed, including taking a seat, handing in homework, reviewing the day's class assignment, working in small groups to complete the assignment, and taking notes about homework, all done while taking every opportunity to talk with a friend about the day's events. This is followed by lunch in the cafeteria with the same friends she sees most days and hangs out with after school. The afternoon class routine is similar to the morning, then the final bell rings and she goes to her after-school activity (science club or cheerleading, depending on the day). After her school day ends, one of her parents or a friend's parent picks up the carpool group and takes each student home.

What is remarkable about Cali is that she lives a typical life at school, at home, and in the community and *has a severe disability. She has friends, homework, life crises, and wardrobe worries just like anyone else her age. The thing that makes her different is that she might not experience these joys of everyday life, if not for the support of other people. Because she has a severe disability, she needs help from other people to do a lot of daily tasks that other people take for granted. Without that support she would face tremendous difficulties in living a typical life. With these supports she lives a life like everyone else and experiences the pleasures and problems that we all face.*

This book is about how to help students with severe disabilities, like Cali, lead typical lives. We will discuss different strategies for helping students with severe disabilities learn and socialize, as well as discuss how these support strategies change with a student's age. However, before we talk more about educational support strategies and inclusion, we need to discuss what makes students with severe disabilities so much like other students, but also unique.

The first chapter in this book focuses on the characteristics and support needs of students with severe disabilities. In it, you will be introduced to the causes of severe disabilities and how these disabilities are manifested. In addition, this chapter will explore the implications of a student's disabilities in terms of effective educational practices. After reading this chapter you will be able to:

- Describe basic characteristics associated with having a severe disability
- Be familiar with the causes and prevalence of severe disabilities
- Understand the interrelationship between abilities and needs
- Name specific assumptions that make educators and students more successful in inclusive settings
- Identify educational supports providing the greatest educational benefit to students with severe disabilities

Teachers encounter a diverse range of students in today's public schools. That diversity stems from a range of sources. Some sources of diversity should be very familiar to the reader, such as family income, parental education level, and ethnicity. Other sources are less apparent, such as culture-specific social expectations or the challenges of becoming bilingual. In other instances, diversity might come from differences in how children develop, such as language delays or precocious reading abilities.

In any particular school or classroom an educator is likely to encounter a fascinating but challenging mixture of students. One of the major trends in American education—which is a reflection of America itself—is the increasing diversity of students in our schools. Within a typical classroom you could encounter any or all of the following students:

- *Paul,* who lives in an impoverished neighborhood, whose parents are multigenerational Euro-Americans, who speaks English as his only language, and who has a severe disability.
- *Ke'Shawna,* who lives in an affluent neighborhood, whose parents are multigenerational African Americans, who speaks English as her only language, and who is typically developing.
- *Jukka,* who lives in a middle-class neighborhood, whose parents are Scandinavian and temporarily living in America, who speaks English and Finnish fluently, and who is typically developing.

- *Cam,* who lives in a working-class neighborhood, whose parents recently immigrated from Vietnam, who is struggling to acquire English as a second language, and who is mathematically precocious.
- *Manuel,* who lives in a middle-class neighborhood, whose parents are second-generation Hispanic-Americans, who speaks English as his only language, and who has a learning disability.

Each of these students brings his or her own unique strengths and needs to the classroom. Each student can contribute to the classroom in a slightly different way and, relatedly, requires a slightly different approach to educational support. Within a classroom, these students will require their teachers to (a) design instructional plans so that each student can make meaningful contact with the curriculum, (b) work with other educators to maximize each student's potential, and (c) understand how a student's family life influences his or her school performance. This increasing diversity in schools requires rethinking how we effectively educate students—and not just some students, but *all* students, including those with severe disabilities (Ryndak & Kennedy, 2000).

This student diversity includes challenges that the educational system has not always embraced and accepted as its responsibility. In the case of students with severe disabilities, most public schools did not provide educational services prior to the mid-1970s. School systems simply did not consider these students worthy of an education. Instead, families and community members were often responsible for providing educational services to students with severe disabilities in non-public-school settings (Dybwad, 1990; Trent, 1994). Those responsibilities shifted to school systems in the 1970s with passage of the Education for All Handicapped Children Act (Public Law 94-142). With the passage of this law, states were required to provide a *free and appropriate public education to all students,* including students who had previously not been served, such as students with severe disabilities (see Smith, 2003, for an in-depth discussion of P.L. 94-142).

P.L. 94-142 was a watershed event for American educational institutions. It promoted consideration of such fundamental issues as:

- What are the goals of an education?
- Who is educable?
- What does "educable" mean?
- How can educational equity and excellence simultaneously be pursued?
- When we say "all," just how encompassing is that word?
- What do our answers to these questions reveal about ourselves, our values, and beliefs?

The changes in educational practices resulting from P.L. 94-142 are still reverberating today.

One of the effects of implementing P.L. 94-142 (and its updated version, the *Individuals with Disabilities Education Act* [IDEA]) has been an emphasis on what is referred to as *"inclusion."* IDEA (1997) explicitly states that students with severe disabilities should be educated in general education settings with their peers without disabilities. This focus on inclusion means that students with severe disabilities are educated in the same settings as other students, learn similar course content, and pursue similar educational goals. This inclusive focus has required substantive changes in how we perceive students with severe disabilities. For example, educators have needed to focus on similarities among a diverse student body, how each student can access the same curricular materials, and how to accommodate individual learning needs. In addition, it has changed what we expect of students with severe disabilities, peers without disabilities, and ourselves as educators. Indeed, this book is a compendium of our current and evolving wisdom about how to effectively include students with severe disabilities into public schools.

As the changes that have taken place during the last several decades continue to unfold, our conceptualization of how students with severe disabilities are educated continues to mature. Viewed within a contemporary perspective, *students with severe disabilities are simply part of the overall diversity of society and schools.* To be able to include students with and without disabilities in general education classrooms is part of the overarching challenge to American society to understand and accept its own diversity. Unfortunately, students with severe disabilities and their families have had to fight for the right to be included in public schools.

Characteristics of Students with Severe Disabilities

So, who are students with severe disabilities? Well, in most respects they are just like everyone else. In fact, students with severe disabilities are as heterogeneous a group of people as can be imagined. They come from every part of society, every ethnic and racial group, all socioeconomic levels, and all faiths. This heterogeneity is one of the most striking characteristics of these students. There are no class, race, political, or religious characteristics that are more, or less, likely to be associated with a person having a severe disability. "They" are just like "us."

However, there are some aspects of having a severe disability that makes this group of students unique. The term *severe disability* refers to a range of characteristics (Sontag & Haring, 1996). As a term, it has emerged from an ongoing dialogue among professionals, family members, and self-advocates (i.e., people with disabilities) about what terminology is most respectful but also descriptive. As with any label for a group of people, it has changed over time and is likely to continue to be refined.

When a student is said to have a severe disability it means several things. First, it means that he or she has a moderate, severe, or profound *intellectual disability* (in the past this was referred to as *mental retardation*). Traditionally, an intellectual disability has been defined as an interaction between intelligence and adaptive behavior (Grossman, 1983). Intelligence quotients are derived from standardized tests such as the *Stanford-Binet* or *Wechsler Intelligence Scale for Children–Revised*. Such measures attempt to estimate the intellectual abilities of a person. Adaptive behavior, such as daily living skills and interpersonal communication, are estimated using tests such as the *Vineland Adaptive Behavior Scales*. A person is generally considered to have a severe disability if both intelligence and adaptive behavior are below average (see Reschly, 1999).

A second aspect of having a severe disability is that it is present *throughout a person's life*. Unlike breaking a leg or catching the flu, having a severe disability is not a temporary condition. This does not mean that certain aspects of the disability cannot be minimized, or even eliminated. What it does mean is that a person's needs are lifelong and do not go away simply because he or she turns a certain age (e.g., when a student graduates from high school).

A third aspect of severe disabilities is the importance of *support from other people*. The concept of *support* is an important one and permeates the content of this textbook. In a real sense, we all require support from other people throughout each day to be successful. For example, think of how many times in a day you receive assistance from another person in order to accomplish some goal. Students with severe disabilities are capable of many of the same things other students can do, but students with severe disabilities require help from others to enhance their capabilities. This need for support is present for all students, but is amplified for students with a severe disability.

Because of the importance of supports, in the 1990s the American Association on Mental Retardation revised how an intellectual disability is defined. Instead of focusing on a person's degree of intellectual disability, the revised definition focuses on the support needs of an individual (Luckasson & Reeve, 2001). Current terminology focuses on how much assistance a person requires from others to lead as normal a life as possible (see Table 1.1). In contemporary special education, people typically talk about a student's support

TABLE 1.1   The Current AAID (formerly AAMR) Definition and Examples of Support Intensity

Level	Description
Intermittent	Support provided on an "as needed" basis. Characterized as episodic in nature. Person does not always need support, or short-term supports are needed during a life transition. Intermittent supports can be of low or high intensity.
Limited	Support provided consistently over time. Characterized as time limited, but not intermittent. May require fewer resources than more intensive support levels.
Extensive	Support provided regularly in at least some environments. Support is ongoing and not time-limited.
Pervasive	Supports provided at a high level of intensity throughout the day, across environments, and not time limited. Typically requires greater resources than extensive support.

Source: Adapted from R. Luckasson et al. (1992). *Mental retardation: Definition, classification, and systems of support.* Washington, DC: American Association on Mental Retardation.

needs, rather than the extent of their disability. This helps focus people's attention on what supports need to be provided to help a student participate in the mainstream of school activities, rather than focus on what they cannot do (see Ferguson & Baumgart, 1991).

Causes of Severe Disabilities

There is no exact estimate of how many people have a severe disability. Studies suggest that between 0.5 percent and 2 percent of the general population has a severe disability (Leonard & Wen, 2002; Roeleveld, Zielhuis, & Gabreels, 1997). However, more precise estimates have been elusive. A major reason for the variability in prevalence rates is the *social construction* of disability (Molloy & Vasil, 2002). Social construction means how a particular society or group of people view a particular idea or concept, with the understanding that different people interpret the world in slightly different ways. Therefore, what constitutes a severe disability to one person may not to another person. Although it is comforting to think that we know exactly what a severe disability is, the truth is that we do not and there are no precise scientific criteria. Hence, all that research can provide in terms of prevalence estimates is a fairly broad estimate.

What is well established about the prevalence of severe disabilities is that they are not part of the typical intellectual ability ("IQ") distribution (referred to as a "normal distribution"). We have been taught by psychologists that all human intelligence falls along a bell-shaped distribution (see Figure 1.1). Most people are average (i.e., 100 IQ points) and the proportion of people who deviate from the average symmetrically declines the farther away you go from the average score. However, when you factor people with severe disabilities into an IQ distribution there is an increase in the number of people falling into the left tail-end of the distribution (Zigler, 1967). Technically, this is referred to as a *bimodal distribution*.

The reason for this bimodal distribution is not entirely understood, but it strongly suggests a biological basis for many instances of severe disabilities. Indeed, as biomedical research has progressed in recent years, the biological basis of many disabilities has been identified (referred to as the *etiology* of the disability). However, even though there is an increasing ability to explain the causes of a disability by reference to biology, the support needs of students with severe disabilities remain the same. So, even though we might be able to explain the genetics and neurobiology of Down syndrome, students with Down syndrome still have educational support needs that require societal intervention. And, as we noted earlier in this chapter, how society responds to those support needs has a pervasive effect on a person's quality of life (Vehmas, 1999). The field of severe disabilities is a fascinating one, in part because of the interplay between the biological causes of disabilities and how society interprets those disabilities and decides to respond (e.g., in terms of educational supports).

Because there is a clear biomedical basis for many severe disabilities and different etiologies express different learning characteristics (referred to as a *behavioral phenotype*) (Hodapp & Dykens, 2001), it is worth reviewing some of the more common causes of severe disabilities. For a more in-depth look into the biomedical causes of disabilities, the

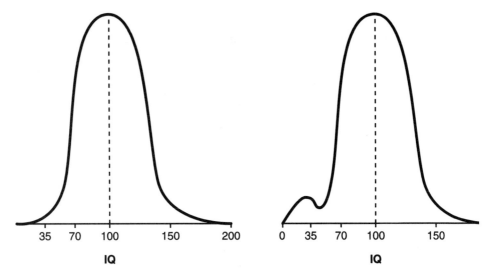

FIGURE 1.1   The panel on the left shows a traditional IQ range that is normally distributed. The panel on the right shows what the actual IQ distribution in society is when you factor in all people. This bimodal distribution suggests that there is a biological basis to the causes of many severe disabilities.

Source: Adapted from Zigler (1967).

reader may want to read Batshaw (2002), from which much of the following material is drawn.

Fragile X syndrome.   The most common identifiable genetic cause of severe disabilities is fragile X syndrome. Prevalence estimates suggest that 1 in 4,000 children have fragile X syndrome. However, not all children who have this syndrome have a severe disability. Because fragile X syndrome is associated with the X chromosome, it is twice as common in males as females. Physical characteristics of this syndrome include an elongated face, large ears, and a prominent jaw. The behavioral phenotype for students with fragile X syndrome include stronger verbal abilities relative to math skills, avoidance of new social situations, increased anxiousness, and increased rates of problem behaviors (Mazzocco, 2000).

Autism.   This syndrome is a neurobiologically based disability with a complex genetic basis that has yet to be adequately characterized. Identification rates for autism are increasing on an annual basis, but the actual prevalence of this syndrome seems to be relatively stable (Lord & Volkmar, 2002). Current estimates suggest a prevalence rate of between 1.2 and 6.3 per 1,000 children, depending on how broad the definition of autism was in a particular study. There are no overt physical characteristics of autism; children with this disability are indistinguishable from students without autism. Behavioral characteristics of students with autism include decreased social interaction, delayed language/communication, and increases in stereotypical and problem behaviors (Dawson et al., 2002).

Down syndrome.   Down syndrome is caused by an alteration in chromosome 21, which results in a well-characterized set of developmental differences. The prevalence of Down syndrome increases with maternal age: the syndrome appears in 1 in 2,000 children of mothers giving birth in their 20s, and 1 in 20 children of mothers in their 40s. Physical features in Down syndrome include small stature, increased weight, decreased muscle tone, characteristic facial features (e.g., rounded face, slanting eyes, and smaller ears), hearing impairments, and an increased risk of congenital heart disease. The behavioral phenotype includes delays in nonverbal cognitive development, problems with speech and language, increased social interests, and fewer problem behaviors than other severe disabilities (Chapman & Hesketh, 2000).

Fetal alcohol syndrome.   The incidence of fetal alcohol syndrome (FAS) is 1.3 per 1,000 children. Unlike most other causes of severe disabilities discussed in this section, FAS is preventable. This syndrome, as the name implies, is the result of maternal alcohol consumption, primarily in the first trimester of pregnancy. Physically, students with FAS have widely spaced eyes and a flattened mid-face. Behaviorally, students with FAS are more likely to be hyperactive, engage in behavior problems, and be impulsive (Steinhausen et al., 2002).

Deaf-blindness.   Students who are deaf-blind have functional impairments in both hearing and vision. The extent of these sensory impairments includes students who are completely deaf and blind, to students who, with correction (e.g., hearing aids or binocular glasses), have functional visual and auditory contact with their environment. Approximately 1 in 5,000 children are deaf-blind. There are a range of etiologies that cause deaf-blindness, and the age at onset ranges from birth to adulthood. Although this type of disability spans the continuum of intellectual functioning (e.g., Helen Keller was deaf-blind), most students who are deaf-blind have multiple disabilities (i.e., physical and intellectual disabilities). The most consistent set of behavioral characteristics associated with this disability are in the areas of communication, mobility, and social interactions (Andrew, 1989).

Nonspecific intellectual disabilities.   The most common type of intellectual disability is referred to as "nonspecific." What this means is that no cause of the disability has been identified. Approximately 10 percent of people with severe disabilities have a nonspecific intellectual disability. Because this is such a heterogeneous grouping of students with no identified etiology, it is difficult to identify specific behavioral phenotypes above and beyond those associated with a particular degree of intellectual disability.

Traumatic brain injury.   This type of disability is acquired through some type of injury to the brain. The resulting brain damage causes changes in behavior that can include an intellectual disability. Approximately 1 in 25 students receive medical treatment for a head injury each year, but only 1 in 500 experience a traumatic brain injury. The degree of disability that a person experiences following a traumatic brain injury can range from very minor changes in intellectual functioning that disappear over time to life-long profound intellectual disabilities (McGarry et al., 2002). In addition, depending on the area of the brain that is damaged, highly idiosyncratic changes in intellectual functioning and behavior can result. Often, along with an acquired intellectual disability, students with traumatic head injuries may also have changes in communication, motor abilities, and emotions (Michaud, Duhaime, & Lazar, 2002).

Supporting Students' Abilities and Needs

Providing educational supports to a heterogeneous group of people with a range of behavioral characteristics is very challenging. Thirty years ago many educators might even have used the word "impossible." However, thanks to a unique combination of advocacy, legislation, and research many of the challenges that students with severe disabilities present educational systems have been overcome. In fact, the expectations for what a student can achieve are largely limited by the skills and imagination of the people who provide support to that individual.

In retrospect, we can identify certain assumptions regarding what constitutes an appropriate education that have helped improve educational practices for students with severe disabilities. One of the most fundamental assumptions that effective educators have regarding this group of students is the importance of *focusing on abilities* as well as needs. Often people have focused only on what a student could not do: the severity of their intellectual disability, the presence of problem behaviors, the lack of friendships, the absence of spoken language, or the presence of physical limitations. Unfortunately, when people only focus on a person's limitations, they miss what is unique about the person and what he or she can accomplish. For this reason, educators need to focus on what a student can do, as well as what he or she still needs to learn.

Another assumption that effective educators adopt is that *all students can learn*. One of the greatest limitations students with severe disabilities have had in public schools is that educators often believed that they could not learn. If an educator adopts this perspective, then it is not surprising if the educational expectations for a student are low or even nonexistent. As was pointed out by Donald Baer (1981), students often live up to the expectations that educators set for them, and if teachers hold little or no expectations for their students, one should not be surprised if students live up to those expectations by achieving very little. It is best if you, an educator, expect progress and growth from all your students, realizing that what constitutes progress and growth has to be defined individually for each student.

A final assumption of effective educators is that all students can make *meaningful contributions to their educational environments*. When inclusive practices first began in the early 1990s, the assumption of many educators was that, although it was acceptable to have students with severe disabilities in general education classrooms, they did not contribute much in those settings. For example, a student with severe disabilities might have worked only with a paraprofessional in the back of the classroom. In the past decade we have learned a great deal about what students with and without disabilities gain from participating in inclusive learning environments. One of those lessons has been that students with severe disabilities contribute a great deal to a classroom both academically and socially. If educators focus on what a student can do and support him or her in achieving those goals, the student can contribute in various meaningful ways to his or her classroom. Often those contributions cannot be predicted by adults, but are appreciated once they begin to occur by all members of a classroom.

In the remainder of this chapter we will review a topic that is at the core of educating students with severe disabilities: *support needs*. Support needs are content areas educators can focus on to encourage a student to grow and develop in inclusive environments to the maximum extent possible. In fact, the remainder of this book largely focuses on how to adequately meet a student's support needs. In a very real sense, the more effective educators are in meeting a student's support needs, the more effectively that student will learn and prosper in inclusive settings.

Support Needs

The term *support needs* refers to ways in which we can describe how students develop and learn in certain situations. As should be evident from our discussion of different etiologies of severe disabilities, there is a range of behavioral phenotypes that are expressed. However, despite this heterogeneity there are several learning patterns that are very likely to exist for students with severe disabilities. Rather than view these characteristics as deficits or excesses, we will discuss them in terms of instructional needs that educators need to take into account when developing support plans for students.

Communication.   Students with severe disabilities communicate with other people in a variety of ways. Sometimes that communication is spoken words, sometimes it is gestural (e.g., signing or facial expressions), and at other times it may be through the use of augmentative or alternative communication systems (see Chapter 7). For many students with severe disabilities, their communication will take on each of these forms. That is, students will use a variety of ways to communicate with others. However, whatever the form(s) a student's communication may take, it is important to pay very close attention to what a person is trying to tell others. One of the greatest challenges of educating a student with severe disabilities is learning to understand what it is he or she wants to say and helping him or her communicate that to others successfully.

Adaptive behavior.   Adaptive behavior refers to things a student can do that will make him or her more independent. For example, teaching a student to read sightwords, walk without assistance, or independently eat a meal are adaptive behaviors. Clearly, the more adaptive behaviors a student has in his or her repertoire, the more things he or she can do without the assistance of others. A key issue in educating students with severe disabilities is how to increase a person's adaptive behavior within the context of the general education classroom (see Chapter 3).

Problem behavior.   In part because of the need to improve a student's communication and adaptive behavior, problem behaviors sometimes become an issue of educational importance. Problem behaviors refer to self-injury (e.g., hand biting), aggression (e.g., hitting others), and/or destroying property (e.g., breaking a window). Often problem behaviors emerge because a particular student does not have an adequate way of communicating with others or lacks skills necessary to complete a task. Chapter 8 of this book focuses on how to identify the causes of problem behavior and develop interventions to reduce these responses while increasing a student's participation in general education settings.

Systematic instruction.   Given that students with severe disabilities take longer to learn skills than most other students, educational researchers have developed techniques for how to systematically teach these students new skills (see Chapter 4). Systematic instruction breaks the learning process down into its elemental parts, allowing teachers and students to understand more clearly what is being taught. Systematic instruction also provides educators with specific techniques that have been demonstrated to facilitate skill acquisition. In addition, the techniques discussed in Chapter 4 show educators how to document and track student progress on instructional goals and objectives. Interestingly, the instructional techniques that work well for students with severe disabilities also work well for students without disabilities, a plus when including students with disabilities in general education settings.

Family-centered practices.   Finally, it is important to acknowledge not only the support needs of students with severe disabilities, but also the support needs of their families. Whether a student is an infant, child, adolescent, or young adult, he or she is part of a family that provides his or her primary supports. Educators have learned that understanding a student's needs within the context of his or her family makes for more successful educational progress and allows families to have critical input into shaping their child's education and his or her future (see Chapter 5).

Social relationships.   Being successful at school, as well as later in life, requires more than acquiring new skills and knowing when to use them. Success also requires being able to get along and interact with other people. Indeed, most people would include their relationships with other people as a key component in having a satisfying life. With the advent of inclusive education the importance of social relationships has moved to the forefront of educational planning. Chapter 6 of this book discusses ways of thinking about social relationships and how to facilitate their development within general education settings.

Sensory and motor needs.   Many students with severe disabilities have other disabilities in addition to their intellectual disability. Some of these additional disabilities manifest themselves as motor needs. For example, some students might have an unsteady gait that makes walking difficult or may have trouble with fine motor skills such as grasping and using a pencil. Other students might have sensory issues that make them more, or less, sensitive to light, touch, smell, sound, or taste. Chapter 9 of this book reviews how educators can assess and plan for sensory and motor needs.

Collaboration.   Clearly, considering the list of support needs given above, to effectively include students with severe disabilities requires a range of expertise that no single human being is likely to possess. Because of these diverse needs, a range of professionals and para-professionals are required for students with severe disabilities. These individuals often include general and special educators, family members, speech pathologists, physical therapists, behavior analysts, and occupational therapists. Having this range of people working with a student requires that adults be able to collaborate with each other (see Chapter 2). In addition, there are logistical issues about inclusive education that require a rethinking of staffing patterns. One of the most important issues in inclusive education is how to meaningfully utilize the skills of paraprofessionals in general education settings. In Chapter 10 of this book we will discuss how to train, manage, and effectively use paraprofessionals to assist collaborative teams in implementing instructional programs and monitoring student progress.

Conclusion

Students with severe disabilities have entered the mainstream of American education after years of being ignored or marginalized by public schools. With the advent of inclusive education, students and their families have new opportunities to learn and interact with peers without disabilities in typical classroom settings. This is a significant step forward for not only students with disabilities, but also their peers without disabilities, who all gain by learning more about the nature of diversity in their local communities.

Current research would suggest that inclusion is a win-win situation for all involved. However, as with any meaningful education goal, inclusive education requires planning and follow-through to be successful. Special educators have needed to rethink what their roles in inclusive schools are. Perhaps the most significant changes relate to collaborating with other professionals in general education environments. Although this has created a new set of job expectations for special educators, it has also opened up a broad range of new opportunities for them and their students. To be effective in inclusive settings, special educators need to focus on the support needs of students with severe disabilities and balance student needs with student strengths. The remainder of this book provides the educator-in-training with essential content knowledge about research-based practices that have been proven to be effective in teaching students with severe disabilities.

References

Andrew, A. K. (1989). Meeting the needs of young deaf-blind children and their parents: II. *Child Care, Health and Development, 15,* 251–264.

Baer, D. M. (1981). A hung jury and a Scottish verdict: "Not proven." *Analysis and Intervention in Developmental Disabilities, 1,* 91–97.

Batshaw, M. L. (2002). *Children with disabilities* (5th ed.). Baltimore: Paul H. Brookes.

Chapman, R. S., & Hesketh, L. J. (2000). Behavioral phenotype of individuals with Down syndrome. *Mental Retardation and Developmental Disabilities Research Reviews, 6,* 84–95.

Dawson, G., Webb, S., Schellenberg, G. D., Dager, S., Friedman, S., Aylward, E., & Richards, T. (2002). Defining the broader phenotype of autism: genetic, brain, and behavioral perspectives. *Developmental Psychopathology, 14,* 581–611.

Dybwad, R. F. (1990). *Perspectives on a parent movement: The revolt of parents of children with intellectual limitations.* Brookline, MA: Brookline Books.

Ferguson, D. L., & Baumgart, D. (1991). Partial participation revisited. *Journal of the Association for Persons with Severe Handicaps, 16,* 218–227.

Grossman, F. (1983). *Classification in mental retardation.* Washington, DC: American Association on Mental Retardation.

Hodapp, R. M., & Dykens, E. M. (2001). Strengthening behavioral research on genetic mental retardation syndromes. *American Journal on Mental Retardation, 106,* 4–15.

Individuals with Disabilities Act (IDEA) Amendments of 1997, P.L. 105-17, 20 §§ 1400 *et seq.*

Leonard, H., & Wen, X. (2002). The epidemiology of mental retardation: Challenges and opportunities in the new millennium. *Mental Retardation and Developmental Disabilities Research Reviews, 8,* 117–134.

Lord, C., & Volkmar, F. (2002). Genetics of childhood disorders: XLII. Autism, part 1: Diagnosis and assessment in autistic spectrum disorders. *Journal of the American Academy of Child and Adolescent Psychiatry, 4,* 1134–1136.

Luckasson, R., & Reeve, A. (2001). Naming, defining, and classifying in mental retardation. *Mental Retardation, 39,* 47–52.

Maccozzo, M. M. M. (2000). Advances in research on the fragile X syndrome. *Mental Retardation and Developmental Disabilities Research Reviews, 6,* 96–106.

McGarry, L. J., Thompson, D., Millham, F. H., Cowell, L., Snyder, P. J., Lenderking, W. R., & Weinstein, M. C. (2002). Outcomes and costs of acute treatment of traumatic brain injury. *Journal of Trauma, 53,* 1152–1159.

Michaud, L., Duhaime, A.-C., & Lazar, M. F. (2002). Traumatic head injury. In M. L. Batshaw (Ed.), *Children with disabilities* (5th ed., pp. 595–617). Baltimore: Paul H. Brookes.

Molloy, H., & Vasil, L. (2002). The social construction of Asperger syndrome: The pathologising of difference? *Disability and Society, 17,* 659–669.

Reschly, D. J. (1999). Assessing educational disabilities. In A. K. Hess & I. B. Weiner (Eds.), *The handbook of forensic psychology* (2nd ed., pp. 127–150). New York: John Wiley & Sons.

Roeleveld, M., Zielhuis, G. A., & Gabreels, F. (1997). The prevalence of mental retardation: A critical review of recent literature. *Developmental Medicine and Child Neurology, 39,* 125–532.

Ryndak, D. L., & Kennedy, C. H. (2000). Meeting the needs of students with severe disabilities: Issues and practices in teacher education. *Journal of the Association for Persons with Severe Handicaps, 25,* 69–71.

Smith, D. D. (2003). *Introduction to special education: Teaching in an era of change* (5th ed.). Boston: Allyn and Bacon.

Sontag, E., & Haring, N. G. (1996). The professionalization of teaching and learning for children with severe disabilities: The creation of TASH. *Journal of the Association for Persons with Severe Handicaps, 21,* 39–45.

Steinhausen, H-C., von Gontard, A., Spohr, H-L., Hauffa, B. P., Eiholzer, U., Backers, M., Willms, J., & Malin, Z. (2002). Behavioral phenotypes in four mental retardation syndromes: Fetal alcohol syndrome, Prader-Willi syndrome, fragile X syndrome, and tuberoses sclerosis. *American Journal of Medical Genetics, 111,* 381–387.

Trent, J. W., Jr. (1994). *Inventing the feeble mind: A history of mental retardation in the United States.* Berkeley: University of California Press.

Vehmas, S. (1999). Newborn infants and the moral significance of intellectual disabilities. *Journal of the Association for Persons with Severe Handicaps, 24,* 111–121.

Zigler, E. (1967). Familial retardation: A continuing dilemma. *Science, 155,* 292–298.

CHAPTER

2

Collaborative Teams

EVA HORN, BARBARA THOMPSON, AND CHELIE NELSON

University of Kansas

To work effectively in supporting students with severe disabilities, educators must *collaborate* with parents, related service professionals, other educators (i.e., regular and special educators), and paraprofessionals. Collaboration is so important it has been defined as the cornerstone of inclusive supports (Odom et al., 2001). This chapter sets the framework for practicing professionals "working and playing together" to maximize their effectiveness in achieving positive outcomes for students with severe disabilities. After reading this chapter you will be able to:

- Define collaboration in the context of inclusive education
- Identify the benefits and purposes of collaboration
- Understand the key components necessary for effective collaboration
- Identify strategies that promote collaborative relationships

What Is Collaboration?

Collaboration is working together for a common end. Increasingly, an effective education for students with severe disabilities requires a range of professionals, paraprofessionals, and community members. Their combined efforts may begin in infancy and continue into adulthood. As more students are educated in inclusive settings, schools have to reconfigure how they operate, placing greater emphasis on cooperation. At the same time, schools must now address the transition needs of young children entering school at age three and again when they become adolescents. Although the individuals involved in a student's life share a general goal—to support the learning of the student—they will vary in their knowledge, perspective, experiences, and training. Not surprisingly, collaboration takes time, energy, patience, and understanding.

Collaboration is more than various individuals working together. It is the process by which individuals with different areas of expertise identify needs and find strategies for solving them. Collaboration can occur between as few as two individuals (e.g., a general educator and special educator), but more often includes a team of individuals who work on behalf of the student with severe disabilities.

First, collaboration requires working effectively with families. All families want teachers who are interested in their children, who will provide them with a safe learning environment, and who are effective instructors. When families are engaged as active members of the school community, significant benefits accrue to students, educators, and the families themselves (Christenson, 1996; Henderson, 1987; Henderson & Berla, 1994; Liontos, 1992). Educators in programs with highly involved families report greater job satisfaction. Family–school collaboration should be characterized by a *transactional* and *individualized* approach that recognizes multiple sources of expertise. In collaboration, families and educators agree on shared goals and work together to advance a student's success. Given the importance of these relationships, family–professional collaboration is the focus of a separate chapter in this book (Chapter 5). In the remainder of this chapter, our focus is on collaboration among professionals involved in educating students with severe disabilities.

Professionals provide a variety of supports to students with severe disabilities. Some of the professionals most commonly involved include special educators, general educators, physical and occupational therapists, communication disorder specialists, administrators, psychologists, school nurses, and paraprofessionals (Orelove & Sobsey, 1996). Although this is a long list, many others may also be team members. Who is involved depends on the nature of the student's abilities and needs. Additional team members can include social workers, vision specialists, orientation and mobility specialists, audiologists, physicians, and dentists.

Forms of Collaboration

As adults work together to achieve a common outcome, each will engage in a variety of actions and take a variety of roles. Three basic forms of collaboration have been described: *consulting, coaching,* and *teaming* (Costa & Kallick, 1993; Fishbaugh, 2000; Idol, Paolucci-Whitcomb, & Nevin, 1994; Morsink, Thomas, & Correa, 1991). Although these types of collaboration are described as distinct, they actually fall along a continuum and share some commonalities. Understanding the basic tenets of each may help educators work together.

Consulting.   A consulting approach involves a triad in which one person (the expert on the topic) provides advice to a mediator (the individual who is a novice on the topic) for the benefit of the student (Idol et al., 1994). This form is an indirect support delivery approach. The consultant does not directly work with the student, but provides information and resources to others who provide direct supports. By design, the consultation model can lead to an inequality, with one party having more expertise, knowledge, or experience than the other does. This inequity can reduce effectiveness if strategies are not implemented to reduce potential negative effects. A key strategy is to have all team members serve as a consultant/expert in their particular area of knowledge, so that no single person is in the role of the "receiver of consultation." In addition, the person doing the consulting should use some

---

BOX 2.1

Consulting

Nina is an itinerant early childhood special education teacher for a large urban school district. Nina completes a quick mental check of her calendar for that day. First there is Hillwood Child Care Center at 8:30 A.M., where she needs to check in with Maho's educational assistant on how the toilet training is coming along and to collect data on Sam's use of adapted signs to request. Then it's on to Brookcreek Center to observe Keith during large motor time to help generate some ideas for supporting him in initiating and sustaining appropriate interactions with his peers. She's got the copy of the peer affection games article that she promised to bring Keith's teacher, Ms. Jeannie. Then it's on to Overbrook Head Start to meet the physical therapist to put together plans for when and how Charlayne can use the pronestander and improve the sitting support for Shelby during snack. Next comes Stepping Stones Preschool for a naptime meeting for which the priority agenda item is strategies for getting Joey to pay attention during circle time. Nina checks that she has her notes on the video clip she made last week. At the last minute she decides to drop in her copy of the tape just as a backup in case the preschool teacher forgets hers. Finally, she checks that she has her materials together for the afternoon orientation visit with Juan, his mother, and the Spanish interpreter about the program Juan will begin attending next week.

---

basic strategies (see Box 2.1). Little (1985) offers six principles for being an effective consultant.

1. Consultants and consultees should share a *common language* that they use in the same ways. Even when professionals use the same words, they sometimes do not understand each other because of idiosyncratic word meanings or "professional speak."
2. The consultant should stay *focused* on the requested information. The agenda has been set by the consultee and should not be changed by the consultant. Adults are most willing to change their behaviors or try something new if they have identified the concern rather than having it identified for them.
3. The consultant should base her advice on *specific events,* rather than personal opinion.
4. Opportunities for *interactive exchanges* of information must occur regularly.
5. There should be no unnecessary surprises in the way the consulting occurs. The consultee should *understand* and be able to *predict* each step in the process. Predictability allows the consultee to have a sense of security and develop trust with the consultant.
6. Finally, *mutual respect* must be communicated and be inherent in any consultant relationship.

Practicing these principles of consulting, using effective interpersonal communication skills, and having strategies for resolving conflicts will reduce the barriers to effective collaboration.

Coaching.   Coaching implies a more interactive approach to collaboration. As in consulting, one member is the expert while the other is the recipient of the expertise. However, the focus in coaching is on effective implementation. Coaching follows the principles of active learning in that information is presented, implementation is modeled, and then practice occurs with feedback. Because of the need to have a person's implementation critiqued, a key issue is trust. In fact, Costa and Kallick (1993) have described coaching as a "critical friendship." The critical friend is a trusted peer who asks questions to gain understanding, provides feedback, and offers insights. Coaching involves the following steps:

1. The learner identifies a topic in which he or she needs assistance.
2. The coach asks questions to understand and clarify the topic.
3. The learner and coach develop an implementation strategy.
4. The coach models implementing the strategy.
5. The learner implements the strategy and discusses his or her performance with the coach. Together they discuss necessary modifications.
6. The coach observes the learner again, providing feedback, raising questions, and critiquing the learner's performance.
7. They discuss the success of the strategy and suggest additional modifications, if necessary.

As with any form of collaboration, the coach must reflect on his or her use of appropriate communication skills to foster mutual respect.

Teaming.   A teaming model requires that the group work in a fully interactive manner. Members of a collaborative team take the lead role as the situation dictates. Further, members of a team share ownership of their collective "work." Thousand and Villa (2000) described a collaborative team as a group of people with a common goal and shared beliefs who work with parity and distributed tasks. This approach, in particular, empowers its members through sharing ownership of problems and solutions. The critical components of effective teams include face-to-face interactions, interdependence, trust, assessment of how the team is working, and individual accountability.

In the forming of teams, several different structures have been identified, including (a) multidisciplinary, (b) interdisciplinary, and (c) transdisciplinary models (Orelove & Sobsey, 1996; Rainforth & York, 1997). These are different teaming approaches that are defined as follows:

- In *multidisciplinary teams,* each professional works separately and in isolation assessing, planning, and implementing student programs by himself or herself. The interventions are planned by different disciplines, can be in opposition to each other, and can be implemented without attention to generalization across settings and people.
- In *interdisciplinary teams,* there is sharing of information by professionals at team meetings in which coordinated decisions about the educational needs of the student are made. However, a limitation of this approach is that intervention continues to be

tied to each discipline's own expertise and orientation, as in the multidisciplinary team model.

■ In *transdisciplinary teams,* one professional—usually the special educator—is responsible for coordinating supports, with the emphasis on embedding the goals of other team members throughout the school day. Implementing this model requires team members to share expertise, engage in role release, and collaborate (Campbell, 1987).

The *transdisciplinary model* extends the potential effectiveness of the other two models and is considered the *preferred method* of coordinating supports for students with severe disabilities (Rainforth & York, 1997). Implementation requires all members to participate in decision-making activities about each student, contributing to problem solving, sharing of expertise, supporting others, and continually updating support approaches to maximize a student's success.

What Are the Purposes of Collaboration?

Collaboration benefits both teachers and students. Johnson and Johnson (1987) have indicated that cooperative work relationships promote higher goal achievement, greater support, and greater satisfaction. Some of the outcomes that occur from collaboration include: (a) sharing pedagogical ideas; (b) achieving a broader view of support options; (c) developing novel, situation-based practices; (d) developing a shared sense of purpose; and (e) obtaining feedback leading to increased teacher efficacy (Weasmer & Woods, 1998).

Research has demonstrated that when students with severe disabilities are provided supports in inclusive schools, this teamwork is beneficial for students, families, and professionals (Lieber et al., 1997). General educators have the opportunity to work with specialists and receive expert advice on learning needs of students. Specialists have the opportunity to work in the classroom where the targeted skills are used by the student. For the student, skills are learned where they will be used. The family can see the learning that occurs as a natural part of the larger school environment.

Across contexts, forms, and disciplines, why people collaborate can be organized into three basic categories: (a) *providing technical assistance,* (b) *collegial development,* and (c) *creating solutions* (Fishbaugh, 2000). Each purpose can be implemented within the context of the three approaches to collaboration previously described and can be used simultaneously within a collaborative relationship. The trick is to match identified need and desired outcome with the appropriate approach.

Technical assistance is defined as providing ongoing information, assistance, and support to address a chronic issue. As students with severe disabilities participate in inclusion schools, general educators need ongoing support from specialists. The physical therapist, for example, may provide regularly scheduled *consultation* visits to evaluate and adjust a student's adaptive equipment. Through this process the student's learning and participation can be enhanced. The general educator can also be certain that the physical environment is arranged appropriately.

Technical assistance may also be implemented via *coaching.* For example, a general education teacher may ask for assistance from the special education teacher in addressing concerns about smooth transitions from one activity to another. Technical assistance on transition using a coaching approach might occur in the following sequence:

1. The general educator requests technical assistance.
2. The general and special educators meet and discuss the current status of the student.
3. The special educator observes student across several transitions.
4. The teachers meet again and discuss possible strategies, with the special educator developing a plan to implement several strategies.
5. The special educator then visits the class and models the strategies.
6. The general educator implements the strategies and reports back to the special educator.
7. When the general educator is ready, the special educator comes to the class to observe and provide additional feedback.
8. This cycle continues as other strategies are introduced or new concerns arise.

Technical assistance may also be implemented within a *collaborative team*. This strategy is used when a need for information arises for all team members. In some cases one team member may have the expertise and can share with the full team, and in others an outside consultant and may be brought in. An example of this latter approach would be a team serving a student with severe disabilities who has a visual impairment. All team members need information on making environmental accommodations, including lighting, positioning, and contrast/color of materials. The vision specialist could provide information to all team members and address the specific concerns of individual team members.

Something similar to technical assistance is *collegial development*. Collegial development refers to professionals supporting each other in their individual development so they become more effective educators. For change to occur, professionals must access new information, practice new skills, and receive feedback from others. Again, as with technical assistance, collegial development can be implemented with each of the models of collaboration.

To illustrate collegial development, we will look at the case of Jerod, an 11-year-old in Ms. DelPraz's sixth-grade class. Jerod has severe disabilities, and a team of adults works with him. The general education teacher (Ms. DelPraz) provides consultation to the other members of the team related to the sixth-grade curriculum. Specifically, Ms. DelPraz provides each team member with written materials about the scope and sequence of the curriculum. During a teacher in-service day early in the school year, she provides specific information across each curricular domain about the desired outcomes for each quarter and plans for activities to support student learning. The team works together collaboratively to learn about the requirements of IDEA in terms of access to the general curriculum for Jerod (see Chapter 3). As the team identifies specific accommodations and modifications needed for Jerod, reciprocal *coaching* by members of the team occurs to ensure that all team members can effectively implement each accommodation or modification.

Another approach, *creating solutions,* focuses on achieving a solution to address an immediate crisis situation through collaboration. Creating solutions differs from technical assistance and collegial development in that it is used when there is an acute as opposed to a chronic situation. In creating solutions, a consultant would respond to a teacher's request for help. For example, a student with severe disabilities who also is technology dependent and medically fragile was included in a third-grade classroom. While a nurse came to the classroom to provide regularly scheduled "tube feedings" and suctioning, the teacher appropriately asked to be trained in the procedures as a backup. The school nurse and the boy's mother provided training for the general and special educators on the procedures, with special emphasis on precautions and handling situations if something goes wrong.

In another approach, *coaching,* a teacher would ask for assistance with an acute situation but would be more actively involved with the solution. Coaching is particularly well suited to situations in which the educators receiving the coaching would be implementing the solution. For example, the same student described above might have an adapted wheelchair but needs to be periodically moved to other positions to support movement and prevent skin sores (see Chapter 9). The physical therapist and special educator would work together with the general educator and paraprofessional through a series of activities to support their implementation of safe lifts, carries, and repositioning techniques.

Barriers to Effective Collaboration

Although few would disagree with the importance of adults collaborating to support students with severe disabilities, many real barriers exist on a daily basis that may prevent them from implementing collaborative practices. Some of these barriers include:

- School climate
- Lack of time
- Lack of expertise and comfort with collaborative skills
- Conflicting beliefs

Each of these barriers is discussed below in detail.

School climate.   One of the most obvious institutional barriers is the physical structure of a school. Teachers and related service personnel can become isolated in school buildings in which they spend most of the day within their own rooms (DeMarrais & LeCompte, 1995; Feiman-Nemser & Floden, 1986). The "hotel-like" structure of schools means that adults seldom see each other except in the hallway, on the playground, or in the lunchroom. This sense that teaching is a private affair also results in the message that one should not "invade" others' teaching space unless invited. This reinforces the belief that competent educators do not need to depend on other adults and that seeking help or assistance is a sign of weakness. The school climate of teaching as a solitary act makes it difficult for educators to see themselves as collaborators (Leonard & Leonard, 1999).

Lack of time.   The importance of time to reflect, to meet with other members of the team, and to plan together cannot be overestimated. A recurring theme in the literature on barriers to effective collaboration is a lack of time (Glickman, 1998; Lieber, Beckman, & Horn, 1999; Raywid, 1993). Research documents that successful schools are those in which the adults discuss, plan, inform, and critique one another. Ongoing interactions among members of a student's team is necessary for continued professional growth and the emergence of a collaborative school culture. Yet without specific time being planned into the school day, neither outcome is likely to occur. Raywid (1993) has noted that meeting time must fit within the school day, and not be tacked onto the end of the day. In addition, meeting time must be allotted in an ongoing, predictable pattern to facilitate meaningful outcomes.

Lack of expertise in collaborating.   Lack of familiarity with the strategies and techniques of working together acts as a barrier to collaboration (Leggett & Hoyle, 1987). Even though good intentions are helpful, they are not enough. Just as the students being supported need both instruction and practice to learn new skills, so do the adults of a team need to learn new strategies.

Conflicting beliefs.   Although team members share a common goal, they will vary in their beliefs on the most effective way to achieve important outcomes. The team members may have different attitudes and values about severe disabilities, about the types of services that should be provided, and about the settings in which services should be provided, different learning priorities, and different expectations about the student's abilities.

Components of Effective Collaboration

Despite numerous barriers, adults working to support students with severe disabilities have found ways to make collaboration a foundational principle. The next section looks at the characteristics of successful collaborative schools.

Joint participation in program development.   Opportunities for being involved in planning, developing, and maintaining a program contributes to the team members' sense of ownership and commitment. In contrast, if some of the adults working with a student with severe disabilities have little input into the development and ongoing implementation of a plan, problems may occur.

Respect for diversity in instructional approaches.   Sharing a teaching philosophy leads to more effective working relationships (Lieber et al., 1999; Shrage, 1990). First, however, each team member must have an open attitude to learn and understand each others' perspectives. As individuals listen and learn, their initial perceptions that "huge differences" exist among team members may be dispelled. Differences may actually be a matter of terminology and specialty area. As the team works together to understand each other's perceptive, each team member will gain new insights into practices and terminology. Ultimately, the team will move closer to a shared belief about how to make things work well for their students.

Perceived "ownership" of students.   As students with severe disabilities are included in general education settings, staff must address whether responsibility for all children are shared by all staff. Research has shown that working relationships are enhanced when general and special educators share responsibility for each student, rather than assuming that the special educator has sole responsibility for the progress of students with severe disabilities (Lieber et al., 1999).

Communication.   A major factor in successful collaborative relationships is effective communication (see Pugach & Johnson, 2001). Communication is the foundation of all interactions between adults. Effective communication enables us to share information and establish a sense of unity with others (Hames & Joseph, 1986). Good communication skills can be viewed as a prerequisite for collaboration. Communication involves a sender, a message, a receiver, and most important, a continuing cycle of changing roles around sender and receiver. Effective collaboration requires using informal and formal strategies (Lieber, Beckman, & Horn, 1999). In some schools, dedicated planning time is provided for staff to meet. Communication can also be enhanced by informal contact among staff members and families. This contact often occurs during arrivals, departures, lunch, and other transition times within the school day.

Changing professional roles and need for clarity.   Working effectively in teams requires members to change their traditional roles and share their disciplinary expertise. The ability of team members to release their previous roles and to adopt others' roles (e.g., a special educator working in another teacher's class as a co-teacher) will impact the quality of inclusive programs. Professionals need to be flexible, recognizing that the specifics of their roles will change from team to team and across time. The most effective teams are those whose team members are able to tolerate some ambiguity and adjust specific roles (see Box 2.2).

Stability of relationships.   Familiarity among adults on the team has a positive impact on collaboration. It makes sense to support the continuation of teams that have been able to work through issues and implement solutions. In these teams a built-in positive atmosphere exists, and a high level of cooperation among members more readily follows. If feasible, administrators should allow team members to continue to work together as students move

---

BOX **2.2**

Changing Professional Roles and the Need for Role Clarification

Maria is a special education teacher in an elementary school. Her students spend much of their day in their homerooms receiving support and specialized instruction from her and her paraeducators in that setting. Maria is generally pleased with how things are going for her students; however, she would like to be more fully integrated into the school. She believes that this would continue to develop her collaborative teaming relationships. In particular, Maria "struggles" somewhat with the fifth-grade cluster teachers. They have been somewhat "cool" to providing more than simple access for the students with severe disabilities. Maria, having grown up in a Cuban community in Miami, is fluent in Spanish. She approaches the fifth-grade cluster leader and offers to provide Spanish "awareness" for fifth graders. The teachers are enthusiastic about this option for their students. Twice weekly, Maria offers Spanish to a group of students from the four fifth-grade classrooms. She works with the cluster teachers to integrate the vocabulary into the current thematic unit. An added benefit is that John, one of her students with severe disabilities who has Spanish as his first language, joins her in the class and serves as her assistant.

through grades within a school. Even when new members are to be added, a strong continuing core team can easily bring in the new members. Assigning a new member a "mentor" significantly accelerates the acculturation of the new member into the "workings" of the team and helps maintain the effectiveness of the team.

Administrative support. Administrators wear many hats, and becoming a collaboration facilitator for staff may seem like one more hat to wear. A strong commitment to supporting all students within the school necessitates a strong commitment to collaboration. Administrators' support contributes to good working relationships among staff members and can remove barriers to effective inclusion. Administrators provide support by recognizing the contributions of individual participants, allocating resources, allowing time for joint planning, and listening to staff. Most important, administrators have many opportunities to establish and clearly communicate a school climate of collaboration. That is, we are all working together to support the success of all of our students. The following story illustrates the impact of "voicing" this message:

> In the context of a very tense individualized educational plan meeting, Drew's parents spoke repeatedly of the supports they hoped to have for their son in elementary school. Many components of the plan required lengthy give-and-take until a solution was achieved. After an hour of tense discussion with only a few issues resolved, Drew's mother said, "I'm not asking for the sun, the moon, and the stars. I just want Drew to be welcomed and wanted so that he can grow and learn." Without hesitation the principal of the school spoke, "You are not asking for anything more than every parent who walks through our school asks for and has a right to." From that moment, the atmosphere shifted, with an acknowledgment that we can do this together. Drew can be a welcomed member of our school community.

Recommendations for Implementation

An increased need for collaboration has occurred in recent years because of the complexity of characteristics of students with severe disabilities and of the need to address their abilities and disabilities within the context of the general curriculum (see Friend & Cook, 1996; Lieber, Beckman, & Horn, 1999; Rainforth & York, 1997; Vandercook & York, 1990). This process is ongoing and changes over time. Below, we list a number of recommendations for facilitating successful collaboration. The suggestions are organized by those most clearly directed toward first building administrators, then teams as a group, and finally the individual team members.

Strategies for Building Administrators

As leaders, administrators play a large part in ensuring that team members with different backgrounds, personalities, and expertise work together to improve student outcomes.

A shared philosophy. Collaborative teams in inclusive schools plan and implement interventions for enhancing student learning. Every inclusive school should have a written philosophy that supports the concept of enhancing outcomes for all students. A written statement, particularly one that team members have contributed to, helps the school keep focused on specific goals and shared beliefs. Developing a shared philosophy is not an easy task. There are significant differences in instructional beliefs among families, general educators, special educators, and related service personnel. Even when these individuals use the same words, they may be talking about different concepts. Because such differences are inevitable, they need to be openly discussed.

Adequate meeting times.   The issue of having adequate time for meetings is a chronic and pervasive problem. The larger the team, the more difficult it is to schedule meetings. If a team is small, possible meeting times are before or after school or during small breaks in the day. With larger teams, it is sometimes necessary for an administrator to provide release time for participants.

Working toward a common goal.   Teams may have a variety of goals, including discussing objectives for individual students or objectives for specific classrooms, but before any meeting the team holds, an agenda should be developed. A variety of forms already exist to help teams construct a meeting agenda that includes meeting objectives, progress toward meeting goals, and assigning tasks to team members (Friend & Cook, 1996; Thousand & Villa, 2000).

Team members' sharing their expertise.   Effective team collaboration requires team members to share their expertise across disciplines. Sharing of expertise requires team members to be both teachers and learners. Often professionals provide training to another team member, who will then deliver the support. Administrators should facilitate the sharing of expertise to ensure that the expectations of roles and responsibilities are defined and understood by all team members.

Team members using collaborative skills.   As team members plan programs and solutions to issues, logistical difficulties and philosophical differences may arise. When this occurs, the team facilitators should be prepared to guide the team through problem-solving techniques (see Box 2.3, p. 28). The team facilitator can work with the team to:

- Identify the problem
- Brainstorm solutions
- Identify the most promising solutions
- Select a solution(s)
- Develop a step-by-step action plan to carry out the solution

Team members should share work.   Although the entire collaborative team may participate in planning, the role of individual team members may vary. Students' programs are almost always carried out by a general education teacher or a co-teaching team. Other team members may participate regularly as itinerant specialists. Whatever the level of involvement, team members should be available to answer questions and offer new ideas. Likewise, team members who serve in an indirect capacity should visit the program regularly to

---

BOX **2.3**

Team Members Using Collaborative Strategies

Reba, a 19-year-old with severe mental retardation and serious emotional disturbance, expressed a desire to go to the local community college the next academic year. At her spring IEP, Reba could not identify an area of interest or possible major related to attending the community college. She stated that she is interested in working in a store, particularly one that sells clothes. Through her special education program, she participated in a range of community job training settings. The one she most enjoyed was a national chain clothing store in the local mall. Reba's father really wanted her to get a job after high school and doesn't see the value in the community college. He says, "She just wants to go there because she likes to socialize." The IEP team, including her father, works together with Reba to modify her postsecondary plans to include the following: Reba will take one class at the community college in the evening in the "retail" program together with one of her high school friends. The work-study teacher at the high school will assist her in getting a full-time job, and the special education program will provide a job coach to support her successful transition into the job. Her father agrees to drive "the girls" to the community college class, since he will also take a class at the same time. The school social worker will work with Reba and her father on finding long-term sources of financial support for transportation to and from work, a job coach, and follow-up support.

---

show their commitment to the student and team. Administrators can support this process by ensuring that all team members understand their roles and know what others expect from them. Often, an administrator's push, praise, and availability is all that it takes to ensure that team members share in the work.

Strategies for Teams

A team is more than different individuals simply working together or being agreeable. A collaborative team requires a process in which people with different areas of expertise work together to identify needs and then find ways to meet those needs. Within this structure, all members of the team are expected to contribute their expertise to the process. Effective teams enhance the likelihood of success by implementing the following strategies.

Concern with mutual goals.   Team members working collaboratively need to focus on the same goals. Thus, the first step in the process needs to be on working together and agreeing on the particular goals for a student.

Recognizing diverse areas of expertise.   Those involved in collaboration recognize their own knowledge and skills, as well as the expertise of others. This does not imply that one person is delegated to dealing with only one aspect of the student with severe disabilities, but it means that team members will rely on the consultation of particular person for specific types of information.

Sharing of expertise.   As teams recognize that members have different expertise, strategies need to be implemented that allow team members to share this expertise. An environment that supports open sharing includes time allocated for input, strategies for ensuring that members have sufficient time to contribute their expertise, and rules for allowing non-judgmental sharing.

Equity among team members.   Team members are considered to be of equal importance to the collaborative process and are expected to work with the same goals in mind. No one team member can claim greater importance in this process than another.

Decision making by consensus.   The collaborative process calls for decisions about curriculum, instruction, and related services to be made through consensus. Groups should deal with issues and resolve them in a way that allows uniform agreement among the decision makers.

Shared responsibility and accountability.   Those engaged in collaboration accept that they share a part of the responsibility for the success of a student. No single person assumes more responsibility for success than another person does; all are jointly accountable.

Strategies for Teachers

Pugach and Johnson (2001) propose that team members who are successful collaborators have several personal and professional skills that contribute to their effectiveness as collaborators. Those teaching students with severe disabilities should learn the skills discussed below.

Having a positive attitude toward change.   Effective teaming requires members to shift their views, learn new skills, and change roles. An open attitude and willingness to try something new by each team member will help facilitate the team achieving a common goal.

Taking initiative.   It's not enough for adults who are working together to be willing to change. Professionals need to take the initiative to make change happen. Although administrators often take the lead at the school level, direct service professionals can play leadership roles as well by making positive things happen for individual students.

Communicating effectively.   Given the critical nature of communication among team members, each team member must reflect on his or her own efforts in this area. Continually developing communication skills will enhance the team's effectiveness. Asking for feedback from others and checking for team members' understanding of content are two critical skills that should occur on an ongoing basis.

Being a flexible and reflective professional.   Flexibility is crucial when groups of adults work together, because change and compromise are necessities. Professionals need to be aware of the quality and effectiveness of their work. When collaborating, each person's practices are brought to the forefront for consideration. This self-reflection provides intellectual stimulation and growth for those who participate.

Enjoying the experience.   Even though collaboration can be difficult, ultimately the outcomes can be worthwhile. Many professionals will enjoy the social nature of collaboration. Successful collaboration requires respect and trust, and these are very rewarding to many people. Collaboration results in the generation of multiple creative solutions. Being an active participant in the creative process can be very gratifying.

Conclusion

As professionals recognize the benefits of collaboration for the students they support, their expectations as educators also change. Although one individual cannot make schools more collaborative, he or she can play a critical role in moving in that direction. It has been argued that professionals working with students with severe disabilities not only need to be technically qualified, but also must be *change agents*. Fullan's (1993) definition of a new professionalism in educators applies here as well and is based on four cornerstones:

- *Personal vision building* in which the professional continually strives to answer, "What difference can I personally make?"
- *Inquiry* must lead our work. Each professional must think about and talk about his or her assumptions and practices of instruction and develop a reflective stance.
- *Mastery* is achieved by practicing continuous learning. "People behave their way into new visions and ideas, not just think their way into them" (p. 13).
- Collaborative environments require that the stereotype of working alone must give way to professionals who *share* their expertise and commitments to improving outcomes for their students.

References

Campbell, P. H. (1987). The integrated programming team: An approach for coordinating professionals of various disciplines in programs for students with severe and multiple handicaps. *Journal of the Association for Persons with Severe Handicaps, 12,* 107–116.

Christenson, S. L. (1996). A report from the school-family committee: Support for family involvement in education. *School Psychologists, 51,* 20–22.

Costa, A. L., & Kallick, B. (1993). Through the lens of a critical friend. *Educational Leadership, 51,* 49–51.

DeMarrais, K. B., & LeCompte, M. D. (1995). *The way schools work: A sociological analysis of education.* White Plains, NY: Addison Wesley Longman.

Feiman-Nemser, S., & Floden, R. E. (1986). The cultures of teaching. In M. C. Wittrock (Ed.), *Handbook of research on teaching* (3rd ed., pp. 505–526). New York: MacMillan.

Fishbaugh, M. S. (2000). *The collaboration guide for early career educators.* Baltimore: Paul H. Brookes.

Friend, M., & Cook, L. (1996). *Interactions: Collaboration skills for school professionals.* New York: Longman.

Fullan, M. G. (1993). *Changing forces: Probing the depths of educational reform.* New York: Falmer Press.

Glickman, C. D. (1998). *Revolutionizing America's schools.* San Francisco: Jossey-Bass Publishers.

Hames, C. C., & Joseph, D. H. (1986). *Basic concepts of helping: A holistic approach* (2nd ed.). East Norwalk, CT: Appleton-Century-Crofts.

Henderson, A. (1987). *The evidence continues to grow: Parent involvement improves student achievement.* Columbia, MD: National Committee for Citizens in Education.

Henderson, A., & Berla, N. (1994). *A new generation of evidence: The family is critical to student achievement.* Washington, DC: National Committee for Citizens in Education.

Idol, L., Paolucci-Whitcomb, P., & Nevin, A. (1994). *Collaborative consultation* (2nd ed.). Austin, TX: Pro-Ed.

Johnson, D. W., & Johnson, R. T. (1987). Research shows the benefits of adult cooperation. *Educational Leadership, 45,* 27–30.

Leggett, D., & Hoyle, S. (1987). Preparing teachers for collaboration. *Educational Leadership, 45,* 58–63.

Leonard, L. J., & Leonard, P. E. (1999). Reculturing for collaboration and leadership. *Journal of Educational Research, 92,* 237–242.

Lieber, J., Beckman, P., & Horn, E. (1999). Working together to provide services for young children with disabilities: Lessons from inclusive preschool programs. In S. Grahman & K. R. Harris (Eds.), *Teachers working together: Enhancing the performance of students with special needs* (pp. 1–29). Cambridge, MA: Brookline Books.

Lieber, J., Beckman, P. J., Hanson, M. J., Janko, S., Marquart, J. M., Horn, E., & Odom, S. L. (1997). The impact of changing roles on relationships between professionals in inclusive programs for young children. *Early Education and Development, 8,* 67–82.

Liontos, L. B. (1992). *At-risk families and schools: Becoming partners.* Eugene, OR: ERIC Clearinghouse on Educational Management.

Little, J. W. (1985). Teachers as teacher advisors: The delicacy of collegial leadership. *Educational Leadership, 43,* 34–36.

Morsink, C. V., Thomas, C. C., & Correa, V. (1991). *Interactive teaming: Consultation and collaboration in special programs.* New York: Merrill/Macmillan.

Odom, S., Schwartz, I. S., & ECRII Investigators (2001). So what do we know from all this? Synthesis points of research on preschool inclusion. In S. L. Odom (Ed.), *Widening the circle: Including children with disabilities in preschool programs* (pp. 154–174). New York: Teachers College Press.

Orelove, F. P., & Sobsey, D. (1996). *Educating children with multiple disabilities: A transdisciplinary approach* (3rd ed.). Baltimore: Paul H. Brookes.

Pugach, M. C., & Johnson, L. J. (2001). *Collaborative practitioners: Collaborative schools* (2nd ed.). Denver: Love.

Rainforth, B., & York, J. (1997). *Collaborative teams for students with severe disabilities: Integrating therapy and educational services* (2nd ed.). Baltimore: Paul H. Brookes.

Raywid, M. A. (1993). Finding time for collaboration. *Educational Leadership, 51,* 30–34.

Shrage M. (1990). *Shared minds: The new technologies of collaboration.* New York: Random House.

Thousand, J. S., & Villa, R. A. (2000). Collaborative teaming: A powerful tool in school restructuring. In R. A. Villa & J. S. Thousand (Eds.), *Restructuring for caring and effective education: An administration guide to creating heterogeneous schools* (2nd ed.). Baltimore: Paul H. Brookes.

Vandercook, T., & York, J. (1990). A team approach to program development and support. In W. Stainback & S. Stainback (Eds.), *Supporting networks for inclusive schooling: Interdependent integrated education* (pp. 95–122). Baltimore: Paul H. Brookes.

Weasmer, J., & Woods, A. M. (1998). I think I can: The role of personal teaching efficacy in bringing about change. *Clearing House, 71,* 245–247.

3

Access to the General Education Curriculum

DIANE L. RYNDAK
University of Florida

FELIX BILLINGSLEY
University of Washington

This chapter focuses on the concept of access to the general education curriculum for students with severe disabilities. Until recently, most students with severe disabilities have been denied access to the general education curriculum by being placed in segregated non-general education settings, by having their instruction limited to less challenging academic content and functional life skills, and by having their assessment procedures and results separated from those of their general education classmates. In spite of the IDEA mandate to provide services in the least restrictive environment, through these practices schools ostensibly established different, separate educational programs, procedures, and systems for students with and without disabilities. Through the concept of access to the general education curriculum (as well as access to district and state tests), the IDEA reauthorization of 1997 begins to break down these dual systems.

What follows is a review of current literature and findings regarding: (a) access to the general education curriculum, (b) why it is important for students with severe disabilities, (c) how educational teams identify what to teach within the context of general education, (d) how an educational team actually provides access to the general education curriculum, and (e) how an educational team assesses performance within the general education context. After reading this chapter you will be able to:

- Define what is meant by "access to the general education curriculum" for students with severe disabilities, including all aspects of the general education experience
- Explain why access to the general education curriculum is critical if students with severe disabilities are to meet their desired outcomes, both short- and long-term

The authors wish to acknowledge the contribution of Lewis Jackson, of the University of Northern Colorado, in the development of the conceptual framework for this chapter.

- Explain why it is critical for students with severe disabilities to have access to the general education curriculum
- Describe processes used by educational teams to identify what to teach a student with severe disabilities
- Describe why the most appropriate instructional content for a student with severe disabilities is a blending of content from the general education curriculum and the student's life outside of school
- Describe how and why school personnel collaborate, reconfigure services in the school, use effective instructional methods for all students, and use adaptations when providing access to the general education curriculum for students with severe disabilities
- Describe four aspects of meaningful assessment for students with severe disabilities, and how each can be addressed while students have access to general education

What Is "Access to the General Education Curriculum"?

Because of the importance of students with severe disabilities acquiring skills in real-life contexts with nondisabled same-age peers, when considering access to the general education curriculum, educational teams must consider for instruction content that goes beyond the traditional interpretation of the word "curriculum." For the purposes of this chapter, therefore, the phrase *general education curriculum* refers not only to the content standards described by states and school districts, but also to the content inherent within participation in all the experiences that comprise general education life (i.e., general education activities, general education settings, and independent functioning across contexts) (Ryndak et al., in press).

With the IDEA 1997 reauthorization, the concept of access to the general education curriculum became prevalent in services for students with special needs. The law refers to this concept by stating that a student's IEP must include:

> a statement of measurable annual goals, including benchmarks or short-term objectives, related to . . . meeting the child's needs that result from the child's disabilities to enable the child *to be involved and progress in the general curriculum.* [emphasis added] (20 U.S.C. section 1414 [A] [ii] [I])

It further states that the IEP must include:

> a statement of the special education and related services and supplementary aids and services to be provided . . . and a statement of the program modifications or supports for school personnel that will be provided for the child . . . *to be involved and progress in the general curriculum* and *to participate in extracurricular and other nonacademic activities.* [emphasis added] (20 U.S.C. section 1414 [A] [iii] [II])

When considering the mandate for access to the general education curriculum, therefore, there are two variables that bear consideration. The first variable is access. What is meant by access, and how can equal access be ensured for all students? The *American Heritage Dictionary of the English Language* (2000) defines access as "the ability or right to approach, enter, exit, communicate with, or make use of [something]." Wordnet (1997) defines access as "the right to obtain or make use of or take advantage of something (as services or membership)." Thus, if two persons have access to a building, then they both are admitted into the same building on an equal basis; if they have access to materials, then they both may obtain and use the same materials on an equal basis. In relation to educational services, if two students have access to academic content (e.g., freshman English, fifth-grade science, third-grade mathematics), then they both are admitted to the course and have access to the same instructional opportunities (including materials, content, and activities) on an equal basis.

To date many schools have provided "access" to general education content by establishing two sets of courses on the same content (e.g., one general education language arts class for students without disabilities taught by a teacher certified in language arts, and one "special class" for students with disabilities taught by a teacher certified in special education). At first glance this may seem appropriate, but upon remembering Chief Justice Earl Warren's words in his judgment in *Brown v. Board of Education* (1954), this dual-class system begins to be less appropriate. He wrote: "Separate educational facilities are inherently unequal. This inherent inequality stems from the stigma created by purposeful segregation which generates a feeling of inferiority that may affect their hearts and minds in a way unlikely ever to be undone." Although speaking about facilities segregated by race, his findings laid the groundwork for today's special education legislation. When considered in light of the new IDEA 97, this practice of dual classes is questioned directly, since both sets of students do not have equal access to the same academic content, instructional materials, and instructional activities. In addition, only students in the general education class have access to a teacher who is certified in the content area.

The second variable that bears consideration is "general education curriculum." In a narrow interpretation, curriculum can refer to a fixed series or sequence of instructional content mastered for the earning of a diploma or degree. In most states this content is delineated in state standards and benchmarks (see McGregor, in press). Many districts expand upon or further delineate their state's standards by developing district curriculum standards. In a less traditional sense *curriculum* refers to every component of the general education experience. Halvorsen and Neary (2001) discussed this concept by stating that "the student's IEP must be addressed within the *context* of the curriculum" (p. 5) and that in inclusive schools "students with severe disabilities can access and experience the multitude of (one hopes) interesting and motivating activities and opportunities available in the general education classroom" (p. 43). Ryndak, Alper, Stuart, and Clark (in press) discussed four aspects of the general education experience, including content, activities, settings, and independent functioning across contexts, which together comprise the experiences of general education students at any given grade level. That is, when considering the general education experiences of a general education student (e.g., a fifth grader), one must consider not only the content included in standards, but also the settings with which the student interacts, the activities in which the student participates, and the use of previously acquired skills that allow the student to function independently.

General Education Content

One aspect of the general education experience is the curriculum content. General education students at each grade level have access to the same content standards, or a core curriculum. At each grade level students are expected to demonstrate competence related to that core curriculum by demonstrating either grade-level performance or proficiency on state or locally determined assessments. It could be appropriate for a student with severe disabilities to demonstrate competence on all, part, or none of the core curriculum content for a given grade level or unit addressed for a given grade level. To determine this, however, all of this content must be considered specifically for each student.

General Education Activities

A second aspect of the general education experience is the set of activities that are common for all students. Such activities could be instructional across settings (e.g., in-class, in-school, and out-of-school activities), logistical (e.g., preparation before or cleanup after instructional activities), social (e.g., interactions in the school, on school grounds, or in field-trip settings), and extracurricular in nature (e.g., club activities or sporting events). As a whole, this set of activities offers students opportunities to: (a) acquire skills and knowledge from the general education curriculum content, (b) demonstrate skills and knowledge incorporated in the general education curriculum content, and (c) participate in common experiences that comprise school life for students of their own age and grade level. The more activities (e.g., class tasks, activities in assemblies, or experiences rushing between classes) that students with severe disabilities have in common with general education classmates, the more they are able to interact with each other about those activities. For example, it is difficult for a any student to join a discussion with classmates about a school-related experience (e.g., a concert in the auditorium, a funny event at a locker, or a stressful situation in the cafeteria) when that student has not participated in the experience with those classmates. In addition to participating in the actual school-related activity, such common experiences also offer opportunities for students to observe and relate to others' behaviors across activities, especially the social norms of their same-age classmates. Without such common experiences, students with severe disabilities have no access to either the educational or social norms that influence every aspect of each student's life.

General Education Settings

A third aspect of the general education experience is the settings, both in and out of school, to which students have access and in which they are expected to function. Even though some commonalities exist across years (e.g., every year students must have access to a bathroom, classrooms, and school hallways), the number, type, and physical layout of settings vary every year. Because of this, each year students must learn to function and participate in the settings used by their grade level. For instance, students must learn: (a) how individual classrooms are structured and organized, (b) where classrooms and other key rooms (e.g., cafeteria or nurse's office) are located in the building, and (c) when and where to attend to self-care needs (e.g., storing personal items or attending to personal hygiene).

Ensuring access to general education curriculum, therefore, must incorporate access to the settings encountered during general education activities, as well as functional participation in those settings.

Independent Functioning across Contexts

A fourth aspect of the general education experience is the use of previously acquired knowledge and skills that are relevant for independent functioning across general education contexts. Such knowledge and skills could reflect standards from the general education curriculum content that were acquired during previous school years (e.g., writing letters). Such knowledge and skills also could reflect skills not traditionally included in general education curriculum standards (e.g., mobility within a classroom, self-care, appropriate behavior, or communication), and could have been acquired either prior to, or concomitantly with, access to the general education curriculum content. In either case, the knowledge and skills continue to be relevant to the general education experience, though they now may be applied in new or more complex applications (e.g., writing words and sentences or moving in a timely manner between rooms for classes during middle school). The consistent continued use of such content allows all students to function independently across general education contexts and to benefit from opportunities to learn content from general education experiences. Though a student with severe disabilities may require additional instruction on such content relevant to independent functioning across general education contexts, this instruction is critical to ensuring access to general education.

Why Is Access to the General Education Curriculum Important?

Many individual pieces of evidence can be cited in support of providing students with severe disabilities access to the general education curriculum. For example, positive and inspiring findings have been reported in relation to the development of literacy (e.g., Ryndak, Morrison, & Sommerstein, 1999), communication and motor skills (e.g., Gee, Graham, Sailor, & Goetz, 1995), social interaction (e.g., Helmstetter, Peck, & Giangreco, 1994), and friendships (e.g., Fryxell & Kennedy, 1995). Perhaps the most compelling reasons for access, however, are found in the situated learning perspective of Lave and Wenger (1991). That perspective suggests that learning occurs within "communities of practice" in which participation is initially "legitimately peripheral," but increases over time in both degree of involvement and complexity. The ability to learn, then, "would develop in close relation to the ability to perform tasks" (Hanks, 1991, p. 21).

In other words, one cannot learn culturally normative, important behaviors in the absence of participation in the environments and activities that are culturally normative and important. It is participation that makes skill acquisition *and* contextually appropriate performance possible. Kliewer (1998) makes this point clearly in the following example:

> Consider the student of Spanish who has received straight As over years of textbook and classroom study. On her first trip to a Spanish-speaking country, she flounders. The people do not speak the language she learned; even if she did know it, they speak too fast; they have

strange nouns that never made the textbook, strange phrases, and even stranger customs. It is all she can do to find a bathroom, and she has great difficulty in even ordering a soft drink! This student's study, which occurred apart from the culture, did not prepare her to participate in the culture. After 6 months' time, however, she flounders less. She has been immersed in the community and that very immersion has been an education more profound than all her years of study combined. Though she will remain, by degree, an outsider, her participation decreases the gap between who she is and what it means to be a part of that culture. Had she been brought up in that culture, of course, the gap would not exist at all. (p. 318)

Similarly, the situated learning perspective suggests that it would not be possible to develop the skills to play a team game (e.g., soccer), to develop mutually supportive relationships with team members, or to learn the unwritten etiquette of the sport without being allowed to participate in the game as a member of the team. For children and youth with disabilities, then, active participation in activities alongside typical individuals is required to develop competence as members of typical but complex communities. Of course, a very significant part of the community of which children and youth are members is the school, and those "typical individuals" include classmates who do not require special education services.

Using Lave and Wenger's (1991) work as a conceptual foundation, Billingsley, Gallucci, Peck, Schwartz, and Staub (1996) described outcome domains for performances and accomplishments that were observed when students with severe disabilities were provided with access to the general education curriculum. Three outcome domains (membership, relationships, and skills) emerged from an examination of extensive qualitative and quantitative data gathered during a two-year follow-along study of 35 preschool through junior high-school students with moderate to severe disabilities who were enrolled full time in general education classes. Billingsley and colleagues (1996) noted that the children in inclusive classrooms achieved many of the outcomes generally associated with exposure to successful special education services (i.e., social/communicative skills, academics, and functional skills). However, they also found that the students developed a variety of personal relationships with their typically developing peers, and that, in varying degree, they achieved membership in formal and informal groups within the classroom and school. Definitions of outcome categories observed within each of the three domains are presented in Table 3.1.

The findings reported by Billingsley and colleagues (1996) indicated that access to the general education curriculum resulted in the kinds of multidimensional effects that, from a situated learning perspective, ought to be achieved through participation. Those effects also were noted to yield holistic advantages that were greater than their parts because they possessed the potential to be transactional and interdependent. That is, participation in the general education curriculum provided the opportunity to gain membership and to develop skills and relationships. Over time, it appeared that increases and improvements in each domain resulted in increases and improvements in the other domains (e.g., improvements in membership facilitated improvements in social relationships and skill development) and resulted in fuller participation in general education. With fuller participation, additional improvements occurred in each of the domains, and so on. For example, a child engaging in a membership activity, such as participating in a class play, also may

TABLE 3.1 Definitions of Outcome Categories

Membership	Relationships	Skills
Role in small group: Student plays an essential role in multiple groups across the school day.	**Play/companionship:** Student engages in reciprocal social interactions with peers.	**Social/communication skills:** The degree of change the student demonstrates in using appropriate social and/or communication skills independently.
Class membership: Student involved in class activities, takes turns with class responsibilities, participates in class privileges, and is active in class routines.	**Helpee:** Student receives and accepts appropriate levels of help from peers. **Helper:** Student offers or provides appropriate levels of help to peers.	**Academic skills:** The degree of change the student demonstrates in using academic skills (e.g., reading, writing, or math).
Friendship cliques: Student is a stable member of a consistent group of friends.		
School membership: Student is involved in schoolwide activities, attends assemblies, and other school functions. **Outside of school activities:** Student is a regular participant in outside of school activities or clubs. Necessary accommodations are present.	**Peer/reciprocal:** Student engages in reciprocal task-related interactions with peers. **Adversarial:** Student is involved in negative interactions with one or more peers.	**Functional skills:** The degree of change the student demonstrates in using skills that increase the student's degree of independence and enable the student to control the environment.

Source: Adapted from Billingsley, Gallucci, Peck, Schwartz, & Staub (1996).

establish or strengthen social relationships and develop useful communication skills (refer also to the experiences of Kliewer's [1998] Spanish student as she more thoroughly participated in the culture of the Spanish-speaking country).

Additionally, it is important to recognize that *each* of the identified domains can contribute substantially to quality of life. The development of skills undoubtedly plays a significant role in promoting independence within and adaptation to residential, community, and vocational settings (see Chapter 15), and possessing feelings of belonging within the community plays a critical role in contributing to a full and meaningful life (see Chapter 6). In fact, Jorgensen and Calculator (1994) interpreted existing research as indicating "one variable that seemed to be more influential than all others in predicting a 'good life'— greater amounts of time spent with people without disabilities who considered the person to be a real friend" (p. 9). The domains, then, are to be equally valued and, where students are removed from inclusive general education contexts in order to achieve only one type of outcome, it is likely that opportunities to achieve outcomes in the other domains will be diminished.

We thoroughly understand that much additional work needs to be done to further strengthen outcomes for students with severe disabilities within the context of general education, particularly in the areas of academic and "functional" skill development (Billingsley & Albertson, 1999). However, given (a) the importance of membership, social relationships, and skill development, (b) their transactional nature, and (c) their interdependence with opportunities to participate, access to the general education curriculum appears not simply recommended, but imperative.

How Do We Identify What to Teach?

When providing educational services for students with severe disabilities, practitioners initially used a "developmental" approach; after all, this was the approach we knew and had used with students who did not require special education services. During the 1970s and 1980s, however, the field moved from a largely "developmental" to a "functional" perspective in identifying instructional targets for students with severe disabilities. During this time a great many commercial curriculum guides intended for use with students with severe disabilities flooded the education market. Those curriculum guides listed skill after skill that should be included in "functional" instructional programs. Soon, however, it became apparent that those guides were insufficient for identifying the unique needs of individual students with severe disabilities, their families, and their life contexts, and the field moved to a more thoughtful perspective to determine what to teach. That approach focused not so much on the assessment of students' strengths and weaknesses when selecting skills for instruction, but on the assessment of current, and likely future, environments in which students lived, worked, and played. Such assessments involved gathering information from many sources, particularly parents, regarding those skills and supports that might provide the best preparation for positive quality-of-life changes in natural environments. Often, a formal process involving *ecological* (or *environmental*) *inventories* was applied that, through direct observation and interviews with several individuals in the student's life, suggested specific needs across school, home, work, and community settings.

Although use of the above practices resulted in instructional content that was more relevant to individual needs than the prepackaged curriculum guide approach that preceded them, the focus was not on today's intent to promote the involvement and progress of students in the general education curriculum. *In order to achieve that involvement and progress, it is important that special educators not revert to a variation of the prepackaged approach that would involve selecting items from the general education curriculum, reducing them to their simplest terms, and then teaching them to students with special needs.* This method for determining what to teach would be very similar to that of pulling items from the commercial curriculum guides of two decades ago. *Rather, the care and thought that were inherent in such processes as ecological inventories must be expanded to encompass the broader experiential base that our students encounter in inclusive school environments.* The task of selecting what to teach, then, is not one of determining which of the skills that form the general education curriculum can be taught to students with severe disabilities. *Rather, the task remains one of identifying instructional content that is likely to lead to participation in valued roles and activities in natural environments, both across general education experiences and outside of school time.*

The ecological inventory process remains valuable; however, because inclusive environments are more complex than segregated settings, and because the intersection of meaningful life-related outcomes and access to the general education curriculum are sought, richer processes that involve the student, special educators, parents, and support professionals are needed (Jackson, Ryndak, & Billingsley, 2000; Ryndak et al., in press; Ryndak, Morrison, & Sommerstein, in press). Those processes, which may involve the focal student, as well as a broad range of significant individuals in the student's life (e.g., classmates, siblings, community members, and general education professionals), incorporate methods such as Choosing Options and Accommodations for Children (COACH; Giangreco, Cloninger, & Iverson, 1998), MAPS (Forest & Lusthaus, 1990), PATH (Pearpoint, O'Brien, & Forest, 1993), and the Osborn-Parnes Creative Problem Solving Method (Giangreco, Cloninger, Dennis, & Edelman, 1994). Inherent in such methods and the overriding process for identifying what to teach is a concern for blending instructional content that addresses critical individual needs, previously viewed as "functional," with content from the general education curriculum (i.e., content, activities, settings, and independent functioning across contexts). Also inherent in these methods and this process is a concern for developing a shared vision for the student's quality of life and modifying educational services to maximize the probability that the vision will be realized. This is accomplished by identifying instructional priorities related to a student's life at home, life in the community, interactions with and acceptance by peers, participation in general education activities, and independence in general education settings. These priorities are then used to develop annual goals that, when met, will improve the student's quality of life by increasing independence and participation in real-life activities with nondisabled peers (Ryndak et al., in press).

As priority educational needs for students are identified, educational teams must also determine which specific annual goals will emphasize independent participation or partial participation in skills and activities across general education experiences and outside of school. The principle of partial participation suggests that even those students with the most extensive cognitive, motoric, and sensory disabilities who may not achieve total independence in their performances can learn to actively participate in activities that are valued and valuable (Ferguson & Baumgart, 1991). Of particular importance when identifying what to teach may be examining whether a student might benefit more from practicing across natural school and community contexts skills and activities that already have been acquired, or benefit more from learning new skills and activities. In addition, where partial participation is considered appropriate, educational teams should examine whether students might benefit from instruction that focuses on *extension skills* (i.e., skills that extend the core skills used in an activity and include such elements as initiation, preparation, and problem solving) and on *enrichment skills* (i.e., skills that are not critical to the performance of the core skills for an activity, but add to their quality).

Following the principle of partial participation ensures that *all* students can take part in those activities that contribute to a rewarding quality of life both across general education experiences and outside of school life. As suggested by the work of Lave and Wenger (1991), active participation is the basic and necessary condition for the future development of social relationships, skill development, and school and community membership.

How Does an Educational Team Provide Access to the General Education Curriculum?

Once educational teams have decided what to teach a student with severe disabilities, their efforts invariably shift to focus on how to provide instruction on that content in a way that ensures the student access to the general education curriculum, while ensuring effective instruction for all students. While Jackson, Ryndale, and Billingsley (2000) discussed many variables that experts describe as required for effective school inclusion, four of these variables relate directly to how educational teams can provide access to general education. These are described below.

Collaboration

Providing access to the general education curriculum requires collaboration among school personnel, including general educators, special educators, related services providers, paraeducators, student support staff, and administrators. Though collaborative styles vary, the outcomes of collaboration are key to effective services. For instance, collaborative efforts should result in the creation of a unified schoolwide culture that supports both: (a) the identification of meaningful instructional content for students with severe disabilities, based on both the general education curriculum and functional needs both in and out of school; and (b) the provision of services that allow effective instruction on that content. This culture should, in effect, equalize power, roles, and responsibilities across general and special educators, so that all school personnel are viewed as collaborative partners in the provision of services for all students. Once viewed this way, school personnel then need the skills that are essential in fulfilling that expectation; therefore, the training and technical assistance needs of all school personnel must be met, so that members of each educational team understand the basic knowledge of (a) general education content and instructional methods (see Chapter 2); (b) special education accommodations, modifications, and instructional techniques (see Chapter 4); and (c) related services approaches (see Chapters 9 and 10). This allows school personnel to communicate more easily by providing a common basic understanding of professional language and concepts and allows school personnel to engage in practices like role release (Rainforth, York, & Macdonald, 1992), in which various team members share specific expertise with each other, so that students may benefit from that expertise even when the specialist is not present. As school personnel develop a better understanding of the expertise provided by others and a better perception of how that expertise can be used to improve a student's participation in the general education curriculum, they can redefine the roles and responsibilities of all adults in the school (e.g., general educators, special educators, related services personnel, paraeducators, volunteers, students, guidance counselors, and behavior specialists).

Reconfiguration of Services

With the redefinition of roles and responsibilities, school personnel then are free to reconfigure services so that students' various needs can be met within the same instructional activity. To accomplish this, educational teams must jointly schedule, coordinate, deliver, and evaluate services for all students within inclusive settings. Schedules for both school personnel and students are critical to this process. For example, school personnel may utilize various forms of block scheduling (Rainforth, York, & Macdonald, 1992) that allow personnel to spend longer periods of time in one classroom or instructional setting, thus decreasing the degree to which their time is fragmented. Educational teams also may utilize forms of role release, so that all school personnel can implement and evaluate instruction across a student's areas of need. Role release allows instruction on one need (e.g., communicating with peers) to occur across the day, with support from a speech/language pathologist, a special educator, a general educator, a paraeducator, a volunteer, a classmate, a cafeteria worker, an administrator, a bus driver, etc. (see Chapter 2). In this way, the student's instructional time is multiplied, while concerns related to skill maintenance and generalization are inherently addressed. In relation to student's schedules, educational team members can verify that instruction related to each annual goal is embedded within instruction that occurs across the student's natural general education contexts. This could mean that a student's instruction on: (a) the use of fine motor skills is addressed when manipulating objects during class activities, when purchasing and carrying lunch in the cafeteria, or when opening the lock on his or her locker; (b) reading letters, words, or sentences is addressed during morning circle, language arts class, school job activities, or reading directions in science class; or (c) use of math computation skills is addressed during math class, work at the school store, or class activities in social studies. The intent is to consider when a skill is needed for completion of any general education activity in any general education setting and embed instruction on that skill when it is needed by the student.

A second strategy for reconfiguring services is for a school to use processes that allow first for the identification of the students' needs for support and identification of the general education locations across the school in which services can meet those needs, and then for school personnel to be assigned roles that fill the students' support needs in those locations (Stetson & Associates, 1998). In this way students are not assigned to service providers; rather, service providers are assigned to sets of students in settings. This may result in school personnel (including special educators and related services personnel) being assigned to co-teach either a class period or an entire day, to provide consultative support to other school personnel (Pugach & Johnson, 1995), or to provide direct instruction in pull-out settings, such as work locations, secondary education contexts, or the community (see Chapters 14 and 15).

Effective Instructional Methods in General Education Classes

Once school personnel are assigned roles on educational teams, they can plan and implement instruction that utilizes instructional methods that are effective for all students. Some general methods are useful in establishing an environment that allows instructional methods to be effective. For example, Christenson, Ysseldyke, and Thurlow (1989) described 10 effective methods used in general education (see Table 3.2). Similarly, McCoy (1995) suggested five factors to consider when organizing instruction: (a) setting expectations, (b) providing instructional feedback, (c) assisting students to organize information, (d) furnishing practice, and (e) delivering systematic incentives. Finally, Mastropieri and Scruggs (1993) summarized the key elements of effective instruction as including daily review, specific techniques for presenting new information (e.g., the SCREAM model: *S*tructure, *C*larity, *E*nthusiasm, *A*ppropriate pace, and *M*aximize engagement), guided practice, independent practice, and formative assessment.

Numerous specific instructional methods have been described, and are useful both when providing new information and when providing opportunities to practice information (see Chapter 4). For example, Fisher, Schumaker, and Deschler (1995) described cooperative learning strategies; Carpenter and King-Sears (1997) described methods for teaching strategies to students; Kataoka and Patton (1989) described the use of an integrated curriculum; and Delisle (1997) described problem-based learning. Numerous researchers discuss various configurations for peer-mediated instruction, including student-to-student tutoring (Gartner & Reissman, 1994), classwide peer tutoring (Greenwood et al., 1987; King-Sears & Bradley, 1995), and cross-age tutoring (Barbetta et al., 1991). When considering effective instructional methods, most are likely to incorporate practices where students are engaged in activities that allow them to interact with others or with manipulatives.

Effective and Meaningful Adaptations

Once an educational team has determined the instructional methods to be used for the general education class, attention can be turned to the adaptations that would allow a student with severe disabilities to successfully participate in the planned instruction. When deciding on adaptations, attention must be given to both the type and level of adaptation used,

TABLE 3.2   General Methods That Allow for the Use of Specific Effective Instructional Methods

Classroom management
Positive school environment
Appropriate instructional match
Clear teaching goals and expectations
High quality of instruction
Instructional support for individual students
Efficient use of time
Substantive student interaction
Monitoring of student understanding and progress
Evaluation of student performance

Source: Adapted from Christenson, Ysseldyke, & Thurlow (1989).

and the aspect of the activity that will be adapted (e.g., materials, devices, equipment, cues, performance expectations, instructional support). Decisions are made based on the student's physical and cognitive needs, the intent of instruction for the student, the materials and activities being used with the student's classmates, the level of intrusiveness of the adaptation, and the possibility of using the adaptation across time and across general education contexts.

How Do Educational Teams Assess Performance?

There are a great many sources of information regarding appropriate methods for assessing the performance of students with severe disabilities (see Chapters 3, 4, 6, and 7). In general, those methods do not differ substantially, because students are being assessed on content that is meaningful to them within general education contexts. However, special educators working within those contexts may note that some general education colleagues may confine assessment only to what students can do independently or under "testing" conditions. Although assessing the adequacy of work performed independently and under "testing" conditions can be helpful, educational teams serving students with severe disabilities are apt to assess performance also (a) under instructional conditions as they provide and then reduce various forms of assistance and consequences, and (b) during naturally occurring opportunities to use knowledge and skills. Such information allows teachers to make more informed decisions regarding the nature of instruction that is needed as the student moves *toward* independence in natural contexts. Fortunately, the benefits associated with assessments that are formative and naturally occurring are beginning to gain visibility within general education (e.g., Ryndak, Morrison, & Sommerstein, 1999).

Because effective assessment methods (e.g., identifying levels of prompts needed during instruction or portfolio assessment strategies) will be highly similar regardless of instructional context, and because of their current wide dissemination, we will not catalog and discuss them individually here. Rather, we will provide some recommendations on six aspects of assessment in general education contexts that we hope will enhance the value of assessments. These recommendations are based not only on comments found within the literature, but also on our own classroom observations and conversations with teachers.

"Authentic" Assessments

In their examination of themes regarding useful practices in inclusive education for students with severe disabilities that emerged from a survey of "experts" in the field, Jackson, Ryndak, and Billingsley (2000) found that respondents offered a single theme related to assessment and reporting student progress: "Use performance-based, authentic, in-context assessments" (p. 136). That is, whether one is using frequency counts, interval measurements, work samples, or portfolio assessments, it was considered critical that assessments upon which instructional decisions will be based be conducted in contexts in which the student is engaged in meaningful activities across settings and that reflect a concern with social validity. Just as students may perform differently under instructional and testing (or "probe") conditions (Farlow, Lloyd, & Snell, 1991), so may they perform differently within highly artificial instructional contexts and within contexts that provide natural motivators and consequences for performance. Therefore, while one might teach certain money management skills during general education math class, additional instruction typically should be conducted within authentic contexts (e.g., when use of money is actually required, as in the school cafeteria or with school vending machines). Because data from assessments that occur within authentic situations reflect behavior under circumstances that are related closely to the criterion environments in which performances will be expected following skill mastery, those data are likely to be most useful in informing program decisions. Similarly, reading instruction might involve small group flash-card practice for vocabulary from a new general education unit and functional activities in the classroom. However, assessment that indicates progress in reading sight words during large group general education activities or when completing those activities would provide the critical data for determining the adequacy of student progress. We recommend a "zero inference" strategy when choosing between assessment under artificial instructional conditions and under authentic conditions, because it cannot be presumed that progress, or lack thereof, under artificial conditions will be associated with similar outcomes in authentic general education contexts.

Stating Objectives

Ensure that performance criteria are stated so that you will know what you are assessing. Objectives in the IEP form the cornerstone of the instructional process, and should therefore receive close attention by those who create them. However, given time constraints and other logistical issues, IEP objectives may not be constructed so as to serve the useful functions for which they were designed, or to communicate the same information to everyone who must use them. This holds true of criterion statements as well as for other elements of the objective. For example, Snell and Brown (2000) offered the following objective for Timothy's arrival program at preschool: "Upon arrival at preschool, Timothy will exit the car, walk to enter the preschool class, greet familiar people, remove and hang his outer garments in the cubby, and select and go to a play activity at a criterion of 10 of 15 steps (67%) during two training sessions (using partial participation on some steps as indicated in the task analysis)" (p. 167). The assessment procedure follows clearly from this objective. The teacher should count the number of steps in the task analysis completed independently by Timothy during each instructional session, and when he completes 10 of the 15 steps for two days, the objective has been completed. Contrast that objective with this one, based on one written for an elementary level student with disabilities included in a general education program: "Talika will respond to "wh-" questions with a maximum of one prompt 90 percent of the time." In this case, one cannot know whether to assess the percentage of "wh-" questions answered within a given instructional session or on a given day, or whether to assess the number of days on which she answers all such questions with a maximum of one prompt. If the latter, then the criterion would refer to 90 percent of days rather than 90 percent of correct responding. In addition, it may be preferable to state objectives and communicate assessment outcomes in terms of number of correct performances out of a specific number. In the case of Talika, 90 percent of correct responding to 20 "wh-" questions might be considered to be an indicator of more general proficiency than correct responding to 90 percent of 10 "wh-" questions. Finally, it is possible to conduct instruction and assessment on this objective without Talika even having access to general education. To ensure that access, the objective should reflect the contexts in which Talika would be required to answer "wh-" questions (e.g., during language arts in her third-grade class or during interactions with general education classmates throughout the school day).

Probing for Generalization

Just as we recommended a "zero inference" strategy in relation to instructional assessment, we also recommend such a strategy in relation to generalized performance. In other words, mastery under instructional conditions does not necessarily indicate the ability to perform skills or demonstrate understanding under conditions other than those in which the skills were learned. Because a failure to achieve generalized performance is a frequently noted outcome for *all* students (Berryman, 1993), generalization probes should be a routine part of the assessment process. Generalization probes essentially are assessments conducted without the prompts and without the artificial consequences that were used during instruction. Typically, such probes are conducted at various times following instructional mastery and occur in natural contexts, including naturally occurring variation in materials, individuals present, cues, and consequences. Generalization probes would help to determine, for example, whether a secondary student who can use a speech synthesis device effectively with general education classmates in science and language arts classes can also use the device among friends at lunch and at extracurricular events, as well as with family members at home and in the community. Data from such probes also can be used in conjunction with decision rules to select instructional practices that have a high probability of promoting generalization, as discussed later in this section. See White (1988) and Ager and Browder (1991) for a thorough discussion of issues involved in assessing generalization.

It should be noted that, although generalization probes typically occur following the achievement of an instructional aim, it is also valuable to probe for skill performance across natural criterion contexts prior to beginning instruction. When students do not use skills under more structured "testing" conditions, but do use those skills in natural contexts, the objectives related to those skills should be considered completed, thereby saving instructional time.

Accuracy versus Fluency

Consider the use of data that allow the assessment of fluency as well as accuracy. Educators traditionally have assessed student behaviors in terms of accuracy (e.g., number or percentage correct) (Kubina & Morrison, 2000). However, using only accuracy as a measure ignores the fact that fluency (i.e., accuracy plus speed) is an extremely important characteristic of effective performance. When only accuracy is measured, we can assess performance only to a limit of 100 percent correct; however, in the real world, 100 percent correct may be entirely insufficient for achieving meaningful changes in quality of life. Natural general education contexts require students to perform beyond a certain accuracy level; they demand accurate performance at certain rates, with certain latencies, or within certain durations (Barrett, 1979). Billingsley, Liberty, and White (1994) have suggested that failure to develop fluent performance may have numerous types of results (see Table 3.3, p. 48, for possible results).

TABLE 3.3   **Possible Results When Students Do Not Develop Fluent Performance**

Result	Examples
Punishing Consequences	A student who takes a lengthy period to answer questions or remarks is later avoided. A student whose gait is too slow arrives after all the seats are taken.
Limitations on Personal Freedom	A students who is not a fluent walker may be confined to wheelchairs by those who do not have the time to "wait" while the student walks.
Restricted Choices	A student who is not taught to chew and swallow fluently may be placed on restricted diets that caregivers can easily handle or that may be fed through gastronomy systems.
Failures to Generalize and Maintain Behaviors	A student who has learned to dress independently but does so very slowly is unlikely to have the opportunity to generalize the skill because others will assist in order to get it done quickly. A student who reads excruciatingly slowly may fail to maintain reading skill because it takes too much effort to do so and the natural pleasure of reading is lost.

Recently, additional benefits of focusing on fluency as an indicator of mastery have been documented (Binder, 1996; Johnson & Layng, 1992). Cited benefits included, for example, improvements in retention and endurance, and the ability to combine skill elements into more complex skill compounds. Educators, therefore, should be encouraged to collect time-based data in the form of rates, durations, or latencies that indicate the speed as well as the accuracy with which learners perform skills in natural general education contexts. They also should be encouraged to express performance aims in terms of acceptable fluency levels within various natural contexts.

Instructional Decisions

Develop or use existing rules to help make instructional decisions. Farlow, Lloyd, and Snell (1991) have indicated that extant data supports the contention that teachers of students with severe disabilities tend to (a) continue instructional programs with no change until maintenance criteria are achieved and (b) frequently fail to tailor instructional strategies to a student's current stage of learning. Further, Liberty, Haring, White, and Billingsley (1988) reported that only 33 to 41 percent of the instructional decisions made by 14 teachers of students with severe disabilities over a two-year period resulted in improved student performance, even when those teachers frequently collected assessment data. Such findings lead us to strongly recommend that educational teams use decision rules to assist in determining whether a change in instructional strategies should be implemented and, if so, what the change should be.

There currently are a variety of field-tested decision rule systems available that are likely to improve the accuracy of instructional decisions. For example, in an investigation of one system, Liberty and colleagues (1988) found that teachers made decisions that resulted in increases in correct responses by students in only 40 percent of cases when decision rules were *not* used. In contrast, when decision rules *were* used, an increase in correct responses was noted in 68 percent of cases.

Decision rule systems have been described in Neel and Billingsley (1989). In addition to those rules that specifically address acquisition and fluency stages of learning, Liberty, Haring, White, and Billingsley (1988) developed and tested effective data-based rules to assist teachers in programming for generalization and maintenance. It is especially good news that decision rules not only can increase the frequency of decisions that improve student performance in general education and other natural contexts, but that their use also can result in substantial decreases in the time educational teams spend planning. See Liberty and Haring (1990) for a review of considerations in the selection and use of data-based decision rules by educational teams.

Anecdotal Records and Portfolios Assessments

Recognizing the importance of broad, quality-of-life outcomes, Brown and Snell (2000) noted that, "recent trends look beyond simple quantitative reports and see each individual within the context of a meaningful life. Measurement strategies must support the evaluation of these important outcomes" (p. 177). Although quantitative data can be employed in documenting broad improvements in quality of life, anecdotal records and portfolio assessment augment traditional assessment methods by adding both breadth and depth to our understanding of the impact of instructional programs on a student's life.

Anecdotal records can alert us to the effects that events and conditions in the natural context have on a student's learning and performance, even when those events and conditions are not explicitly a part of the student's instructional program. Anecdotal records also can provide a basis for modifying data collection practices by documenting possible negative effects that those practices might have on the social relationships and classroom membership of students with severe disabilities within the general education contexts.

Portfolios put "meat on the bones" of quantitative data by providing student work samples that may include final products, as well as works that reflect steps toward those products. The items included in the portfolio can range from samples of students' work to logs of activities, to videotapes, to teachers' notes; in other words, a portfolio can include virtually any evidence that reflects the student's performance in meaningful activities in natural contexts. Such qualitative data provide an excellent mode of communication with parents and other educational team members regarding the progress of students. Qualitative data can also assist the educational team in determining whether the instructional program is achieving outcomes that are likely to make a difference in promoting independence, friendships, and dignity. For discussions of portfolio assessment, see Hanline and Fox (1994) and Wesson and King (1996).

Conclusion

For students with severe disabilities "access to the general education curriculum" refers not only to access to the content standards described by states and school districts, but also access to the content inherent within participation in all the experiences that comprise general education life (i.e., general education activities, general education settings, and independent functioning across contexts). Access to all of the general education experiences is critical for students with severe disabilities because of (a) the importance of membership, social relationships, and skill development, (b) their transactional nature, and (c) their interdependence with opportunities to participate in the natural age-appropriate communities of practice—that is, general education contexts. Without access to all general education experiences, students with disabilities have limited opportunities, if any, to participate and learn in the contexts that are vital to their participation in life. When identifying what to teach, educational teams identify instructional content that is likely to lead to participation in valued roles and activities in natural environments, both across general education experiences and outside of school time. This content reflects both the general education curriculum and a student's life outside of school. In order to provide effective instruction on that content, school personnel must collaborate, reconfigure services in the school, use effective instructional methods for all students, and use effective and meaningful adaptations when appropriate. Finally, effective strategies must be used to assess a student's performance in relation to meaningful measures, including acquisition, generalization, and maintenance of skills within activities that are important to the student, both in general education contexts and outside of school.

A word of caution is in order here. As school personnel begin to provide access to the general education curriculum for students with severe disabilities it becomes obvious that change in one component of a school leads to concomitant changes in other components. As indicated by Sarason (1990), changes are "so embedded in a system of interacting parts that if [one thing] is changed, then changes elsewhere are likely to occur" (p. 16). Consistent with this, Fullan and Miles (1992) indicated that if a school is to be successful at changing one aspect of their services (e.g., providing access to the general education curriculum for students with severe disabilities), then it must "focus on the development and interrelationships of all the main components of the system simultaneously—curriculum, teaching and teacher development, community, student support systems, and so on" (p. 751).

References

Ager, C. L., & Browder, D. M. (1991). Assessment of integration and generalization. In D. M. Browder, *Assessment of individuals with severe disabilities* (pp. 273–303). Baltimore: Paul H. Brookes.

American Heritage Dictionary of the English Language (4th ed.). (2000). Boston: Houghton Mifflin.

Barbetta, P. M., Miller, A. D., Peters, M. T., Heron, T. E., & Cochran, L. L. (1991). Tugmate: A cross-age tutoring program to teach sight vocabulary. *Education and Treatment of Children, 14,* 19–37.

Barrett, B. (1979). Communitization and the measured message of normal behavior. In R. York & E. Edgar (Eds.), *Teaching the severely handicapped* (vol. 4, pp. 301–318). Columbus, OH: Special Press.

Berryman, S. E. (1993). Learning for the workplace. In L. Darling-Hammond (Ed.), *Review of research in education* (pp. 343–404). Washington, DC: American Educational Research Association.

Billingsley, F. F., & Albertson, L. R. (1999). Finding a future for functional skills. *Journal of the Association for Persons with Severe Handicaps, 24,* 298–302.

Billingsley, F. F., Gallucci, C., Peck, C. A., Schwartz, I. S., & Staub, D. (1996). "But those kids can't even do math": An alternative conceptualization of outcomes for inclusive education. *Special Education Leadership Review, 3,* 43–55.

Billingsley, F. F., Liberty, K. A., & White, O. R. (1994). The technology of instruction. In E. C. Cipani & F. Spooner, *Curricular and instructional approaches for persons with severe disabilities* (pp. 81–116). Boston: Allyn and Bacon.

Binder, C. (1996). Behavioral fluency: Evolution of a new paradigm. *Behavior Analyst, 19,* 163–197.

Brown, F., & Snell, M. E. (2000). Measurement, analysis, and evaluation. In M. E. Snell & F. Brown, *Instruction of students with severe disabilities* (5th ed., pp. 173–206). Columbus, OH: Merrill.

Carpenter, S. L., & King-Sears, M. E. (1997). Strategy instruction. In D. F. Bradley, M. E. King-Sears, & D. M. Tessier-Switlick, *Teaching students in inclusive settings: From theory to practice* (pp. 283–321). Boston: Allyn and Bacon.

Christenson, S. L., Ysseldyke, J. E., & Thurlow, M. L. (1989). Critical instructional factors for students with mild disabilities: An integrative review. *Remedial and Special Education, 10,* 21–31.

Delisle, R. (1997). *How to use problem-based learning in the classroom.* Alexandria, VA: Association for Supervision and Curriculum Development.

Farlow, L. J., Lloyd, B. H., & Snell, M. E. (1991). The relationship between student performance under training conditions and under probe conditions and the implications for interpretation of student performance data. *Journal of the Association for Persons with Severe Handicaps, 16,* 85–93.

Ferguson, D. L., & Baumgart, D. (1991). Partial participation revisited. *Journal of the Association for Persons with Severe Handicaps, 16,* 218–227.

Fisher, J. B., Schumaker, J. B., & Deschler, D. D. (1995). Searching for validated inclusive practices: A review of the literature. *Focus on Exceptional Children, 28,* 1–20.

Forest, M., & Lusthaus, E. (1990). Everyone belongs with the MAPS Action Planning System. *Teaching Exceptional Children, 22,* 32–35.

Fryxell, D., & Kennedy, C. H. (1995). Placement along the continuum of services and its impact on students' social relationships. *Journal of the Association for Persons with Severe Handicaps, 20,* 259–269.

Fullan, M., & Miles, M. (1992, June). Getting reform right: What works and what doesn't. *Phi Delta Kappan, 73,* 745–652.

Gartner, A. J., & Reissman, F. (1994). Tutoring helps those who give, those who receive. *Educational Leadership, 52,* 58–61.

Gee, K., Graham, N., Sailor, W., & Goetz, L. (1995). Use of integrated general education and community settings as primary contexts for skill instruction for students with severe multiple disabilities. *Behavior Modification, 19,* 33–58.

Giangreco, M. F., Cloninger, C. J., Dennis, R. E., & Edelman, S. W. (1994). Problem-solving methods to facilitate inclusive education. In J. S. Thousand, R. A. Villa, & A. I. Nevin (Eds.), *Creativity and collaborative learning: A practical guide to empowering students and teachers* (pp. 321–346). Baltimore: Paul H. Brookes.

Giangreco, M. F., Cloninger, C. J., & Iverson, V. S. (1998). *Choosing outcomes and accommodations for children: A guide to educational planning for students with disabilities* (2nd ed.). Baltimore: Paul H. Brookes.

Greenwood, C. R., Dinwiddie, G., Bailey, V. I., Carta, J. J., Dorsery, D., Kohler, F. W., Nelson, C., Rotholz, D., & Schulte, D. (1987). Field replication of classwide peer tutoring. *Journal of Applied Behavior Analysis, 20,* 151–160.

Halvorsen, A. T., & Neary, T. (2001). *Building inclusive schools: Tools and strategies for success.* Boston: Allyn and Bacon.

Hanks, W. F. (1991). Foreword to J. Lave & E. Wenger, *Situated learning: Legitimate peripheral participation.* Cambridge: Cambridge University Press.

Hanline, M. F., & Fox, L. (1994). The use of assessment portfolios with young children with disabilities. *Assessment in Rehabilitation and Exceptionalities, 1,* 40–57.

Helmstetter, E., Peck, C. A., & Giangreco, M. F. (1994). Outcomes of interactions with peers with moderate or severe disabilities: A statewide survey of high school students. *Journal of the Association for Persons with Severe Handicaps, 19,* 263–276.

Individuals with Disabilities Education Act Amendments of 1997, 20 U.S.C. § 1400 *et seq.* (U.S. Government Printing Office, 1997).

Jackson, L., Ryndak, D. L., & Billingsley, F. F. (2000). Useful practices in inclusive education: A preliminary view of what experts in moderate to severe disabilities are saying. *Journal of the Association for Persons with Severe Handicaps, 25,* 129–141.

Johnson, K. R., & Layng, T. V. J. (1992). Breaking the structuralist barrier: Literacy and numeracy with fluency. *American Psychologist, 47,* 1475–1490.

Jorgensen, C. M., & Calculator, S. N. (1994). The evolution of best practices in educating students with severe disabilities. In S. N. Calculator & C. M. Jorgensen (Eds.), *Including students with severe disabilities in schools: Fostering communication, interaction, and participation* (pp. 1–25). San Diego: Singular.

Kataoka, J. C., & Patton, J. R. (1989). Integrated curriculum. *Science and Children, 16,* 52–58.

King-Sears, M. E., & Bradley, D. (1995). Classwide peer tutoring: Heterogeneous instruction in general education classrooms. *Preventing School Failure, 40,* 29–36.

Kliewer, C. (1998). The meaning of inclusion. *Mental Retardation, 36,* 317–322.

Kubina, R. M., & Morrison, R. (2000). Fluency in education. *Behavior and Social Issues, 10,* 83–99.

Lave, J., & Wenger, E. (1991). *Situated learning: Legitimate peripheral participation.* Cambridge, England: Cambridge University Press.

Liberty, K. A., & Haring, N. G. (1990). Introduction to decision rule systems. *Remedial and Special Education, 11,* 32–41.

Liberty, K. A., Haring, N. G., White, O. R., & Billingsley, F. F. (1988). A technology for the future: Decision rules for generalization. *Education and Training in Mental Retardation, 23,* 315–326.

Mastriopieri, M. A., & Scruggs, T. E. (1993). *A practical guide for teaching science to students with special needs in inclusive settings.* Austin, TX: Pro-Ed.

McCoy, K. M. (1995). *Teaching special learners in the general education classroom* (2nd ed.). Denver: Love.

McGregor, G. (In press). Access to general education and state standards. In D. Ryndak & S. Alper (Eds.), *Curriculum and instruction for students with significant disabilities in inclusive settings* (2nd ed.). Boston: Allyn and Bacon.

Neel, R. S., & Billingsley, F. F. (1989). *IMPACT: A functional curriculum handbook for students with moderate to severe disabilities.* Baltimore: Paul H. Brookes.

Pearpoint, J., O'Brien, J., & Forest, M. (1993). *PATH: A workbook for planning positive possible futures.* Toronto: Inclusion Press.

Pugach, M. C., & Johnson, L. J. (1995). *Collaborative practitioners: Collaborative schools.* Denver: Love.

Rainforth, B., York, J., & Macdonald, C. (1992). *Collaborative teams for students with severe disabilities: Integrating therapy and educational services.* Baltimore: Paul H. Brookes.

Ryndak, D. L., Alper, S., Stuart, C., & Clark, D. (in press). Identifying curriculum for students with severe disabilities in general education contexts. In *AAMR research to practice series: Innovations.* Washington, DC: American Association on Mental Retardation.

Ryndak, D. L., Morrison, A. P., & Sommerstein, L. (1999). Literacy before and after inclusion in general education settings: A case study. *Journal of the Association for Persons with Severe Handicaps, 24,* 5–22.

Sandler, A. G. (1999). Short-changed in the name of socialization? Acquisition of functional skills by students with severe disabilities. *Mental Retardation, 37,* 148–150.

Sarason, S. (1990). *The predictable failure of educational reform.* San Francisco: Jossey-Bass Publishers.

Snell, M. E., & Brown, F. (2000). Development and implementation of educational programs. In M. E. Snell & F. Brown, *Instruction of students with severe disabilities* (pp. 115–172). Columbus, OH: Merrill.

Stetson and Associates. (1998). *A step by step approach for inclusive schools: Together is better!* Tallahassee: Florida Department of Education.

Strully, J., & Strully, C. (1985). Friendships and our children. *Journal of the Association for Persons with Severe Handicaps, 10,* 224–227.

Wesson, C. L., & King, R. P. (1996). Portfolio assessment and special education students. *Teaching Exceptional Children, 28,* 44–48.

White, O. R. (1988). Probing skill use. In N. G. Haring (Ed.), *Generalization for students with severe handicaps: Strategies and solutions* (pp. 129–142). Seattle: University of Washington Press.

Wordnet. (1997). Princeton, NJ: Princeton University.

4 Systematic Instruction

**JAMES W. HALLE, JANIS CHADSEY,
SUZANNE LEE, AND ADELLE RENZAGLIA**
University of Illinois

This chapter focuses on concepts and strategies involved in planning and delivering instruction to students with severe disabilities. In a generic sense, all teaching involves identification of intended outcomes for students, assessment of student skills and knowledge, and planning and implementation of activities designed to assist students in acquiring and practicing targeted skills. Research-supported practices for instruction of students with severe disabilities are based in what is referred to as systematic instruction. After reading this chapter you will be able to:

- Define systematic instruction as a means of facilitating student learning
- Identify the types of outcomes related to systematic instruction that should be documented
- Understand the key components of systematic instruction
- Identify instances when specific systematic instructional techniques should be used

Elements of Systematic Instruction

Definition

One way systematic instruction can be distinguished from other approaches to planning and teaching is by its emphasis on approaching instruction from a behavioral paradigm. A key feature of systematic instruction is frequent, precise measurement of an observable and measureable "outcome" of instruction. Considerable attention is given to carefully defining what students will learn and be able to do and the circumstances under which they will be able to apply their new skills and knowledge.

Another essential component in systematic instruction is its focus on developing an intervention package including both antecedents and consequences that are selected to increase the probability that learning occurs and that changes in skills will be maintained and generalized. Educators using a systematic-instruction approach integrate principles of learning and instruction with knowledge about their students and how they learn best. From this information, educators create a very detailed plan for teaching and for evaluating the effectiveness of instruction.

Sometimes educators' decisions about student learning and when to move on in the curriculum are made based on the calendar—a certain amount of time is allocated to covering particular content, then the educator must move on to other areas to ensure that all areas are covered during the school year. In contrast, in a systematic instruction approach, students are assessed on the intended outcomes before instruction begins (i.e., the baseline) and then continue to be assessed on a frequent basis as they are being taught. Instruction and measurement continue hand in hand until the student can perform the skills at the targeted level rather than ending at a particular date on the calendar.

Importance

It is important to use a systematic-instruction approach with students with severe disabilities for a number of reasons. Most compelling is that students with severe disabilities are unlikely to learn with other, less precise types of instruction. Indeed, systematic instruction was developed because these students failed to learn when presented with the typical educational curriculum and instructional strategies. Systematic instruction requires that a learning task be broken down into parts (task analysis) and taught using carefully designed antecedent and consequence strategies that assist students in focusing on the relevant parts of the task, enabling them to respond correctly. This micro-analysis of teaching, coupled with frequent measurement of student progress, allows educators to identify more readily whether their teaching is effective and to adjust their instructional programs as needed to ensure student progress. This systematic approach is particularly important for students with severe disabilities because they generally require more frequent opportunities to practice skills correctly to ensure acquisition and maintenance of high-priority skills. Finally, a critical feature of systematic instruction is its strong data-based orientation. Assessment data permit an objective determination of (a) where to begin instruction and (b) the effects of instruction.

In the remainder of this chapter, we will describe (a) principles that guide the implementation of systematic instruction; (b) characteristics of behavior targeted for instruction; (c) five strategies for programming consequences (i.e., events that occur subsequent to the behavior of interest); (d) various types of reinforcers and how they are identified; (e) scheduling of reinforcers to enhance maintenance of behavior; (f) means of promoting generalized use of new skills; (g) strategies for modifying antecedents (i.e., events that precede the behavior); and (h) methods for evaluating the effects of systematic instruction.

Guiding Principles

Decades of research on effective instruction with individuals with severe disabilities have produced a number of guiding principles for designing systematic instructional programs. These principles guide educators in developing instructional plans that have the greatest likelihood of student learning and include: (a) teaching meaningful and functional skills, (b) errorless learning, (c) facilitating attention to relevant stimuli, (d) providing frequent opportunities to respond, and (e) providing a positive learning environment. The components of a well-developed instructional program should incorporate these principles.

For instruction to achieve the label "systematic," it must encompass an overall plan (Box 4.1 illustrates an overall plan for Jesse). Referred to as a curriculum, this plan prescribes what is to be taught. Curriculum (what to teach) can be separated from instruction (how to teach); however, we believe the two are so intricately tied to one another that we want to provide at least some cursory guidelines for curriculum. In fact, the specific target behaviors discussed throughout this chapter could not be determined without identifying a more global curriculum. Motivation for learning is increased when the skills taught are meaningful to the student. Identifying and teaching skills that are useful now and will continue to be useful in the future are critical for students who do not learn as rapidly as others. Given the relatively few years students spend in school, the time must be used well. Teaching skills in meaningful contexts, settings containing materials that represent those in the natural environment and activities that are targeted as high priority for participation, likely will result in quicker acquisition, lasting maintenance and increased generalization to similar situations (Horner, Dunlap, & Koegel, 1988; Stokes & Baer, 1977). For students with severe disabilities, the connection between skills and meaningful applications must be made from the onset of instruction, increasing the likelihood of acquisition and minimizing the time needed for facilitating maintenance and generalization. (For additional information on functional and socially valid skills, see Brown et al., 1979; Wehman, Renzaglia, & Bates, 1985).

The role of errors in learning has been a point of discussion among educators. However, the research with individuals with intellectual disabilities consistently has supported an errorless learning format (Alberto & Troutman, 1999; Wolery, Bailey, & Sugai, 1988) in which instruction is programmed specifically to eliminate the probability of errors in responding. One potential negative outcome of instruction that includes frequent errors is the development of a "failure set" on the part of the student. This means that the student, after making frequent errors and failing to acquire the targeted information, becomes anxious when provided with instruction in a similar context and with similar content to that in which failure has been experienced. This anxiety may produce avoidance behavior (misbehavior or distracting behavior) that results in the student escaping the instructional interaction or in the student becoming distressed (e.g., looking away, frowning, perspiring, crying, or the like) when presented with instruction.

A second potential undesirable outcome of instruction that includes frequent errors is the development of error patterns. That is, if students are not learning the information relevant to the task presented, they might respond by using a strategy that is not relevant to the task at hand but has worked for them in the past. For example, students might respond to a two-choice discrimination task using position if they don't understand the task. If they always pick the choice on the right, they will be correct about 50 percent of the time, strengthening the use of this strategy and developing an error pattern. On the other hand, instruction that is errorless or near errorless provides a positive instructional interaction in which the student experiences success based on responding correctly to the task presented.

Using instructional strategies that facilitate the student's attention to the relevant features or stimuli of the task is another guiding principle of good instruction. Successful task performance requires the student to attend to the features of the task that are critical to performing the task correctly and not to other stimuli that might be present in the materials or

BOX **4.1**

Jesse

Jesse is a third-grade student in Mr. Marsh's class at Fairview Elementary School. Jesse shares his strong interest in videogames, game character trading cards, and action figures with many of his third-grade classmates. Throughout the school day in Mr. Marsh's room, Jesse receives special education services designed by Ms. Smythe, his special education teacher. Because Jesse has severe disabilities, he requires an individualized curriculum focused on developing skills in caring for himself and helping around the house, participating actively in a variety of leisure-recreation skills, and becoming more independent in the community.

One of the objectives on Jesse's IEP is using money. Jesse's parents want him to independently purchase one or two items in a number of situations, such as buying a snack at the concession stand at his brother's high school football games, buying trading cards at a local "superstore," or getting a snack at a neighborhood convenience store. Ms. Smythe wanted to design an instructional program to teach purchasing skills to Jesse that would ensure that he could perform the skills in the wide variety of situations important to Jesse and his family. She also wanted to ensure that Jesse had frequent opportunities to practice the purchasing skills while also keeping him together with his classmates in Mr. Marsh's room to the greatest extent possible.

Working collaboratively with Mr. Marsh, Ms. Smythe designed an instructional program that involved teaching Jesse and several of his classmates in multiple community settings (to enhance generalization). Ms. Smythe and Mr. Marsh identified skills from the general academic third-grade curriculum that students could practice in community settings such as those in which Jesse needed to receive instruction. Some of the skills identified included calculating price per unit on grocery items at the superstore to compare to price per unit on similar items at a convenience store and analyzing the nutrition facts on labels of popular snack items to identify more and less healthful snacks.

Mr. Marsh and Ms. Smythe planned for community-based instruction to occur three afternoons each week during "workshop time." During this class time, all Mr. Marsh's students worked on independent or small group projects across various subject areas; Mr. Marsh used this time to work with individual children or small groups of students. On these three days each week, Ms. Smythe takes Jesse and another student or two into the community for instruction. During this session, Ms. Smythe provides instruction to Jesse's classmates on their targeted skills and teaches Jesse to purchase items using a "next dollar" strategy. She uses a *most-to-least intrusive response-prompting hierarchy* and capitalizes on naturally occurring reinforcers to maintain newly acquired skills. Furthermore, Ms. Smythe assesses Jesse's performance on a regular basis by conducting probes. On the two days each week in which no community-based instruction occurs during workshop time, Ms. Smythe or a teaching assistant conducts instruction in Mr. Marsh's room in a simulation context of a board game or other small-group activity.

Ms. Smythe is pleased to see Jesse's independence in purchasing increase across the weeks. As she inspects the graphed probe data she collects regarding Jesse's performance, it appears that he will achieve the criterion level identified in his IEP if his current *trend* continues. His parents report that they, too, have seen his skills and confidence improve when he is with them in the community. Mr. Marsh enthusiastically awaits their turn for community-based instruction. Mr. Marsh notes that several students who had been struggling in math problem solving have improved significantly because of the opportunities the community-based instruction provides for them in more naturally occurring contexts.

context of the task and do not have any relevance to correct performance. For example, size, shape, and color do not have any relevance to determining ordinal position, such as first in line. However, students might associate color with ordinal position (e.g., if first in line is always red) if the educator doesn't systematically vary irrelevant features of the task. If students respond to a request to identify the "first in line" by identifying the red object, they will make errors. Frequent errors are closely related to students' lack of attention to the relevant features or stimuli of the task.

Another principle of good instruction is to provide students with frequent opportunities to respond to the instructional task. The more trials that are provided to the student, the more opportunities the student has to practice the skill and to learn by receiving feedback, and the more rapidly the student will acquire new skills. However, this is sometimes difficult because the targeted skills often do not occur naturally on a frequent basis. For example, if the target skill is bed making, this occurs naturally once a day, and good instruction might suggest multiple trials daily for learning to occur at an adequate rate. Therefore, an educator would have to be creative to provide frequent opportunities for the student to receive instruction on bed making. Perhaps the educator would ask the student to make all of the beds in a house, or return with the student to the bedroom throughout the day to find that the bed has been unmade by someone and needs to be remade. Skills such as use of money to purchase items at the drugstore occur naturally even less frequently than once daily. Practicing the target skills in simulated environments (in the classroom or school at large) in addition to instruction in natural environments would be another way to increase the opportunities to engage in the task.

Finally, a positive learning environment is crucial to positive outcomes of the educational process. A positive learning environment encompasses the prior guiding principles, but also includes structure and routines, sensitive instructional pacing, high expectations for student performance, and constructive and positive feedback. Providing structure to the learning context, including rules for behavior and routines for completing activities, enhances the predictability of the environment. Also strategic planning of activities that alternates sedentary instructional tasks with more active, movement-oriented tasks may create a more positive learning environment. Instructional pacing that is geared to the amount of time students require to respond may produce optimal outcomes—too rapid and students become fatigued or frustrated, too slow and disruptive behavior becomes more likely. High expectations for student performance goes hand in hand with constructive and positive feedback. Educators' high expectations assure optimal rates of learning when students' efforts are acknowledged with either constructive feedback to assist with future performance, if incorrect, or positive feedback to reinforce correct responding.

A-B-Cs as a Fundamental Approach to Instruction

Long ago, the researchers embracing an operant explanation of human behavior adopted the A-B-C equation in which A = *antecedent* events that "set the occasion" for the target behavior, B = the target *behavior,* and C = the *consequences* produced by the target behavior (Skinner, Reynolds, others). Although simplistic, this equation provides a powerful tool for determining immediate influences (the As and the Cs) on behavior (the B), whether it be in the context of assessing why behavior is occurring or in the context of changing behavior. Identifying, refining, and modifying antecedents and consequences are the *fundamental operations* of systematic instruction that produce learning of new concepts and acquisition of new skills. Much of the remainder of this chapter is organized by these three overarching factors: antecedents, behavior, consequences. Thus, we begin this section by describing characteristics of behavior targeted for instruction. Then we turn to a discussion of five types of consequences that influence behavior and provide detailed information about (a) reinforcers and their identification, (b) schedules of reinforcement and their contribution to maintenance of behavior, and (c) generalization of behavior. Finally, we summarize information about antecedents and how they can be arranged to influence behavior. Antecedents covered include *prompting* and *prompt-fading* strategies that when programmed effectively lead to acquisition of skills at the appropriate time and place, an outcome referred to as *stimulus control.*

Characteristics of Behavior Targeted for Instruction

Operationalizing or pinpointing target behavior.   Fundamental to systematic instruction is *behavior.* We cannot determine a goal or an outcome, assess current performance, or evaluate progress without first defining the focus of instruction in behavioral terms. Professionals often refer to this process as *operationalizing* or *pinpointing* behavior. Kazdin (1982) cites two criteria that define a behavior: it must be observable and measurable. Observable means that you can see it, hear it, or touch it. Measurable means that you can record some dimension of it such as its frequency, intensity, or duration. Once the focus of instruction is identified in behavioral terms, it is clear when it has occurred and when it has not and it can be monitored to see if it is changing with instruction (see section on evaluation). Although educators sometimes have difficulty with the process of operationalizing or pinpointing behavior, it is helpful to remember that whatever descriptor they have used to characterize the child, it necessarily was based on behaviors they had observed in the child. This is the only way we come to know something about another person. Thus, if an educator refers to a child as *confident,* this label is used because the educator observed particular behaviors in the past. Therefore the process is one of working backward: what behaviors of the child lead to the descriptor the educator is using to describe the problem/focus. As an example, if educators target self-esteem as a focus of instruction, they will need to operationalize the term *self-esteem* because it does not meet the definition of behavior; it's neither observable nor measurable. Behaviors that might define self-esteem will vary with the individual, but might include any of the following: attempting a difficult task or attending longer to it, disagreeing with the majority in one's peer group, making statements like "I did well on my math quiz today!" or answering questions in large group discussions. Similarly, if reducing the frequency of *autistic behavior* is the goal, specific behaviors need to be identified and might assume the form of being alone during free play, not making eye contact when interacting with another, or repeated hand flapping (back and forth movement at the wrist). The importance of defining learning targets in behavioral terms cannot be overstated; systematic instruction depends on this critical prerequisite.

Discrete and chained target behaviors.   In the process of identifying target behaviors, a distinction needs to be made between those targets that are discrete and those that are chained. Discrete targets are single responses such as coming when called or learning to say "hello" when introduced to a new person. Chained targets involve multiple responses and might include tasks like brushing teeth, getting dressed, or making a bed. Each of these tasks encompasses multiple behaviors. For example, when brushing teeth, students need to (a) pick up the brush, (b) open the toothpaste, (c) place a ribbon of paste on the bristles, (d) turn on the water, (e) moisten the brush, (f) brush the upper left quadrant of the mouth in a circular motion on three surfaces (the inside, the outside, and the bottom), (g) brush the other three quadrants (you get the idea). In summary, when learning targets are identified, they need to be categorized as either discrete or chained; if they are chained targets, the specific steps or responses need to be identified prior to instruction. The process of identifying multiple steps in a chained target is identical to what others refer to as *task analysis*.

Consequences of Behavior

In the A-B-C equation, the C represents consequences. Consequences are events that occur after behavior and are implemented contingently and immediately. Contingent means they depend on the occurrence of the target behavior; the consequence should be delivered *only* after the behavior has occurred. The timing of the consequence is important, because if it is not delivered immediately after the behavior, the relationship between behavior and its consequence may not be established. If the consequence is delayed, another behavior may occur before the consequence, and this latter behavior, instead of the target, will be influenced. After a behavior is acquired, immediacy of the consequence becomes less relevant for most students.

At this point, it is important to digress to consider the possibility that consequences for our behavior are occurring all the time, whether we realize it or not, and these consequences influence the likelihood that our behavior will continue or change. For example, when a student raises her hand to ask the educator a question and the educator does not see the raised hand, hand raising may become less likely. After raising her hand, if the same student yells to the educator, "I have a question!" and the educator approaches her, yelling for attention may become more likely. Certainly this is not the educator's intended outcome, but naturally occurring consequences do influence behavior.

In contrast to naturally occurring consequences, in systematic instruction consequences are implemented in a planful or systematic way. (Later we discuss a strategy to promote the maintenance of newly acquired target behavior that encompasses transferring from planned to natural consequences.) Different types of consequences are available depending on the educator's goal. At least five classes of consequences can be distinguished: positive and negative reinforcement, extinction, and positive and negative punishment.

If a response occurs that the educator wants to encourage, then either positive or negative reinforcement ought to be considered. *Positive reinforcement* describes a relationship between behavior and its consequences such that when a behavior occurs and is followed by the *presentation* of a *pleasant* event, the behavior is more likely to occur in the future. Whenever an educator praises or delivers a sticker for a correct response, positive reinforcement *may* be operating. *Negative reinforcement* describes a relationship between behavior and its consequences such that when a behavior occurs and is followed by the *removal* of an *unpleasant* event, the behavior is more likely to occur in the future. Whenever an educator allows a student to select a preferred activity contingent on completing a worksheet, she is *attempting* to employ negative reinforcement. Please note that both types of reinforcers produce the same outcome: an increase in the rate of the target behavior. The distinction lies in whether the consequence is *presented (and pleasant)* or *removed (and unpleasant)*. Two important caveats require mention (a) the person who determines whether the consequence is pleasant or unpleasant *must be* the student and (b) whether reinforcement has occurred can be determined *only* after the effect on behavior is measured—this is the reason that we italicized the words *may* and *attempting* above.

If a response occurs that an educator wants to discourage, then any of the remaining three classes of consequences might be considered. Extinction is the third class of consequences, but is distinguished by its lack of consequence. *Extinction* describes a relationship between behavior and its consequence such that a behavior that has been reinforced previously no longer is reinforced—the reinforcing consequence is withdrawn. For example, an educator determines that Dana, a child with a severe disability, spits to gain the attention (laughter and pointing to Dana) of two peers who sit next to her. The educator moves Dana to the other side of the room close to peers who will not look at or say anything to Dana when she spits. In this example, peer attention was the reinforcing consequence for spitting and it was removed by changing Dana's seat assignment. When employing extinction, three considerations are critical. First, be sure to identify the reinforcer for the target behavior; it cannot be assumed that attention is always the reinforcer. Second, like reinforcement, extinction is defined by its effect on behavior, so only when behavior is reduced in frequency can extinction be claimed. Third, if attention is the reinforcer, one must be prepared to withhold it no matter what behavior occurs because under conditions of extinction a student's behavior may worsen in an effort to regain the lost reinforcement. If educators cannot "stay the course," their attention to more coercive forms will reinforce worse behavior.

Extinction is only one means of reducing or eliminating behavior; punishment offers two additional classes of consequences that produce this same outcome. In systematic instruction punishment has a somewhat different definition than that used in everyday conversation. Like the other classes of consequences, punishment is defined by its effect on behavior rather than its form. That is, we cannot know by watching a father yell at his toddler son for running across the street whether the yell functioned as a punishing consequence until we observe the future occurrence of this behavior. Only if it becomes less likely did the yell function as a punisher. Like reinforcement, two classes of punishment can be distinguished. *Positive punishment* describes a relationship between behavior and its consequences such that when a behavior occurs and is followed by the *presentation* of an *unpleasant* event, the behavior is less likely to occur in the future. Whenever an educator frowns and tells students they are too noisy during silent reading, positive punishment is operating (if noise levels during silent reading decrease in the future). *Negative punishment* describes a relationship between behavior and its consequences such that when a behavior occurs and is followed by the *removal* of a *pleasant* event, the behavior is less likely to occur in the future. Whenever an educator removes students from an enjoyable activity because they did not follow the rules and requires them to "sit out," negative punishment has occurred (if they increase their rule following in the future). *Presentation* and *removal* are key operations distinguishing positive and negative punishment just, as they were with reinforcement. In systematic instruction positive punishment often includes facial expressions, negative feedback (e.g., "No, don't touch the card"), or tone of voice. Negative punishment is synonymous with time-out and response-cost procedures. Time-out literally means *time out from reinforcement* and defines a strategy in which, contingent on an unwanted behavior, a student is removed from a reinforcing activity or situation. For this strategy to be effective, the "time-in" situation (i.e., the one from which the student is removed) must be more reinforcing than the time-out situation. Response cost defines procedures in which something of value is removed from a student contingent on an unwanted behavior. Fines by removing points or minutes of recess are examples of response cost.

Types of reinforcers and how they are identified.   Reinforcers are critical to the success of systematic instruction. Whenever instruction occurs, we need to ensure that the students are motivated to learn, or in other words, that reinforcers are available for accurate responding. Due to the critical role reinforcers play in SI, their identification becomes an important goal. Educators have developed three strategies to facilitate this identification process. The first is ask the student or someone who is very familiar with the student to list potential reinforcers (preferences). This process is facilitated by providing them with categories or types of reinforcers. In this way, many possibilities can be cued that may not have been considered. The two major categories are primary and secondary reinforcers. Primary reinforcers are those with which we are born—our survival depends on them, and they are unlearned and include food, water, sleep, shelter, and sex. Secondary reinforcers are items or events that become reinforcers by being paired repeatedly with another reinforcer, either primary or secondary. Within the major category of secondary (also referred to as conditioned) reinforcers are four subcategories: social, tangible, activity, and generalized reinforcers. Praise, toys, favorite games, and money respectively are examples of each subcategory. These potential reinforcers derive their value by being paired with other valued events. For example, money is paired with a multitude of valued items and events that are purchased.

A second strategy for identifying potential reinforcers is observation. We can learn a great deal about what students enjoy and value simply by watching them in unstructured situations, ones in which they are free to behave as they wish with no demands or restrictions. Ideal situations are free play or recess, when many items and activities are available and students are free to choose. Simply recording the items (or person) selected and time spent engaging with them can provide an indication of their reinforcing value.

A third method for determining reinforcers is referred to as systematic preference assessment and entails providing students with an opportunity to choose or to engage with items thought to be preferred. This process is often conducted in a trial format and provides as an outcome a prioritized list or hierarchy of preferred items and activities. In this method students are presented with items thought to be preferred and they select the one they want. This method permits a comparison among many preferred items/activities. (For a more elaborate discussion of preference assessments, please refer to Alberto & Troutman, 1999, or Reichle, York, & Sigafoos, 1991.)

Schedules of reinforcement and maintenance of behavior.   Once reinforcers have been identified, it is important to make a systematic determination of *when* contingent reinforcement will be scheduled or provided. We already know that to be contingent, reinforcers must occur immediately after the target response. However, this does not imply that every response is reinforced. In SI, we apply labels to situations in which we intend to reinforce (a) every target response (continuous reinforcement or CRF schedule) or (b) a subset of target responses (intermittent schedule of reinforcement). Decisions about whether to use continuous or intermittent schedules depend on the purpose or goal of instruction. For example, if we are beginning to teach a new behavior, we would want to reinforce every correct response (CRF) to strengthen the relationship between the response and its consequence. After the response is acquired, we likely would change to an intermittent schedule so the student does not anticipate a reinforcer after every response and to anticipate naturally occurring schedules of reinforcement. If the response is important, we don't want the student to stop engaging in it when reinforcement is not provided. (Remember, this is the definition of extinction.) To prevent extinction of the response, we are attempting to develop tolerance for the student to continue responding in the absence of the reinforcer. This notion is referred to as resistance to extinction or maintenance of behavior (discussed later).

Two examples demonstrate the power of schedules on the maintenance of behavior in the absence of reinforcement. Consider the situation in which you are thirsty and you place a dollar in a vending machine and push the button signaling a preferred drink. It accepts your dollar, but no drink is delivered. How many times would you continue to "feed" the machine with dollars? Probably not very many because the schedule of reinforcement operating with a vending machine is a CRF—every response (insert dollar and push button) is reinforced. In contrast to the schedule operating with a vending machine, let's consider that operating with a slot machine: each lever pull produces the possibility of a big cash jackpot; however, experience reveals that most lever pulls do not produce a jackpot. Thus, the schedule of reinforcement operating with a slot machine is intermittent. If we pose the same question as above—how many times would you continue to "feed" the machine with dollars?—the answer would be very different. The gambler hopes to win the jackpot with every lever pull, but knows that many responses may be needed prior to the jackpot. The concept of schedules of reinforcement has dramatic implications for the maintenance of behavior acquired with SI.

Generalization of behavior.   In SI, instruction is conducted in a careful and planful manner. Often the conditions under which teaching occurs do not match those operating in everyday situations. That is, we may arrange conditions to optimize instructional outcomes. Thus, a crucial feature of systematic instruction is to anticipate the multiple situations in which the target behavior ought to occur and to plan for this in the design of the instructional program to enhance the probability that the student will use the skill in the desired situations. Generalization refers to use of the skill in situations in which training never occurred. For example, if we are teaching a young boy to use the telephone, we may use a toy phone that looks like a real phone because it is convenient to do so—we can keep it in the classroom, we can use it anytime we want without interfering with others' use, and if it breaks, replacement is inexpensive. However, such simulations may produce a problem with generalization. That is, the child may acquire adept phone skills (dialing, greeting, obtaining needed information) with the simulated phone, but may not perform the same way with a real phone.

Years ago, Stokes and Baer (1977) generated nine strategies for promoting generalization. Their major conclusion was that generalization of behavior is not a passive phenomenon that simply can be expected when new behavior is acquired; rather, it needs to be actively and systematically planned and programmed. A few of their strategies may be instructive. They recommend *teaching multiple examples* of a generalizable concept or lesson "until the induction is formed" (p. 355). In other words, when teaching the concept *dog,* examples of dogs might be introduced and labeled "dog" until such time that the student could identify new examples as dogs (and differentiate other animals that are not dogs). A more sophisticated application of teaching multiple examples is general-case programming (Horner, Sprague, & Wilcox, 1982). In this strategy the range of situations in which the behavior ought to occur is identified, examples are drawn from this range, and the behavior is taught in these sample situations. Finally, situations that were not part of training are assessed to determine if the behavior now occurs in these generalization situations.

Another one of Stokes and Baer's generalization-promotion strategies is *programming common stimuli.* This strategy entails introducing an object or event present during the instruction of a target behavior as a cue for the behavior in other situations in which generalization is desired. Thus, in the example of the girl who learned to yell instead of raise her hand, if we want her to raise her hand during group instruction situations, educators might say, "Please raise your hand if you need my help," just as they did during the original instruction, before all group instruction situations.

Introduction to natural maintaining contingencies is a third strategy for promoting generalization. In this strategy, control of the behavior is transferred from the educator to contingencies that naturally operate in the students' everyday environment. Thus, for example, when an educator teaches a student whose speech is unintelligible to point to pictures of objects or activities to request them, this new way of requesting is likely to generalize because when the student points to a picture of a desired item outside of training, any listener is likely to understand and thus honor the request. In fact, this strategy ought to drive much of our teaching; we need to identify contingencies operating in our students' everyday environments that will naturally (without our intervention) support newly acquired behavior.

Antecedent Strategies

In the A-B-C equation, the A represents antecedents. Prompts and arranging the physical environment are examples of antecedent events and now will be discussed in detail by describing stimulus control, prompting, and prompt-fading. Box 4.2 illustrates the A-B-C process.

BOX **4.2**

Dennis

Mr. Douglas is a middle school special education teacher. Several of his students with severe disabilities spend about an hour each day participating in work experiences in nearby community businesses. Dennis, an eighth-grade student, is learning a variety of skills during his experience at a small restaurant. One of the most important skills targeted for Dennis is learning to set tables. Mr. Douglas developed a table-setting routine that was acceptable at the restaurant and with Dennis's parents so Dennis could use the same skills at home to set the table for family meals.

To monitor the effectiveness of his instructional program, Mr. Douglas decided to collect information about how accurately Douglas followed the steps of the table-setting routine, as well as how quickly he completed the task. Before he began teaching, Mr. Douglas observed Dennis setting tables several times, both at the restaurant and in his home. He recorded and plotted these data for several days to get good idea of how well Dennis could perform the skills before instruction (baseline) (see Figure 4.1, p. 66).

Mr. Douglas designed an instructional program to teach table setting to Dennis. One feature of his program was a *stimulus prompt*—a small piece of an index card with a picture of correctly positioned silverware to which Dennis could refer when he was uncertain. Dennis was taught to keep this prompt card in his pocket where he could easily reach it when needed. To assist Dennis in learning the steps of the task analysis, Mr. Douglas selected a most-to-least intrusive prompt-fading hierarchy using first a direct verbal prompt paired with pointing (e.g., "Place the plate here" while pointing to the proper spot on the table), then fading to an indirect verbal prompt (e.g., "Think about what is placed next to the fork—that's what you need next"), and then removing the response prompts altogether, allowing Dennis the opportunity to perform each step of the task analysis without assistance. Mr. Douglas taught this instructional program each day Dennis worked at the restaurant. Once every four opportunities, Mr. Douglas implemented a probe trial at the restaurant to assess Dennis's learning. Once every two weeks, he conducted a probe trial at Dennis's home to see whether Dennis could generalize or transfer his table-setting skills from the restaurant to his home.

Figure 4.2 (p. 66) shows Dennis's progress in learning table setting during the semester. At first, Dennis's progress in learning to perform the steps of the task seemed slow. Mr. Douglas evaluated the graphed data on an ongoing basis and was considering making some changes to the prompting system when Dennis's probe data began to show an increasing trend. As shown in Figure 4.2, soon after Dennis's accuracy increased, his speed increased as well. Mr. Douglas continued to monitor Dennis's performance in setting the table at home as well. He was very pleased to see that the skill was generalizing to his home setting as well.

Mr. Douglas was pleased with Dennis's progress with this instructional program. The restaurant manager was impressed with how quickly Dennis showed improvement and that he was soon able to perform the skill as accurately and quickly as other restaurant employees. Mr. Douglas concluded that the combination of a cue card and most-to-least prompting hierarchy seemed to be particularly effective for Dennis and decided to use it when designing other instructional programs for Dennis.

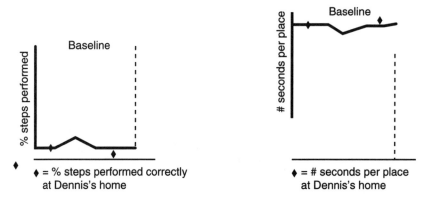

FIGURE 4.1   Dennis's table-setting performance before instruction was begun.

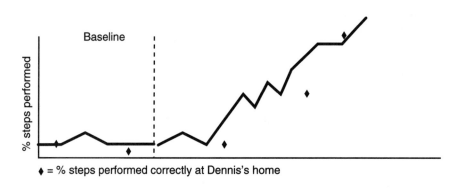

♦ = % steps performed correctly at Dennis's home

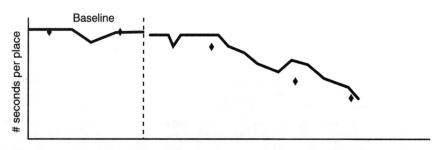

FIGURE 4.2   Dennis's table-setting performance during instruction.

Stimulus control.   Key to students' successful acquisition, maintenance, and generalization of any skill is their response to the stimuli that are intended to set the occasion for task performance. Stimulus control operates when antecedent stimuli reliably set the occasion for specific skill performance. Stimulus control refers to the predictable relationship that exists between antecedent stimuli, behavior performance, and positive consequences. Ultimately, all instructional programs ought to have a desired outcome of skill performance given naturally occurring environmental stimuli. For example, when a student is acquiring the skills to answer the phone, he or she does not know to pick up and answer the phone when it rings. In fact, someone usually has to tell the student to answer the phone because it is ringing. Over trials of instruction to answer a ringing phone, however, the student begins to associate the ringing of the phone with the skill/behavior of answering, which is predictably related to the positive consequence of someone on the other end talking (assuming this is positive to the student). When this relationship has been established, the ringing phone is said to exercise stimulus control over phone answering. The ring is a discriminative stimulus for phone answering and signals to the student that phone answering will be positively reinforced with someone on the other end talking. Also by this point the student should have learned that answering a silent phone, one that is not ringing, will not result in someone on the other end talking.

Educators usually use additional antecedent stimuli to assist a student in knowing when and how to perform correctly. Frequently, the additional stimuli include verbal instructions to perform the desired skill when the natural antecedents occur. When a student has dirty hands, a educator might say, "Your hands are dirty; please go wash them," or when the lunch bell rings, the educator might say, "There's the lunch bell; please line up to go to the cafeteria." However, over time the educator is likely to expect the students to perform these tasks in response to the environmental cues, without being told (e.g., wash hands because they are dirty, line up for lunch when the bell rings). For this to happen, the natural environmental cues must become discriminative stimuli for the desired performance; for example, the students must learn the relationship between bell ringing, lining up for lunch, praise from educator/eating lunch. Assuming praise and/or eating lunch are positive to the student, lining up to go to lunch will occur when the bell rings, once the relationship has been established. The antecedent stimuli, provided by the educator, that are paired with the natural environmental cues and assist the student in correct performance are called *prompts.*

Prompts

Prompting is a strategy that facilitates both errorless learning and attention to the relevant task features or stimuli. Prompts are stimuli or stimulus events that are paired with the natural environmental cues to facilitate correct responding. The two categories of prompts are stimulus prompts and response or instructional prompts.

Stimulus prompts.   Arranging the environment to signal the student to behave or respond in certain ways given specific contexts can be stimulus prompts. For example, positioning materials for a task in an order that corresponds to the order in which the task should be completed serves as a prompt for correct task completion. This might be done with laundry materials, placing spot remover first on a shelf, then detergent, followed by bleach, and finally fabric sheets for the dryer. The order of laundry supplies is a prompt for ordering the steps involved in doing the laundry. Arranging a classroom so that specific areas are associated with certain behavior (e.g., independent work, socialization) and only that type of behavior serves as a stimulus prompt. Another type of environmental arrangement would be placing a novice student next to a peer who would serve as a competent model (e.g., in the cafeteria line, putting a student who has not learned how to go through the line and request food, pay, and take a seat in line behind a peer who has mastered these steps). The competent peer model may serve as a prompt for the student.

Stimulus prompts can be added to natural cues of a task with the intent of assisting a student in responding correctly. For example, picture cues frequently accompany written words for those who are in the acquisition stage of learning to read words (e.g., in recipe reading). *Pictures serve as stimulus prompts for the written word. The assumption is that the student can identify the picture that accompanies the word and, over repeated trials, stimulus control will transfer to the word alone, resulting in the student reading the word. Picture prompts have also been used to facilitate following a schedule and completing daily living and vocational tasks, among other skills.*

Other types of stimulus prompts include using color codes to assist a student in completing tasks (e.g., using a color code to indicate the stove temperature for baking, color coding numerals to assist the student in numeral recognition), increasing intensity of relevant cues (e.g., putting key words in bold), and using auditory signals (e.g., buzzers to signal lunchtime when clock reading would be the natural cue). In any case, when using stimulus prompts, the educator must develop a plan for withdrawing the extra stimuli so that the student is eventually responding to the natural environmental stimuli. A gradual process of withdrawing the extra stimuli would facilitate errorless learning. *For example, color codes can be gradually faded until the extra color is no longer there, or the intensity of the stimuli might be gradually reduced until the natural intensity sets the occasion for correct responding (e.g., bolded key words become lighter over trials).*

Although the use of stimulus prompts may require some preparation, a benefit is that the prompts are built into the materials or environment and, therefore, would not require extra educator time in the instructional interaction. In fact, with effective stimulus prompts and eventual prompt fading, a student may be able to acquire a task without any additional direct instructional time from the educator. In addition, some stimulus prompts may be acceptable as long-term adaptations for a student (e.g., picture prompts for recipe reading might never be faded).

Response or instructional prompts.   Systematic use of response or instructional prompts is basic to effective instruction. Response prompts are those extra cues or assistance an educator provides in an instructional interaction. What defines an instructional prompt is that the educator's assistance is provided either at the same time as the natural cues for the task or after the natural cues, but before the student responds. The purpose of these prompts is to assist the student in responding and to reduce or eliminate errors.

The types of response prompts include verbal prompts, gestures, models, or physical guidance. Within each of these types of prompts, a continuum exists. For example, verbal prompts can be direct (e.g., "Pick up your shirt"), questioning (e.g., "What do you do with your shirt?"), confirmational (e.g., "That's right, you pick up your shirt"), qualitative (e.g., "Pick up your shirt, gently"), or indirect (e.g., "What do you do next?"). The degree of assistance varies with each of these types of verbal prompts, and the appropriateness of the prompt must be judged based on the skills and needs of the student. Similar continua exist for gestures and physical prompts. A gesture prompt could vary from very intrusive and obvious (e.g., hand waving and full-body gestures) to less intrusive (e.g., a point) to very subtle (e.g., an eye glance). Similarly, physical prompts might range from a very subtle gentle tap to full physical guidance through hand-over-hand assistance to complete a task. Critical to selecting a prompt is knowing that it is functional for the student. That is, the prompt must assist the student in responding correctly. Therefore, an indirect verbal prompt such as "What comes next?" should not be selected unless the student knows what comes next when asked and then can perform it. If this type of assistance is not functional for the student, it is not a prompt, and perhaps a different type of verbal prompt (e.g., a direct verbal such as "Pick up your shirt") or an entirely different type of prompt such as a gesture (e.g., educator points to the shirt) should be selected. As with stimulus prompts, the goal of an instructional interaction using response prompts should be to teach the student to respond to the natural cues for the task; student success would be achieved only when the student no longer requires the educator's prompts. Therefore, systematic strategies must be employed to fade the assistance needed by the student.

Response Prompt-Fading Systems

A number of response prompt-fading systems have been developed and described in previous literature. These systems fall into three general categories, least-to-most intrusive prompting, most-to-least intrusive prompting, and time-delay.

Least-to-most intrusive prompt systems. Least-to-most intrusive prompt systems allow the student the opportunity to perform a task with the greatest degree of independence before providing more assistance. This would be accomplished by first identifying a hierarchy of prompts from least assistance for the individual student to the most assistance that might be needed for that student. This sequence of prompts is available on each trial of the task. However, the educator would begin the instructional interaction by allowing the student the opportunity to perform with the least assistance, and if he or she did not or could not, the educator would provide the next, more intrusive prompt and continue this way until a correct response was obtained. One example might be with a hierarchy of prompts that would include (a) a direct verbal prompt, (b) a direct verbal paired with a point, and (c) a direct verbal paired with full-physical guidance. In this example, the student would be given the opportunity to respond to the natural cue of the task, and if he or she did not perform or began to make an error, the educator would provide the direct verbal prompt. If the student still did not respond or began to make an error, the educator would provide the direct verbal prompt along with the point prompt and so on. Another example of a least-to-most hierarchy might be within physical prompts including (a) a slight tap, (b) guidance from the elbow, and (c) full-physical guidance through hand-over-hand contact. The expectation is that as the student acquires the skill being taught, he or she will perform with less assistance, thus fading out the need for prompts.

Least-to-most intrusive prompt hierarchies should be designed to meet the needs of the individual student. Regardless of the prompts selected, the prompt hierarchy should result in correct responding. Therefore, the final prompt in the hierarchy must be functional to the student. In addition, since prompts are designed to prevent errors, any errors should be interrupted and the next prompt in the hierarchy should be provided. If errors are allowed to occur, the prompts become error corrections and do not serve the purpose for which they are designed.

Most-to-least intrusive prompt systems.   Most-to-least intrusive prompting systems are developed with the assumption that a student or the task being taught would benefit most by being provided initially with the most assistance that might be necessary and then gradually reducing the amount of assistance over trials. As with a least-to-most intrusive system, in a most-to-least intrusive system, a hierarchy of prompts must be selected. In fact, the same hierarchy might be selected that was described above for a least-to-most intrusive system: (a) a direct verbal prompt, (b) a direct verbal paired with a point, and (c) a direct verbal paired with full-physical guidance. However, with a most-to-least intrusive system of prompting, the initial prompt used is the most intrusive prompt in the hierarchy (e.g., a direct verbal paired with full-physical prompt). The rationale for this approach is that the student responds to the most intrusive prompt in the hierarchy with the least likelihood of errors; therefore this prompt will be used initially to ensure errorless learning.

When using a most-to-least intrusive prompt hierarchy, a predetermined method of moving up the hierarchy of prompts must be established with the purpose of fading assistance and increasing independence. The method of fading might involve a predetermined number of trials at the most intrusive prompt level (e.g., 10 trials with a full-physical prompt) then moving to a less intrusive prompt for a predetermined number of trials (e.g., 10 trials with a point prompt) and so on up the hierarchy of prompts until the student is performing independently. When using a most-to-least intrusive prompt hierarchy, an error correction procedure must be developed prior to instruction because as the educator moves up the hierarchy of prompts, the student may make errors in responding. For example, when the educator moves from a full-physical prompt to a point prompt in the example above, the student might make an error even though a point prompt is provided. When the error is made, the educator must correct the error before moving on to the next trial; this might be done with providing feedback along with a full-physical prompt (e.g., educator says, "No, that is not first in line. Point to the first in line" and gives a hand-over-hand assistance to point to the first in line). When selecting a procedure for error correction, the educator must be certain that the error will be corrected effectively and efficiently, and the student should not receive reinforcement as if he or she had completed the trial with a prompted correct response. Additionally, if frequent errors are made, perhaps the prompts were faded too quickly and moving back to a more intrusive prompt might be considered.

As with a least-to-most intrusive hierarchy, the prompts selected for the most-to-least intrusive hierarchy can be any combination depending on the needs of the student and the type of tasks being taught. Prompts can be within a type (e.g., verbal) or across types of prompts. An important variable related to prompt selection is that the most intrusive prompt must be functional for the student at the onset of instruction so as to promote error-less learning.

Time-delay systems. A final method of prompt fading entails delaying the introduction of the prompt. Time delay refers to a process of inserting time between the natural cues (the desired discriminative stimuli) for the task and the presentation of the prompt that might assist the student in performing correctly. Time-delay systems can be implemented in many different ways. One type of time-delay system is a progressive delay procedure. In progressive delay, a prompt that is functional to the student is selected and presented with the natural cues for the task either at the same time (no delay) or quickly (e.g., one-second delay) after the natural cues so that responding would not be possible before prompt delivery. Then over trials the prompt is progressively delayed so that the student has an increasing opportunity through increased amounts of time to anticipate and make a correct response before the prompt is delivered. For example, a progressive delay procedure might involve beginning instruction by providing the prompt with no delay, then progressing to a two-second delay then to a four-second delay and to a final six-second delay. In this way the student through anticipation of the correct response will be more likely to respond with increasing prompt delays, eliminating the need for a prompt.

Another type of time delay is a constant delay procedure in which the delay remains the same (e.g., four-second delay before delivering the prompt) throughout instruction and across trials. The rationale for this procedure is the same as for a progressive delay, that the student will anticipate a correct response across trials and eliminate a need for the prompt.

Any type of prompt can be used in a time-delay system as long as the prompt selected is functional to the student. Additionally, the delays should be selected to meet the needs of the student considering the complexity and difficulty of the task. As with any prompt-fading system, the purpose of time delay procedures is to facilitate errorless learning. Therefore, procedures should be selected keeping this in mind. Furthermore, as with a most-to-least intrusive hierarchy, error correction procedures must be developed prior to instruction because of the potential for errors once the prompt is delayed. With a time-delay procedure, errors can be made before prompt delivery when the prompt is delayed or after prompt delivery if the prompt does not provide enough assistance for correct responding. If frequent errors occur after the prompt is delivered, the type of prompt chosen must be examined. If the errors occur before prompt delivery, the size of the delay should be evaluated. In all cases, procedures should be selected that are likely to promote errorless learning.

Assessing the Effects of Systematic Instruction

The best way to assess the effects of systematic instruction is through the evaluation of data that are collected on an ongoing basis. The first step in collecting data is to make certain that the student's target behavior is operationally defined so that it is observable and measurable. If two people can agree when the behavior occurs and when it does not occur, then the behavior has probably been carefully defined. For example, it would be easier for two people to collect data on requesting when it is defined as "Emily touches a picture of CD player in her communication book after being asked what she wants to do" than it would be to agree on "Emily makes requests."

After the behavior is defined, then the behavior is measured over time. There are many different ways to measure behavior, but the measurement system selected depends on how the behavior is defined. For example, in the above illustration of Emily, we might want to measure and record the number of times Emily touches a picture of her CD player when given the opportunity to do so (i.e., when she is asked what she wants to do); this measurement system would be called *response-per-opportunity* and would be represented by a *percent*. If we wanted to measure the number of times Emily initiated a request for her CD player over the course of a school day without being asked what she wanted to do, this measurement system would be called *frequency*. If we were concerned about the length of time that it took Emily to actually touch the picture of the CD player when asked to do so, we would measure the *latency* of her response (i.e., the amount of time between us making the request and Emily touching the picture). We could also measure *duration* if we were interested in the length of time that Emily kept her finger on the picture. Space precludes a thorough discussion of all the different types of measurement systems and their advantages and disadvantages, so other sources can be consulted for more detail (e.g., Alberto & Troutman, 1999).

After data are collected on the target behavior, educators must evaluate the data in order to make decisions about the effectiveness of their instructional strategies. There is no reason to collect data if they are not evaluated on an ongoing basis. It is only through the evaluation of data that educators can decide if learning is occurring. If it does not appear that students are learning, then educators must change their instructional strategies.

Sometimes educators may think that collecting and evaluating data is fruitless and a waste of time. However, a number of research studies have shown that educators make better instructional decisions for their students when they collect and evaluate student performance data (Farlow & Snell, 1989; Fuchs & Fuchs, 1986; Meyer & Janney, 1989). Collecting and evaluating student performance data is one of the most important jobs we do as educators because it ensures that more of our time is spent using effective rather than ineffective teaching strategies.

Collecting Data during Baseline, Instruction, and Generalization Sessions

Data need to be collected during baseline, instruction, and generalization sessions. During baseline, the educator collects data on the target behavior when the student has an opportunity to perform it, but *before* providing instruction to the student. Baseline data are collected so that educators can see how well the student performs the target behavior before instruction. Later, educators can compare student performance on the same behavior after instruction. In this way, educators can determine if their instructional strategies helped students to learn. Generally, educators should collect baseline data until they are stable (i.e., there is no upward or downward trend and little variability), which may take several days (three to five at a minimum).

Usually, baseline data are collected in the setting with the people and materials that will be used during instruction. However, it is also a good idea to collect generalization data during baseline conditions. Generalization data, or probes, provide the educator with information on whether the student can perform the target behavior under natural circumstances without educator assistance, instruction, or reinforcement. For example, we might collect baseline data in the classroom on a student's selection of the right amount of money to pay for various items. At the same time, we would also want to conduct a few generalization probes in the stores (e.g., grocery, hardware) where the student will have to purchase items. During instruction, educators should continue to conduct several generalization probes to see if the student will perform the skill in community stores.

In a recent study conducted by Smith, Collins, Schuster, and Kleinert (1999), baseline data were collected on four adolescents' table cleaning in a classroom. A task analysis of table cleaning had been developed, and through a multiple-opportunity method, students were given a chance to complete all of the steps associated with the task analysis, but no instruction was given on any step. Data were collected for a minimum of three baseline sessions and researchers noted if the steps were done correctly or incorrectly.

Prior to and following the instruction, generalization probe sessions occurred in three settings: school cafeteria, educators' lounge, and a local church. Data were collected on whether steps in the task analysis of cleaning tables were performed correctly or incorrectly. In addition, the educator also conducted observational learning probe sessions to assess whether the students could perform the nontargeted tasks of preparing and putting away the cleaning materials in the classroom setting by just observing the educator completing these tasks.

Because baseline and generalization performance was very low for all four students, instruction was needed. During instruction, Smith and colleagues (1999) recorded the type of prompt required for successful completion of the steps of the task analysis of cleaning tables. A system of least prompts and multiple exemplars was used as the instructional procedure, and data were collected on the level of the prompt used: (a) independent, (b) verbal prompt, (c) model prompt, and (d) physical prompt.

The results from the Smith and colleagues (1999) study showed that the system of least prompts and multiple exemplars was successful in teaching four students to clean tables under both instructional and generalization conditions. In addition, all four students showed increases in completing the tasks of preparing and putting away materials through observational learning. So in this study, baseline data consisted of correct and incorrect responses that could be converted to percent or frequency of steps completed correctly according to the task analysis of table cleaning. The same type of data was collected during generalization probes, but under different conditions than those used during baseline. And during instruction, the type of data recorded included the level of prompt used when the student made an error or did not respond.

Evaluating Data

As stated previously, the reason data are collected is to make decisions about student learning. If students are not learning, then instructional strategies need to be changed. The best way to evaluate data is to plot the raw data (e.g., frequency counts, percent, duration) onto a visual display, such as a graph. In this way, data that have been collected over several days can be inspected visually over time to see if student progress has occurred. There are many conventions for plotting data, such as the information that appears on the vertical and horizontal axis. Again, space precludes an in-depth discussion of data-plotting conventions and the reader should consult other sources (e.g., Alberto & Troutman, 1999; Wolery et al., 1988).

After data are plotted, they can be inspected visually to see if learning has occurred. Educators need to compare student performance during baseline to student performance during instruction. There are two primary features of the data that need to be considered. First, educators should look to see if there is a change in the *level* of data (i.e., an increase in performance) when baseline is compared to instruction. Let's assume that educators were trying to increase the length of time (i.e., duration) that Fred worked at the computer in a bank. If Fred worked an average of 15 minutes during baseline, and then after the first several days of intervention, he worked an average of 30 minutes, we would say that a shift in the level of performance had occurred (i.e., from 15 minutes to 30 minutes) and we would assume that our intervention was successful. However, gathering data for several days after intervention may not tell the whole story about student learning. If our goal were to help Fred work at the computer for an hour at a time without a break, we would need to measure his progress over time until our goal was reached. Consequently, we would need to evaluate the second primary feature of the data, which is called the *trend*.

The trend refers to the overall direction that the data path takes, and the direction can be one that is increasing, decreasing, or flat, showing no trend (Kazdin, 1982). In addition, it is also important to look at the variability of data points around the trend. Consider the data displayed in Figure 4.3a. In this figure, Julie was taught to read words. Data were gathered on the percentage of words read correctly. Before instruction, Julie's baseline data were flat; she needed instruction. After instruction, Julie quickly learned to read her words correctly. Her data show an increasing trend line during instruction, which would tell an educator that no changes need to be made to Julie's instructional program.

In Figure 4.3b, Dan was taught to complete the steps associated with his grooming procedure after he completed PE class. During baseline, Dan's performance was poor on the percent of steps completed correctly according to the task analysis. After instruction, there seemed to be a slight increase in trend, but then the trend decreased to almost baseline levels. Clearly, an educator would need to make a change in Dan's instructional program. How might an educator change Dan's program? Visual inspection of the data path and an analysis of the responses and errors Dan made (Horner, Bellamy, & Colvin, 1984) might offer some clues about what to change first so that Dan could be successful. In Dan's case, it could be that the steps in the task analysis were too large for him to complete successfully or the cues or prompts given to Dan at certain steps might not be effective. Additionally, the type and schedule of reinforcement might not be appropriate, or something else in Dan's life that was not a part of the instructional program could be impacting the data.

In Figure 4.3c, Lisa was taught to initiate requests for food items during snack. After low baseline levels and the implementation of the instructional procedures, Lisa's data path showed little or no trend, nor was a change in level evident. With this scenario, the

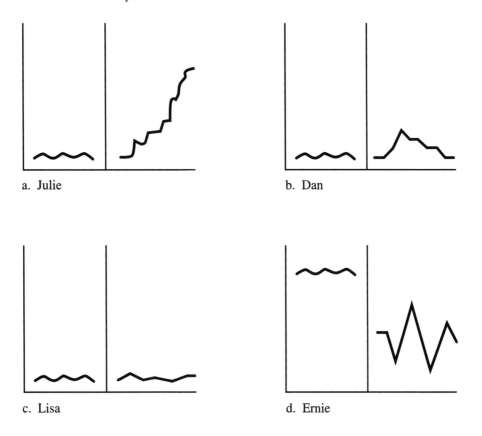

a. Julie

b. Dan

c. Lisa

d. Ernie

FIGURE 4.3 **Examples of increasing, decreasing, flat, and variable data trends.**

educator would again want to change the instructional procedures and, depending upon Lisa's responses, could consider manipulating the same antecedent or consequent events suggested for Dan.

Finally, in Figure 4.3d, the educator was implementing a procedure to decrease the number of times that Ernie shrieked during class. After a high baseline performance and the implementation of the instructional procedures, a clear change in level occurred, but the data path was variable. Sometimes it seemed that the intervention was working well and sometimes its effect was unclear. Again, the educator could make several hypotheses about what might be causing the variable data. For example, the variable performance could be related to the inconsistent implementation of the procedures or to the use of different reinforcers across days, some more highly preferred.

Data need to be evaluated consistently over time in order to see if students are learning. If students are not learning, then educators need to change their teaching strategies until learning does occur. By consistently evaluating student data, educators will become more effective instructors and student learning will be enhanced.

Special Considerations

Some educators may think that they can collect data on only one student at a time. As much of our teaching may occur in group formats, it is important to realize that data can be collected on more than one student during an instructional session. For example, if students take turns responding in a group, educators can collect data on each student's behavior by having carefully organized data-collection sheets. As each student responds, educators can simply record performance. This can be accomplished even if students are learning different skills. The trick to collecting data is to be well organized before teaching begins, so that all the necessary teaching and data-collection materials are readily available. Additionally, as with all types of learning, the more educators practice collecting data, the easier it will become. Educators should also realize that it might not always be necessary to collect data every day or on every response. It may be that learning can be evaluated effectively when data are collected a few days a week or are sampled for brief periods of time instead of across the entire day.

Some educators may worry that the act of collecting data (e.g., following students around in order to record behaviors on a data sheet attached to a clipboard) may be intrusive and cause undue attention to students who are being educated in inclusive environments. Data do not always have to be gathered by recording behavior on data sheets attached to clipboards. Educators can collect data in a variety of ways, such as wearing golf counters to count behavior, transferring pennies or beans from one pocket to another as a behavior occurs, or moving brightly colored beads (like an abacus) up a leather strip, which might be attached to a bracelet. Audiotapes and videotapes offer additional means of gathering data that can be stored until educators have time to listen or watch.

Conclusion

It is essential to assess the effects of systematic instruction by collecting and evaluating data on an ongoing basis. If educators carefully define a student's behavior; select the appropriate measurement system; collect data during baseline, instruction, and generalization sessions; plot the data on a graph; and evaluate the level and trend of the data path, they will be more effective educators, and students with severe disabilities will learn more.

References

Alberto, P.A., & Troutman, A. C. (1999). *Applied behavior analysis for teachers* (5th ed.). Upper Saddle River, NJ: Prentice-Hall.

Brown, L., Branston, M. B., Hamre-Nietupski, S., Pumpian, I., Certo, N., & Gruenewald, L. (1979). A strategy for developing chronological-age-appropriate and functional curricular content for severely handicapped adolescents and young adults. *Journal of Special Education, 13,* 81–90.

Carnine, D. (1997). Bridging the research-to-practice gap. *Exceptional Children, 63,* 513–521.

Farlow, L. J., & Snell, M. E. (1989). Teacher use of student performance data to make instructional decisions: Practices in programs for students with moderate to profound disabilities. *Journal of the Association for Persons with Severe Handicaps, 14,* 13–22.

Fuchs, L. S., & Fuchs, D. (1986). Effects of systematic formative evaluation: A meta-analysis. *Exceptional Children, 53,* 199–208.

Horner, R. H., Bellamy, G. T., & Colvin, G. T. (1984). Responding in the presence of nontrained stimuli: Implications of generalization error patterns. *Journal of the Association for Persons with Severe Handicaps, 9,* 287–295.

Horner, R. H., Dunlap, G., & Koegel, R. L. (1988). *Generalization and maintenance: Lifestyle changes in applied settings.* Baltimore: Paul H. Brookes.

Horner, R. H., Sprague, J. & Wilcox, B. (1982). Constructing general-case programs for community activities. In B. Wilcox & G. T. Bellamy (Eds.), *Design of high school programs for severely handicapped students* (pp. 61–98). Baltimore: Paul H. Brookes.

Kazdin, A. E. (1982). *Single-case research designs: Methods for clinical and applied settings.* New York: Oxford University Press.

Meyer, L. H., & Janney, R. (1989). User-friendly measures of meaningful outcomes: Evaluating behavior interventions. *Journal of the Association for Persons with Severe Handicaps, 14,* 263–270.

Reichle, J., York, J., & Sigafoos, J. (1991). *Implementing augmentative and alternative communication.* Baltimore: Paul H. Brookes.

Smith, R. L., Collins, B. C., Schuster, J. W., & Kleinert, H. (1999). Teaching table cleaning skills to secondary students with moderate/severe disabilities: Facilitating observational learning during instructional downtime. *Education and Training in Mental Retardation and Developmental Disabilities, 34,* 342–353.

Stokes, T. F., & Baer, D. M. (1977). An implicit technology of generalization. *Journal of Applied Behavior Analysis, 10,* 349–367.

Wehman, P., Renzaglia, A., & Bates, P. (1985). *Functional living skills for moderately and severely handicapped individuals.* Austin, TX: Pro-Ed.

Wolery, M., Bailey, D. B., & Sugai, G. M. (1988). *Effective teaching: Principles and procedures of applied behavior analysis with exceptional students.* Boston: Allyn and Bacon.

5 Families

AMY L. CHILDRE
Georgia College and State University

The information shared in this chapter will provide insight into families, particularly the families of students with severe disabilities. In the field of education there is growing recognition of the importance of involving families in the education of their children. To achieve family involvement, family–educator partnerships must be fostered. Through this chapter, the importance of family–educator partnerships to the education of students with severe disabilities will be highlighted. While exploring the benefits of involving parents in the education of their children, ways for communicating with and tools for engaging families to build those necessary partnerships will be discussed.

After reading this chapter you should be able to:

- Describe how education laws relate to parent participation in education
- Recognize benefits of parental involvement in education
- Understand the family systems perspective and use the information to support parent-educator relations
- Apply family-centered techniques to support parent–educator partnerships and to empower families
- Implement processes to support family involvement in educational planning
- Utilize support and information organizations as an educator and family resource

What Are Families?

Given the ever-changing dynamics of today's society, families can no longer be easily characterized or defined. Increasing divorce rates, highly mobile societies, and changing values have impacted the organization of families (Hanson & Carta, 1996). What is your own definition of family? Certainly your definition is colored by the lens of your own family and life experience, as is each different family you will encounter. Families may define themselves as a group brought together by blood, marriage, or adoption; a unit sharing responsibilities for one another and working together toward common goals; or in a number of other ways that characterize their own function and structure. Today's families include non-traditional heads of households, single-parent families, stepchildren and adopted children, nuclear families, extended families, and a range of other diverse structures. Despite this variance in how families are structured and defined, families have commonalities such as a family head, rituals and routines, place of home, ways of showing affection, and means of protecting the family. These commonalities open our eyes to and broaden our understanding of other families.

Why Are Families Important to the Educational Process?

Beginning with P.L. 94-142 (Education for All Handicapped Children Act, 1975) and with each subsequent reauthorization of the law, family involvement in educational planning has been mandated with increasing emphasis. P.L. 94-142 set the basis for involving families in the educational process by including parents as members of the team developing the individualized education program (IEP) and by mandating informed parental consent for program placements and changes. In 1986, a subsequent revision, P.L. 99-457, required the development of individualized family service plans (IFSP) for families with children birth to age three. In 1990, IDEA acknowledged the importance of families in the transition process by requiring family involvement in individualized transitions plan (ITP) planning for children at age 16. The most recent revision, Individuals with Disabilities Education Act (IDEA) Amendments of 1997, incorporated more options and requirements for family involvement to further include parents and value their input and decisions.

Additional support for family involvement has been provided through the Families of Children with Disabilities Support Act of 1994, P.L. 103-382, which was passed as part of the reauthorization of the Elementary and Secondary Education Act of 1965, P.L. 89-313. This law requires states to collaborate with families to determine support strategies that will be implemented by state agencies that provide services to families. Efforts are to be coordinated across all agencies, including schools.

The rationale behind these laws represents an implicit set of values. These values are a reflection of changes in societal attitudes over the past three decades wherein fundamental human rights of persons with disabilities and the importance of family to their functioning have been acknowledged (Wehmeyer, Morningstar, & Husted, 1999). The law affirms that parents should be decision makers in a child's life and supports the belief that family involvement leads to optimal child development outcomes. Although the law outlines a set of minimum requirements that may result in passive participation from families, it provides families with the opportunity for active maximal involvement in their child's education.

Legislation supports family involvement, but actual options or roles that families may fulfill in the educational process are not delineated. Instead the law provides an open door for parent involvement in the educational process. Prior to the passage of P.L. 94-142 in 1975, the families' rights and their voice in educational planning were not guaranteed. Historically, family involvement was not solicited and families entered the educational arena as advocates pushing for changes in educational options for their children. Family advocacy efforts and grassroots efforts are largely responsible for the monumental changes that have occurred during the last several decades. Through family advocacy, lawful mandates, and court decisions, families now can fulfill myriad roles within the educational process. Some of the roles families engage in include gathering information, collaboration, decision making, advocation, support, intervention, and volunteerism (Sailor, Kleinhammer-Tramill, Skrtic, & Oas, 1996).

Family involvement in such roles is considered a best practice across all ages and child learning levels (Defur, Todd-Allen, & Getzel, 2001). Leaders in the field of special education advocate involving families in educational planning, supporting the impetus of the law. Research documents improved outcomes in child and family functioning as a result of family participation. These outcomes have been observed in home, school, and community environments. Positive results from family involvement include improved quality of life for the student; skill generalization to new situations and environments; modification of child behavior and gains of functional skills; more positive transition outcomes; development of advocacy skills for both parent and child; commitment to in-home placements; improved home functioning through routines and coping; and parent perception of having a higher degree of control within the service system (Agosta & Melda, 1996; Alper, Schloss, & Schloss, 1996).

Now, after considering these outcomes, let's reflect on the actual responsibilities when families fulfill the aforementioned roles of gathering information, collaboration, decision making, advocation, support, intervention, and volunteerism. As information gatherers, families collect medical, social, behavioral, and academic information for the educational system to assist in planning. As collaborators, parents practice listening, understanding, and working cooperatively with educators to identify priorities and achieve mutual goals. As decision makers, families determine services to be received within the school system, nonschool resources and programs to pursue, and their own level of involvement within all of these services. As advocates, families educate others about their children and families, make requests of education and medical professionals, and research and share information about their children's disability. As supporters, families provide necessary resources to educators, be it adaptive equipment, school supplies, or money for community-based outings. As interventionists, families follow through with educational or therapeutic interventions and provide continuity to the educational setting supporting skill generalization. As volunteers, families engage in the classroom by observing as well as by assisting with teaching, therapy, and informal assessments. Given the variety of ways a parent may be involved, it is clear the extent to which families can impact the education provided to their children.

What Processes Are Involved in Understanding Families?

Understanding the Family within

Choices families make regarding the roles they fulfill in their children's education are in part determined by who each member is as both an individual and a family member. To better understand families and their involvement or lack of involvement, the educator must have some concept of the families' needs and basic interworkings. Prior to intervening with families or working to support or increase family involvement, one must understand the complex nature of families who have a member with a disability.

Until recently the literature described family adaptation to a child with a severe disability from a pathogenic viewpoint. The assumption maintained focus on negative impacts of disability, asserting that families were irreparably damaged and burdened by the addition of a member with a disability (Buck, 1950; Singer & Powers, 1993). With the growing recognition of successful adjustment experienced by parents, family adaptation has shifted to emphasize the positive aspects of family functioning (McDermott, 2000; Scorgie & Sobsey, 2000). When faced with the challenge of a disability, families show resilience, utilizing coping strategies to adjust. Families self-reporting of the use of coping strategies includes developing professional and social support networks, focusing on the present, finding meaning through reframing, and relying on religious beliefs. Through this resilience families see their experiences as providing them opportunities to grow personally. In current research, families discuss their personal growth, including increased flexibility, tolerance, selflessness, and compassion, more meaningful relationships, and more positive outlook on the world (Sandler & Misretta, 1998; Sobsey, 2001).

Interestingly, research shows that family utilization of coping strategies, particularly reframing and social support, is highly predictive of family strengths and outcomes (Hanline & Daley, 1992; Judge, 1998). This ability to reframe or positively reappraise situations and to utilize the resource of social support has been shown to be more beneficial to family adjustment than reliance on professional supports. The coping strategy that research has shown to hinder family adjustment is passive appraisal. Waiting for a problem to go away, engaging in activities to avoid issues, and keeping one's feelings from others are all examples of avoidance responses that are indicative of a passive appraisal approach. This avoidance approach can have a negative impact on family adjustment to disability and family sense of competence.

To develop a deeper understanding of families and their adaption to disability as a family, one must explore the interworkings of families. A family systems perspective can organize our understanding of family characteristics, interactions, functions, and life cycles (Turnbull & Turnbull, 2001). With the birth or diagnosis of a child with severe disabilities, families are impacted across all aspects of their family framework. The impact is variable dependent upon the families' ability to adapt. Changes in family characteristics, interactions, and functions affect parents, siblings, and even extended family members. The repercussions of a member with a severe disability may continue throughout the lifespan of the child or even throughout the life of any member involved. Box 5.1 (p. 82) describes a sibling whose outlook on life and life ambitions have been shaped by what she learned from her brother with severe disabilities.

In addition to a member with a disability, another factor that affects all aspects of the framework is culture. Culture has an immense influence on basic characteristics of the family, how members interact, functions that members assume, and roles across the life cycle. Educators must have understanding of the basic components of family—characteristics, interactions, functions, and life cycles—and how they are influenced both by a member with a disability and by culture to effectively interact and work with families.

BOX **5.1**

Karen's Story

Karen's older brother Matthew was born with severe disabilities. Matthew was blind, had severe physical disabilities, required a feeding tube, and did not communicate. From birth his family saw him as a special and unique member of the family. Through the years Matthew has had a tremendously positive impact on his parents and his sister, Karen. Matthew's parents found meaning in his disability and instilled this positive view of disability in Karen. Matthew passed away as a young adult, and even now, he is still influencing Karen's life.

"Matthew had an impact on me from an early age. I knew he was different from other siblings during elementary school, but I was not ashamed. It would upset me when other kids would make fun of those in special education. My parents explained to me that my brother was different but special and that he still had a purpose. They never stated that purpose, but after I got older and after Matthew passed away, I knew his purpose. He gave me a passion for working with people with disabilities and taught me how to be sensitive to people who are different. If I did not have a brother like Matthew, I would not be where I am today. Some people ask if he was a burden because he required so much time and care. We never saw it that way. To our family it was a privilege to give him time and care. In return Mathew gave me a sense of humility and a desire to give to others."

Karen is now a sophomore in college and plans to major in special education. She spends her summers and breaks volunteering at Camp Hawkins, a summer camp for children with special needs, and at Matthew's Time, a respite care weekend established by Georgia Baptist Children's Home in honor of her brother. Karen's goal is eventually to direct such a program. She attributes her life ambitions to the influence her brother had and continues to have on her life.

Characteristics of family.   The characteristics of the family encompass not only family attributes (e.g. size, structure, socioeconomic status, geographic location), but also personal characteristics of each member (e.g. mental and physical health, coping strategies, exceptionality) and the special challenges that each family faces (e.g., poverty, abuse, parent with a disability). The diversity among families is illustrated in trends such as the steady increase of single-parent homes and mothers employed outside the home as well as the widening income gap between skilled and unskilled laborers. These trends place tremendous pressure on families who are struggling to meet basic needs. Some family characteristics are static while others are ever evolving in response to changes in some aspect of the family system framework. The addition of a family member with a disability to any family can impact changes in family characteristics.

Possible changes in characteristics that a family may encounter are numerous, and the changes can affect any and all aspects of characteristics—attributes, personal characteristics, or special challenges. The size and structure of a family may change due to disability. The addition of a member with a disability may prompt family members to form bonds to include extended family to support new and special needs; for other families the additional stress may contribute to family separation or divorce. Dealing with disability can affect coping strategies by compelling family members to establish supports in friends, neighbors, churches, and other organizations; or it may cause the family as a whole or as individual members to withdraw or to learn to rely on self-sufficiency.

Interactions within the family.   Family interactions refer to the relationships between individual family members and among subgroups within the family unit. This includes parental, marital, sibling, and extended family relationships. How the family interacts determines how they respond to needs and to challenges such as those associated with a member with a severe disability. Two elements are key to family interactions: adaptability and cohesion.

Adaptability refers to the capability of a member or family to adjust in response to stress or demands. Adaptability exists on a continuum from rigid and unchanging to constant change, instability, and confusion. A family exhibiting adaptability would adjust the functions of individual family members as needed to meet the needs of a member with a disability. Families at extreme ends of the continuum may, for example, require the mother to perform all caregiving needs for the child with a disability or at the opposite end, the family may never delineate responsibilities for members and determine routines, and hence chaos is constant and daily needs are not satisfactorily met.

Cohesion refers to the level of emotional support and dependence among family members, ranging along a continuum from disengagement to enmeshment. Consider a parent or a sibling who withdraws from the family in reaction to a member with a disability; this is indicative of disengagement. At the other extreme, enmeshed family members may not have any outside support or interests and rely solely on one another to the point that it becomes detrimental to healthy family interactions.

Family interactions and characteristics are closely linked. Generally, as interactions change reciprocal changes occur in family characteristics; that is, adjustments in one aspect of the family framework affect all other components of the framework. For instance, a mother's lack of adaptability in response to increased demands may stress her mental and physical health and may place her family at increased risk of poverty and abuse. So, clearly, challenges in her family interactions affect the status of her family's characteristics.

Functions of the family.   Families strive to meet the collective needs of their members by performing eight primary functions: spiritual, economic, daily care, affection, socialization, self-esteem, education, and recreation (Turnbull, Summers, & Brotherson, 1984). Each function is distinct, but at the same time interdependent so that difficulties or benefits in one area of functioning resonate through other functions. For instance, in a single-parent family in which the parent is meeting economic needs by working two jobs, children may focus time on supporting the family's daily-care needs; the functions that both parent and children perform may leave limited time for recreational or educational activities. Thus, efforts to meet economic needs may inadvertently impact educational and recreational pursuits. This interdependence of function also applies to the impact a child with a disability may have on the functions individual members perform within the family. A parent may feel it necessary to terminate employment to meet the child's needs at home, or another parent may have to seek additional employment to pay for the child's medical needs. Siblings may be expected to fulfill adult roles to assist in caregiving for their sibling with a disability. In the case of the family whose structure has changed in response to the child's disability (e.g., through divorce, separation, addition of a caregiver or extended family member), all members may modify the functions they perform in the family.

Life cycle of the family.   The life cycle component of the framework is based on the presumption that family life revolves around a sequence of developmental stages (Turnbull & Turnbull, 2001). These stages center around the growth of children into adults and how families adapt and change as they transition through these stages. Major life events such as birth, preschool, elementary school, middle school, high school, college, jobs, and marriage guide this cycle. Life events such as these signal shifts in roles and responsibilities of family members. So as the family transitions across each life event, the family characteristics and functions are altered. A child with a severe disability can affect the life cycle in ways different from children without disability. With the birth or diagnosis of a child with a severe disability, the typical life cycle is transformed. First, the child may not be expected to transition through all of the typical life events, particularly graduating high school and moving on to an independent life and starting the cycle with one's own family. Also, parents must rethink their role as parent and the functions that will be required, including the possibility that they will have to provide care for their child even after he or she reaches adulthood, possibly for the remainder of the child's life. Coming to terms with these issues can take time, and educators may encounter parents still working through these issues. As students reach transition points (e.g., entering middle school) educators must be sensitive the issues parents are facing (e.g., leaving a comfortable, positive situation to enter a new and unknown situation; fear child may not be accepted by peers during adolescence).

Culture and the family.   To further complicate understanding an individual family and the family system framework, one must also consider cultural background. Culture's influence on family structure, interactions, and functions is evident prior to and after the entrance of a member with a disability. Different cultures hold varying views about the roles of different family members and about how children should be raised and disciplined. Sibling roles and cultural expectations vary given gender, age, and birth order; even sibling bonds are influenced by culture (Harry, Day, & Quist, 1998). Each culture maintains different means of verbal (e.g., slang, level of familiarity) and nonverbal communication (e.g., eye contact, physical proximity, gestures). Educator knowledge of this diversity and how these differences influence interactions can be useful in building lines of communication with families.

Consider the following brief information, which illustrates the extent of variations that may exist among families due to cultural differences. The basic family structure of many Americans of Anglo-European descent is the nuclear family, with the father as head of household; for persons of African descent, family may mean a larger network including extended family and friends with a nontraditional head of household such as a grandmother. In family interactions, female Asian family members may be expected to be more passive and less vocal than men, and children more conforming and responsible. The family function of older children of some African and Pacific Island cultures is to assume caregiving responsibility for younger children. This is in contrast to Anglo-European culture, where children's function is to enjoy childhood and assume limited responsibility. These are all in contrast to Asian culture, where responsibility is focused on learning and achieving.

As these examples demonstrate, culture heavily influences the family framework. Culture also is a strong variable influencing how disability is perceived and addressed within the family framework. Culture affects the adjustment to and even acknowledgment of disability within a family and can be a determining factor in the medical and educational interventions sought. The coping strategies each family employs to cope with disability are heavily influenced by culture (Hanline & Daley, 1992). Hispanic and African American families often utilize the strategy of reframing. They are able to change their frame of reference to see the positive aspects of disability, which assist them in maintaining a sense of family pride and respect. Anglo-American families tend to rely on social and professional supports to cope with disability.

Understanding the Family and Outside Interactions

Educators must recognize the significance of each family's framework and culture, and must understand the impact this has on the family's interactions with outside people and organizations. In making requests of families, determining priority goals for students, and providing opportunities for involvement in educational planning and interventions, educators must understand who families are. To further develop understanding of these interactions, one can consider two theories that seek to explain individual and family choices: environmental press and needs hierarchies (Dunst, Johanson, Trivette, & Hamby, 1991). Environmental press refers to the influences an environment has on shaping, or pressing, behavior. Circumstances and individuals interact to push behavior in specific directions. One's environment and experiences (i.e., all aspects of the framework, culture, and experiences outside the family) interact to affect all aspects of one's life: interactions, educational pursuits, parenting decisions, recreational activities, and vocational choices. For instance, a person surrounded by family and friends who value education may pursue the benefits of schooling, whereas a person who has peers and family who do not value education may not excel in school or may choose not to pursue education beyond the legally required age. Needs hierarchies put each individual's needs on a continuum of least to greatest importance. Those unmet needs of greatest importance serve to shape an individual's behavior and interactions with his environment. Persons focus their time and energy on meeting needs they view as important rather than needs that outsiders value. In the hierarchies of needs, one family may rank the purchase of electronic games and video equipment as priority over adapting their home for wheelchair access for their child.

Dunst and colleagues (1991) propose a needs hierarchy perspective of environmental press to explain the failure of some families with children with disabilities to become involved in educational planning and intervention. Parents are not intentionally oppositional or apathetic when they rank education as a low priority. As educators, we must recognize that supporting educational priorities may be difficult for some families. Education is not the only function that families must perform. The focus for families is meeting the needs that they see as priority and for some education is low on the continuum. Unmet needs take precedence, directing behaviors toward fulfilling self-identified needs and goals. If parents are having difficulty providing the family with food and shelter, they may view attending an IEP meeting or gains in fine motor skills for their child as having little significance.

Moreover, a family's needs may affect behavior and interactions with the educational system in additional ways. Many times a lack of agreement or consensus between what educators and families see as priority needs sets the occasions for conflict and families' withdrawing of their support of educational programs (Dunst, Trivette, & Deal, 1988). This often causes families to be viewed as apathetic and uncooperative. In reality this lack of compliance is symptomatic of a much larger issue—the educational system's failure to enable parents to be involved, to listen to the family voice, and to reach consensus on educational plans and programs prior to moving forward. What has often been interpreted as apathy within minority and lower socioeconomic groups has been found to be mistrust of the system. Low-income minority families often withdraw from working with schools because they do not trust the decisions made by educators and feel they have no power to have their needs met. Yet other families avoid involvement due to discomfort within and lack of understanding of the educational process. In situations where families feel like outsiders, many will limit their involvement in such experiences.

Educational systems often do not recognize the ability they have to influence families and family interactions, whether it be positively or negatively. Communications, requests, and criticisms made from school to home can place undue pressure on families and further stress the family framework. Support, recognition, and praise can be a factor in affirming and building family strengths. Educators must realize the impact their exchanges can have on family interactions and how that can reverberate to other aspects of the family framework.

How Do You Implement Practices That Support Families and Inclusive Practices?

Although research supports family involvement and the literature discusses this ideal, families typically remain uninvolved or at best participate passively. The intent of P.L. 94-142 and each reauthorization was for families to proceed through educational planning as active participants, but the majority of families still today function only at the legally required level of informed consent. Family participation not mandated by law occurs at low levels (Defur, Todd-Allen, & Getzel, 2001). For both educators and families, initiating nonrequired involvement is not the norm.

Broadening Understanding of Family and Family Participation

The initial step to supporting families is for educators to broaden their understanding of families and their perceptions of how families should participate in their children's education. To broaden understanding of families, educators must work at understanding families and removing the barriers that exist to family involvement. First, educators must be familiar with the family system and how it is manifest in each family. A particularly critical piece is recognition of the cultural perspective of each family. This certainly does not mean adopting that culture but being aware of how it might impact the family interactions and how they might perceive the child with the disability and educational interventions. Be cautious, though, not to stereotype members of a particular culture. One must attend to heterogeneity within any family or group, being aware of unique characteristics and differences (Harry, Rueda, & Kalyanpur, 1999). Second, educators must develop skills for supporting family–educator communication and partnerships. Many educators enter the teaching profession to work with students rather than families. Since the key factor to student mastery of skills is parent involvement, educators must recognize that working with families is crucial. Workshops and courses in teacher preparation programs are available to educators so that they may develop competence in working with families. Finally, negative educator perceptions of family involvement in education must be transformed (Defur, Todd-Allen, & Getzel, 2001). For a variety of reasons, some educators are opposed to family control in educational decision making. Some educators do not want to relinquish full control; others view families as lacking in the knowledge required to make competent decisions—and clearly communicate this attitude to families. Educators must realize the benefits of involving parents and that their success with the student hinges on family support. To make this shift in attitudes, educators must develop empathy for families, become more flexible in working with families, and reconstruct their viewpoint and acceptance of families (see Table 5.1). No matter the barriers, families are all too aware of the imbalance of power and lack of equality in educational decision making for their children. Changes in working with families must occur so that families are supported within the educational system.

TABLE 5.1 Educator Attitudes Supporting Families

Developing Empathy	Becoming Flexible	Reconstructing Viewpoints
Listen and show concern when talking with families.	Keep involvement options flexible, recognizing that what works for each individual family may be different.	Exhibit an attitude of humility.
Do not pity families.		View informing and educating families as an integral part of working with students.
Seek to understand the family's experiences.	Value and respect the viewpoints of each family.	Be nonjudgmental.
Be sensitive to the pain and emotion unique to each family.	Do not impose your own values on families.	Eliminate the view that the professional viewpoint is superior.
Avoid imposing guilt and shame on families.	Be patient.	Appreciate the knowledge that families possess and can share.
Strive to see through the family's eyes.	Support families by guiding them to appropriate support options.	Accept families as equal partners.
Listen for commonalities with families.	View concerns as an opportunity to problem solve with families.	Focus on strengths.
		Be open to learning from families.

Source: Adapted from T. M. Jones, J. A. Garlow, H. R. Turnbull III, & P. A. Barber. (1996). Family empowerment in a family support program. In G. H. S. Singer, L. E. Powers, and A. L. Olsen (Eds.), *Redefining family support: Innovations in public-private partnerships* (p. 96). Baltimore: Paul H. Brookes.

Supporting Families and Building Partnerships

The majority of today's schools are child focused, but the movement is toward family-centered services. Recognition is growing of the impact of educational services on students with disabilities when families are actively involved in designing and supporting programs (Sailor, Kleinhammer-Tramill, Skrtic, & Oas, 1996). Family-centered practices are key to supporting families so that family–educator partnerships may be established. A family-centered approach is based on the following assumptions: (a) building trust is a basis to partnerships; (b) open communication is an essential component to family–educator relationships; (c) focus is on enabling and empowering the family and student; and (d) a collaborative problem-solving approach is used to resolve issues and problems. These principles are key to building partnerships (Powell, Batsche, Ferro, Fox, & Dunlap, 1997).

Trust.   Educators must work to establish trust so that families feel comfortable communicating and sharing in interactions with the school (Defur, Todd-Allen, & Getzel, 2001). A first step is letting go of a personal agenda so that one can "hear" parents' desires and concerns. Educators must let go of their preset expectations of families. A step further is to personalize relationships through open, honest, and personal communication. One teacher for students with severe disabilities has had repeated success establishing trusting relationships with parents. She connects with families by sharing of herself through conversations of personal stories and through nontraditional contacts such as evening phone calls. All of her conversations incorporate a personal element such as taking interest in the family, asking questions, and making comments about issues other than the student. Parents respond by opening up to this teacher to share family information and to seek out the teacher in problem solving. Mutual sharing of personal information and stories builds trust. Maintaining confidentiality of that information further supports the trusting relationship. Educators must recognize that this trust takes time to build through repeated contacts and interactions.

Communication.   Communication is key to overcoming difficulties and building working partnerships with families. Open and honest communication between families and educators builds upon trust, creating a firm foundation for a successful alliance (Defur, Todd-Allen, & Getzel, 2001). Educators must be aware of how they are communicating both nonverbally and verbally in interactions with families. Nonverbal communication includes facial expressions, gestures, and body language. A person can convey concern, interest, and acceptance just by touching another's hand, maintaining eye contact, and smiling.

Verbal communication, any type of verbal response, can be used to support or shut down interactions. There are three types of verbal responses that educators should be able to use to support interactions: (a) paraphrasing, (b) questioning, and (c) summarizing (Turnbull & Turnbull, 2001). Paraphrasing is restating a family's message in your own words. This can serve the purpose of affirming the family's statement or to check that you accurately understand what the family is conveying. Questioning includes both closed and open-ended questions. Closed questions should be used sparingly because they tend to elicit yes-no or short responses. Open-ended questions often lead families into sharing. One should be cautioned against using questions that seem to place blame or focus on deficits (e.g., "Why did you not send Harold's braces today?" "What do you see as the most important problems your child is having?"). Summarizing is reiterating the most important aspects of a discussion or conversation as a way of finalizing and confirming what has been discussed. Summarization should be used at the end of any meeting or contact with family members. It is particularly useful in tying together rambling meetings or phone calls as a means of checking that all are in consensus on what was discussed and agreed upon.

When engaged in any verbal or written exchange with families, educators must pay particular attention to use of jargon. Educators become so comfortable with daily use of acronyms and special education terminology that they forget that others do not have this same familiarity and knowledge. Communications with families must be presented so that they may be understood—in one's native language and in terms that one can comprehend. Particularly with written exchanges, one must be cognizant of the literacy level and comprehension level of the audience. For instance, a note sent home to a family with limited literacy skills might be written in simpler language than a note written to a family with a high education level.

Another important aspect of communication is listening skills. Families must feel that they are being heard, or else lines of communication will be fractured. Educators should practice active listening, which involves making eye contact, using varied facial expressions, asking questions, making comments, and sharing in the dialogue (Turnbull & Turnbull, 2001). Through listening, one can reflect on and respond to the families' communication to convey understanding, concern, and empathy.

Empowerment. Family-centered practice recognizes that child success is interconnected with family success. For this reason, it is of utmost importance that educators use interactions with families as opportunities to empower them with skills to be successful. Receiving help can be debilitating for some in that it promotes a sense of others' control of one's life. Opportunities for offering help must be viewed as opportunities to empower families. Families must be supported to gain skills and knowledge so that they can navigate the educational and social systems competently (Dunst, Trivette, & Deal, 1988). So when educators are aware of family problems, they must provide families with the resources, contacts, and knowledge to solve their own problems. Educators take on the role of supporter rather than expert. As families develop skills to meet their own needs and as they experience success in resolving their own problems, families will become empowered. An additional component of empowerment is the principle of reciprocity. As families become empowered and self-determined, they begin to recognize how they can contribute to others, particularly others in similar situations (Powell, Batsche, Ferro, Fox, & Dunlap, 1997).

Collaborative problem solving. Collaboration is the process of families and educators working together toward common goals. The collaboration process is evidenced by partners stating views, critiquing views of others, asking questions, expressing disagreement, negotiating, and demonstrating support. Collaboration is essential to problem solving. When a problem arises, families and educators must collaborate so that they reach mutually agreeable solutions. Partners must develop a basic trust so that collaborative problem solving can occur (Walker & Singer, 1993). When educators are on the receiving end of a complaint, they must first exercise the communication techniques discussed previously (e.g., active listening, paraphrasing) to understand the issue or problem. To actually solve a problem, the steps followed are identifying the problem, generating solutions, evaluating solutions, collaborating to negotiate solutions, and determining roles in acting on the problem (Lichtenstein, 1993). Educators must openly communicate with families frequently to determine that solutions are satisfactorily being met.

Consider how trust, communication, empowerment and problem solving work together. When an educator takes the opportunity to call a family member about a child's accomplishment or to send a note of thanks, families are supported and strengthened by this affirmation. This family may have been struggling with what seemed minimal progress in the child's skills, and this positive action on the part of the educator may support the family in reframing their view of the child's progress, being proud of the small accomplishments. On the other hand, if educators take occasion to contact parents only to register negative complaints, educators are not only driving a wedge between themselves and families and minimizing the possibilities of collaborative partnerships, but they may have a negative effect on family interactions. In one instance, an elementary educator called repeatedly to complain that the sibling of her student, a young girl with severe disabilities, was avoiding his sister at school. The teacher demanded that the parents address the problem. For these parents, who were already aware of the sibling acceptance issue but had no solutions, these complaints only added to their mounting anxiety. Consider the effect this stress could have on parental, sibling, and spousal relationships, particularly if the relationships were already fractured. Educators must first build trusting relationships with families so that they may communicate openly. Then educators must work with families to solve problems, enabling families to be part of the solution.

Including Families in Educational Planning

In educational planning, attention is currently on an approach that applies family-centered principles but moves a step beyond. This approach, termed *person-centered planning,* was initially used with persons in the adult service system for life planning but is now being used with school-age children. The basic assumptions of person-centered planning are: (a) viewing the student with disabilities as a whole, considering personal history rather than assessment information to understand the individual; (b) focusing planning on capacities and opportunities as opposed to deficiencies and impossibilities; (c) choices and independence for the individual; (d) building a network to share ideas and collaborate on plans; (e) inclusion within natural environments that will provide natural supports; and (f) networking of services and agencies to better meet the needs of the individual (Mount & Zwernick, 1989; Pearpoint, O'Brien, & Forest, 1995). Some of the many published person-centered tools include Personal Futures Planning (Mount, 1995; Mount & Zwernik, 1989), MAPS (Forest & Pearpoint, 1990), PATH (Pearpoint, O'Brien, & Forest, 1995), and Essential Lifestyle Planning (Smull & Harrison, 1992).

Although the person-centered planning process was initially developed as a meeting outside of IEP planning, the benefits of incorporating this approach within educational planning have been recently recognized. Student Centered IEP Planning (Childre, 1998) is one such process; it takes aspects of several different person-centered tools and adapts them to meet the requirements of IEP meetings. Integrating person-centered planning within IEP meetings serves to achieve multiple purposes. Since person-centered planning was originally used outside of educational planning, combining the two different planning meetings makes person-centered planning accessible for all families. This new version of planning takes the focus off the legal document and places it on participation. The family and student are critical to the process—family participation is the central hub. See Figure 5.1 to see how student-centered IEP planning utilizes both family and student input as a

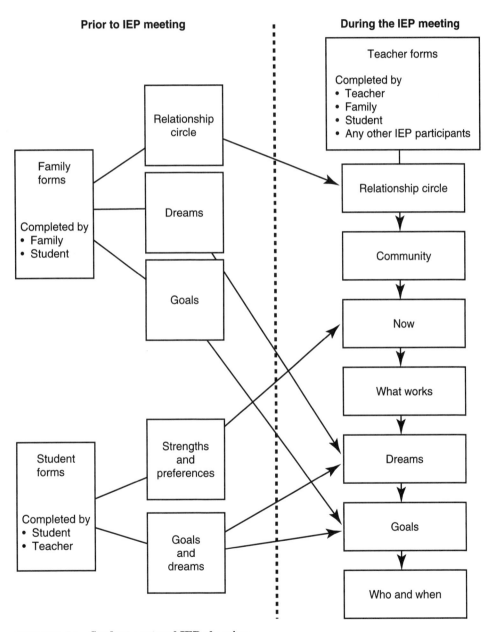

FIGURE 5.1 Student-centered IEP planning.

basis for the IEP meeting. The role of the family is built in; no matter which person-centered tool is used, in all versions the person with the disability and the family are the experts. In this type of planning the team works together toward a joint understanding of reality for the student by considering student capacities and present needs and environments. Families and, if possible, the student share their dreams and goals for the future. The team then problem solves to determine services and goals that should be targeted today so that future dreams may be reached. Emphasis is then placed on determining responsibilities for putting the plan into action. Family satisfaction in using this approach has been overwhelmingly positive, and unequivocally preferred over traditional IEP planning. Educators also recognize the impact of this collaboration. In Box 5.2 you can read how one adolescent's life was changed by person-centered planning.

In preparing for IEP planning, educators must be sensitive to the needs of families. Always provide parents with multiple options for meetings. Not all families will be able to arrange their schedules to attend meetings. To support family involvement, educators should offer multiple options for meeting dates and times and consider nontraditional meeting places (e.g., fast-food restaurant, student's home, community center). If it is not possible for families to attend meetings, optional means of participation should be pursued. For instance, family input may be garnered through an informal telephone conversation, e-mail, simple questionnaire, or note between school and home.

B O X   **5.2**

Sharing Dreams

"My dream for Donna is that she will meet a friend who will be a true friend to her—one who will not draw back because of her physical or verbal limitations, but who instead will be strong for Donna and pull out the best in her." This was a mother's dream for her child, shared during a person-centered IEP meeting. This mother took the planning seriously and shared from the heart. Other members of the team also took it seriously and set out to achieve these dreams. Unfortunately, despite the best efforts, the dream was not reached during middle school. Peers came and went with no one ever connecting with Donna on a personal level. Donna transitioned to the high school and the dream continued unrealized. The heartfelt words shared by this mother never left the teacher. After changing jobs to teach at a university, the teacher became involved in a student organization that promotes friendships between people with and without disabilities. Remembering the mother's words, she contacted the family to see if Donna could join. This time everyone could see the dream was within reach. At one of the organization's outings, Donna clicked with a college student, Cynthia, and a friendship blossomed. They have been inseparable friends for several years now. Donna's mother declares that not only has Donna gained a friend, she feels she herself has gained a daughter. Cynthia says that she and Donna have a sort of unspoken connection. Mention Cynthia's name and Donna just smiles. The teacher thinks all of this was sparked by the person-centered planning meeting. "Knowing the family's dreams keeps pushing you forward. You do not want to stop until you help them reach those dreams."

Assisting Families in Making Informed Choices

In working with families and in developing educational plans, educators will have multiple opportunities to share their expertise and knowledge. One particular issue that is central to the education of students with severe disabilities and that educators should address with families is inclusion. Educators may encounter families who are not aware of the benefits of inclusion and who maintain opposition due to their negative perceptions. To enable families to make clearly informed decisions about placement, families should be aware of the benefits and disadvantages of any environment. The first step towards expanding parental views is to be aware of their primary concerns. Parents express the following concerns regarding inclusion (Palmer, Fuller, Arora, & Nelson, 2001):

- Will the type and level of my child's disability prevent him or her from benefiting from inclusion?
- Will the regular education teacher and students be overtaxed and negatively impacted by my child with a severe disability?
- Will the regular education curriculum meet the developmental needs of my child?
- Will my child miss out on specially trained personnel, services, and individual attention in an inclusive placement?

Once aware of family concerns, educators can inform families so that they have the knowledge to evaluate situations and make choices in the education of their children. Educators should share the benefits that other families observe in inclusive settings: appropriate peer models; gains in social, language, and motor skills; acceptance by peers; and opportunities for the family to meet and develop relationships with other children and parents (Bennett, Lee, & Lueke, 1998).

Communication and sharing information with families should also be part of the educational planning process. Use of person-centered planning can assist in opening the doors to sharing among all parties. In communicating and planning with families, educators must listen for concerns that may be of issue for families. Educators should be particularly aware of the possibility of increased concerns at transition points (e.g., preschool to elementary school, high school to the community). (For discussion of issues at various ages, see Chapters 11 through 15.) As mentioned in the discussion of the family life cycle, transitions can be the most stressful points for families because they are facing so many unknowns. Some of the following approaches and resources can be used by educators to support families and provide information to address their concerns.

Creating Multiple Opportunities for Involvement

Educators must consider family involvement in education from a broad viewpoint. Family involvement in educational planning is only one piece of the partnership puzzle. Families can be involved in other aspects of their children's education. Various techniques and approaches exist that an educator may employ to build family partnerships and to involve families (Jackson, Ryndak, & Billingsley, 2000). Research points to the atmosphere created by the school as a crucial variable in family involvement. When schools have an open-door policy with families, this creates an accepting, welcoming climate in which families are comfortable. Educators should put effort into educating themselves about the involvement options parents may have not only in school and at home, but also in the community.

First, educators should create an inviting environment in the classroom and throughout the school. This includes opportunities as well as invitations for families to be involved. As one parent shares, "I knew there were different programs for parents at our school, but I did not feel welcome and did not start participating until I was invited." To begin, simply look at your classroom for ways that you can involve parents. Can parents serve as room assistant or teacher volunteer for a day? Can families join the class for community-based instruction outings? Would families like to facilitate school–home communication through a daily notebook? Would families like to implement motor, feeding, behavioral, or other interventions at home? Would families like to use e-mail or phone calls to stay in contact or to conduct educational planning?

Next look at your school for involvement opportunities. Offer families opportunities to volunteer with after-school programs, speak to other classes about their occupations or about disability awareness, serve on the school council, or speak to the school faculty or the school board about the impact of inclusion on the student and family.

Finally, look to the community. There are numerous local, state, and national organizations through which families can both provide and receive support. Support is available for both parents and siblings.

Parent support.   A variety of organizations exist as sources of information on disability and parenting, advocacy services, and parent training. All of these types of support serve to empower families with knowledge and skills to work with their children or to navigate the education system. Organizations funded through the U.S. Department of Education include parent training and information centers in each state and community–parent resource centers in underserved urban communities. Technical assistance to the parent and training information centers is coordinated nationally through the PACER Center (http://www.pacer.org). The government has also funded organizations to serve as clearinghouses disseminating information to families and educators. National Information Center for Children and Youth with Disabilities (NICHCY) (http://www.nichcy.org) and the Beach Center on Families and Disabilities (http://www.lsi.ukans.edu/beach/beachhp.htm) serve as clearinghouses and are leaders in providing a broad array of services and information. A comprehensive listing of these and other parent support organizations and services has been compiled by Turnbull and Turnbull (2001). The listing notes pertinent contact information (i.e., addresses, phone numbers, e-mail addresses, websites) so that families and educators may easily access the support.

A popular grassroots organization typically run by volunteer efforts is the Parent to Parent Program. The program was started by Fran Porter, a parent of a child with a disability, in honor of the help she had received from other parents who shared with her their personal experience. In Parent to Parent, one-to-one matches are made between "new" and "veteran" parents on the basis of similar disability and family experience. Those involved offer testimony to the strength gained from listening and talking to parents who have "been there before" and successfully managed the situation (Turnbull & Turnbull, 2001). Programs in many states and regions have websites. Another program based on a similar premise is Parents Helping Parents. These services support families in moving out of the receiver role in services to be providers to other families. Families are viewed as competent and capable of contributing to other families who face similar situations. As a result of serving in such a role, self-esteem and self-confidence increase, which supports families in becoming more self-determined.

Sibling support.   Families function as a system, and siblings are an integral part of that system and must not be overlooked when working with families who have a member with a severe disability. As students with severe disabilities become school age and enter public schools, new concerns and questions may arise with their siblings (Powell & Gallagher, 1993). What is the special education program? Why does my sibling's room look different? Will my friends accept my sibling? Will I need to help take care of my sibling at school? Educators can assist in addressing sibling issues in a number of varying ways. The foremost way that educators can address these issues is by supporting inclusion for the sibling with severe disabilities (Harry, Day, & Quist, 1998). Inclusion will place the sibling with disabilities in a normalized setting in which acceptance can be modeled; information can be shared about disabilities, special needs, and equipment; and multiple interaction opportunities can be provided. A variety of literature has been written for children to foster understanding and acceptance of children with disabilities. Both the National Information Center for Children and Youth with Disabilities (http://www.kidsource.com/NICHCY/literature .html) and Powell and Gallagher (1993) have developed comprehensive lists of children's literature related to disability and to siblings. Literature can be integrated into the curriculum in any classroom, especially inclusive classrooms, to support recognition of the uniqueness, contribution, and feelings of all individuals. As siblings age, educators may invite siblings (with parent permission) to be involved in educational planning meetings. Siblings often have insight into their sibling's special needs that may be overlooked by adults. Throughout the school years, educators must take care not to overwhelm siblings with additional responsibilities of caring for their sibling while at school. For instance, unless the sibling desires, it is not his responsibility to teach his sibling or to be the social intermediary.

An additional way that educators can address the special needs of siblings is to provide resources to the family. More is being researched and written on the impact disability has on the siblings within a family. In response to this recognition various newsletters, workshops, and support groups have been developed. The Sibling Information Network Newsletter, published quarterly, is written for children who have a sibling with a disability (Sibling Information Network, A.J. Pappanikou Center, 62 Washington Street, Middletown, CT 06475; 203-344-7500). A special support program and newsletter, Sibling Squabble, has been developed by Parents Helping Parents to bring attention to the unique needs of siblings who have a family member with a disability (Parents Helping Parents, 3041 Olcott, Santa Clara, CA 95054-3222; 408-288-5010). The most distinctive sibling workshop model has been developed by Don Meyer. These workshops, "Sibshops," provide both emotional support and information to siblings through a variety of interactive and engaging activities. Resource material is available so that families, educators, or other advocates can sponsor workshops in their own communities (Meyer & Vadasy, 1994).

How Do You Assess the Effectiveness
of Your Practices with Families?

Educators most often assess the impact of their practices with families informally in a qualitative manner. Educators assess their success with families by judging or measuring family responses to invitations; the level of cooperation with requests; agreement or disagreement with goals, objectives, and daily instruction; the amount of support given their work; perceived level of success of efforts to guide or influence families; and amount of help provided to families and the families' acceptance of this help (Walker & Singer, 1993). Assessments such as these are more consistent with a child-focused rather than a family-centered delivery model of service because the teacher is the sole person making these judgments. Does this mean that an educator should not informally assess parent interactions? Certainly not; educators should continually assess their work with families, but they should also seek means of input from parents about their perceptions of involvement and partnerships. When using a person-centered approach to educational planning, parent satisfaction with educator efforts and student progress are naturally voiced in the process. Thus, informal assessment is built into this approach. This approach builds comfort and trust so that families can voice their opinions and ideas for change.

Other more formal assessments, surveys, and questionnaires exist to gather various information on family perceptions and family functioning. Specific instruments have been developed for the purpose of assessing family satisfaction and family attitudes toward inclusion. The Parent Attitudes Toward Inclusion (PATI) Scale measures family perception of inclusion practices and teacher support (Palmer, Borthwick-Duffy, & Widaman, 1998). A number of additional instruments have been developed to measure aspects relative to family functioning and support. An extensive list of measures of social support and family functioning has been compiled by Dunst and Trivette (1985). Another analysis of measures, this one focused on family quality of life, was completed by Hughes, Hwang, Kim, Eisenman, and Killiam (1995). For educators working within a system with a family-centered approach to services, these measures could provide much insight for guiding service provision.

Educators may choose one of these instruments to provide a more objective analysis of practices with families or they may tailor their own instrument. By reviewing these instruments, educators can create their own surveys or questionnaires tailored to assess the particular aspects of family functioning, inclusion, or collaboration in which they are interested. In administering some of these instruments, the option of anonymity and confidentiality should be offered so that families can respond openly without worrying that they may hurt or offend their children's educators.

Conclusion

Without the support of families, our efforts as educators will produce limited results. Educators must work to build the bonds with families that create and continually strengthen partnerships. As educators learn to recognize and respect the variances in families and implement family-centered practices, they can begin to understand families, their children, and their unique needs. As partners, families and educators can share their resources so that the partnership and the family are empowered to achieve the goals and dreams they and the student envision.

References

Agosta, J., & Melda, K. (1996). Supporting families who provide care at home for children with disabilities. *Exceptional Children, 62,* 271–282.

Alper, S., Schloss, P. J., & Schloss, C. N. (1996). Families of children with disabilities in elementary and middle school: Advocacy models and strategies. *Exceptional Children, 62,* 261–270.

Bennett, T., Lee, H., & Lueke, B. (1998). Expectations and concerns: What mothers and fathers say about inclusion. *Education and Training in Mental Retardation and Developmental Disabilities, 33,* 108–122.

Buck, P. S. (1950). *The child who never grew.* New York: Day.

Childre, A. (1998). Student centered planning and IEP meetings: Parent perceptions before and after implementation (Doctoral dissertation, Vanderbilt University, 1998). *UMI Dissertation Abstracts,* 9915077.

Defur, S. H., Todd-Allen, M., & Getzel, E. E. (2001). Parent participation in the transition planning process. *Career Development for Exceptional Individuals, 24,* 19–36.

Dunst, C. J., Johanson, C., Trivette, C. M., & Hamby, D. (1991). Family-oriented early intervention policies and practices: Family-centered or not? *Exceptional Children, 58,* 115–126.

Dunst, C. J., & Trivette, C. M. (1985). *A guide to measures of social support and family behaviors.* Chapel Hill: University of North Carolina, Technical Assistance Development System.

Dunst, C., Trivette, C., & Deal, A. (1988). *Enabling and empowering families: Principles and guidelines for practice.* Cambridge, MA: Brookline Books.

Forest, M., & Pearpoint, J. (1990). *Everyone belongs: Building the vision with MAPS—The McGill Action Planning System.* Toronto: Center for Integrated Education.

Hanline, M. F., & Daley, S. E. (1992). Family coping strategies and strengths in Hispanic, African-American, and Caucasian families of young children. *Topics in Early Childhood Special Education, 12,* 351–366.

Hanson, M. J., & Carta, J. J. (1996). Addressing the challenges of families with multiple risks. *Exceptional Children, 62,* 201–212.

Harry, B., Day, M., & Quist, F. (1998). "He can't really play": An ethnographic study of sibling acceptance and interaction. *Journal of the Association for Persons with Severe Handicaps, 23,* 289–299.

Harry, B., Rueda, R., & Kalyanpur, M. (1999). Cultural reciprocity in sociocultural perspective: Adapting the normalization principle for family collaboration. *Exceptional Children, 66,* 123–136.

Hughes, C., Hwang, B., Kim, J., Eisenman, L. T., & Killiam, D. (1995). Quality of life in applied research: A review and analysis of empirical measures. *American Journal on Mental Retardation, 99,* 623–641.

Jackson, L., Ryndak, D. L., & Billingsley, F. (2000). Useful practices in inclusive education: A preliminary view of what experts in moderate to severe disabilities are saying. *Journal of the Association for Persons with Severe Handicaps, 25,* 129–141.

Judge, S. L. (1998). Parental coping strategies and strengths in families of young children with disabilities. *Family Relations, 47,* 263–268.

Lichtenstein, J. (1993). Help for troubled marriages. In G. H. S. Singer & L. E. Powers (Eds.), *Families, disability, and empowerment: Active coping skills and strategies for family interventions* (pp. 285–315). Baltimore: Paul H. Brookes.

McDermott, J. (2000). *Babyface: A story of heart and bones.* Bethesda: Woodbine.

Meyer, D. J., & Vadasy, P. F. (1994). *Sibshops: Workshops for siblings of children with special needs.* Baltimore: Paul H. Brookes.

Mount, B. (1995). *Capacity works: Finding windows for change using personal futures planning.* New York: Graphic Futures.

Mount, B., & Zwernik, K. (1989). *It's never too late, it's never too early: A booklet about personal futures planning.* St. Paul: Minnesota Governor's Planning Council on Developmental Disabilities.

Palmer, D. S., Borthwick-Duffy, S. A., & Widaman, K. (1998). Parent perceptions of inclusive practices for their children with significant cognitive disabilities. *Exceptional Children, 64,* 271–282.

Palmer, D. S., Fuller, K., Arora, T., & Nelson, M. (2001). Taking sides: Parent views on inclusion for their children with severe disabilities. *Exceptional Children, 67,* 467–484.

Pearpoint, J., O'Brien, J., & Forest, M. (1995). *PATH: A workbook for planning positive possible futures, planning alternative tomorrows with hope for schools, organizations, businesses, and families* (2nd ed.). Toronto: Inclusion Press.

Powell, D. S., Batsche, C. J., Ferro, J., Fox, L., & Dunlap, G. (1997). A strength-based approach in support of multi-risk families: Principles and issues. *Topics in Early Childhood Special Education, 17,* 1–26.

Powell, T. H., & Gallager, P. A. (1993). *Brothers and sisters: A special part of exceptional families* (2nd ed.). Baltimore: Paul H. Brookes.

Sailor, W., Kleinhammer-Tramill, J., Skrtic, T., & Oas, B. K. (1996). Family participation in new community schools. In G. H. S. Singer, L. E. Powers, & A. L. Olson (Eds.), *Redefining family support: Innovations in public-private partnerships* (pp. 313–332). Baltimore: Paul H. Brookes.

Sandler, A. G., & Misretta, L. A. (1998). Positive adaptation in parents of adults with disabilities. *Education and Training in Mental Retardation and Developmental Disabilities, 33,* 123–130.

Scorgie, K., & Sobsey, D. (2000). Transformational outcomes associated with parenting children with disabilities. *Mental Retardation, 38,* 195–206.

Singer, G. H. S., & Powers, L. E. (1993). Contributing to resilience in families. In G. H. S. Singer & L. E. Powers (Eds.), *Families, disability, and empowerment: Active coping skills and strategies for family interventions* (pp. 1–25). Baltimore: Paul H. Brookes.

Smull, M., & Harrison, S. B. (1992). *Supporting people with severe reputations in the community.* Alexandria, VA: National Association of State Mental Retardation Program Directors.

Sobsey, D. (2001). Dale Evans and the great rescue: A parent's view. *Mental Retardation, 39,* 401–404.

Turnbull, A. P., Summers, J. A., & Brotherson, M. J. (1984). *Working with families with disabled members: A family systems approach.* Lawrence: University of Kansas, Kansas Affiliated Facility.

Turnbull, A., & Turnbull, R. (2001). *Families, professionals, and exceptionality: Collaborating for empowerment.* Upper Saddle River, NJ: Prentice-Hall.

Walker, B., & Singer, G. H. S. (1993). Improving collaborative communication between professionals and parents. In G. H. S. Singer & L. E. Powers (Eds.), *Families, disability, and empowerment: Active coping skills and strategies for family interventions* (pp. 285–315). Baltimore: Paul H. Brookes.

Wehmeyer, M. L., Morningstar, M., & Husted, D. (1999). *Family involvement in transition planning and implementation.* Austin, TX: Pro-Ed.

6 Social Relationships

CRAIG H. KENNEDY
Vanderbilt University

This chapter focuses on an often overlooked but critically important aspect of all our lives—*social relationships*. Until recently, when educators thought about supports for students with severe disabilities, they tended to focus on skill building. That is, to make students more *independent*. However, there is a growing appreciation among educators that along with becoming more independent, a student also needs to learn how to rely upon, relate to, and help others. In other words, to become more *interdependent*.

What follows is a review of current findings regarding the nature of social relationships, what they provide to students, and how they can be improved. After reading this chapter you should be able to:

- Describe different types of social relationships and explain why they are important
- Understand how social relationships develop
- Identify key elements in facilitating and maintaining social relationships
- Implement a range of strategies to improve the social lives of your students
- Make decisions about how to help your students benefit from their social relationships

What Are Social Relationships?

There are two easy answers to this question: "It's obvious, we all have them and know what they are," and "Defining social relationships is like defining the meaning of life—it's not possible." Although each of these views has a kernel of truth to it, to arrive at a useful understanding of what social relationships are we will need to go beyond these easy answers.

Most researchers attempting to understand social relationships have focused on two interrelated aspects of our social lives: (a) patterns of contact and (b) subjective satisfaction. First, and perhaps most fundamentally, social relationships are based on *contact patterns* between two people. For example, two students might see each other in class on a regular basis, or that contact may be more intermittent such as two students getting together for lunch once a week. The contact between two students does not need to be direct for a social relationship to exist (e.g., people regularly stay in contact with each other through e-mail messages). From this perspective, a student's social life can be understood as a collection of interactions with other people.

Researchers are using several aspects of social contact patterns to capture important aspects of what we mean when we talk about social relationships (Newton, Olson, & Horner, 1995; Kennedy, in press; Staub, Peck, Galluci, & Schwartz, 2000). Figure 6.1 shows one way of visualizing aspects of social contact patterns. The most intuitive level of Figure 6.1 is that social relationships are based on *social contacts*. The notion of a social interaction can be described as how often two students interact, how long each interaction lasts, what particular day(s) those interactions occur on, and so on.

Another area of interest in describing social relationships is what occurs between students when they interact. Figure 6.1 refers to this as *social support*. Argyle (1993) noted that for people to repeatedly interact they must gain something from an interaction. These social supports include helping others (e.g., lending someone a pencil), exchanging information (e.g., learning a new joke), and emotional support (e.g., comforting someone in distress). (We will talk more about social support in the next section on why social relationships are important.)

Along with social interactions and social support, Figure 6.1 also includes something called *social networks*. A social network simply refers to the different patterns of interaction among students. For example, Nan, Steve, Laura, and Janice might individually interact with each other on a regular basis, but rarely get together as a group. Although these individuals rarely interact as a group, we can still think of them as highly interconnected with one another (i.e., a social network).

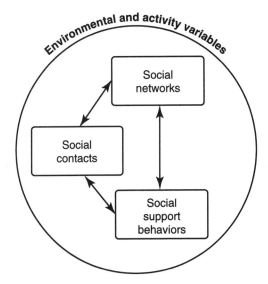

FIGURE 6.1   A conceptual approach to assessing adolescent social interactions.

Finally, it is important to note that social interactions, social supports, and social networks occur within a *context*. Whether we are simply trying to assess someone's social interactions or trying to help him or her develop a richer social life, it is important to pay attention to where students interact and what they do when interacting. As a collection, then, when we talk about students' social relationships in this chapter, we will be describing them in terms social interactions, social supports, social networks, and the contexts in which they exist.

Clearly, there is more to what we think of as a social relationship than describing patterns of social interaction. A second important aspect of social relationships is a student's *subjective satisfaction* with his or her social life. A consistent finding from research on this topic is that there is substantial variation among students regarding what constitutes a desirable social life. Some individuals prefer to interact with a small number of people, but interact frequently with them; others prefer to interact with a large number of people, but less frequently. The point is that there is not a specific number of people or number of interactions per day that mark a good social life. Instead, what a particular student perceives as a *satisfactory social life* needs to be identified and evaluated on an individual basis.

Along with an individual's personal preferences regarding the nature of his or her social relationships is how the student interprets specific relationships. Although more complex schemes have been developed for categorizing relationships, a reasonable way of thinking about this is to place them on a continuum from *acquaintances* to *friends*. The difference between these two end points is a student's subjective labeling of a relationship. The importance of this distinction being the greater social importance given to people considered as friends. As in the definition of personal preferences (e.g., the size of a social network), how a student labels his or her social relationships is a matter of individual preference. It should also be noted that a student's social needs are not static, but change over time and should be repeatedly assessed (Staub et al., 2000).

If we put all these pieces of the social relationship puzzle together, we begin to have a basis for describing the social life of students. For a specific student we can identify the other people with whom the individual interacts, how frequently they interact, if others are involved, where they interact, what they are doing, the types of social supports that occur, and who is perceived as a friend. Such a range of descriptors provides educators with a picture of what a student's social life is like and suggests how future supports may need to be arranged to facilitate and/or maintain social relationships.

Why Are Social Relationships Important?

Social relationships are important because of the numerous benefits that are derived from them (Sarason & Duck, 2001). It is well established that people with a satisfactory social life are healthier, happier, and more active than those who have less satisfactory social lives. In addition, when people are faced with a difficult challenge (e.g., illness, injury, or unemployment) a supportive social network can help them overcome many of the negative effects of such events. These outcomes make sense because along with the gratification that is derived from a satisfactory social life there are many direct benefits that people receive from social relationships. In the remainder of this section we will discuss three areas that have been identified by researchers as reasons that social relationships are important: (a) social support, (b) membership/belonging, and (c) personal happiness.

Social support refers to the behaviors that are a part of social interactions (Cohen & Underwood, 2000). For example, a student's pencil point might break during English class and the person next to her might lend her a pencil sharpener. Or a student who uses a wheelchair may have trouble negotiating his way through an entrance and another student might help him navigate through the door. In addition to social behaviors that produce clear material benefits, social support can also include behaviors that have a more emotive role. For example, a child might be crying because his toy was taken from him, and another child comes over and gives him a hug. Or an adolescent girl might be starting a painful menses and one of her friends confides to her that she, too, has the same health concerns.

Researchers categorize social support into six categories: (a) emotional support, (b) companionship, (c) access to others, (d) information sharing, (e) material assistance, and (f) choice making. Table 6.1 lists definitions of these social supports and provides additional examples.

TABLE 6.1   Social Supports: Definitions and Examples

Emotional Support: Comforting a person during positive or difficult events
- Give a hug when the student is upset
- Listen to student's verbal or gestural communication
- Show basic courtesy (e.g., apologize for bumping)

Companionship: Interacting within a shared context
- Talk with each other directly or following a greeting
- Smile while working on parallel tasks/activities
- Tell a joke to another person

Access to Others: Introducing a person to a new acquaintance
- Be introduced to a new classmate
- Delegate another person to help a student with a task
- Bring a student to a club meeting

Information: Communicating about recent/forthcoming events or activities
- Tell about events going on at school
- Tell about a movie
- Tell about a specific place for recreation or shopping

Material Aid: Providing a person with physical assistance or items
- Help get things out of a backpack
- Push a person's wheelchair
- Loan school supplies

Decision Making: Helping with arriving at personal choices
- Present options for task/activity
- Assist in making choices about activity
- Encourage student to follow classroom rules

Source: Adapted from S. Shukla, C. H. Kennedy, and D. Fryxell. (1995). *Social interaction checklist.* Honolulu: University of Hawaii.

One of the goals of an educator should be to increase a student's access to social support and improve his or her ability to provide social support to others. The defining characteristic of having a severe disability is a person's need for increased assistance from other people. Typically, this need for support is present throughout a person's life. This need for social support makes having an adequate social network critical for people with severe disabilities. The more people involved in a student's life and the greater their commitment, the more likely the student is to receive the social support that will help improve his or her quality of life.

Along with providing access to, and opportunities to give, social support, social relationships also form the basis for *belonging and membership* (Murray-Seegert, 1989). What is meant by belonging and membership is a sense of "connectedness" with other people. This connectedness is typically characterized as being stable and something that is shared by the individuals involved. In addition, people describe belonging and membership as characterized by a sense of equality among the individuals involved, mutual respect for one another, and reciprocity of social supports. Not surprisingly, people often report that a sense of belonging and membership is one of the most important benefits of having social relationships.

Belonging and membership emerge at a number of different levels. Clearly an important part of having social relationships is having a circle of friends that you feel a part of (Haring & Breen, 1992). Along with these friendship networks, it is important for students to be valued members of the classes they attend. Similarly, school membership is an important issue (see Schnorr, 1990). Finally, students need to be a part of their family and community. At each of these levels it is important to realize that belonging and membership, like social relationships in general, require active efforts to create and maintain them.

Finally, despite all the discussions focusing on defining what social relationships are and how we benefit from them, whether a person is satisfied with his or her social life is a fundamentally subjective and individual issue. Ultimately, the goal of educators is to improve a student's *happiness*. Because a satisfactory social life is an important aspect of happiness, teachers need to be aware of a student's perception of the adequacy of his or her social relationships (Strully & Strully, 1985).

What Processes Are Involved in Social Relationships?

What makes social relationships develop? This question can be partially answered based on existing research, but no definitive answer can currently be given to what causes social relationships to form and endure. However, we do know enough about social relationships to outline processes that influence how a person develops a satisfactory social life. This knowledge comes from researchers studying a wide range of ages, including early childhood, preadolescence, adolescence, and adulthood (Meyer, Park, Grenot-Scheyer, Schwartz, & Harry, 1998; Odom, McConnell, & McEvoy, 1992). This section will discuss four general areas relating to social relationship development and maintenance: (a) how relationships develop, (b) balancing independence and interdependence, (c) types of social interactions, and (d) variables that influence the course of a relationship.

How Social Relationships Develop

Social relationships follow a predictable pattern (Goldstein, Kaczmarek, & English, 2001; Jackson & Rodriguez-Tomé, 1993). This pattern can be described as having three broad stages that occur in a fixed sequence. The first stage focuses on *initial social encounters*. This initiation phase is based on students first being introduced to each other, typically through another person who is familiar with both individuals. Of course there are other ways in which students meet; however, in school contexts the predominant way in which students first meet one another is through a peer or teacher facilitating the initial interaction. This first phase is generally brief, just one to three interactions, with either of two outcomes occurring. One outcome is that unilaterally, by mutual agreement, or other circumstances, the two individuals stop interacting with each other. The second outcome is that students move into the second stage of social relationship development. Current estimates for students with severe disabilities is that approximately 55 percent of the peers who are initially met go on to the second stage of social relationships. This number is not too different from the literature on social relationships between typically developing peers, which suggests that 35 percent of interactions move into the second stage. This slightly higher percentage for students with severe disabilities probably relates to the planned nature of many of their initial social interactions.

This second phase of social relationship development focuses on establishing *mutually preferred interaction contexts*. After students have met, they try out different activities with one another, sometimes in new settings. In essence, people try out different places where interactions can occur, what activities they can engage in, and how each person enjoys those interaction contexts. This phase provides a vehicle for (a) expanding the array of opportunities for interacting, (b) identifying what are preferred and nonpreferred contexts, and (c) making implicit and/or explicit decisions about what form the relationship will take in the future. These relationships either dissolve over time or go on to become durable social relationships (the third stage of relationship development). The reasons for relationships not continuing are multiple, but students report reasons such as conflicting schedules, changing interests, and membership in new peer groups. Indeed the majority of social relationships do not extend beyond the second phase. This pattern is consistent for students whether they have a disability or not, and are a natural part of how our social lives are constituted.

Most people providing support to students with severe disabilities tend to focus on the final stage of social relationship development—establishing *durable relationships*. These are relationships that are typically described as friendships and are the most satisfactory of relationships. Along with the emergence of sustained social interaction and the self-identification of these relationships as friendships, something else happens. As people continue to interact a routine develops, with people getting together at similar times, on similar days, and engaging in similar activities. This "routinization" is a hallmark of durable relationships. People tend to fall into a pattern of opportunities to interact with one another. For example, two children may always play the same game (e.g., hopscotch) during the morning recess period. Or two adolescents may belong to the same school club (e.g., French culture) and interact each time the club is scheduled to meet.

Data from research on inclusive schools suggests that 15 percent of the peers that students with severe disabilities meet will develop into longer-term relationships (Kennedy,

Shukla, & Fryxell, 1997). Again, this percentage is similar to data reported for students without disabilities (Buhrmester, 1990). However, it is important to note that a student's social relationships are dynamic, and change over time is a natural part of the process. Although there are certainly exceptions to the stages just described, these stages are useful for helping educators think about how social relationships develop.

Balancing Independence and Interdependence

The development of social relationships is influenced in part by the *social competence* of the individuals. Social competence refers to a student's ability to effectively interact and maintain social interactions. One aspect of social competence is a student's ability to independently engage in a set of behaviors that are referred to as "social skills." The more *independent* a person is in initiating social interactions, taking turns during social episodes, and providing reciprocal social support, the more likely the person is to self-determine a social life he or she is happy with. Therefore, teaching students to be as independent as possible is an important goal for educators.

However, too much of an emphasis on independence in social interactions may be counterproductive (Kennedy, in press). If educators focus exclusively on teaching students to be independent, particularly students with severe disabilities, educators may be setting up "readiness traps." That is, if an individualized education program (IEP) team focuses on a child learning prerequisite skills (e.g., making eye contact or reducing challenging behavior) prior to being allowed to interact with students without disabilities, there is a strong risk that months, even years, may pass before the student is allowed to interact with his or her peers. Although certain social interaction skills are useful in facilitating social interactions, the costs of waiting for a child to learn prerequisite skills before interacting with peers without disabilities may be too great (e.g., Ferguson & Baumgart, 1991; Strully & Strully, 1985).

An alternative to this readiness trap is for teachers to strike a balance between promoting independence and interdependence. What is meant by *interdependence* is a child or student being able to work collaboratively with others to accomplish a common goal (a second aspect of social competence). For example, three preadolescents may be surfing the Internet for a class project on tropical rain forests. Within the context of this interaction there are multiple roles and responsibilities (e.g., what search engine to select, who moves the mouse, and who decides what information to download). Finding a role for a student with severe disabilities that allows a central role in the interaction (e.g., controlling the mouse) may facilitate his or her participation in the activity by making each student interdependent to achieve success. This type of social context places the emphasis not on a student being independent, but on learning how to participate in activities with others.

Contexts and Types of Social Interaction

Where we interact and what we do are closely linked. For example, two children interacting inside a synagogue engage in very different behavior than on the playground at school. This is in part because of the activities available for people to interact around, along with distinct social expectations about what are, and what are not, appropriate behaviors. Children or youth who are socially competent learn what behavior to engage in depending on the context.

In school settings there are three broad contexts within which social interactions occur: (a) classroom-based activities, (b) recess/breaks/mealtimes, and (c) brief interactions in other settings. We will review each of these and note what types of behaviors are typically engaged in within these different contexts and the types of social interactions they facilitate. For example, the social interactions that occur while waiting in line for the school bus have specific characteristics that differ from interactions during a collaborative social studies project.

The majority of a student's school day is spent in *classroom-based activities*. Hence, these contexts become important settings for encouraging social interactions. However, what social interactions are permissible in these contexts depend on a range of variables, including the grade level of the classroom, the types of learning situations provided by the general education teacher, and the use of peer supports. More social interaction is permissible in prekindergarten and early elementary school than, for instance, high school. Typically, the higher the grade level, the less social interaction is encouraged during class activities. However, moderating this grade-level effect on social interaction opportunities are the types of teaching strategies educators use (see Chapters 11 through 15). For example, using a cooperative learning strategy provides opportunities for social interaction that whole-class instruction does not permit. Finally, the use of peer supports, discussed in the next section of this chapter, is a strategy that allows for social interactions between students with severe disabilities and their peers without disabilities across a range of learning contexts and instructional situations.

The most common types of social support that occur in classroom settings are access to others, information sharing, material assistance, and choice making (Kennedy et al., 1997). Although emotional support and companionship are important and also occur in these contexts, the demand of classrooms structure the types of behaviors that occur within them.

Another important context for social interaction at school occurs during *recess, breaks, and meals*. These situations differ as students move along the prekindergarten to high school and transition continuum (see chapters in Section Two), but there are also common characteristics. Out-of-class activities, whether playtime (prekindergarten), recess (elementary/middle school), or breaks (high school and work), allow people to engage in much less structured interactions. Typically, a student is allowed to select the type of activity that he or she wants to engage in and that, in part, determines what peers are available. In addition, the focus of these social contexts is more likely to emphasize emotional support and companionship through collaborative interactions.

Mealtimes are similar to breaks except that there is a common activity (i.e., eating a meal or snack). These contexts provide students with opportunities to be together in a similar activity. In addition, along with the eating of the food itself, mealtimes typically provide a rich set of opportunities for social interaction. Like break times, the social support behaviors that are engaged in are less task oriented and emphasize emotional support and companionship.

Along with classroom activities and break/meal times, students also have opportunities to interact with one another when *transitioning from one classroom to another and arriving at, or leaving, school.* For example, a student may have an opportunity to say hello to half a dozen peers when going from English class to math class. These opportunities are typically transient, but provide many opportunities for students to interact briefly by exchanging social greetings.

One final note on the types of social interaction that occur in classrooms, during breaks, and transitions. Several researchers have noted the importance of *reciprocity* in social interactions (Meyer et al., 1998; Strain, Odom, & McConnell, 1984). What is meant by reciprocity is the equal exchange of social supports between two people. For example, during a class project one student might lend another a pencil and the recipient of the pencil might offer to give the other student a piece of paper. In this scenario each student is providing something to the other; that is, they are reciprocating social support. Or reciprocity can be as simple as one student saying hello to another student after that individual initiates a greeting. Students with severe disabilities may need to be taught when and how to act reciprocally. An important area for assessment is to identify opportunities for students to learn to provide social supports to others (we will talk more about this in the next section).

Another goal to consider when providing opportunities for students with severe disabilities to interact with their peers is the "role" that each person takes in the interaction. Staub and colleagues (2000) and Meyer and colleagues (1998) have referred to this issue as the degree to which social interactions are *vertical* versus *horizontal*. A vertical interaction means that one person is serving in a dominant, supervisory, or instructional capacity, while the other person is the recipient of those actions. For example, a "peer tutor" interaction places one person in the role of teacher, while the other assumes the role of student. A horizontal interaction is one in which the students share a common or equal role within the activity. For example, one student might cut figures for an art project and the other might arrange those pieces on a page.

Some researchers have noted that when peers without disabilities begin to interact with students with severe disabilities, there is a tendency for the peer without disabilities to adopt a vertical role when interacting with the student with disabilities (Giangreco, Edelman, Luiseli, & MacFarland, 1997). This suggests, just as with reciprocity, that educators should take an active role in facilitating interactions to make sure there is a balance of vertical and horizontal roles and that the student with disabilities is supported to assume as many diverse roles as possible. Most people report that a healthy relationship involves multiple roles and an important part of facilitating social interactions is an awareness of the different roles that students can have.

Facilitating Social Relationships

Now that we have reviewed what researchers know about defining social relationships, why they are important, and the processes that influence their development, in the next section we will focus on what educators can do to facilitate social relationships. An important first step is assessing when opportunities for social interaction may occur during the school day. Once places, times, activities, and people have been identified, a set of strategies needs to be selected to facilitate interactions.

Assessing Opportunities for Interaction

Assessment in educational settings is a necessary first step in identifying targets for intervention. Without this type of information the development of support strategies becomes "hit or miss." With reasonable assessment information educators can focus their efforts on specific contexts that will provide students with the optimal set of opportunities to further their social development.

Several key elements are necessary for conducting an assessment of social interactions. Those elements, in the order they should be conducted, are:

Step 1. Identify the student who is being assessed. Focusing on a specific student allows for the collection of information that is unique to that person's strengths and needs. If a general assessment that does not identify a specific student is conducted, the information may not be relevant for a particular individual.

Step 2. Identify the times and settings to be assessed. Knowing when and where to conduct assessments specifies what the potential contexts for support strategies are. For example, is the assessment being conducted for a student who is new to the school? If so, then assessments may need to occur throughout the school day. Is the assessment being conducted for a student with a well-established support plan? If so, then assessments should focus on contexts that require refinement or additional support strategies.

Step 3. Identify what aspects of a person's social life you want to assess. Is the primary interest in increasing the number of people that a student meets? Or is the primary focus on maintaining already established social relationships? Using the educational team's cumulative knowledge of a student's social life allows for the selection of target areas. Table 6.2 offers a list of questions to ask to brainstorm on improving a student's social life. A good starting place is to ask, "Who does the student interact with?" This question will not only

---

TABLE 6.2 Social Life Assessment Questions and Suggestions

1. List the people with whom you interact.
   - A. Is each person a friend or acquaintance?
   - B. How many times per week do you interact with each person?
   - C. In what setting(s) do you interact with each person?
   - D. What activities do you engage in when you interact with this person?
   - E. Does this person know any of the other people you interact with?

2. What areas of your social life could be improved?
   - A. Would you like more interactions with a particular person?
   - B. Would you like to interact with this person in new settings?
   - C. Would you like to do different activities with this person?
   - D. Would you prefer individual or group activities?
   - E. Would you like to meet new people?

provide information regarding whom a student interacts with, but will also facilitate questions about how often they interact, where they interact, what they do, and what type of social network exists. Given this information, support personnel are in a better position to know what aspects of a student's social life could be improved.

Step 4.   Formal and informal information gathering is necessary to assess a student's social life. Once the educational team has identified areas where a student's social life can be improved and/or maintained, identifying what the student is currently experiencing at school is important for accurate decision making. There are a number of ways to gather this information—some very simple, some more sophisticated. When gathering assessment information, it is important to remember that, in general, the more effort that goes into information gathering, the more likely the information is to be accurate. On the other hand, the less time spent on gathering assessment information, the sooner support plans can be developed. As with many aspects of teaching, an educator needs to strike a balance between these competing issues.

Appendix 6.1 (pp. 118–119) lists various measurement strategies that can be used to assess social relationships. The appendix lists different types of information that an educational team might be interested in and different measurement strategies that can be used, and provides a reference for obtaining more detailed information about a specific measurement system. Although it is beyond the scope of this chapter to discuss each measurement system individually, the references provided allow readers to follow up on particular measurement strategies by consulting the books and journal articles listed in the appendix.

In Step 3 the target information for assessment was identified (e.g., a student's social interaction frequency in math class could be improved). Using Appendix 6.1 the next step is to identify possible measures of student social interaction. In general, measurement systems vary from verbal or written questions to direct observations of a student (with the latter typically being more accurate but more time consuming). For instance, asking the student with disabilities, his or her peers, the general education teacher, and/or a paraprofessional a series of questions may be all that is necessary. This information could be gathered either orally or in writing (e.g., an e-mail message). Or an observational system could be used by a paraprofessional during class to gain more direct counts of social interaction. Box 6.1 has an example of how this process might be used.

Assessment information is gathered until the educational team believes that it has accurate information. For oral or written questions, this might mean gathering information from two or three people in a class. Or, for direct observation, gathering data may last for two to five days. The amount of assessment information is largely a matter of how much information needs to be gathered to have assembled a believable picture of a student's social life given the areas targeted for improvement.

Step 5.   Once assessment information has been collected it will need to be summarized and interpreted (see Chapter 4). How the information is summarized is largely based on the questions identified in Step 3. For example, the scenario outlined in Box 6.1 focuses on identifying what class period(s) had high and which had low levels of social interaction, using a combination of direct observation and interviews. The results of the assessment indicated high levels of social interaction in all but two class periods (math and physical

---

BOX **6.1**

Assessing Peter's Social Interactions across the School Day

Peter has autism and a severe intellectual disability. He is 6 years old and is new to his elementary school and the first-grade classroom he is attending. Peter tends to be gregarious, but his frequent social initiations generally focus on specific interests like dinosaurs and cars. He has been in school a month with a variety of support strategies that, in general, seem to be effective academically and socially. However, there are reports that in some classes his frequency of social interaction is very low. Mr. Washington, the special education teacher on Peter's interdisciplinary team, has been asked to assess these concerns and report back to Peter's support team. Initially, Mr. Washington uses the Social Contact Assessment Form (see Appendix 6.1) to identify Peter's level of social interaction in each class. Mr. Washington identified an adult in each class who could collect the information each day for one week and taught each person how to complete the scale. The results of the initial assessment showed that Peter had frequent social interactions in all but two class periods—math and physical education (PE). Using a similar process, Mr. Washington then employs the Engagement Scale (see Appendix 6.1) to identify the grouping arrangements and contexts for social interaction in the math and PE classes. After assessing these classes for a week, it was clear that Peter was working alone in those classes. Mr. Washington then scheduled individual meeting times with the math and PE teachers to discuss Peter's participation in each class. The results of the unstructured interviews were very different. Peter's math teacher said that she primarily provided instruction to her class using a standard lecture and overhead format, so Peter's social interaction patterns were similar to those of the other students. When asked if she would consider using alternative instructional formats, the math teacher indicated she would be interested, but that she would need consultation from other teachers on Peter's team. In PE, Mr. Washington discovered that the instructor had never worked with a student with autism and was unsure how to deal with Peter. The PE teacher's primary support strategy for Peter was to have him work with a paraprofessional during the PE class. Asked if he would be interested in trying peer support strategies in his class, the PE teacher said he was unsure what that was or how it worked, but would be willing to meet with the interdisciplinary team to discuss the possibility. Mr. Washington then took this information to the interdisciplinary team to help them make a more informed decision about improving Peter's social interactions.

---

education). This finding led to subsequent discussions and observations in those two classes suggesting that instructional formats were a barrier to greater participation in the class and this resulted in less frequent social interactions with peers without disabilities. Summarized information needs to then be reviewed and discussed by key members of the educational team. After a "snapshot" of a student's social life has been obtained and areas for improvement identified, strategies for facilitating those areas for improvement can be implemented with greater effectiveness and efficiency.

Facilitating Interactions

Table 6.3 (p. 112) lists five barriers to social interaction and social relationship development, as well as support strategies that educators often use to overcome those barriers. Researchers

TABLE 6.3   Barriers to Social Interactions and Relationships and Suggested Strategies

1. Access to general education settings

    Facilitating inclusive placements

2. Access to peers without disabilities in general education settings

    Peer supports

    Classroom participation

3. Access to the general education curriculum

    Adaptations/modifications

4. Skills for facilitating interactions

    Pivotal activity skills

    Reciprocity skills

    Teaching interdependence

5. Access to specific peers over time

    Class scheduling

    Alternative school interaction opportunities

    Afterschool interaction opportunities

have identified *access to general education settings* as a critical barrier to social relationship development (Haring & Breen, 1992; Kennedy et al., 1997). This is a concern because most students without disabilities are in general education settings, so opportunities for interaction are maximized by participating in those settings. If the assessment of a student's social relationships indicates few interactions and little participation in general education settings, then the suggested strategy is increased access to general education settings. Strategies for accomplishing this are present throughout this book, particularly in Part 2 and Chapters 2, 3, and 10 from Part 1.

A second barrier is *gaining access to peers* without disabilities in general education settings. As Giangreco and colleagues (1997) note, simply placing a student with severe disabilities into general education settings does not ensure the occurrence of social interactions. If students are currently attending general education classes and participating in other regular settings (e.g., the cafeteria) but interactions are infrequent, then *peer support* and *classroom participation* strategies might be useful (Janney & Snell, 1997; Salisbury, Galluci, Palambaro, & Peck, 1995).

Peer supports refer to strategies that facilitate social interactions in general education settings between students by allowing peers without disabilities to provide direct support to the student with a severe disability under the supervision of adults (Goldstein et al., 2001; Haring & Breen, 1992; Hunt et al., 1997; Kamps, Potucek, Lopez, Kravits, & Kemmerer, 1997; Odom et al., 1992). This strategy complements and extends the role of paraprofessionals outlined in Chapter 10 by Giangreco and Doyle. Generally, there are four steps to creating and implementing a peer support program. First, peers without disabilities are

---

BOX **6.2**

Developing Peer Supports for Natasha in Math Class

Natasha is taking Ms. Cherry's seventh-grade pre-algebra class. Natasha is 11 years old, has attended her middle school for one year, and has made several friends. She has an electric wheelchair to move around, complete use of her upper body, typical sensory abilities, and a severe intellectual disability. She is new to the math class, as are most of the other students. Along with Natasha, there are 25 students in the math class; three have a learning disability and one a moderate intellectual disability. A paraprofessional, Ms. Jones, has been assigned to assist Ms. Cherry in supporting this range of student needs. Natasha's math class last year was the one class where she had few social interactions with peers without disabilities, so Natasha's instructional team wants to assess potential opportunities in her new math class for social interaction. Before the first class, the paraprofessional scans the enrollment sheet to see if Natasha knows any of her peers in the class; none are identified, so Ms. Cherry makes an announcement at the end of the first class that she is looking for volunteers to be peer supports for Natasha. She outlines the expectations and roles of peer supports, emphasizing the importance of helping one another be successful. This process results in two peers, Tonisha and Roger, who volunteer to be peer supports and who are friends of friends of Natasha, but have not met her in the past. Everyone agrees that the peers will take weekly turns serving as supports for Natasha. Three IEP goals are identified for Natasha: answering "wh-" questions, speaking clearly, and independently maneuvering her wheelchair in the classroom. Ms. Jones, in consultation with Ms. Cherry, identifies curricular adaptations for Natasha that can be applied across daily and weekly lecture plans. These adaptation strategies are then taught to Tonisha and Roger to use during class. Ms. Jones and Ms. Cherry agree that it is best if Ms. Jones checks in with the peer supports every 10 minutes to ask if they need help, check on the appropriateness of interactions (Tonisha tends to be off-task), and monitor the acquisition of IEP goals. In addition, Roger and Tonisha are asked to write down any questions or concerns they have at the end of each week and give the feedback form to Ms. Cherry. Ms. Jones does the same, but orally, for Natasha.

---

recruited to a serve as peer supports. Researchers have identified several strategies for accomplishing this, including classroom announcements requesting volunteers, identifying peers without disabilities who know or have previously worked with the student with disabilities, rotating opportunities among peers in the classroom, and offering extra credit for students who serve as peer supports.

Then, once a peer(s) has been identified, teachers need to identify what IEP goals are going to be focused on in the classroom. A third step in the peer support process is facilitating access to the general education curriculum. This step focuses on strategies for providing the student with disabilities opportunities to learn the same content material (e.g., a lesson on tropical rain forests) as other students in the class (see Chapter 3). Often in peer support programs access to the general education curriculum is provided by having a paraprofessional or teacher outline for the peer supports what types of adaptations need to be made and then supervising the peers in making adaptations for the student with severe disabilities (see Box 6.2). The fourth step is to establish a regular schedule for monitoring the peer support program, providing feedback to each of the students, and soliciting information regarding what is working and what needs to be modified to make the peer support program more effective. For example, the peer support group might be monitored by a paraprofessional every 15 minutes during class, and once a week the students with and without disabilities are given the opportunity to make suggestions for improving instruction.

Another set of strategies for facilitating interactions with peers without disabilities focuses on maximizing classroom participation using techniques other than peer support programs (Janney & Snell, 1997; Salisbury et al., 1995). One such strategy is *cooperative learning groups* (see Putnam, 1998). Cooperative learning groups provide an excellent opportunity for interactions within the context of learning opportunities and have been shown to increase social interactions. A second strategy is identifying specific classroom roles that the student with disabilities can assume. For example, a student might be assigned to check student attendance each day, check that homework has been handed in, or distribute/collect textbooks during the class. A third strategy identified by Salisbury and colleagues (1995) is identifying *opportunities during class scheduled for interactions*. These times are different from cooperative learning and classroom roles in that they are not instructional times, but instead are opportunities for less structured socialization. Often teachers provide these times either at the beginning of class or toward the end of the class period.

A third barrier to social interactions listed in Table 6.3 is *access to the general education curriculum*. We have talked a little about how peer supports can be used to access the curriculum; however, there are number of strategies that have been developed that facilitate access. Chapter 3 by Ryndak and Billingsley provides a discussion of how to gain access to the general education curriculum and why it is critical for successful inclusion.

A fourth barrier to social interactions is the need for students with severe disabilities to learn *new skills for facilitating interactions* with peers. Along with support strategies that compensate for a student's disabilities, educators also want to focus on the development of new skills. One approach to skill development associated with improved social interactions is to teach students *pivotal skills for participating in activities*. Most social interactions are based around an activity (e.g., surfing the Internet or playing in a sandbox). Certain skills are required to engage in the activity, and typically each of the partners share or alternate the responsibility for executing those skills. Teaching a student some of the skills necessary for participating in an activity gives them a central role in the social interaction that is valued by others (Breen & Haring, 1991). For example, if a student with disabilities is playing a computer game with a student without disabilities, teaching the student with disabilities to move the cursor with the mouse or hit the return key to advance the game to the next step gives that person a key role in the activity.

A related approach is to teach students *reciprocity skills* during social interactions. Most sustained social relationships contain a high level of reciprocity. Indeed, taking turns initiating interactions, choosing activities, and complementing the other person are behaviors that are expected in relationships. Explicitly identifying and teaching students these skills has been shown to increase the richness and length of social interactions (Kohler & Fowler, 1985). For example, teaching a student to say hello when another student greets him or her increases the likelihood of a more elaborate social interaction. Or teaching a child to offer a toy to another student and ask if he or she wants to play increases the likelihood of an interaction.

Finally, teaching students *interdependence* can increase the frequency and quality of social interactions. Interdependence is different from participation or reciprocity skills in that this approach to skill development focuses on cooperation and collaboration between students (Kennedy, in press). As noted earlier, most social interactions are based around some type of activity. If you think of an activity as producing some desired set of outcomes, identifying ways that students can collaborate to obtain those ends can be a way of facilitating social interactions. For example, making sandwiches for lunch can be viewed as a collaborative endeavor for facilitating social interactions through interdependence training, as well as a way to make something good to eat. Students can be taught how to negotiate what steps will be conducted by whom, whether a person will need additional help, what steps will require two or more people to complete, and how they will share the end product. The idea of interdependence training incorporates elements of pivotal skills and reciprocity skills into a larger context of cooperative interaction.

The final barrier to social interactions listed in Table 6.3 focuses on strategies to make sure that a student has *access to specific friends and acquaintances over time*. Even when educators are successful in facilitating the development of social interactions, active efforts need to be made to support the relationship. School contexts change from semester to semester and year to year in terms of scheduling and classroom placements. Because these changes can disrupt opportunities for social interaction between particular students, they are a concern. An important logistical issue that can disrupt social relationships is *class scheduling*. In preschool settings this is often focused around changes in age groupings; in elementary school this concern arises when grade levels change; and in middle school and high school this concern arises each semester/quarter when class schedules change. When these inevitable changes occur, educators need to identify specific relationships that are important to the student with severe disabilities and be proactive in arranging schedules so that continued opportunities for interaction will be available. For example, in a high school setting a student with severe disabilities and his or her teacher might ask the student's best friend what classes he or she is going to take when enrolling for the fall semester so that they can take one or two classes together in the upcoming school year.

An additional set of opportunities for interaction occur in relation to non-classroom-based opportunities for interaction. These *alternative school interaction opportunities* exist throughout the school day, largely in between classroom periods/blocks or activities. One such set of opportunities exists in transitions from one class period to the next. Although these opportunities are brief and transient, they provide a rich opportunity for brief greetings and exchanges of social amenities. Recesses, breaks, or play periods provide opportunities for more prolonged interactions around recreation activities. Regularly scheduling opportunities for students to "play" together or "hang out" are important elements in constructing a student's schedule (Haring & Breen, 1992). In addition, of course, there are daily opportunities around mealtimes (lunch, snack, and so on). Again, actively scheduling for times, days, locations, and specific individuals to interact with, along with additional supports that a student might need, is an important strategy for promoting social interactions and social relationships. One additional set of social interaction opportunities that occur outside of the classroom is *afterschool activities*. School dances, sporting events, fundraisers, and related social gatherings are important opportunities for social interaction and help define a school as a community center.

Conclusion

Building a social life for any student requires active efforts to develop social relationships and sustain them over time. A systematic approach requires that opportunities for interaction be assessed not only throughout the school day, but also in terms of extracurricular events. Knowing when, where, and who—the results of assessment—makes creating regular opportunities for social interaction easier and more successful. However, educators also need to actively use strategies for facilitating social interactions, such as peer supports, to ensure that students with and without disabilities receive frequent and appropriate opportunities to interact with one another. In addition, because social relationships are very dynamic and school schedules routinely change, educators need to actively plan for future opportunities for social interaction for their students in order to ensure that relationships have a chance to continue over time.

References

Argyle, M. (1993). *Experiments in social interaction.* Brookfield, VT: Dartmouth Publishing.

Breen, C. G., & Haring, T. G. (1991). Effects of contextual competence on social initiations. *Journal of Applied Behavior Analysis, 24,* 337–347.

Buhrmester, D. (1990). Friendship, interpersonal competence, and adjustment in preadolescence and adolescence. *Child Development, 61,* 1101–1111.

Cohen, S., & Underwood, L. G. (2000). *Social support measurement and intervention: A guide for health and social scientists.* New York: Oxford University Press.

Ferguson, D. L., & Baumgart, D. (1991). Partial participation revisited. *Journal of the Association for Persons with Severe Handicaps, 16,* 218–227.

Fisher, D., Sax, C., & Pumpian, I. (1999). *Inclusive high schools: Learning from contemporary classrooms.* Baltimore: Paul H. Brookes.

Giangreco, M., Edelman, S., Luiselli, T., & MacFarland, S. (1997). Helping or hovering? Effects of instructional proximity on students with disabilities. *Exceptional Children, 64,* 7–18.

Goldstein, H., Kaczmarek, L., & English, K. M. (2001). *Promoting social communication: Children with developmental disabilities from birth to adolescence.* Baltimore: Paul H. Brookes.

Haring, T. G., & Breen, C. G. (1992). A peer-mediated social network intervention to enhance the social integration of persons with moderate and severe disabilities. *Journal of Applied Behavior Analysis, 25,* 319–334.

Hunt, P., Farron-Davis, F., Wrenn, M., Hirose-Hatae, A., & Goetz,-L. (1997). Promoting interactive partnerships in inclusive educational settings. *Journal of the Association for Persons with Severe Handicaps, 22,* 127–137.

Jackson, S., & Rodriguez-Tomé, H. (1993). *Adolescence and its social worlds.* Hillsdale, NJ: Lawrence Erlbaum Associates.

Janney, R. E., & Snell, M. E. (1997). How teachers include students with moderate and severe disabilities in elementary classes: The means and meaning of inclusion. *Journal of the Association for Persons with Severe Handicaps, 22,* 159–169.

Kamps, D. M., Potucek, J., Lopez, A. G., Kravits, T., & Kemmerer, K. (1997). The use of peer networks across multiple settings to improve social interaction for students with autism. *Journal of Behavioral Education, 7,* 335–357.

Kennedy, C. H. (in press). Social interaction interventions for youth with severe disabilities should emphasize interdependence. *Mental Retardation and Developmental Disabilities Research Reviews.*

Kennedy, C. H., Shukla, S., & Fryxell, D. (1997). Comparing the effects of educational placement on the social relationships of intermediate school students with severe disabilities. *Exceptional Children, 64,* 31–47.

Kohler, F. W., & Fowler, S. A. (1985). Training prosocial behaviors to young children: An analysis of reciprocity with untrained peers. *Journal of Applied Behavior Analysis, 18,* 187–200.

Meyer, L. H., Park, H. S., Grenot-Scheyer, M., Schwartz, I. S., & Harry, B. (1998). *Making friends: The influences of culture and development.* Baltimore: Paul H. Brookes.

Murray-Seegert, C. (1989). *Nasty girls, thugs, and humans like us: Social relations between severely disabled and nondisabled students at high school.* Baltimore: Paul H. Brookes.

Newton, J. S., Olson, D., & Horner, R. H. (1995). Factors contributing to the stability of social relationships between individuals with mental retardation and other community members. *Mental Retardation, 33,* 383–393.

Odom, S. L., McConnell, S. R., & McEvoy, M. A. (1992). *Social competence of young children with disabilities: Issues and strategies for intervention.* Baltimore: Paul H. Brookes.

Putnam, J. W. (1998). *Cooperative learning and strategies for inclusion* (2nd ed.). Baltimore: Paul H. Brookes.

Salisbury, C. L., Gallucci, C. L., Palombaro, M. M., & Peck, C. A. (1995). Strategies that promote social relations among elementary students with and without severe disabilities in inclusive schools. *Exceptional Children, 62,* 125–137.

Sarason, B. R., & Duck, S. (2001). *Personal relationships: Implications for clinical and community psychology.* Chichester, England: John Wiley & Sons.

Schnorr, R. (1990). Peter? He comes and goes . . . First graders' perspectives on a part-time mainstreamed student. *Journal of the Association for Persons with Severe Handicaps, 15,* 123–140.

Staub, D., Peck, C. A., Gallucci, C., & Schwartz, I. (2000). Peer relationships. In M. E. Snell & F. Brown (Eds.), *Instruction of students with severe disabilities* (5th ed., pp. 381–409). New York: Merrill/Prentice-Hall.

Staub, D., Spaulding, M., Peck, C. A., & Gallucci, C. (1996). Using nondisabled peers to support the inclusion of students with disabilities at the junior high school level. *Journal of the Association for Persons with Severe Handicaps, 21,* 194–205.

Strain, P. S., Odom, S. L., & McConnell, S. R. (1984). Promoting social reciprocity of exceptional children: Identification, target behavior, selection and intervention. *Remedial and Special Education, 5,* 21–28.

Strully, J., & Strully, C. (1985). Friendship and our children. *Journal of the Association for Persons with Severe Handicaps, 10,* 224–227.

APPENDIX 6.1

Types of Measures for Assessing Social Relationships

1. Access to General Education Settings

   Engagement Scale. Hunt, P., Farron-Davis, F., Beckstead, S., Curtis, D., & Goetz, L. (1994). Evaluating the effects of placement of students with severe disabilities in general education versus special classes. *Journal of the Association for Persons with Severe Handicaps, 19,* 200–214.

   Schedule Analysis Instrument. Hunt, P., Farron-Davis, F., Beckstead, S., Curtis, D., & Goetz, L. (1994). Evaluating the effects of placement of students with severe disabilities in general education versus special classes. *Journal of the Association for Persons with Severe Handicaps, 19,* 200–214.

   Setting Utilization Matrix. Haring, T. G., & Breen, C. (1989). Units of analysis of social interaction outcomes in supported education. *Journal of the Association for Persons with Severe Handicaps, 14,* 255–262.

   Social Contact Assessment Form. Kennedy, C. H., & Itkonen, T. (1994). Some effects of regular class participation on the social contacts and social networks of high school students with severe disabilities. *Journal of the Association for Persons with Severe Handicaps, 19,* 1–10.

2. Social Interaction Patterns

   Ecological Inventory of Social Skills. Browder, D. M. (1991). *Assessment of individuals with severe disabilities* (2nd ed.). Baltimore: Paul H. Brookes.

   MS-CISSAR. Carta, J. J., Greenwood, C. R., Shulte, D., Arreaga-Mayer, C., & Terry, B. (1988). *Code for instructional structure and student academic response— Mainstream version.* Kansas City: University of Kansas, Juniper Gardens Children's Project.

   Nondisabled Peer Interview. Staub, D., Peck, C. A., Gallucci, C., & Schwartz, I. (2000). Peer relationships. In M. E. Snell & F. Brown (Eds.), *Instruction of students with severe disabilities* (5th ed., pp. 381–409). New York: Merrill/Prentice-Hall.

   Performance-Based Assessment of Social Competence. McConnell, S. R., & Odom, S. L. (1999). A multimeasure performance-based assessment of social competence in young children with disabilities. *Topics in Early Childhood Special Education, 19,* 67–74.

Social Contact Assessment Form. Kennedy, C. H., & Itkonen, T. (1994). Some effects of regular class participation on the social contacts and social networks of high school students with severe disabilities. *Journal of the Association for Persons with Severe Handicaps, 19,* 1–10.

Social Interaction Checklist. Kennedy, C. H., Shukla, S., & Fryxell, D. (1997). Comparing the effects of educational placement on the social relationships of intermediate school students with severe disabilities. *Exceptional Children, 64,* 31–47.

Social Interaction Observations. Haring, T. G., & Breen, C. G. (1992). A peer-mediated social network intervention to enhance the social integration of persons with moderate and severe disabilities. *Journal of Applied Behavior Analysis, 25,* 319–334.

Student Participation in General Education Settings. Rainforth, B., York, J., Macdonald, C. (1997). *Collaborative teams for students with severe disabilities* (2nd ed.). Baltimore: Paul H. Brookes.

Valued Outcomes Information System. Newton, J. S., Ard, W. R., Horner, R. H., & Toews, J. D. (1996). Focusing on values and lifestyle outcomes in an effort to improve the quality of residential services in Oregon. *Mental Retardation, 34,* 1–12.

3. Friendship Networks

Peer Survey. Helmstetter, E., Peck, C. A., Giangreco, M. F. (1994). Outcomes of interactions with peers with moderate or severe disabilities: A statewide survey of high school students. *Journal of the Association for Persons with Severe Handicaps, 19,* 263–276.

School-Based Social Network Analysis Form. Fryxell, D., & Kennedy, C. H. (1995). Placement along the continuum of services and its impact on students' social relationships. *Journal of the Association for Persons with Severe Handicaps, 20,* 259–269.

Social Network Analysis Form. Kennedy, C. H., Horner, C. H., & Newton, J. S. (1990). The social networks and activity patterns of adults with severe disabilities: A correlational analysis. *Journal of the Association for Persons with Severe Handicaps, 15,* 86–91.

Social Preference Survey. Hall, L. J. (1994). A descriptive assessment of social relationships in integrated classrooms. *Journal of the Association for Persons with Severe Handicaps, 19,* 302–313.

Sociometric Peer Rating. Asher, S. R., Singleton, L. C., Tinsley, B. R., & Hymel, S. (1979). A reliable sociometric measure for preschool children. *Developmental Psychology, 15,* 443–444.

7 Communication

ANN N. GARFINKLE AND ANN P. KAISER
Vanderbilt University

This chapter focuses on important skills through which we express ourselves and understand others—communication skills. Considerable theoretical and empirical research has been conducted to understand the acquisition of speech and language skills in typically developing children. Similarly, studies have been conducted that assess the effectiveness of interventions designed to teach speech and language or alternative and augmentative systems of communication to students with severe disabilities. Many of these interventions, however, focus primarily on the development of expressive communication skills, not on receptive skills. That is, the interventions focus on teaching students to send a message, but do not improve their skills for receiving or understanding a message. After reading this chapter you should be able to:

- Define what is meant by "communication"
- Explain why communication is so critical to social interactions and learning
- Describe the various forms that communication can take
- Understand general principles that will help guide the development and implementation of communication interventions for students with severe disabilities in inclusive classrooms
- Have knowledge of several empirically supported communication interventions that can be implemented in inclusive classrooms

As researchers have examined the experiences of students with severe disabilities in inclusive settings, it has become clear that in addition to the communication skills traditionally taught, it is also important to ensure that students with severe disabilities develop relationships and are viewed by their classmates as a member of the class (Schwartz, 2000; Schwartz, Garfinkle, & Davis, 2002; Schwartz, Staub, Gallucci, & Peck, 1995). There is increased recognition that students with severe disabilities need to learn meaningful and functional expressive and receptive communication skills for use in peer interactions. In addition, peers need support and encouragement to communicate with students who have disabilities (Ferguson, 1994).

For students with severe disabilities, their functional use of communication and the form it takes will be affected by their cognitive and linguistic skills as well as by their social skills. Cognitive skills provide the basis for learning associations, memory, and recall. Cognition is foundational for the linguistic skills and symbolic use required to produce and understand even simple communicative messages. Thus, in order to help students with severe disabilities become competent communicators, cognitive skills, social skills, and communicative skills must all be targeted for intervention.

This chapter focuses primarily on communication skills with limited discussion of cognitive and social skills (see Chapters 3, 4, and 6 for interventions on skills in these domains). The chapter discusses five basic steps for planning and implementing communication interventions for students with severe disabilities. Within each step, principles are given to help guide the interventionist in making the decisions required to plan individualized intervention programs for students with severe disabilities.

What Is Communication?

Communication is the social exchange of information using symbols or signs to represent meaning. Although communication is not unique to humans, it is one of the most severe distinguishing features of human behavior. Communication is a social act requiring at least two partners for the exchange of information. To exchange information, both partners must be able to understand meanings (receive messages) and express meanings (send messages). Meanings are defined by the shared contexts of the speaker and the listener and by their rule-governed use of a shared system of symbols and signs. Human symbolic communication can be extremely complex. The production and understanding of linguistic systems in a social context is governed by rules related to phonology (sound systems), lexicon (vocabulary), morphology (markers of meanings appended to words, such as plurals [-s, -es] and past tense [-ed]), syntax (sentences and their components), and pragmatics (social use in context). Use of signs (manual signing such as American Sign Language), computer-based augmentative communication systems, or picture-based systems (e.g., the Picture Exchange Communication System [PECS; Bondy & Frost, 1994]) simplifies some aspects of communication, but the core requirements of shared meaning defined by context and governed by rules remain.

Why Is Communication Important?

Communication is an essential skill for a successful life (Guralnick, 1997). Language provides the framework for thinking about people, objects, experiences, and ideas in the past, present, and future (Goldstein & Woods, 2002). Shared language allows people to identify with groups and to develop, share, and maintain a culture. At a more basic level, language and communication allow people to express needs and desires in social exchanges. Environmental factors such as a family's capacity to provide meaningful experiences, the family's physical and mental health, the family's educational level, the community the family lives in, and the resources available to the family in the community all contribute the child's learning of communication skills (Sameroff & Chandler, 1975; Sameroff & Fiese, 1990). For students with severe disabilities, interventions to teach communication skills are likely to be a critical factor in students' social interactions and their quality of life.

Communication and Problem Behavior

The relationship between communication skills and problem behavior is not completely understood in all populations (Hester & Kaiser, 1998). For children with severe disabilities, however, there is a well-documented link between the two. In a classic study, Carr and Durand (1985) demonstrated that by teaching students with problem behavior appropriate communicative skills, instances of the inappropriate behavior sharply declined. A decrease in inappropriate behavior was documented even though the problem behavior itself was not the target of intervention. This relationship between communication skills and behavior has been replicated by several researchers (e.g., Davis, Brady, Williams, & Hamilton, 1992; Durand & Carr, 1992; Koegel, Koegel, & Surratt, 1992; Wacker et al., 1990). For students with severe disabilities, acting-out behaviors may be their most effective form of communication. Teaching more standard forms of communication gives students acceptable, effective alternatives for expressing their needs.

Communication and Inclusion

Participation in inclusive educational settings requires communication with others. While the forms and contexts for communication will vary according to the age of the student and the type of inclusive classroom, the need for communication as a basis for participation is a constant. Communication is central to inclusion, to the teaching and learning that will occur in inclusive settings, and to the social transactions among students and between teachers and students. The typical communication abilities and social engagement strategies of students with severe disabilities challenge teachers, assistants, and other students when students with severe disabilities are included in ongoing classroom activities in a meaningful and natural way.

Teaching communication to students in an inclusive setting is unique and offers unusual benefits as well as challenges. The availability of peers who are competent communicators and who can learn and use strategies to support communication by students with severe disabilities is an obvious advantage. Typical student peers can offer models of communication, partners for conversation, and a ready reference point for teachers working with students who have severe disabilities. At the same time, these typical peers compete with students with severe disabilities for teacher time and attention. Typical peers engage more easily. They are easier to understand, more persistent in their bids for teacher attention, and likely to override the more tentative communications of students with severe disabilities. Teachers must regulate their own attention to be sure that students with and without severe disabilities have equitable access and opportunities for responding.

The range of activities in the regular classroom presents many opportunities for learning for students with severe disabilities. For teachers, the range of activities and the range and discrepancies in students' learning goals and rates of progress may make effective communication intervention for students with severe disabilities especially challenging. Teaching in natural environments, using activity-based, incidental teaching strategies, requires a high level of teacher skill and careful planning. In the context of inclusive classrooms, it may be difficult to give students with severe disabilities sufficient opportunities to learn and practice communication skills while addressing the instructional needs of all the class members. Teachers may be particularly challenged to concurrently provide instruction on communication skills and meet students' academic goals while supporting students with severe disabilities in developing social relationships and group membership. However, addressing communication in its natural context—in social interaction—is essential to achieving instructional goals and valued social outcomes.

Individualized Communication Needs

Students with severe disabilities need instruction in communication that is tailored to their unique abilities and to the social and learning contexts of the inclusive classroom. Four dimensions of support are of particular importance: (a) shared communication modes; (b) opportunities for learning and use of communication in instructional and social contexts of the classroom; (c) effective, comprehensive instruction that includes ongoing assessment; and (d) support to peers in communicative interactions with students with severe disabilities. These supports for learning new communication skills parallel what students with severe disabilities will need to participate in inclusive educational settings: a means of communication that is understood by peers and adults with whom the student interacts; ongoing support in communicating; and individualized accommodations in instruction that take into account communication abilities.

Social opportunities to use receptive and productive communication skills are at the core of both learning and participation in the inclusive classroom. Use and refinement of communication is socially motivated. When the classroom offers opportunities for academic and social interaction that students find reinforcing, there will be functional opportunities for instruction and for spontaneous social use of newly learned forms. The importance of the inclusive setting as a context for promoting fluency, generalization, and maintenance of communication skills cannot be understated. While it is possible to teach initial acquisition of new forms outside of social context (e.g., using direct instruction in one-on-one teaching sessions), fluency, generalized use over time, and integration of communication skills into the student's social and behavioral repertoires require practice in everyday conversations. Functional, social opportunities for communication are one of the most important features of inclusive classrooms; however, insuring sufficient opportunities for teaching and learning requires planning and monitoring.

Successful instruction and functional use of the communication skills depend on the selection of a communication mode that fits both the students' abilities (e.g., oral, motor, cognitive, and linguistic; see Warren & Reichle [1992] and Beukelman & Miranda [1998] for detailed discussion of the selection of a mode for communication). Communication also depends on the abilities of adults and peers to engage in social and instructional exchanges with the student using that mode. The communication mode must be transparent to partners. That is, it must be understandable and usable by adults and peers or it will not support natural, ongoing social communication, academic instruction, or naturalistic teaching and learning. All communication partners may need some level of training to make a mode useful in social conversation. The amount of training partners will need is one of the important considerations in choosing a mode and designing a fully inclusive classroom.

Students with severe disabilities need receptive communication skills, as well as productive communication skills. Support for receptive communication in inclusive settings parallels support for productive communication. Students with severe disabilities may not be able to understand the modes of communication used by their peer and adult conversational partners. Most students with severe disabilities will understand more spoken language than they use. When students use an alternative communication form (e.g., signs, PECS, natural gestures), they must have receptive communication skills in this mode. Instruction to increase their receptive communication skills in spoken language and the alternative mode should be planned. Students will need to learn specific strategies to mediate social communication when they are unable to understand what is being said. For example, students will need to be able to ask a partner to repeat a message, give more information, or demonstrate their meaning through actions. Planning must provide opportunities for learning and practicing receptive skills in conversations. In addition, accommodations in instruction and interventions to increase social interaction must take into account students' receptive communication ability and teach essential skills.

Inclusive classrooms are one part of students' lives. The communication goals, modes, and strategies for instruction in the classroom should be consistent with families' and students' valued outcomes. It is expected that student's communication goals will reflect the family's culture, the family's uniqueness, and the family's values. Collaboration between family members and school personnel to select a mode of communication, immediate and long-term goals for instruction, and strategies to support generalization, maintenance, and development over time is central to the interventions that will be implemented in the classroom. Collaboration with families starts during the assessment of student progress and continues through the refinement of instructional and support strategies.

Teaching Communication Skills

Teaching communication skills to learners with severe disabilities requires a level of precision and planning beyond what is necessary for learners without severe disabilities. The general approach to teaching, however, is similar to that used with other populations and for skills in other domains. This general approach to teaching consists of five basic steps:

1. Conduct comprehensive and ongoing assessments of student's skills.
2. Select intervention targets (goals and objectives).
3. Provide instruction to teach the targeted skill; instruction is not finished until all stages of learning have been addressed.
4. Monitor the frequency, intensity, and fidelity of instructional and intervention procedures.
5. Monitor the student's progress in learning and using the targeted skills.

In this chapter, we propose a set of principles to gauge intervention planning and implementation. These are general principles but not specific directives. The heterogeneity

TABLE 7.1 Steps and Principles for Intervention Planning and Implementation

Step 1: Assessing Communication Skills

    Principle 1: Use reliable and valid assessment
    Principle 2: Assess communication skills in multiple environments with multiple partners
        on multiple occasions
    Principle 3: Assess the environment
    Principle 4: Assess the skills of the communicative partners
    Principle 5: Link assessment information to goal and intervention selection

Step 2: Select Communicative Goals and Objectives

    Principle 6: Teach behaviors that are foundations to communication
    Principle 7: Teach receptive and expressive skills
    Principle 8: Teach skills for the present and the future

Step 3: Select Communicative Interventions

    Principle 9: Use interventions with empirical support
    Principle 10: Select a mode of communication that can be learned quickly
    Principle 11: Prepare and support communicative partners

Step 4: Measure the Intervention Intensity and Fidelity

    Principle 12: Measure learning opportunities
    Principle 13: Measure instructional fidelity

Step 5: Conduct Ongoing Monitoring

    Principle 14: Monitor student progress
    Principle 15: Repeat the process

of the population of students with severe disabilities and importance of immediate context on the form and functions of communication limit the usefulness of specific directives. These principles are summarized in Table 7.1.

Principles for Assessing Communicative Skills

Assessment is an ongoing process whereby information is collected to determine the student's current communication skills and related competencies. Traditionally, assessments were conducted only on a student's level of communication and understanding of speech (Prizant & Schuler, 1987). It is now recognized that the student's skills, the context of the communication, existing supports for communication, and the skills of the communicative partners must also be assessed (Schwartz, Garfinkle, Joseph, & McBride, 1998).

    Principle 1: Use a variety of reliable and valid assessment tools to assess the student's skills. Different assessment tools are needed to provide the range of information needed for planning effective interaction. Tools should be selected based on the purpose of the assessment. Typically, a variety of observational and direct testing methods will be used to gather information about the student's current skill level. Observational methods will include several language/communication samples. These running records of student communication acts should be taken during ongoing, regularly occurring activities as well as in one-on-one interactions with a responsive adult. Direct testing assessments may include the use of assessment designed specifically to test communication skills (e.g., the Peabody Picture Vocabulary Test [PPVT]; Dunn & Dunn, 1981), but many students with severe disabilities may not have the prerequisite skills for responding to standardized tests. Alternative functional means will be needed to assess vocabulary and semantic/syntactic knowledge. When students are able to respond on such tests, use of item-level information (i.e., specific skills student exhibits during testing) will be more useful than standard scores in planning intervention. Information from norm-referenced tests should be considered as one data point describing students responding under a specific set of circumstances, not as definitive of student overall ability. Depending on the goal of the assessment and the age of the student, norm-referenced, curriculum-referenced, and criterion-referenced assessments may be useful. Integrating information from these assessments should yield a picture of the student's specific communication profile in adult-supported, focused interactions. Interactions of testing may be needed to identify precise instructional targets. For example, the PPVT might be used to determine students' general receptive vocabulary when drawings of pictures are the stimulus. Parent report on the McArthur Communication Development Inventory (Fenson et al., 1991) can indicate words the student uses or understands at home. Communication samples from the classroom indicate words the student uses in interactions with teachers and peers. Analysis of the classroom context and the information obtained from norm-referenced tests, parents, and observation can indicate vocabulary skills to be examined in criterion-referenced tests. Crais and Roberts (1996) and Loeb (1997) provide detailed information about specific communication assessments.

Principle 2: Plan to assess the student's skills in multiple environments, with multiple partners, on multiple occasions. A hallmark of valid assessment is repeated measurement. This is particularly important for assessing the communication skills of students with severe disabilities, which may vary considerably based on context. The skills and interests of the communicative partner will affect the communicative performance of the student with severe disabilities. Measurement over time can describe student's typical communication and identify the factors affecting performance. In inclusive classrooms, it is important to assess the student's interactions with adults and a variety of peers across instructional and social contexts. Differences in performance related to context indicate opportunities to teach for increased fluency and generalization of communication skills.

Principle 3: Assess the student's learning environments. The schedule of activities, the social communication demands embedded in activities, the instructional format and the communication demands associated with instruction, and the transitions and routines that structure students' time in the classroom are aspects of the environment to be examined. Creating an activity by social communication demand matrix (see Figure 7.1, p. 127) and using a discrepancy analysis approach (McCormick, Loeb, & Schiefelbush, 1997) to compare the social communicative behavior of the student with severe disabilities to the behavior of typical students in each activity will provide a general framework for intervention. Students' interests, current level of engagement, and the adequacy of their existing communicative responses in activities of the classroom will be used to focus the targets for instruction. Adult skills in mediating environment to provide opportunity and support for communication and access to communication partners should also be evaluated.

FIGURE 7.1 Activity by social communication demand matrix.

Activity	Social Communication Demands	Supports
Arrival from bus/entry into class	■ Greet teacher and peers ■ Respond to greetings ■ Answer simple social questions about home activities	■ Teacher initiates greeting ■ Classroom routine ■ Use picture book from home
Large group activity	■ Introduce self/say name ("I'm Jane") ■ Participate/respond in calendar routines ■ Answer questions from teacher	■ Verbal prompts needed ■ Peer modeling ■ Use picture display
Math and reading clinic	■ Request materials ■ Ask for assistance ■ Indicate when finished	■ Time delay as prompt ■ Arrange environment to promote requests ■ Peer modeling
Playground	■ Enter play ■ Ask for turn ■ Comply with peer requests	■ Assign peer buddy ■ Scripts
Lunch	■ Indicate choices of goods ■ Ask for assistance	■ Time delay as prompt
Small group	■ Request peer share materials ■ Respond to peer requests for materials	■ Peer dispenses materials
Art and music centers	■ Request materials ■ Indicate choices ■ Comment on own and others' work	■ Arrange materials to promote requests ■ Routine for commenting ■ Embedded in activity
Depart for bus	■ Say good-bye to teacher and peers ■ Greet bus driver and monitor	■ Classroom routine for departure ■ Prompt driver and monitor to make eye contact, wait for greeting

Principle 4: Assess the skills of the student's potential communicative partners. The skills and strategies expected for adult partners will be somewhat different than those expected to be used by peers. Assessing adult skills should focus on (a) their skills as communication partners for students with disabilities, (b) their skills in teaching new communication forms and functions across activity contexts, (c) their skills in adapting instruction in other domains to match student's current communication abilities, and (d) their skills in supporting and facilitating ongoing communication between students with severe disabilities and typical students. Assessing peer skills includes determining (1) their current levels and mode of communication skill, (2) their ability to adapt to the communication needs of

the student with severe disabilities (e.g., fluency in the student's mode, ability to understand communication acts by the student, interest and persistence in communicating with the student), and (3) naturally occurring opportunities for peer communication in the classroom. The activity by social communication demand matrix can be used to analyze peer communication in context, and observations of interactions can be used to determine peer skills in a manner similar to the assessment of the student with severe disabilities.

Principle 5: Link assessment to selecting communication goals, intervention strategies, and monitoring student's progress. Assessing the student's skill level, planning interventions, and monitoring the student's progress are overlapping activities (Bricker & Woods Cripe, 1992; McCormick, 1997). The assessment information should lead directly to the intervention goals. Thus, it is important that the level of assessment matches the level of intervention. The student's progress should be measured to ensure that progress is being made. The results of this monitoring are then incorporated into the assessment information that again is used to determine intervention goals. This loop is essential for the effective intervention on communication skills in students with severe disabilities.

Principles for Selecting the Communication Goals and Objectives

After the assessment information has been gathered and analyzed, goals for intervention need to be selected. The ultimate goal of communication interventions for students with severe disabilities is to increase the student's level of functional communication. Communication is functional when it is useful in the context in which communication is happening and is helping the communicator to share information with a partner or partners. Goals should be specific to the student with severe disabilities and take into account the student's skill level, interests, and environment. Family preferences and cultural influence should also guide the development of communication goals.

Principle 6: Target behaviors that are foundational to communication. Many skills are important to successful communication. Cognitive and social skills are foundational to communication. Engagement with activities, social initiations, persistence, responsiveness, attention, turn taking, repair of communicational breakdowns, conversational maintenance, and extension are aspects of successful communicative interactions and potential intervention goals. Students with severe disabilities may exhibit skills that span the complete developmental range. For example, some students may not yet exhibit consistent social initiations to peers. Communication intervention for these students begins with establishing social engagement via initiations and responses using a simple mode such as natural gestures or picture exchanges. Most students with severe disabilities who have foundational social skills make few initiations. Their initiations are often difficult for communicative partners to understand, because of poor articulation or use of an augmentative system of communication. When the initiations of students with severe disabilities cannot be understood or are not responded to, the communication opportunity is lost. The core question for determining foundational skills for communication is "What ancillary skills does this student need to communicate effectively now?" While intervention may eventually address many aspects of cognitive and social behavior, the immediate goal will be to provide the student with skills and strategies that allow more functional and successful communication with everyday communication partners. Students with severe disabilities must be taught to persist in their communication attempts and to recognize when they need to change their strategy in order to successfully deliver their message. These skills must be explicitly taught to students with severe disabilities.

Principle 7: Target receptive and productive communication skills. The majority of empirical work conducted on enhancing communication skills with students with severe disabilities has been focused on productive or expressive skills. It is equally important to target receptive communication skills. Receptive skills are difficult to assess and teach because of the confluence of receptive skills and compliance skills that affects performance in both testing and natural communication contexts. The range of receptive skills parallels the range of expressive skills and includes understanding of social meanings (greetings, refusals and protests, requests for action and information, comments) understanding of vocabulary or specific symbol meanings, and understanding of complex, multisymbol messages (sentences, sequences of signs). Performance of receptive skills will be influenced by context. Intervention to promote receptive skills will include providing instruction and adult-mediated supports for students to acquire receptive understanding of social, lexical, and syntactic forms across communication contexts.

Principle 8: Target skills for immediate communication and for the development of future skills. Students with severe disabilities will have both short-term and long-term communication goals. Short-term goals are skills the student uses immediately. Short-term goals should be specific to the classroom context and have specific detailed examples of use in context. These targets should be determined by the student's current skills, the interests and the social and instructional demands of the classroom environment. If the targets are not appropriate to the classroom, then the student with severe disabilities will get insufficient practice with that target. Short-term targets should be referenced to long-term targets. Long-term targets are skills that will help the student develop, generalize, and integrate complex communication skills into an extended social communication repertoire.

Principles for Selecting Interventions to Teach Communication Skills

Once the assessment information has been used to develop short-term and long-range communication goals, the teacher and other members of the educational team need to select an intervention to teach the target skills. The intervention should be empirically supported and likely to be able to be implemented given contextual factors.

Principle 9: Use instructional strategies that have empirical support. There are many interventions that have support from the research literature. These strategies range from direct teaching to naturalistic strategies. A list of empirically supported strategies and a brief description of the procedure is presented in Table 7.2 on pages 130–131.

Before implementation of an intervention can begin, the learning environment must be arranged so that the student with severe disabilities is likely to communicate. A list of environmental arrangement strategies can be found in Table 7.3 (p. 132). The basic goal of these strategies is to ensure that the student has something to communicate about (interesting materials), that there will be opportunities to request those items (items may be kept in sight but out of reach), and that there are multiple opportunities for practice requesting each

TABLE 7.2 Summary of Empirically Supported Communication Interventions

Name of Intervention	Brief Description	Reference
Shaping	Systematically reinforcing closer and closer approximation of the target communicative behavior.	Carr & Kologinsky, 1983
Prompting	Assistance that is provided to the student to increase the likelihood of producing a correct response.	
Fading	The gradual removal of prompts such that students are independent in their responding.	
Reinforcement	An event following the behavior that is likely to increase the probability of the response being repeated.	
Direct instruction	Teacher-led explicit instruction of specific communication skills.	Goldstein & Cisar, 1992; Krantz & McClannahan, 1993
Routines and script training	Structured intervention where interactions between students are scripted and then taught specifically to students.	Koegel, O'Dell, & Koegel, 1987; Laski, Charlop, & Schreibman, 1988
Natural language paradigm	A procedure designed for use in a natural environment that follows the child's lead.	Ostrosky & Kaiser, 1991
Environmental arrangement	These strategies are described in Table 7.3.	Kaiser, 1990
Milieu Teaching	A naturalistic approach that uses the environmental arrangement strategies described in Table 7.3, a responsive interaction style and the use of elicited models, mand models, time delay, and incidental teaching strategies.	
Choice making	The adult presents the student with a choice of materials or activities.	Rogers-Warren & Warren, 1980
Mand model	The adult initiates this procedure by presenting the student with a verbal request related to the student's interest and communication goal.	

Technique	Description	Citation
Topic continuation	When the student initiates, the adult uses comments, questions, familiar topics, or routine communication exchanges to support and extend the interaction.	
Time delay	Once the child makes a request for an item, the adult blocks access and maintains eye contact and an expectant look (for approximately 5 seconds) with the student so that the student has an opportunity to produce a more sophisticated communicative behavior.	Halle, Marshall, & Spradlin, 1979
Incidental Teaching	This strategy relies on the child requesting the adult's assistance and the adult using the opportunity to require a more elaborate communicative response.	Hart & Risley, 1968
Interactive modeling (recasting, interactive language instruction, focused stimulation)	Provides frequent and salient exposure to target communication skills.	Cole & Dale, 1986
Situated pragmatics	Instruction that focuses on providing students with information to understand the social context of communication.	Duchan, 1995
Scaffolding (includes setting the stage, using Semantic Maps, providing extensions, using questions, emphasizing and reviewing old information, restating and sum-marizing, using flowcharts, and using repetition)	Supporting a student to use communication in a more complex way than he or she could without the assistance.	Silliman & Wilkinson, 1994; Westby & Costlow, 1991
Observation learning	The student watches as a peer models a specific language target, and then has the opportunity to repeat this target.	Goldstein & Brown, 1989; Hepting & Goldstein, 1996
Augmentative and alternative communication systems	Any one of a number of nonverbal communications systems (may include gestures, pictures, computer voice output systems) taught to students using a variety of prompting strategies to augment or supplant spoken communication.	Beukelman & Miranda, 1998

TABLE 7.3   Environmental Arrangement Strategies

Interesting materials: Materials and activities are available that are interesting to the student.

Out of reach: Interesting materials are kept within view but out of reach.

Inadequate portions: Materials are held back or distributed in small portions.

Choice making: A choice of two materials or activities are presented.

Assistance: Students need to ask for help in order to have access to preferred materials or activities.

Unexpected situations: Something that violates a known routine creates an unexpected situation.

material (insufficient portions). Ostrosky and Kaiser (1991) present an in-depth discussion about how to use each of these strategies.

Once the physical environment has been arranged to elicit and promote communication attempts by the student with severe disabilities, a particular intervention should be selected to teach each short-term and long-term goal. Naturalistic interventions like Milieu Teaching are ideally suited to teaching students with severe disabilities in inclusive settings. Milieu Teaching is a collection of strategies—such as model procedures (Alpert & Kaiser, 1992), mand-model procedures (Warren, McQuater, & Rogers-Warren, 1984), time-delay procedures (Halle, Marshall & Spradlin, 1979), and incidental teaching procedures (Hart & Risley, 1968)—that take advantage of student interest and teach functional communication skills. Figure 7.2 provides an overview of Milieu Teaching, and Kaiser (1990) provides a precise explanation of how to use Milieu Teaching with students with severe disabilities.

Principle 10: Select a mode that can be learned quickly. To participate in inclusive classrooms, students with severe disabilities must have an effective mode of communication. Immediate functional use is the foremost goal of communication intervention. Select-

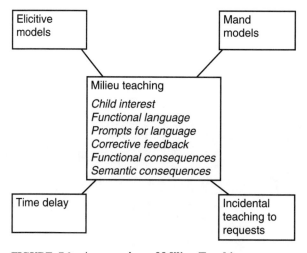

FIGURE 7.2   An overview of Milieu Teaching.

ing a mode that is relatively easy for a given student to use in the classroom is essential. If students have already begun to use inappropriate behaviors to communicate, then the new communication mode must be as fast and as efficient at communicating the students' needs and wants as the students' current inappropriate behavior. For some students with severe disabilities this mode may be spoken, or verbal, communication; for others it may be an augmentative or alternative communication system (AAC).

There are a variety of AAC systems commonly used by students with severe disabilities, including natural gestures, signs, communication boards, books of photographs, line drawings, the alphabet, and computer-based voice output systems (Light & Binger, 1998). The AAC system should be matched to the particular student's needs and abilities (see Beukelman & Mirenda, 1998, for an assessment procedure) and the system must be useful and supported in the inclusive classroom. That is, the system must: (a) be used with a reasonable degree of fluency by the students across contexts; (b) be understood and used by partners with little training or expertise; and (c) be a system for which naturalistic learning opportunities can be arranged.

One example of such a system is the Picture Exchange Communication System (PECS; Bondy & Frost, 1994). PECS does not prescribe the particular form of pictures to be used (e.g., line drawings, photographs, or computer-generated symbols). It does prescribe a multiphase procedure of prompting and prompt-fading techniques that results in the student learning to communicate independently via the exchange of symbols with a communicative partner (Bondy & Frost, 1994; Schwartz, Garfinkle, & Bauer, 1998). A summary of the phases of the PECS protocol is found in Table 7.4.

PECS may be especially well suited for use in an inclusive classroom because it is often acquired quickly (Schwartz, Garfinkle, & Bauer, 1998). The protocol includes procedures for teaching persistence in social communication. The symbols are portable and are easily understood by most untrained communicative partners (Bauer & Garfinkle, 1997). Students with severe disabilities have been taught to communicate via PECS with other

TABLE 7.4   PECS Intervention Phases

Phase 1: Identify interesting materials, activities, or food.
Phase 2: Teach students to exchange the symbol.
Phase 3: Teach distance and persistence.
Phase 4: Teach discrimination between and among symbols.
Phase 5: Teach "sentence building."
Phase 6: Teach "PECS with Peers."
    Step 1: Make sure the student is fluent in phases 1–5 above.
    Step 2: Arrange the environment so children will need to request materials from one another.
        Step 2a: Make sure peers have materials preferred by the target child.
        Step 2b: Make sure the target child has materials preferred by other students.
    Step 3: Support peer-to-peer.
    Step 4: Make sure there are these sorts of interactions across peers, materials, and environments.

students who have other disabilities and students who are typically developing (Garfinkle & Schwartz, 2002). When PECS is used in combination with environmental strategies such as those described earlier, communication with peers can be taught and maintained in the context of ongoing classroom activities. (See Garfinkle and Schwartz [2001] for a step-by-step description of this procedure.)

Principle 11: Prepare and support conversational partners. An inclusive setting provides opportunities for students with severe disabilities to interact with a variety of communicative partners, including trained adults, untrained adults, and peers. Adults who interact regularly with the student with severe disabilities (e.g., classroom teacher, paraprofessionals, therapists) need strategies to facilitate everyday communication and to support acquisition of short-term and long-term communication goals. One such strategy is a responsive conversational style (Kaiser, Hancock, & Hester, 1998). A responsive conversational style includes systematically establishing joint or mutual attention to signal the availability of a conversational partner, to balance turn-taking in social exchanges, to provide contingent responsiveness to communication attempts, and to demonstrate positive affect toward the communication partner during social interaction. Adults employing the components of responsive conversational style support the student with severe disabilities by following his or her lead, providing opportunities to take turns, and providing specific and general positive consequences for communication. Kaiser and Delaney (2001) provide an accessible and thorough description of responsive communication strategies.

Inclusive school environments provide opportunities for interaction with other adults (e.g., school administrators, cafeteria workers, hall monitors, bus drivers, and so on) in addition to the teachers and instructional personnel in the student's class. These adults may play an important role in the student's daily life at school but are not likely to be trained in communicative intervention techniques or in responsive communication strategies. For students with severe disabilities, interactions with these adults are important occasions for learning and using communication skills. Teacher planning and support for both the student and the adult in these interactions will be needed. Such occasional contacts with adults who are not as familiar with individual students' specific communication goals and skills underscore the importance of the students' use of a mode that is easily understood by others. Also, interacting with unfamiliar adults will require students to be persistent in communicating their messages and to utilize repair strategies to ensure their messages are understood correctly. Interactions with these adults in the school setting can provide an important bridge to successful communication in the community outside the school.

One of the great advantages of inclusive educational settings is the availability of typically developing peers. Proximity to typically developing students does not ensure communication interactions between students with severe disabilities and their peers. The environment must be arranged to create opportunities, facilitate social engagement, and extend the brief naturally occurring exchanges. The amount of structure and support a student will need to engage in social interactions with typical peers depends on the skills of the students involved. There are a wide variety of interventions to help facilitate the interaction. Brown, Odom, and Conroy (2001) present a hierarchy of intervention strategies that have been successful for increasing interactions between students with severe disabilities and their classroom peers. Brown and colleagues (2001) describe classwide naturalistic techniques as well as direct teaching techniques. Arranging the environment so students have to communicate is an example of a classwide intervention. One example of a structured direct teaching technique is the use of social scripts, which are used to help support participation and balance the turns between the student with disabilities and the typically developing peer (see, e.g., Charlop & Milstein, 1989; Goldstein & Cisar, 1992; Goldstein & Kaczmarek, 1992; Kranz & McClannahan, 1993). Garfinkle and Schwartz (2001) describe a strategy that combines environmental arrangement techniques with direct teaching methods to facilitate communication between children who use AAC systems and their typically developing peers.

All intervention techniques designed to facilitate communication between students with severe disabilities and their typically developing peers require that the communication mode used by the student with severe disabilities is understood by peers. Peers may need to be taught to recognize and understand the communicative behaviors of the student with severe disabilities. In order for peers to communicate with a student who has severe disabilities, they may need to learn to read nonverbal forms of communication, including direct eye gaze and facial expression. Instruction on reading communicative nonverbal behavior can be conducted in a large group format or taught systematically in naturally occurring social contexts. It is the teaching adult's responsibility to ensure that both students with severe disabilities and typical students are successful in their communicative interactions and to provide the level of support needed to ensure this success.

Principles for Measuring the Intensity and Fidelity of the Intervention

In order for students with severe disabilities to meet their short-term and long-term communication skill objectives, they must receive enough high-quality intervention for learning to occur.

Principle 12: Measure the number of instructional opportunities. When direct teaching techniques are used, instructional opportunities are relatively easy to measure, because the adult plans and initiates teaching episodes. When naturalistic techniques are used in everyday environments, instructional opportunities are more difficult to plan in advance and thus more difficult to measure. Naturalistic techniques use the initiations of the student as the occasion for teaching. Students with severe disabilities have limited interests and few skills and strategies for initiating to adults. Consequently, they make severely fewer initiations than students who are typically developing or who have less severe disabilities.

To balance the smaller number of spontaneous student initiations, teachers of students with severe disabilities must plan specific but naturally occurring opportunities throughout the school day when the student will have the opportunity to practice communicating and will receive instruction related to his or her communication goals. The first step in assessing student progress in an intervention is to determine the number of times the student with disabilities participated in the targeted activity and received instruction. Counting the total number of instructional episodes and the opportunities to practice skills during the school day provides an indication of the intensity of instruction. Student performance changes can be evaluated accurately only when the amount of instruction is specified.

Principle 13: Measure instructional fidelity. Instructional fidelity is the degree to which the intervention was implemented as planned. Use of empirically supported interventions increases the likelihood of teaching a student targeted communication skills. However, unless the intervention is implemented with sufficient integrity, it will not be effective and the student will not learn. For this reason, frequent instructional fidelity checks are essential. Billingsley, White, and Munson (1980) present a useful strategy for conducting treatment fidelity checks. This approach involves delineating all of the steps of the intervention, writing the steps out, and using this to create a checklist to record the actual behavior that occurred by the interventionist during the intervention. The higher the level of agreement between the steps of the intervention and the interventionist's behavior, the higher the instructional fidelity.

Principles for Monitoring Student's Progress on Communication Goals and Objectives

Ongoing assessment is required to ensure that students with severe disabilities are making progress toward their communication goals and objectives (Wolery, 1996). Assessment of student performance in the classroom during instruction and during ongoing activities that do not include communication instruction can be used along with other formal assessment information to select new intervention goals.

Principle 14: Monitor students' progress. In order to determine if students with severe disabilities are making progress toward their short- and long-term goals and objectives, it is important to collect data. Data on student communication behavior must be collected frequently to make accurate judgments about student learning. Data collection must be planned and systematic and must occur regularly. Data on student progress together with data on learning opportunities and intervention fidelity will indicate if expected progress is being made. When data collection is carefully designed, the information collected can assist the teacher in determining if student progress is satisfactory. If less than desirable progress is being made, then the data should help to explain why this is the case. These possible explanations then help inform the type of change that may need to be made in the intervention so that the student will learn. Wolery (1996) provides a precise description of how to monitor student's learning and use this information to make instructional decisions.

Principle 15: Continue the process. After data have been collected, summarized, and analyzed, instructional decisions must be made. The data may indicate that the communicative goals have been reached and it is time to develop new goals. Alternatively, the data may indicate that the student is making satisfactory progress but that the student has not yet met his or her goal; or the data may indicate that the student is not making satisfactory progress, and changes in goals, intervention techniques, or implementation of the intervention may be warranted. Periodic assessment and systematic decision making are part of the process of teaching communication skills using the steps and principles delineated above. The stages of learning (initial acquisition, fluency, generalization, maintenance, and integration) are part of the continuing instructional process. A communication skill that is successfully acquired in a supportive classroom context (e.g., greeting the teacher when entering the room after the teacher greets the student) can be extended to new settings (the bus) and new people (the bus monitor) where natural supports are present (the bus monitor routinely greets students when they get on the bus each morning). The array of communication skills that are systematically being extended and integrated into students' skill repertoire can be extensive. Once again, a system for tracking and monitoring instruction and student performance will be essential to long-term student success.

Conclusion

Most students with severe disabilities will need support in learning and using communication skills. The specific form of the communication (speech or an augmentative system) is less important than the student's functional communication with adults and peers in everyday classroom activities. Teachers of students with severe disabilities in inclusive settings are challenged both to support students' use of their current communication skills and to implement interventions to expand students' communications skills. Inclusive settings provide rich and varied opportunities for authentic communicative exchanges between students with severe disabilities and their typically developing peers; however, teachers must ensure that these exchanges occur regularly and with sufficient support to assure success for all students. When teachers use empirically supported interventions with sufficient intensity and fidelity, students with severe disabilities in inclusive classrooms can learn functional communication skills and use communication to develop important social relationships as members of their class and the community.

References

Alpert, C. L., & Kaiser, A. P. (1992). Training parents as milieu language teachers. *Journal of Early Intervention, 16,* 31–52.

Bauer, J. & Garfinkle, A. N. (1997, November). *Beyond basic training: PECS use in the classroom and at home.* Paper presented at the American Speech-Language and Hearing Association, Boston.

Beukelman, D. R., & Miranda, P. (1998). *Augmentative and alternative communication: Management of severe communication disorders in children and adults.* Baltimore: Paul H. Brookes.

Billingsley, F. F., White, O. R., & Munson, R. (1980). Procedural reliability: A rationale and an example. *Behavioral Assessment, 2,* 229–241.

Bondy, A., & Frost, L. (1994). The picture exchange communication system. *Focus on Autistic Behavior, 9,* 1–19.

Bricker, D., & Woods Cripe, J. J. (1992). *An activity-based approach to early intervention.* Baltimore: Paul H. Brookes.

Brown, W. H., Odom, S. L., & Conroy, M. A. (2001). An intervention hierarchy for prompting young children's peer interactions in natural environments. *Topics in Early Childhood Special Education, 21,* 162–175.

Carr, E. G., & Durand, V. M. (1985). Reducing behavior problems through functional communication training. *Journal of Applied Behavior Analysis, 18,* 111–126.

Carr, E., & Kologinsky, E. (1983). Acquisition of sign language by autistic children II: Spontaneity and generalization. *Journal of Applied Behavior Analysis, 16,* 297–314.

Charlop, M. H., & Milstein, J. P. (1989). Teaching autistic children conversational speech using video modeling. *Journal of Applied Behavior Analysis, 22,* 275–285.

Cole, K. N., & Dale, P. S. (1986). Direct language instruction and interactive language instruction with language delayed preschool children: A comparison study. *Journal of Speech and Hearing Research, 29,* 206–217.

Crais, E. R., & Roberts, J. E. (1996). Assessing communication skills. In M. McLean, D. B. Bailey & M. Wolery (Eds.), *Assessing infants and preschoolers with special needs* (2nd ed.). Englewood Cliffs, NJ: Merrill.

Davis, C. A., Brady, M. P., Williams, R. E., & Hamilton, R. (1992). Effects of high-probability requests on the acquisition and generalization of responses to requests in young children with behavior disorders. *Journal of Applied Behavior Analysis, 25,* 905–916.

Duchan, J. F. (1995). *Supporting language learning in everyday life.* San Diego: Singular.

Dunn, L. M., & Dunn, L. M. (1981). *Peabody Picture Vocabulary Test-Revised.* Circle Pines, MN: American Guidance Service.

Durand, V. M., & Carr, E. G. (1992). An analysis of maintenance following functional communication training. *Journal of Applied Behavior Analysis, 25,* 777–794.

Fenson, L., Dale, P. S., Reznick, J. S., Thal, D., Bates, E., Hartung, J. P., Pethick, S., & Reilly, J. S. (1991). *Technical manual for the MacArthur Communication Development Inventories.* San Diego: San Diego State University.

Ferguson, D. L. (1994). Is communication really the point? Some thoughts on interventions and membership. *Mental Retardation, 32,* 7–18.

Garfinkle, A. N., & Schwartz, I. S. (2002). *PECS with Peers: Increasing Social Interactions in Integrated Preschool Settings.* Unpublished manuscript.

Garfinkle, A. N., & Schwartz, I. S. (2001). "Hey, I'm talking to you": Teaching children to use AAC systems with their peers. In S. Sandall & M. Ostrosky (Eds.), *Young Exceptional Children Teaching Monograph* (vol. 3). Chicago: Sopris West.

Goldstein, H., & Brown, W. H. (1989). Observational learning of receptive and expressive language by handicapped preschool children. *Education and Treatment of Children, 12,* 5–37.

Goldstein, H., & Cisar, C. L. (1992). Promoting interaction during sociodramatic play: Teaching scripts to typical preschoolers and classmates with handicaps. *Journal of Applied Behavior Analysis, 25,* 265–280.

Goldstein, H., & Kaczmarek, L. (1992). Promoting communicative interaction among children in integrated intervention settings. In S. F. Warren & J. Reichle (Eds.), *Communication and language intervention series: Causes and effects in communication and language intervention* (vol. 1, pp. 81–112). Baltimore: Paul H. Brookes.

Goldstein, H., & Woods, J. (2002). Promoting communication competence in preschool age children. In M. R. Shinn, H. M. Walker, & G. Stoner (Eds.), *Interventions for academic and behavior problems II: Preventive and remedial approaches.* Bethesda, MD: National Association of School Psychologists.

Guralnick, M. J. (1997). *The effectiveness of early intervention.* Baltimore: Paul H. Brookes.

Halle, J. W., Marshall, A. M., & Spradlin, J. E. (1979). Time delay: A technique to increase language use and facilitate generalization in retarded children. *Journal of Applied Behavior Analysis, 12,* 431–440.

Hart, B. M., & Risely, T. R. (1968). Establishing the use of descriptive adjectives in the spontaneous speech of disadvantaged preschool children. *Journal of Applied Behavior Analysis, 1,* 109–120.

Hepting, N. H., & Goldstein, H. (1996). Requesting by preschoolers with developmental disabilities: Videotape self-modeling and learning of new linguistic structures. *Topics in Early Childhood Special Education, 16,* 407–427.

Hester, P. P., & Kaiser, A. P. (1998). Early intervention for the prevention of conduct disorder: Research issues in early identification, implementation, and interpretation of treatment outcomes. *Behavioral Disorders, 24,* 58–66.

Kaiser, A. P. (1990). A two-fold model of environment: Implications for early language learning. In S. R. Schroeder, *Ecobehavior analysis and developmental disabilities: The twenty-first century* (pp. 141–153). New York: Springer-Verlag.

Kaiser, A. P., & Delaney, E. M. (2001). Responsive conversations: Creating opportunities for naturalistic language teaching. *Young Exceptional Children Monograph Series No. 3,* 13–23.

Kaiser, A. P., Hancock, T. B., & Hester, P. P. (1998). Parents as co-interventionists: Research on applications of naturalistic language teaching procedures. *Infants and Young Children, 10,* 46–55.

Koegel, R. L., Koegel, L. K., & Surratt, A. (1992). Language intervention and disruptive behavior in preschool children with autism. *Journal of Autism and Developmental Disorders, 22,* 141–153.

Koegel, R. L., O'Dell, M. C., & Koegel, L. K. (1987). A natural language teaching paradigm for nonverbal autistic children. *Journal of Autism and Developmental Disorders, 17,* 187–200.

Krantz, P. J., & McClannahan, L. E. (1993). Teaching children with autism to initiate to peers: Effects of a script-fading procedure. *Journal of Applied Behavior Analysis, 26,* 121–132.

Laski, K., Charlop, M., & Schreibman, L. (1988). Training parents to use the natural language paradigm to increase their autistic children's speech. *Journal of Applied Behavior Analysis, 21,* 391–400.

Light, J. C., & Binger, C. (1998). *Building communication competence with individuals who use augmentative and alternative communication.* Baltimore: Paul H. Brookes.

Loeb, D. F. (1997). Language theory and practice. In L. McCormick, D. F. Loeb, & R. L. Schiefelbusch (Eds.), *Supporting children with communication difficulties in inclusive settings: School-based language intervention* (pp. 43–70). Boston: Allyn and Bacon.

McCormick, L. (1997). Ecological assessment and planning. In L. McCormick, D. F. Loeb, & R. L. Schiefelbusch (Eds.), *Supporting children with communication difficulties in inclusive settings: School-based language intervention.* Boston: Allyn and Bacon.

McCormick, L., Loeb, P. F., & Schiefelbusch, R. L. (1997). *Supporting children with communication difficult in inclusive settings: School-based language intervention.* Boston: Allyn and Bacon.

Ostrosky, M. M., & Kaiser, A. P. (1991). Preschool classroom environments that promote communication. *Teaching Exceptional Children, 23,* 6–10. Reprinted in K. L. Freiberg (Ed.) (1992), Annual editions: Educating exceptional children (6th ed., pp. 158–161). Guilford, CT: Dushkin Publishing Group.

Prizant, B., & Schuler, A. (1987). Facilitating communication: Theoretical foundations. In D. J. Cohen & A. M. Donnellan (Eds.), *Handbook of autism and pervasive developmental disorders* (pp. 289–300). New York: John Wiley & Sons.

Rogers-Warren, A. K., & Warren, S. F. (1980). Mands for verbalizations: Facilitating the display of newly trained language in children. *Behavior Modifications, 4,* 361–382.

Sameroff, A., & Chandler, M. (1975). Reproductive risk and the continuum of caretaking causality. In F. Horowitz (Ed.), *Review of Child Development Research* (vol. 4, pp. 187–244). Chicago: University of Chicago Press.

Sameroff, A., & Fiese, B. H. (1990). Transactional regulation and early intervention. In S. J. Meisels & J. P. Shonkoff (Eds.), *Handbook of early childhood intervention* (pp. 119–149). New York: Cambridge University Press.

Schwartz, I. S. (2000). Standing on the shoulders of giants: Looking ahead to facilitating membership and relationships for children with disabilities. *Topics in Early Childhood Special Education, 20,* 123–128.

Schwartz, I. S., Garfinkle, A. N., & Bauer, J. (1998). The Picture Exchange Communication System: Communicative outcomes for young children with disabilities. *Topics in Early Childhood Special Education, 18,* 144–159.

Schwartz, I. S., Garfinkle, A. N., & Davis, C. A. (2002). Arranging preschool environments to facilitate valued social and educational outcomes. M. R. Shinn, H. M. Walker, & G. Stoner (Eds.), *Interventions for academic and behavior problems II: Preventive and remedial approaches* (pp. 455–468). Bethesda: National Association of School Psychologists Publications.

Schwartz, I. S., Garfinkle, A N., Joseph, G., & McBride, B. (1998). Communication and language disorders. In P. Howlin (Ed.), *Behavioral approaches to problems in childhood.* London: Mac Keith Press.

Schwartz, I. S., Staub, D., Gallucci, C., & Peck, C. A. (1995). Blending qualitative and behavior analytic research methods to evaluate outcomes in inclusive schools. *Journal of Behavioral Education, 51,* 93–106.

Silliman, E. R., & Wilkinson, L. C. (1994). Discourse scaffolds for classroom intervention. In G. P. Wallach & K. G. Butler (Eds.), *Language learning disabilities in school-age children and adolescents* (pp. 27–52). New York: Merrill/Macmillan.

Wacker, D. P., Steege, M. W., Northup, J., Sasso, G., Berg, W., Reimers, T., Cooper, L., Cigrand, K., & Donn, L. (1990). A component analysis of functional communication training across three topographies of severe behavior problems. *Journal of Applied Behavior Analysis, 23,* 417–429.

Warren, S. F., McQuarter, R. J., Rogers-Warren, A. K. (1984). The effects of teacher mands and model on the speech of unresponsive language-delayed children. *Journal of Speech and Hearing Research, 49,* 43–52.

Warren, S. F., & Reichle, J. (1992). The emerging field of communication and language intervention. In S. Warren & J. Reichle (Eds.), *Causes and effects in communication and language intervention.* Baltimore: Paul H. Brookes.

Westby, C. E., & Costlow, L. (1991). Implementing a whole language program in a special education class. *Topics in Language Disorders, 11,* 69–84.

Wolery, M. (1996). Monitoring child progress. In M. McLean, D. B. Bailey, & M. Wolery (Eds.), *Assessing infants and preschoolers with special needs.* Englewood Cliffs, NJ: Merrill.

8 Positive Behavior Supports

ROBERT E. O'NEILL
University of Utah

I recall the tearful phone call requesting help, from a former university student of mine now teaching in a public elementary school setting. One of her students, a young girl named Keisha who is labeled as having autism, had "blown up" during lunchtime in the cafeteria, and had ended up throwing food and hitting and kicking several other students before others were able to intervene. The upset parents of the other students were calling the school and this educator about what had happened, and the school principal wanted to suspend or expel the girl. Meanwhile the girl's parents were angrily questioning the educator about how and why she had let this incident happen.

Students with significant disabilities sometimes exhibit serious problem behaviors such as self-injury, aggression toward others, and property destruction. My former student's experience illustrates the difficulties faced by families and school personnel in supporting students who exhibit such behaviors in school settings. This chapter will provide information about the prevalence and impact of such behaviors, offer an overview of the conceptual foundations of positive behavioral supports, and describe assessment and programmatic strategies that can be used to support students engaging in such behaviors in classroom settings. After reading this chapter you should be able to:

- Describe the general prevalence of severe problem behaviors and their impact on students, their families, and educators and support providers working with them
- Describe key concepts and definitions regarding positive behavioral support
- Describe and implement a variety of strategies for conducting a functional assessment of situations involving severe problem behaviors
- Describe the overall process for developing and specific components of implementing comprehensive behavior support plans

Portions of this chapter are from R. E. O'Neill. (In press). Positive behavioral supports. In J. J. McDonnell, M. H. Hardman, and A. M. McDonnell, *Introduction to persons with moderate and severe disabilities: Educational and social issues* (2nd ed.). Boston: Allyn & Bacon.

Whose Problem Is It Anyway?

As a beginning point it is interesting to think about the different terms that have been used in the literature over the years to describe problem behaviors in educational settings. For example, such behaviors frequently used to be labeled "maladaptive." However, in more recent times it has become clear that such troubling behaviors may indeed be very adaptive for the students exhibiting them, as they may result in achievement of various desired outcomes (e.g., getting out of an undesired situation, gaining social attention/interaction). Currently, a range of terms are used, including difficult behaviors, destructive behaviors, and challenging behaviors. This chapter employs the term *problem behavior,* as an indication that a wide range of behaviors may be considered a problem by various people, given a particular situation or context.

This leads to an issue that has frequently been examined from both conceptual and practical points of view; that is, *who* decides what is a problem behavior and therefore in need of intervention and support? Clearly there are some behaviors, such as the aggression and disruption exhibited by Keisha and described in the opening vignette, that create such potential or actual physical danger to individuals or damage to the environment that it is clear they need to be addressed to maintain health and safety. However, there may be a broad range of other behaviors that fall into more of a "gray area," with different persons in a student's life (parents, educators) having different perspectives on the need for intervention (Kazdin, 2001). For example, a student who frequently rocks while sitting in a chair or emits loud vocalizations in regular classroom settings may not be physically hurting anyone, but his or her behavior may have other negative effects on social interactions or academic learning that would be of concern. Most researchers and clinicians have recommended that decisions about the need for intervention and support be made by groups of relevant persons, such as IEP or multidisciplinary teams. To the greatest extent possible these should include the student with significant disabilities and his or her family members.

How Prevalent Are Severe Problem Behaviors?

Research has been conducted with different groups of people in various settings to attempt to determine how often problem behaviors are exhibited by children and adults with significant disabilities. Differences in the types of participants, definitions of behaviors, and other methods used in this research make it somewhat difficult to draw hard-and-fast conclusions, but these studies provide general estimates of prevalence. For example, Horner, Diemer, and Brazeau (1992) surveyed 162 educators of 1,535 school-age students with significant disabilities in the state of Oregon. The educators reported that 12 percent, or 184, of the students exhibited significant problem behaviors, with 59 percent of that subgroup exhibiting multiple types of behaviors (e.g., self-injury and aggression). Roughly similar percentages have been reported in studies involving adults with significant disabilities (see Borthwick-Duffy, 1994).

A number of studies have demonstrated a relationship between problem behaviors and such things as where people live and the severity of their disabilities. Children and adults living in more restrictive living arrangements such as large institutional settings and group homes are more likely to exhibit such behaviors in comparison with those living in less restrictive settings such as parental homes or semi-independent apartment living (Bruininks, Olson, Larson, & Lakin, 1994). This type of finding is usually interpreted to indicate the end result of a process in which students or persons exhibiting more severe problem behaviors gradually end up in more restrictive settings such as self-contained classrooms.

Life Impact

As exemplified in the vignette involving my former student, severe problem behaviors can have a variety of negative physical, social, educational, and economic consequences. Self-injurious and aggressive behaviors of children and adults with significant disabilities can result in significant pain, injury, and emotional stress both for the persons themselves and for families and staff providing support to them (Bromley & Emerson, 1995). Participation in less restrictive school settings, work environments, residential programs, and other community settings may be jeopardized, and as mentioned above, there may be increased risk for readmission to public residential facilities (see Schroeder, Rojahn, & Oldenquist, 1991). Providing necessary staffing, programmatic, and medical support results in greatly increased costs. A study by the National Institutes of Health in 1991 found that the annual cost of services for people with mental retardation in the United States who exhibit self-injury, aggression, or property destruction *exceeds $3.5 billion* per year (NIH, 1991). Along with the additional costs, a major concern is that such behaviors may place persons with significant disabilities at greater risk for abusive treatment by support staff.

A Shift in Perspective on Providing Behavioral Support

Given the challenges posed by severe problem behaviors, it's not surprising that professionals such as educators and school personnel consistently identify help in managing such behaviors as their primary technical assistance need (Reichle, 1990). For many years school- and community-based intervention strategies have predominantly revolved around reinforcement of appropriate behaviors, punishment of problem behaviors, and exclusion strategies (Repp & Singh, 1990). More recently, concern with the lack of effectiveness and the reactive and restrictive aspects of such procedures has led to a more positively oriented and comprehensive approach (Horner et al., 1990). This approach includes, in part, an emphasis on early intervention and prevention, access to appropriate normalized activities and lifestyle, provision of good instruction on adaptive skills, interventions involving multiple components, and an emphasis on careful functional assessment as a basis for selecting and implementing intervention and support strategies (Dunlap et al., 1993). Together these components have frequently come to be referred to as positive behavioral support (PBS) (Carr et al., 1999; Koegel, Koegel, & Dunlap, 1996).

Current Definitions and Features of Positive Behavioral Support

Table 8.1 (p. 144) presents several basic descriptions, or definitions, of PBS. These and other authors have elaborated on the critical common themes or features of this approach.

TABLE 8.1   Sample Definitions of Positive Behavioral Support (PBS)

"Positive behavioral support refers to the broad enterprise of helping people develop and engage in adaptive, socially desirable behaviors and overcome destructive and stigmatizing responding." (Koegel, Koegel, & Dunlap, 1996, p. xiii)

"Positive behavior support is a values-driven approach to solving problems that educators can use effectively across a variety of settings." (Bambara & Knoster, 1998, p. 1)

"The goal of PBS is to apply behavioral principles in the community in order to reduce problem behaviors and build appropriate behaviors that result in durable change and a rich lifestyle." (Carr et al., 1999, p. 3)

"A positive behavioral supports approach emphasizes the use of a collaborative problem-solving process to develop individualized interventions that stress prevention of problem behaviors through the provision of effective educational programming." (Janney & Snell, 2000, p. 2)

Broadened Perspective on Outcomes of Behavioral Support

A primary goal of behavior modification and management procedures has been the reduction in the frequency, intensity, and/or duration of targeted problem behaviors. While change in problem behavior is a critical outcome, proponents of PBS have in addition emphasized the need to look at the broader impact of behavioral support in terms of changes in educational, residential, vocational, and social outcomes (Kennedy, in press; Sugai et al., 2000). For example, a student's problem behaviors may be occurring less frequently, but this positive outcome is limited if he or she is not progressing in other areas such as learning new skills and developing peer social relationships.

Functional Assessment

One of the most significant components of PBS is the refocusing of attention on understanding the full range of setting, antecedent, and consequence variables that are related to a student's problem behaviors (Iwata et al., 1994; Repp & Horner, 1999). Recent years have seen a literal explosion of writing, research, and materials in the area of functional assessment (Johnston & O'Neill, 2001; Witt, Daly, & Noell, 2000). This resurgence is exemplified by the inclusion of language in the reauthorized Individuals with Disabilities Education Act that specifically requires functional behavioral assessments in particular situations. The basic theme is that we have no business significantly intervening in a student's situation unless we first have as clear an understanding as possible of the range of things that may be positively and negatively influencing his or her behavior (O'Neill et al., 1997). For example, students who have difficulty communicating in conventional ways may engage in problem behavior to express what they want and need; that is, the behavior may serve a communicative function or purpose (Durand, 1990). Based on such assessment information support plans that make sense can then be developed and implemented (Bambara & Knoster, 1998).

Focus on Preventive and Educative Supports

Previous research on and application of behavior interventions have been characterized as overly reactive, with an emphasis on punishment when problem behaviors occurred. While both positive and negative consequences have a significant role to play, PBS places a heavy emphasis on strategies to prevent the occurrence of problem behaviors, and to teach and promote adaptive behaviors that can serve as positive alternatives for a student. Prevention may focus on changes in medical supports, such as treatment for allergies or changes in medication levels, and classroom variables such as changes in curricular or instructional strategies (Luiselli & Cameron, 1998). In the area of positive alternative behaviors the greatest emphasis has been on teaching communicative skills and behaviors (e.g., use of speech, signing, electronic devices) to allow students to indicate what they need and want, instead of engaging in problem behaviors to achieve such outcomes (Carr et al., 1994; Reichle & Wacker, 1993).

Comprehensive Support Plans

Applied behavior analysis has always emphasized the importance of the context in which behavior occurs, including the broader and more specific environmental events preceding behavior, and the events or consequences which follow it (Baer, Wolf, & Risley, 1968). PBS has built on this approach and added a values-based component with regard to looking at the places people live, what they spend their time doing, their social relationships, and how those things can affect a person's behavior. The variables that affect problem behaviors can range from very specific, such as the type of instructional activity in a classroom setting, to very broad, such as the student's family interactions in the home setting. The field has been moving away from what we might call the "magic bullet" approach, where parents and educators attempt to identify a single technique or strategy that will make the difference or solve a problem. Instead, there has been increased recognition of the fact that situations involving lengthy and complex histories of problem behaviors will require a comprehensive approach (Repp & Horner, 1999). That is, along with the preventive, educative, and consequence components described above, educators may also need to understand and address broader physical/medical and lifestyle issues in home, school, and other community settings in order to eliminate the conditions that contribute to problem behavior.

Evaluation of Support Outcomes

Applied behavior analysis has a lengthy history of emphasizing concrete and objective methods of measuring changes in behavior related to support and intervention (Baer et al., 1968). This continues to be a critical component of PBS. It is important to have data and information that can allow judgments about the effectiveness of support and guide decisions about changes that may be needed to maximize its impact. However, as mentioned above, PBS includes evaluation of a range of outcomes including, but not limited to, changes in problem behavior. In the classroom setting these would include effects on a students' skill acquisition and social and leisure activities, and their overall happiness and satisfaction (Clarke, Worcester, Dunlap, Murray, & Bradley-Klug, 2002).

Functional Assessments and Comprehensive Positive Behavioral Support

PBS has developed to the point where there are substantial similarities across different authors' models for conducting assessments and providing support.

Overall Life Assessment and Planning

Either prior to or as part of a comprehensive functional assessment, many authors and practitioners have recommended that consideration be given to assessment and planning concerning broader lifestyle issues and concerns (Janney & Snell, 2000; O'Neill et al., 1997). What are the goals of the student and his or her family with regard to school, work, and community outcomes and activities? How are those goals going to be met, and what kinds of supports will be necessary to do so? This type of planning will typically require input from parents, family members, classmates, friends, neighbors, support staff, and other community members (see Horn et al., Chapter 2). Such groups can meet with the student in question, usually with a group leader to facilitate the process, and identify relevant goals and strategies for achieving them. In some cases this type of planning will identify lifestyle factors that, when changed, will create positive effects with regard to problem behaviors, thus decreasing the need for more focused and elaborate assessment and intervention strategies (Risley, 1996).

Example of behavioral support: Pamela.   Pamela is a 10-year-old who has been labeled as having severe mental retardation and autism. She communicates mainly via gestures, a few formal signs, and picture arrays to which she can point to indicate wants and needs. Pamela is currently living at home with her parents and two younger siblings and attends her neighborhood elementary school. She spends about half of her time working on her IEP goals in a regular education class, and the other half in various school jobs and community-based instructional activities. Her family and educators are concerned about her screaming, self-injury, and aggressive behavior (hitting and/or kicking others). They conducted two meetings following the Big Picture Planning process delineated by McDonnell, Mathot-Buckner, and Ferguson (1996). This allowed them to identify Pamela's current situation and possible future preferences with regard to living situation, possible work activities, social relationships, transportation and community access, and resource management. This served as the foundation for identifying a range of IEP goals and objectives that could be pursued in both school and community settings. Based on this information and additional functional assessment activities (see below), a variety of support and intervention strategies were implemented for Pamela.

Functional Assessment and Analysis

As described above, there has been a tremendous resurgence of interest in strategies for conducting functional assessments of problem behaviors as a basis for developing and implementing support plans (Repp & Horner, 1999). Conceptual and technological development of such strategies has been the focus of literally hundreds of workshops, journal articles, books, manuals, CD-ROMs, and other materials. Although approaches may differ with regard to specific details and methods, there is general agreement on the main critical components of the process. These include gathering relevant information via a variety of means, developing hypotheses about the variables influencing the behaviors and the functions or purposes they serve, and using these hypotheses as a basis for the development and implementation of support plan strategies (Foster-Johnson & Dunlap, 1993).

While speakers and authors may sometimes use the terms *functional assessment* and *functional analysis* relatively interchangeably, there has been a developing consensus on the need to differentiate between these procedures. Functional assessment is now considered to be a broader, more inclusive term that refers to a range of activities in which someone may engage to gather information to improve the effectiveness and efficiency of a behavior support plan (O'Neill et al., 1997). These activities might include interviewing people, having them complete rating scales, checklists, or questionnaires, or conducting systematic observations in particular situations. *Functional analysis* is a subset of these procedures that comes under the broader functional assessment umbrella. A functional analysis entails conducting controlled systematic presentations of environmental events (antecedents and/or consequences for problem behaviors) and collecting data to determine their effects on problem behaviors. These presentations are usually carried out in the context of a structured experimental design, in order to allow for clear conclusions about the relationships among environmental events and the problem behaviors (Iwata, Vollmer, & Zarcone, 1990; Wacker et al., 1999).

Functional assessment outcomes. O'Neill and colleagues (1997) identified five major outcomes of the assessment process. These are: (a) identification of the full range of problem behaviors of concern, and how they may be related to or interact with one another, (b) identification of the broader setting events and more immediate antecedent events leading to problem behaviors, (c) identification of the outcomes or consequences that appear to be reinforcing and maintaining the behaviors, (d) synthesis of this information into succinct summary statements or hypotheses, and (e) some level of systematic observational data that can confirm or disconfirm the hypotheses. Again, the main idea is that with this information in hand educators and caregivers can then choose strategies that will be logically related to *why* the behaviors are occurring, or the functions they are serving for the individual.

Functional assessment methods in the classroom. Functional assessment methods are generally classified into three main categories. A frequent first step for educators and teams is the use of *indirect,* or *informant,* assessments. These involve gathering information from relevant persons (parents, educators, the "target student" himself or herself) via interviews, rating scales, checklists, and/or questionnaires. Table 8.2 (p. 148) presents a list and description of commonly used tools of this type and sample items or questions from each (source citations are provided in the chapter's reference list). While research has indicated that such instruments and procedures can provide valid and important information to educators, it has also indicated that they may also provide information that is less trustworthy and helpful (Johnston & O'Neill, 2001). The basic message is that this type of data gathering can be critical, but should rarely if ever be relied upon as the sole source of information in the assessment process. These approaches can help in developing initial hypotheses about

TABLE 8.2 Tools and Instruments That Have Been Used for Indirect/Informant Functional Assessment

Tool/Instrument	Description	Sample Items
Motivation Assessment Scale (MAS—Durand & Crimmins, 1992)	16-item rating scale focusing on functions of an individual's behavior (attention, escape from undesired activities, obtaining tangibles, and sensory stimulation); primarily used with individuals with more severe developmental disabilities	2) Does the behavior occur following a request to perform a difficult task? 4) Does the behavior occur whenever you stop attending to this person?
Problem Behavior Questionnaire (PBQ—Lewis, Scott, & Sugai, 1994)	15-item rating scale focusing on functions of behavior in classroom settings (peer and educator attention, escape from undesired activities); primarily used with students in regular education classroom settings	4) When the problem behavior occurs do peers verbally respond or laugh at the student? 13) Will the student stop doing the problem behavior if you stop making requests or end an academic activity?
Functional Analysis Screening Tool (FAST—Iwata, 1994)	27-item yes–no response scale focusing on functions of behavior; primarily used with individuals with more severe developmental disabilities	4) The behavior often occurs when the child has not received much attention. 10) The behavior often occurs when you inform the person that he or she cannot have a certain item or engage in a particular activity.
Student-Assisted Functional Assessment Interview (Kern, Dunlap, Clarke, & Childs, 1994)	52-item guideline for interviewing students to identify instructional and curricular variables that may influence problem behaviors in classroom settings	1) When do you think you have the fewest problems with your behavior in school? 7) If you had the chance, what activities would you like to do that you don't have the opportunity to do now?
Functional Assessment Interview Form (FAI—O'Neill et al., 1997)	29-section interview format to identify a range of physical, setting, antecedent, and consequence variables that may influence problem behavior	A2) Which of the behaviors described above are likely to occur together in some way (i.e., a chain or a sequence)? C4) What *activities* are most and least likely to produce the behaviors?

behavior that can then be validated via additional procedures. It is critical that the student who is the focus of the assessment be a part of this process, to the extent that it makes sense. If he or she has the social and communicative skills to participate in an interview type of interaction with an appropriate person, this input would be very important to paint a complete picture of the situation.

A second strategy frequently used by educators and teams, either along with or after indirect assessment, is *systematic observation* that involves recording structured data on the occurrence of behavior and related environmental events during routines and activities in typical settings such as the classroom or at home. A wide range of procedures for collecting such data has been described in the behavioral and educational literature. These include such things as antecedent-behavior-consequence (A-B-C) recording, interval recording, scatterplot recording, and other formats, such as the Functional Assessment Observation form (O'Neill et al., 1997). Figure 8.1 (p. 150) presents an example of a detailed A-B-C type of format in which different antecedents, behaviors, and consequences can be noted during ongoing time periods. Each behavior episode and its related antecedents (what happens before the behavior), consequences (what happens after the behavior), and functions (why the behavior occurs, or motivation) are noted by a different number. These data collection formats share common strategies in that they typically involve recording (i.e., marking on a data sheet) the occurrence of relevant antecedents to the problem behaviors, the behaviors themselves, and the consequences or results that follow them. These data can then be analyzed to identify consistent relationships among problem behaviors and categories of environmental events (Repp, 1999). For example, the data pattern in Figure 8.1 indicates that the student's aggressive behavior appears to be motivated by escaping from task demands, while screaming and self-injury are motivated by gaining social attention. This information is used to help decide on the accuracy and validity of hypotheses initially developed from indirect assessments.

The third major category is *experimental functional analysis,* which was described above (Iwata, Vollmer, Zarcone, & Rodgers, 1993). In this procedure environmental events are presented or withdrawn during relatively short sessions (5 to 15 minutes) to assess their influence on behavior. These might include obtaining desired items or activities, escaping from aversive situations (e.g., work requests), or obtaining social interaction. During these sessions observational data are collected on the frequency of problem behaviors in the different conditions. For example, antecedent events may be manipulated, such as the presentation of particular tasks or activities like listening to music or doing a math worksheet. Alternatively, different social responses (e.g., social attention) can also be provided when the student engages in a problem behavior to assess whether it increases the likelihood that the behavior will occur. Typically, these kinds of manipulations are systematically controlled in order to develop the best possible explanation of what variables are contributing to the occurrence of a problem behavior and why a person is engaging in it. These types of functional analyses have been used in both regular and special education classroom settings to help develop and validate hypotheses about the functions or purposes of problem behaviors (Northup & Gulley, 2001; Sterling-Turner, Robinson, & Wilczynski, 2001).

Is there a best approach?   There has been considerable debate about the most effective and efficient methods for conducting functional assessments. As mentioned above, indirect

Time	Antecedents	Behavior(s)	Consequences/Responses	Potential Function(s)
9:00 – 9:30	1 2	1 2	1 2	1 2
9:30 – 10:00				
10:00 – 10:30	3 4	3 4	3 4	3 4
10:30 – 11:00	5	5	5	5

FIGURE 8.1 Positive behavior support.

assessments may not always provide valid information. Some authors have contended that the experimental functional analysis approach provides the most precise and reliable data. Others have expressed concerns about these approaches, such as safety problems and the need for trained personnel and resources to be able to carry them out effectively (Sturmey, 1995). To help respond to these concerns there is a substantial need for further research on the comparative validity of different assessment methods (Cunningham & O'Neill, 2000). In addition, recently enacted legal requirements have resulted in increasing logistical demands for assessment services in educational and other service settings (Sugai et al., 2000). This has created a substantial challenge for service providers as they attempt to identify and implement procedures that will be effective but can also be done within the time and resource constraints present in schools and other service settings (Drasgow, Yell, Bradley, & Shriner, 1999). Until further research and practice produce additional data-based guidance, the best approach is likely to be one that is individualized to particular situations, begins with less time- and resource-intensive strategies, and moves on to more demanding procedures as needed.

Final hypotheses/summary statements. As described above, the final outcome of the assessment process should be one or more hypotheses that characterize the range of situations and functions concerning an individual's behavior. Table 8.3 (p. 152) presents examples of such hypotheses or summary statements that include broader setting events, more immediate antecedent factors, the different types of behaviors of concern, and the functions or purposes that they appear to serve in those situations (O'Neill et al., 1997). Note that there are multiple statements for some students, illustrating the fact certain behaviors may occur in one situation for one reason, but similar or other behaviors may occur in other situations for other reasons. It is critical to make sure that the full range of situations is identified so that they can all be taken into consideration in designing and implementing support strategies. For example, with Pamela, situations involving task or activity demands, difficult peer interactions, and recess activities were all problematic and involved multiple types of problem behaviors and reinforcers.

Functional assessment as an ongoing process. It is important to keep in mind that functional assessment is not something that occurs once and never has to be repeated. Like all people, students with significant disabilities may experience changes over time with regard to their situations, preferences, and behavior. Therefore, various aspects of the assessment process may need to be periodically revisited to ensure that assessment outcomes and support strategies continue to be relevant and up to date (O'Neill et al., 1997).

Developing and Implementing Assessment-Based Comprehensive Behavioral Support Plans

A critical issue that has arisen in the field is that practitioners may be able to carry out an effective behavioral assessment, but often struggle with how to use that information to bridge the gap into developing and implementing a plan. Although a variety of frameworks have been developed to help practitioners move through this process, they are all based on

TABLE 8.3   Examples of Hypotheses/Summary Statements Concerning Problem Behaviors

Student	Behaviors	Hypotheses/Summary Statements
Monique	Cursing, property destruction, aggression	When Monique has not had much sleep and is asked to do a nonpreferred activity in her classroom, she will curse, tear up materials, and hit the teacher in order to escape the task demands.
Jackie	Spitting, hitting	When Jackie wants to maintain access to the cassette player at the end of a music activity, she will spit at and/or hit the teacher in order to maintain access to the music.
Randy	Rocking, drumming	In situations with low levels of activity or attention Randy will rock back and forth and drum on things in order to obtain internal stimulation.
Pamela	Screaming, self-injury, aggression	When Pamela's medication levels are low and she is asked to do independent seatwork, she is likely to begin screaming and/or hitting herself to get educator attention. When Pamela has fought with her siblings at home and is teased by her classmates, she will curse at and/or hit them in order to stop the aversive teasing. When Pamela wants to control the game/activity during recess, she will scream at and/or hit her classmates to try to get them to do what she wants them to do.

similar basic principles (Bambara & Knoster, 1998; O'Neill et al., 1997; Witt, Daly, & Noell, 2000).

Plans must be based on assessment results.   The whole point of functional assessment is to allow us to understand the things that influence a person's problem behavior so that we can make a difference. Consequently, the hypotheses or summary statements must be incorporated into the plan and guide the selection of strategies that are used with the student.

Behavioral support plans typically focus on our behavior.   Parents, educators, and other caregivers may often want a consultant or expert to do something to or with a student that results in stopping the occurrence of the problem behavior. However, in most cases behavior support plans will mainly describe the changes that parents, educators, and others must make in the environment or their own behavior to reduce the likelihood of problem behavior. Behavior support is about what *we* do differently to construct an environment that supports appropriate behavior and allows a student to be more successful. This doesn't mean that support shouldn't involve things that might have a more direct effect on an individual (e.g., counseling or medication). However, even these kinds of strategies will require support by a variety of other persons to be effective (e.g., providing reminders to take medication).

Plans should be technically sound.   Behavior plans must be based on empirically established principles and procedures of applied behavior analysis. However, they must be comprehensive with regard to including strategies that aim at proactively *preventing* behaviors, as well as *reacting* to them when they occur. Proactive strategies can help make the behaviors irrelevant. For example, if the aversive classroom demands that have been contributing to a student's behavior can be removed or modified to be less aversive, then there will be no need for him or her to engage in the behaviors. On the reactive side it is important that, to the extent possible, educators or caregivers do not reinforce the individual when he or she engages in problem behaviors.

Plans should fit the settings where they will need to be implemented.   In recent years there has been increasing attention paid to the factors that might influence whether support providers can and will implement the strategies called for in a plan. This can be thought of as the "goodness of fit" of a plan for parents or educators. It is important to determine whether support providers have the values, skills, and resources to effectively carry out the necessary strategies (Albin, Lucyshyn, Horner, & Flannery, 1996; Kennedy, Long, Jolivette, Cox, Tang, & Thompson, 2001). For example, an educator coping with 25 to 30 students in a classroom will have difficulty implementing intervention procedures that call for frequent ongoing contact with one particular student. This issue highlights the need for all relevant persons to be involved in the assessment and plan-development process. This allows parents, educators, and others to provide input on what they think is most important and doable within given settings and situations.

Severity of behavior versus intensity of intervention.   It is typically recommended that the intrusiveness or aversiveness of potential interventions be matched to the severity of the behavior, and that interventions follow a least-to-most hierarchy in terms of intrusiveness or aversiveness (Bailey, Wolery, & Sugai, 1988). That is, more extreme interventions such as physical restraint or corporal punishment should only be considered in situations involving truly dangerous self-injurious or aggressive behavior, and only after less intrusive or restrictive interventions have been competently and exhaustively attempted. In addition, any more intrusive or aversive interventions must be carried out in the context of strategies designed to develop and positively reinforce alternative appropriate behaviors (Emerson, 1995). In making such decisions it is critical that team members such as educators and parents become knowledgeable about the rules and regulations that govern the use of intervention procedures at federal, state, and local school district levels.

The Competing Behavior Perspective

Based on previous work by Horner and Billingsley (1988), O'Neill and colleagues (1997) described a competing behavior model for laying out assessment results and guiding intervention and program development. This model involves delineating a given hypothesis/

summary statement describing a problem behavior, and then doing two things: (a) identifying the *desired behavior* that a student should be exhibiting in a given situation (completing work, attending to the educator), and (b) identifying at least one *appropriate
alternative behavior* that the student could perform that would produce the same outcome
as the problem behavior (asking for attention or a break from an activity). These behaviors
have been referred to as "functional equivalents" to problem behaviors (Carr, 1988). The
task of the group planning support is then to identify factors in a multitude of areas that will
make the desired and alternative behaviors more likely to occur, and the problem behaviors
less likely to occur. As described above, strategies need to be considered in four areas:
broader setting events, more immediate antecedent events, teaching and/or prompting
skills/behaviors, and consequences for appropriate and problem behaviors (Bambara &
Knoster, 1998).

"Setting event" interventions.   In some respects we are still in the early stages of developing effective strategies for the evaluation and management of broader "setting events"
(also referred to as "establishing operations"). There are good conceptual frameworks for
how such events influence the likelihood of problem behaviors, and some examples of how
interventions in such areas might be successful (Kennedy & Meyer, 1998). Horner,
Vaughn, Day, and Ard (1996) delineated proactive and reactive strategies for dealing with
influential events. These general strategies are outlined in Table 8.4 (p. 155), and specific
examples for Pamela are presented in Table 8.5 (p. 156). There is a great need for ongoing
research in these areas to develop more effective assessment and intervention practices.

More immediate antecedent event strategies.   Quite a range of strategies fall into this
more proactive category, some of which have received substantial empirical support (see
examples for Pamela in Table 8.5). For instance, offering choices can help to mitigate
problem behaviors in situations involving less preferred activities (Dunlap et al., 1994;
Vaughn & Horner, 1997). Several studies have been done on behavioral momentum or high
probability request sequences, in which a student is asked to respond to multiple requests
to which they are likely to respond and get reinforced before being asked to do a task or
activity that has been more problematic (Davis & Brady, 1993). There is a wide range of
potential curricular and instructional modifications that fit into this category as well.
Changes in task length, difficulty, content, and other variables can have positive effects on
problem behaviors (Dunlap & Kern, 1993). Several studies in recent years have examined
the effects of providing access to preemptive or noncontingent reinforcement; that is, students are provided with periodic social attention or breaks from task demands in order to
prevent the occurrence of problem behaviors motivated by those outcomes. Over time the
schedules of reinforcement can be extended so it does not need to be so frequently provided. Lastly, two straightforward approaches are: (a) to simply remove, if possible, the
problematic stimuli that are setting off the problem behaviors (e.g., changing IEP goals to
eliminate a problematic task/activity), and (b) to make sure to prompt appropriate alternative behaviors *before* the problem behaviors occur.

Teaching/prompting appropriate alternative behaviors.   This approach has received a
great deal of attention from researchers and practitioners (Carr et al., 1994). The main

TABLE 8.4   **Proactive and Reactive Strategies for Dealing with Influential Setting Events**

Strategy	Examples
Minimizing the Likelihood of Setting Events (Proactive)	Preventing the occurrence of problematic events, such as managing peer conflict at home or on the playground; ensuring adequate rest/sleep; treating and resolving medical problems (e.g., ear infections); adjusting levels of psychoactive medications
Neutralizing the Effects of Setting Events (Reactive)	Mitigating the influence of events that have already occurred, such as allowing a student a "cool-down" period (e.g., take a walk, listen to music) after a playground or bus altercation; providing medication to a student who is ill
Withholding Stimuli That Set Off Problem Behaviors (Reactive)	Minimizing or eliminating (at least temporarily) events that frequently lead to problem behaviors, such as not engaging in a demanding academic or work activity when someone is in an agitated state
Increase Prompts for Desired Behavior (Reactive)	Increasing prompts and reminders for appropriate alternative behaviors (e.g., signing to ask for a break) when it is known that a student is in a problematic state
Increase Value and Quantity of Reinforcers for Desired Behaviors (Reactive)	Increasing the quantity and quality of rewards or reinforcement that will be made available for the occurrence of appropriate behaviors, such as letting a student know he or she can have 15 minutes of free time with the computer when he or she usually gets only 10 minutes of free time with the computer

Source: Adapted from Horner, Vaughn, Day, & Ard (1996).

focus for students with significant disabilities has been on teaching social communicative behaviors that can replace and serve the same function as problem behaviors; this is known as functional communication training (Durand, 1990; see examples for Pamela in Table 8.5). For example, an individual might be taught to use verbal phrases ("Please talk to me"), signs or gestures, or other alternative communication methods to request attention, a break, help with a task, or a desired item or activity (see Garfinkle & Kaiser, Chapter 7). These responses are taught with typical modeling and prompting strategies. Initial reinforcement by honoring the requests is critical, as is trying to ensure that there is minimal or no reinforcement for problem behaviors (O'Neill & Sweetland-Baker, 2001). Over time, delays can be implemented so that requests don't have to be honored by caregivers so quickly or frequently.

TABLE 8.5   Summary of Behavioral Support Strategies for Pamela

Setting Event Strategies	Antecedent Strategies	Teaching/ Promoting Alternative Behaviors	Consequence Strategies	Crisis Management	Data Collection/ Evaluation
■ Increased doctor visits to check medication levels	■ Preemptive/ noncontingent social attention ■ Proactive prompting to engage in appropriate social interactive behaviors	■ Teach hand waving to recruit attention ■ Sign "Stop" and walk away from teasing ■ Use picture book to initiate social interactions	■ Honoring communicative responses ■ Responses to social initiations/ interactions ■ Ignore/move away from inappropriate behavior ■ Block and sit alone for aggressive behavior	■ Not applicable	■ Ongoing A-B-C data collection ■ Weekly meetings to review data and make programming decisions

Acceptable consequences for appropriate and problem behaviors.   While there has been less emphasis in recent years on reactive consequence strategies, they are still a critical component of a comprehensive plan (see examples for Pamela in Table 8.5). Reinforcement for appropriate behaviors should be programmed in both more natural (e.g., responding to communicative requests) and more structured ways (e.g., point/token systems) as needed (Williams, Williams, & McLaughlin, 1989). As mentioned, research has demonstrated that reinforcement for problem behaviors must be minimized or prevented in order for other strategies to be maximally effective. Finally, appropriate acceptable consequences for punishment and reduction of problem behavior should be considered (Iwata, 1988). These might include procedures such as reprimands, response cost, and time-out from reinforcement (O'Brien, 1989). There has been a massive volume of discussion and debate on this topic. Support providers need to ensure that in making decisions about potentially intrusive and aversive procedures they are following: (a) best practice guidelines for selecting and implementing such interventions, (b) full input from students with significant disabilities and their families and caregivers, and (c) all applicable legal guidelines and restrictions at local school district and state levels (Christian, Luce, & Larsson, 1992).

Crisis/emergency support.   Again, while most emphasis should be on proactive and educative procedures, even with appropriate positive strategies in place some individuals will sometimes exhibit behavior of such intensity or severity it will be necessary to intervene in very intrusive ways, such as brief physical restraint (Carr et al., 1994; Walker,

Colvin, & Ramsey, 1995). It is critical that such procedures only be implemented by support persons who have been thoroughly trained in their use, and that they are carried out in accord with all applicable legal and regulatory guidelines. It is very important that everyone involved keep in mind that the sole purpose of such procedures is the protection of the individual and others around him or her. These *are not* procedures that should be expected to bring about any positive behavior change (Carr et al., 1994; LaVigna & Donnellan, 1986).

Data collection/evaluation. A hallmark of applied behavior analysis is ongoing data collection that allows for decision making about the success of support plans (see Halle et al., Chapter 4). There needs to be some type of ongoing data collection and review so that educators can decide whether to maintain, modify, or terminate a support plan or one or more of its components (see examples for Pamela in Table 8.5). It is very important that those persons responsible for collecting data (educators, classroom assistants, parents) are regularly involved in reviewing the summarized data and contributing to the decision-making process.

Future Directions in Behavioral Support in Educational Settings

Broader Perspectives on Implementing Behavioral Support

In recent years researchers and practitioners have begun to develop and implement broader systemwide approaches to behavioral support. For example, Sugai, Horner, and their colleagues have been running a federally funded national center on Positive Behavioral Interventions and Supports (Sugai et al., 2000). The main focus of this center is to provide information, training, technical assistance, and research on schoolwide systems for supporting the full range of students presenting behavioral challenges in the schools, including students with significant disabilities and those labeled as having emotional/behavioral disorders. Often referred to as Effective Behavioral Support (EBS), this approach emphasizes the need for considering multiple systems within a school (schoolwide; specific settings such as playground or cafeteria; classroom; individual assessment-based programs) and how they need to be structured to effectively support the full range of more and less behaviorally challenging students in school settings (Lewis & Sugai, 1999). Demonstrations of the effectiveness of these comprehensive approaches are beginning to accumulate in the literature (Taylor-Greene et al., 1997), and provide important direction for future research and application.

Continued Development of Functional Assessment Technology

As mentioned above, there are still a number of challenges that remain with regard to identifying the most effective and efficient functional assessment strategies in school, home, and community settings. Fortunately, this is an area receiving considerable attention from both researchers and practitioners. Down the road, support providers should expect to see fairly concrete recommendations concerning which types of assessment procedures will be effective and most easily carried out with which kinds of individuals and situations (Cunningham & O'Neill, 2000). In addition, new technology should become available to facilitate the functional assessment process in terms of both training and implementation (Liaupsin, Scott, & Nelson, 2001).

Research into Practice: Where the Rubber Meets the Road

Recent years have seen a growing consensus concerning the development of a valid and effective set of principles and procedures comprising PBS (Scotti & Meyer, 1999). However, a sizeable gap still remains between the cutting edge in research and practice and what is actually available to many educators and students with disabilities and their families (Schwartz, 1997). This problem is part of the larger issue of a lack of resources and services for students with developmental disabilities and their families (Lakin, 1998). However, short of a massive infusion of money and other resources, there are still a variety of avenues for attacking this problem. Better information can be disseminated to the general public concerning what they should expect with regard to competent behavioral services. Information on appropriate behavioral assessment and support services needs to be more effectively included in pre- and inservice training for a range of relevant professionals including educators and school psychologists (O'Neill et al., 2001; Vollmer & Northup, 1997). Finally, more training and information can be made available to parents and families to allow them to work effectively with professionals as they collaborate to support their children in home, school, and community settings (Fox, Vaughn, Dunlap, & Bucy, 1997; Vaughn et al., 1997).

Conclusion

The development of the approach known as PBS represents a unique integration of personal values and empirically based procedures from behavior analysis. This combination allows educators, other practitioners, families, and researchers to pursue important, socially valid goals for students with severe disabilities, and to do so from a solid grounding of effective principles and procedures.

References

Albin, R. W., Lucyshyn, J. M., Horner, R. H., & Flannery, K. B. (1996). Contextual fit for behavior support plans: A model for "goodness of fit." In L. K. Koegel, R. L. Koegel, & G. Dunlap (Eds.), *Positive behavioral support: Including people with difficult behavior in the community* (pp. 81–98). Baltimore: Paul H. Brookes.

Baer, D. M., Wolf, M. M., & Risley, T. R. (1968). Some current dimensions of applied behavior analysis. *Journal of Applied Behavior Analysis, 1,* 91–97.

Bailey, D. B., Wolery, M., & Sugai, G. (1988). *Effective teaching: Principles and procedures of applied behavior analysis for exceptional students.* Boston: Allyn and Bacon.

Bambara, L. M., & Knoster, T. (1998). *Designing positive behavior support plans.* Washington, DC: AAMR.

Borthwick-Duffy, S. A. (1994). Prevalence of destructive behaviors: A study of aggression, self-injury, and property destruction. In T. Thompson & D. B. Gray (Eds.), *Destructive behavior in developmental disabilities: Diagnosis and treatment* (pp. 3–23). Thousand Oaks, CA: Sage.

Bromley, J., & Emerson, E. (1995). Beliefs and emotional reactions of care staff working with people with challenging behavior. *Journal of Intellectual Disability Research, 39,* 341–352.

Bruininks, R. H., Olson, K. M., Larson, S. A., & Lakin, K. C. (1994). Challenging behaviors among persons with mental retardation in residential settings: Implications for policy, research, and practice. In T. Thompson & D. B. Gray (Eds.), *Destructive behavior in developmental disabilities: Diagnosis and treatment* (pp. 24–48). Thousand Oaks, CA: Sage.

Carr, E. G. (1988). Functional equivalence as a mechanism of response generalization. In R. H. Horner, G. Dunlap, & R. L. Koegel (Eds.), *Generalization and maintenance: Life-style changes in applied settings* (pp. 221–241). Baltimore: Paul H. Brookes.

Carr, E. G., Horner, R. H., Turnbull, A. P., Marquis, J. G., McLaughlin, D. M., McAtee, M. L., Smith, C. E., Ryan, K. A., Ruef, M. B., & Doolabh, A. (1999). *Positive behavior support for people with developmental disabilities: A research synthesis.* Washington, DC: AAMR.

Carr, E.G., Levin, L., McConnachie, G., Carlson, J. I., Kemp, D. C., & Smith, C. E. (1994). *Communication-based intervention for problem behavior: A user's guide for producing positive change.* Baltimore: Paul H. Brookes.

Christian, W. P., Luce, S. C., & Larsson, E. V. (1992). Peer review and human rights committees. In J. K. Luiselli, J. L. Matson, & N. N. Singh (Eds.), *Self-injurious behavior: Analysis, assessment, and treatment* (pp. 352–366). New York: Springer-Verlag.

Clarke, S., Worcester, J., Dunlap, G., Murray, M., & Bradley-Klug, K. (2002). Using multiple measures to evaluate positive behavior support: A case example. *Journal of Positive Behavior Interventions, 4,* 131–145.

Cunningham, E., & O'Neill, R. E. (2000). A comparison of results of functional assessment and analysis procedures with young children with autism. *Education and Training in Mental Retardation and Developmental Disabilities, 35,* 406–414.

Davis, C. A., & Brady, M. P. (1993). Expanding the utility of behavioral momentum with young children: Where we've been, where we need to go. *Journal of Early Intervention, 17,* 211–223.

Drasgow, E., Yell, M. L., Bradley, R., & Shriner, J. G. (1999). The IDEA amendments of 1997: A schoolwide model for conducting functional behavioral assessments and developing behavior intervention plans. *Education and Treatment of Children, 22,* 244–266.

Dunlap, G., dePerczel, M., Clarke, S., Wilson, D., Wright, S., White, R., & Gomez, A. (1994). Choice making and proactive behavioral support for students with emotional and behavioral challenges. *Journal of Applied Behavior Analysis, 27,* 505–518.

Dunlap, G., & Kern, L. (1993). Assessment and intervention for children within the instructional curriculum. In J. Reichle & D. P. Wacker (Eds.), *Communicative alternatives to challenging behaviors: Integrating functional assessment and intervention strategies* (pp. 177–208). Baltimore: Paul H. Brookes.

Dunlap, G., Kern, L., dePerczel, M., Clarke, S., Wilson, D., Childs, K. E., White, R., & Falk, G. (1993). Functional analysis of classroom variables for students with emotional and behavioral disorders. *Behavioral Disorders, 18,* 275–291.

Durand, V. M. (1990). *Severe behavior problems: A functional communication training approach.* New York: Guilford.

Durand, V. M., & Crimmins, D. (1992). *The motivation assessment scale administration guide.* Topeka, KS: Monaco & Associates.

Emerson, E. (1995). *Challenging behaviour: Analysis and intervention in people with learning difficulties.* Cambridge, UK: Cambridge University Press.

Foster-Johnson, L., & Dunlap, G. (1993). Using functional assessment to develop effective, individualized interventions for challenging behaviors. *Teaching Exceptional Children, 25,* 44–50.

Fox, L., Vaughn, B. J., Dunlap, G., & Bucy, M. (1997). Parent-professional partnership in behavioral support: A qualitative analysis of one family's experience. *Journal of the Association for Persons with Severe Handicaps, 22,* 198–207.

Horner, R. H., & Billingsley, F. F. (1988). The effect of competing behavior on the generalization and maintenance of adaptive behavior in applied settings. In R. H. Horner, G. Dunlap, & R. L. Koegel (Eds.), *Generalization and maintenance: Life-style changes in applied settings* (pp. 197–220). Baltimore: Paul H. Brookes.

Horner, R. H., Diemer, S., & Brazeau, K. C. (1992). Educational support for students with severe problem behaviors in Oregon: A descriptive analysis from the 1987–1988 school year. *Journal of the Association for Persons with Severe Handicaps, 17,* 154–169.

Horner, R. H., Dunlap, G., Koegel, R. L., Carr, E. G., Sailor, W., Anderson, J., Albin, R. W., & O'Neill, R. E. (1990). Toward a technology of "nonaversive" behavioral support. *Journal of the Association for Persons with Severe Handicaps, 15,* 125–132.

Horner, R. H., Vaughn, B. J., Day, H. M., & Ard, W. R. (1996). The relationship between setting events and problem behavior: Expanding our understanding of behavioral support. In L. K. Koegel, R. L. Koegel, & G. Dunlap (Eds.), *Positive behavioral support: Including people with difficult behavior in the community* (pp. 381–402). Baltimore: Paul H. Brookes.

Iwata, B. A. (1988). The development and adoption of controversial default technologies. *The Behavior Analyst, 11,* 149–157.

Iwata, B. A. (1994). The FAST: Functional Assessment Screening Tool. Unpublished instrument. Gainesville: Center for the Study of Self-Injury, University of Florida.

Iwata, B. A., Dorsey, M. F., Slifer, K. J., Bauman, K. E., & Richman, G. S. (1994). Toward a functional analysis of self-injury. *Journal of Applied Behavior Analysis, 27,* 197–209. (Reprinted from *Analysis and Intervention in Developmental Disabilities, 2,* 3–20, 1982).

Iwata, B. A., Vollmer, T. R., & Zarcone, J. R. (1990). The experimental (functional) analysis of behavior disorders: Methodology, applications, and limitations. In A. C. Repp & N. N. Singh (Eds.), *Perspectives on the use of nonaversive and aversive interventions for persons with developmental disabilities* (pp. 301–330). Sycamore, IL: Sycamore.

Iwata, B. A., Vollmer, T. R., Zarcone, J. R., & Rodgers, T. A. (1993). Treatment classification and selection based on behavioral function. In R. Van Houten & S. Axelrod (Eds.), *Behavior analysis and treatment* (pp. 101–125). New York: Plenum.

Janney, R., & Snell, M. E. (2000). *Behavioral support.* Baltimore: Paul H. Brookes.

Johnston, S., & O'Neill, R. E. (2001). Searching for effectiveness and efficiency in conducting functional assessments: A review and proposed process for educators and other practitioners. *Focus on Autism and Developmental Disabilities, 16,* 205–214.

Kazdin, A. E. (2001). *Behavior modification in applied settings* (6th ed.). Belmont, CA: Wadsworth.

Kennedy, C. H. (2002). Toward a socially valid understanding of problem behavior. *Education and Training of Children, 25,* 142–153.

Kennedy, C. H., Long, T., Jolivette, K., Cox, J., Tang, J. C., & Thompson, T. (2001). Facilitating general education participation for students with behavior problems by linking positive behavior supports and person-centered planning. *Journal of Emotional and Behavioral Disorders, 9,* 161–171.

Kennedy, C. H., & Meyer, K. A. (1998). Establishing operations and the motivation of problem behavior. In J. Luselli & M. Cameron (Eds.), *Antecedent-based approaches to reducing problem behavior* (pp. 329–346). Baltimore: Paul H. Brookes.

Kern, L., Dunlap, G., Clarke, S., & Childs, K. (1994). Student-assisted functional assessment interview. *Diagnostique, 19,* 29–39.

Koegel, L. K., Koegel, R. L., & Dunlap, G. (Eds.). (1996). *Positive behavioral support: Including people with difficult behavior in the community.* Baltimore: Paul H. Brookes.

Lakin, K. C. (1998). On the outside looking in: Attending to waiting lists in systems of services for people with developmental disabilities. *Mental Retardation, 36,* 157–162.

LaVigna, G. W., & Donnellan, A. M. (1986). *Alternatives to punishment: Solving behavior problems with non-aversive strategies.* New York: Irvington.

Lewis, T. J., Scott, T., & Sugai, G. (1994). The Problem Behavior Questionnaire: An educator-based instrument to develop functional hypotheses of problem behavior in general education classrooms. *Diagnostique, 19,* 103–115.

Lewis, T. J., & Sugai, G. (1999). Effective behavior support: A systems approach to proactive schoolwide management. *Focus on Exceptional Children, 31,* 1–24.

Liaupsin, C. J., Scott, T. M., & Nelson, C. M. (2001). *Functional behavioral assessment: An interactive training module.* Longmont, CO: Sopris West.

Luiselli, J. K., & Cameron, M. J. (Eds.). (1998). *Antecedent control: Innovative approaches to behavioral support.* Baltimore: Paul H. Brookes.

McDonnell, J. J., Mathot-Buckner, C., & Ferguson, B. (1996). *Transition programs for students with moderate/severe disabilities.* Pacific Grove, CA: Brooks/Cole.

National Institutes of Health (NIH) (1991). *Treatment of destructive behaviors in persons with developmental disabilities.* Washington, DC: National Institutes of Health.

Northup, J., & Gulley, V. (2001). Some contributions of functional analysis to the assessment of behaviors associated with attention deficit hyperactivity disorder and the effects of stimulant medication. *School Psychology Review, 30,* 227–238.

O'Brien, F. (1989). Punishment for people with developmental disabilities. In E. Cipani (Ed.), *The treatment of severe behavior disorders: Behavior analysis approaches* (pp. 37–58). Washington, DC: AAMR.

O'Neill, R. E., Horner, R. H., Albin, R. W., Sprague, J. R., Storey, K., & Newton, J. S. (1997). *Functional assessment and program development for problem behavior: A practical handbook* (2nd ed.). Belmont, CA: Wadsworth.

O'Neill, R. E., Johnson, J. W., Kiefer-O'Donnell, R., & McDonnell, J. J. (2001). Preparing educators and consultants for the challenge of severe problem behavior. *Journal of Positive Behavior Interventions, 3,* 101–108.

O'Neill, R. E., & Sweetland-Baker, M. (2001). An assessment of stimulus generalization and contingency effects in functional communication training with two students with autism. *Journal of Autism and Developmental Disorders, 31,* 235–240.

Reichle, J. (1990). *National working conference on positive approaches to the management of excess behavior: Final report and recommendations.* Minneapolis: Institute on Community Integration, University of Minnesota.

Reichle, J., & Wacker, D. P. (Eds.). (1993). *Communicative alternatives to challenging behaviors: Integrating functional assessment and intervention strategies.* Baltimore: Paul H. Brookes.

Repp, A. C. (1999). Naturalistic functional assessment with regular and special education students in classroom settings. In A. C. Repp & R. H. Horner (Eds.), *Functional analysis of problem behavior: From effective assessment to effective intervention* (pp. 238–258). Belmont, CA: Wadsworth.

Repp, A. C., & Horner, R. H. (Eds.). (1999). *Functional analysis of problem behavior: From effective assessment to effective intervention.* Belmont, CA: Wadsworth.

Repp, A. C., & Singh, N. N. (1990). *Perspectives on the use of nonaversive and aversive interventions for people with developmental disabilities.* Sycamore, IL: Sycamore.

Risley, T. R. (1996). Get a life! Positive behavioral intervention for challenging behavior through life arrangement and life coaching. In L. K. Koegel, R. L. Koegel, & G. Dunlap (Eds.), *Positive behavioral support: Including people with difficult behavior in the community* (pp. 425–437). Baltimore: Paul H. Brookes.

Schroeder, S. R., Rojahn, J., & Oldenquist, A. (1991). Treatment of destructive behavior among people with mental retardation and development disabilities: Overview of the problem. In *Treatment of destructive behaviors in persons with developmental disabilities* (pp. 125–171). Washington, DC: National Institutes of Health.

Schwartz, I. S. (1997). It is just a matter of priorities: A response to Vaughn et al. and Fox et al. *Journal of the Association for Persons with Severe Handicaps, 22,* 213–214.

Scotti, J. R., & Meyer, L. H. (1999). *Behavioral intervention: Principles, models, and practices.* Baltimore: Paul H. Brookes.

Sterling-Turner, H. E., Robinson, S. L., & Wilczynski, S. M. (2001). Functional assessment of distracting and disruptive behaviors in the school setting. *School Psychology Review, 30,* 211–226.

Sturmey, P. (1995). Analog baselines: A critical review of the methodology. *Research in Developmental Disabilities, 16,* 269–284.

Sugai, G., Horner, R. H., Dunlap, G., Hieneman, M., Lewis, T. J., Nelson, C. M., Scott, T. M., Liaupsin, C., Sailor, W., Turnbull, A. P., Turnbull, R., Wickham, D., Wilcox, B., & Ruef, M. (2000). Applying positive behavior support and functional assessment in schools. *Journal of Positive Behavior Interventions, 2,* 131–143.

Taylor-Greene, S., Brown, D., Nelson, L., Longton, J., Gassman, T., Cohen, J., Swartz, J., Horner, R. H., Sugai, G., & Hall, S. (1997). School-wide behavioral support: Starting the year off right. *Journal of Behavioral Education, 7,* 99–112.

Vaughn, B. J., Dunlap, G., Fox, L., Clarke, S., & Bucy, M. (1997). Parent-professional partnership in behavioral support: A case study of community-based intervention. *Journal of the Association for Persons with Severe Handicaps, 22,* 186–197.

Vaughn, B., & Horner, R. H. (1997). Identifying instructional tasks that occasion problem behaviors and assessing the effects of student versus educator choice among these tasks. *Journal of Applied Behavior Analysis, 30,* 299–312.

Vollmer, T. R., & Northup, J. (1997). Applied behavior analysis and school psychology: An introduction to the mini-series. *School Psychology Quarterly, 12,* 1–3.

Wacker, D. P., Cooper, L. J., Peck, S. M., Derby, K. M., & Berg, W. K. (1999). Community-based functional assessment. In A. C. Repp & R. H. Horner (Eds.), *Functional analysis of problem behavior: From effective assessment to effective support* (pp. 32–56). Belmont, CA: Wadsworth.

Walker, H. M., Colvin, G., & Ramsey, E. (1995). *Antisocial behavior in school: Strategies and best practices.* Pacific Grove, CA: Brooks/Cole.

Williams, B. F., Williams, R. L., & McLaughlin, T. F. (1989). The use of token economies with individuals who have developmental disabilities. In E. Cipani (Ed.), *The treatment of severe behavior disorders: Behavior analysis approaches* (pp. 3–18). Washington, DC: AAMR.

Witt, J. C., Daly, E. M., & Noell, G. (2000). *Functional assessments: A step-by-step guide to solving academic and behavior problems.* Longmont, CO: Sopris West.

CHAPTER

9   Sensory and Motor Needs

SALLY ROBERTS
University of Kansas

This chapter focuses on the sensory and motor needs of students with multiple disabilities. Students with severe and multiple disabilities have remained a challenge to educators. They are typically nonverbal and have varying levels of sensory, motor, and health disabilities. Using traditional assessment measures, they often evidence overall levels of development of six months or less regardless of their chronological ages. Moreover, they may display only minimal response to visual and auditory stimuli.

What educators believe about their students, and the relationship between those beliefs and the resulting translation into exemplary classroom practices, has long been a topic of research (Soto & Goetz, 1998). Understanding and facilitating active learning for students with multiple disabilities in inclusive settings requires that educators have a basic philosophy that includes the following:

- All students despite the extent of their disabilities have a right to an education in a least restrictive environment.
- The needs of these students are multiplied by the extent and number of their disabilities, and these needs must be responded to both individually and collectively.
- Students must be viewed as a whole rather than by their individual disabilities.
- Every student has value and the potential to learn.

Educators who embrace this philosophy will be better able to create a learning environment and instructional activities that will ultimately result in an appropriate and valuable educational program for students with multiple disabilities despite the challenges their disabilities present. After reading this chapter you should be able to:

- Understand what is needed to support students with sensory, motor, and health needs in inclusive settings, including enhancing their potential for achievement and fulfillment in school and daily living activities

- Describe the processes involved in responding to the sum of the student's needs and how these needs interconnect
- Identify the necessary key team members and promote effective communication and collaboration among them
- Develop and assess the effects of good instructional methodology and teaching practices that take all of the student's individual needs into consideration
- Be sensitive to the unique needs and challenges faced by parents and educators of this population

Who Are Students with Multiple Disabilities?

No single definition can be ascribed to this population; however, IDEA regulations define multiple disabilities as follows:

> *Multiple disabilities means concomitant impairment (such as mental retardation–blindness, mental retardation–orthopedic impairment, etc.), the combination of which causes such severe educational problems that they cannot be accommodated in special education programs solely for one of the impairments. The term does not include deaf-blindness. (34 C.F.R. Sec. 300: [b][6])*

IDEA regulations further define this population by describing the various services that are required:

> *. . . children with disabilities who, because of the intensity of their physical, mental, or emotional problems, need highly specialized education, social, psychological, and medical services in order to maximize their full potential for useful and meaningful participation in society and for self-fulfillment. (34 C.F.R. Sec. 315.4 [d])*

While it is difficult to determine a single definition of students with multiple disabilities, for the purpose of this chapter the following six categories of characteristics described by Turnbull, Turnbull, Shank, Smith, and Leal (2002) will be used:

1. Students with severe disabilities in intellectual functioning as indicated by their academic skills and levels of alertness
2. Those who need to develop adaptive skills, particularly in the self-care and social skills areas
3. Those who exhibit significant delay in motor development as a result of a sensorimotor disability such as cerebral palsy
4. Students with disabilities of hearing and vision
5. Students who experience health care problems including the need for gastrostomy tube feeding, respiratory support, and therapy, and who require numerous medications for health maintenance
6. Those students who are nonverbal and do not use a formal symbolic means of communication

Overview of the Characteristics of Sensory and Motor Disabilities

Sensory Disabilities: Vision

The range and severity of vision loss among students with multiple disabilities varies greatly and may be influenced by the environment, the presence of additional disabilities, and the type of vision impairment. Vision problems can be classified into three separate types: refractive (problems with the physical components that allow the eye to focus), diseases of the anterior visual pathways (interference of the transmittal of light or the inability of the retina to receive light), and diseases of the visual cortex (problem with transmitting the electrical impulse to the visual cortex or the brain's inability to interpret the visual images it receives) (Sacks & Silberman, 1998). Diseases of the visual cortex—cortical visual impairment (CVI)—differ considerably from ocular impairments, as do intervention strategies to promote residual vision. CVI is often referred to as *cortical blindness,* a bilateral vision loss where normal pupillary response is present and an eye examination indicates no other abnormalities in the physical components of the eye (i.e., lens, cornea, retina) (Whiting, Jan, Wong, Ferrell, & McCormick, 1985).

Sensory Disabilities: Hearing

Hearing involves gathering sound from the environment and then interpreting this auditory information. The hearing mechanism comprises the outer, middle, and inner ear, and the location and nature of the dysfunction in the auditory pathway will determine the degree and type of hearing loss (Batshaw, 2002). A lesion in the outer or middle ear results in a conductive hearing loss—an inability to conduct sound to the inner ear. Problems in the inner ear result in a sensorineural hearing loss—difficulty with receiving and transferring the auditory stimulus into nerve impulses, transmitting sound to the brain, and/or interpreting the auditory message once the brain receives it. Hearing is evaluated in terms of loudness and pitch, and hearing loss is defined in terms of degree—mild, moderate, moderate-severe, severe, and profound. The obvious implication of hearing loss in students with multiple disabilities is the effect on their ability to receive and transmit language.

Motor Disabilities

Cerebral palsy is the most common cause of motor impairment seen in children with multiple disabilities. Cerebral palsy refers to a disorder of movement and posture that is due to a nonprogressive abnormality of the immature brain (Batshaw, 1997). The motor impairments associated with cerebral palsy are also classified according to their distribution (e.g., hemiplegia—arm and leg involved on same side of the body) and by physiological type (e.g., spasticity—resistance to stretch, increased muscle tone, clonus) (Dormans & Pellegrino, 1998). Sensory impairments are very common in students with cerebral palsy and can often be overlooked in our efforts to deal with the motor problems. Dormans and Pellegrino (1998, p. 52) state, "there is a high incidence of visual impairments, including myopia (i.e., nearsightedness), amblyopia (i.e., loss of vision related to disuse, often referred to as "lazy eye"), loss of vision in segments of the visual field (especially in children with hemiplegia), and cortical blindness (i.e., loss of vision caused by abnormalities of the brain rather than abnormalities of the eye or the optic nerve)." Oculomotor problems such as strabismus are also common in students with cerebral palsy (Menacker, 1993). Thus, the probability of accompanying sensory problems in combination with their motor disability most certainly impacts learning in students with multiple disabilities.

What Processes Are Involved in Providing an Education to Students with Sensory and Motor Needs?

Several factors are critical to the provision of services to students with multiple disabilities, particularly when these disabilities involve vision and hearing loss and motor impairment. First, having information about the various disabilities is critical. Knowledge leads to a lessening of fear of the unknown and provides the educator with the tools to develop appropriate instructional activities. Soto and Goetz (1998) reported the importance of a teacher's sense of self-efficacy in relationship to its influence on teacher practice and student outcomes. Research has shown that a teacher's feelings of efficacy influence, among other things, their classroom performance, acceptance of students, and persistence with low achievers. Hill (1999) suggests that educators need three sources of knowledge to feel a higher sense of efficacy: (a) knowledge of one's skills and ability to practice those skills in the classroom; (b) regular meetings to share both concerns and successes; and (c) opportunities for direct support that provides both information and feedback about their capabilities of successfully implementing the skills they have learned.

Second, collaboration and communication among the many individuals involved with the student must occur. Transdisciplinary team planning and service delivery is the preferred method of assuring that the various and complex needs of these students are met effectively (Campbell, 1987; Orelove & Sobsey, 1991; Rainforth, York, & Macdonald, 1992).

Finally, school-level administrators and the overall educational system must be positively involved in the process of serving students with multiple disabilities (Lipsky & Gartner, 1997). Administrators must also be receptive to and supportive of having students with multiple needs in their buildings and classrooms. This includes being willing to provide time for collaboration among team members as well as necessary resources, and evidencing a positive attitude toward serving all students.

Gathering Information and Knowledge

Rainforth (2000) described college students' responses to the Concerns-Based Adoption Model: Stages of Concern and Intervention Questionnaire (Hord et al., 1987), a tool she utilizes in her graduate training program. This is a staff development model that delineates the seven stages of concern through which teachers progress as they work through movement to an educational innovation (e.g., use of a new curriculum). The questionnaire consists of 35 statements that are associated with stages of concern around the dimensions of *Self*, *Task*, and *Impact*. Rainforth reports that the initial questionnaire administration (at the beginning of a university course on inclusive education for students with severe disabilities) most often shows that course participants' greatest concerns are clustered in the areas related to *Self,* which Hord and colleagues (1987) indicated was most typically seen in "nonusers." She states that while mean level of Self-Concerns does not decrease significantly from precourse levels, "there consistently has been a large reduction in the Task Concern of Management suggesting that course participants do learn strategies that they believe will allow them to succeed at educating students with severe disabilities" (p. 89). These results seem to suggest that providing a knowledge base to educators who work with students who have multiple disabilities can increase both comfort levels and feelings of competence.

Information gathering about sensory and motor needs can occur in a variety of ways. Team members including families conduct comprehensive assessments together. Regular team meetings provide ongoing transfer of information, knowledge, and skills among members. Team members make a commitment to teach, learn, and work together across disciplines (Orelove & Sobsey, 1991).

Collaboration and Communication

Educational teams for students with multiple disabilities will, out of necessity, involve many members. When taking into consideration all of the separate needs of students with multiple disabilities (i.e., vision, hearing, speech/language, motor, health, and so on), the numbers of professionals who will be part of the student's educational team can include the following: parents, regular and special educators, paraprofessional/intervener, occupational and physical therapists, speech/language pathologist, vision specialist, hearing specialist, orientation and mobility specialist, dietitian, school nurse, school psychologist, and administrator. In addition, good communication between the team and medical health-care providers will be essential. The logistics of communication among all of these individuals, let alone scheduling regular meetings, is daunting. No one person, however, can effectively respond to the diverse needs of students with multiple disabilities. Collaborative teaming is designed to create a feeling among members that everyone is responsible for the student. A "sink or swim together" attitude emphasizes pooling diverse knowledge, skills, and resources to provide for the needs of the student.

Johnson and Johnson (1987) and Thousand and Villa (1992) suggest no more than six or seven members as an optimal size for collaborative groups. As is obvious from the list of possible members above, educational teams for students with multiple disabilities will be much larger than the recommended size. Moreover, the sheer numbers will hamper the chances that regular meetings can be scheduled around the variety of schedules involved. The need for ongoing communication and problem solving remains critical, however. It is suggested that team members find alternative methods of communicating, with face-to-face meetings only scheduled quarterly or as a specific need arises. Using current available technology such as e-mail, digital still and video cameras, and multimedia portfolios showing student progress can help keep team members informed and interacting. For example, nonsymbolic communication cues can be listed in a multimedia communication dictionary, the development of which represents the collaborative effort of families, caregivers, and educators to define the communicative forms and functions utilized by the student (Siegel-

Causey & Bashinski, 1997). This will ensure appropriate and consistent response to identified communicative cues by all of the student's communicative partners.

Administrative Attitudes

System change outcomes often describe results that affect the structure and activities of
organizations rather than individuals. Administrative support has been identified as the
most powerful predictor of changing teacher attitudes towards individuals with disabilities
and inclusive education (Villa et al., 1996). While states and local educational agencies may
support the philosophy of serving students with multiple disabilities in inclusive classroom
settings, successful implementation of appropriate services requires the ongoing involvement and support of building administrators. Principals, superintendents, and directors of
special education are critical participants in serving students with multiple disabilities.
They have the power to provide funding, resources, and time for collaboration. Turnbull
and colleagues (2002) suggest that the school reform movement has increased administrators' power and influence within their individual school districts and communities at large.
This empowerment can be advantageous to efforts to serve students with multiple disabilities. Thus, it is critical that administrators be viewed as informed partners and team members in the development and implementation of programming. While it is unlikely that
district wide administrators will take an active role in the individual student's program,
building-level administrators should be encouraged to be active participants in both planning and problem solving. Moreover, they should be viewed as partners rather than adver-
saries. Regular communication is recommended, and principals should be thanked and
complimented for positive contribution to the team and not accessed only when a need or
problem arises. A proactive interaction is always better than one that is reactive.

Implementing Systematic Programming in Inclusive Settings with Students with Multiple Disabilities

The old medical model traditionally used by related service providers in the past to address
the specific needs of students with multiple disabilities tended to divide the child into separate problem areas (Campbell, 1987). It is critical, however, for all educational team members to view students as the "sum of their parts" rather than a specific separate disability.
For example, the vision specialist must take into consideration the student's hearing, motor,
and communicative needs when developing and implementing a vision program. Programs
for students with multiple disabilities involve transdisciplinary IEP development, systematic instruction that takes into consideration all aspects of the student's disability, curricular accommodation and adaptation, and sensitivity to the unique needs and challenges that
families and caregivers of these students face (see Chapter 2). The following section will
provide the reader with some specific instructional methodologies in the areas of assessment, training the use of residual and alternative senses, orientation and mobility, motor
skills training including positioning and handling as it relates to instructional needs, and
addressing nutritional and medical care in the school setting.

Functional Assessment of Hearing and Vision

Meaningful outcomes are assessed as those that are "functional" for students. Opportunities to use skills must occur every day for students with multiple disabilities and will determine how well they function in a given environment as well as help them gain access to additional environments (Haring, 1988). Schwartz (1995) states that although it is relatively common to identify self-care skills as functional skills, it is also important to consider functional skills in other domains. Functional assessment by definition looks at how individuals use a particular skill within their environment. Thus, it is essential to assess, as well as train, visual and auditory skills within a context. Information about a student's hearing and vision may be available from a medical professional (e.g., ophthalmologist, audiologist, ear-nose-throat specialist). As described earlier, this information will provide hearing or visual sensitivity, if acuity information was attainable, but will most likely not give the educator a true picture of how the student uses his or her residual (remaining) sensory capabilities. For example, a student may be diagnosed as having a moderate-severe hearing loss across all of the frequencies (i.e., pitches). This will give information about hearing sensitivity (how loud a sound must be for the individual to respond), but it does not tell us whether he or she can recognize and respond to a specific auditory stimulus in the school setting. Additionally, the visual or hearing mechanisms may be intact, but in the classroom environment the student functions as though he has no hearing or vision at all.

Functional hearing and vision assessment should occur within a naturally occurring context. It is designed to evaluate response to sound or visual stimuli informally while considering additional disabilities. For example, if a motor response is required to indicate recognition of a visual or auditory stimulus and the student has cerebral palsy—limiting the ability for voluntary movement—an alternative indicator may be required. Examples of alternative responses might be pupillary dilation, cessation of movement including stereotypic or repetitive movements, heightened or lowered body tone, visual localization toward the stimulus, or increased levels of alertness.

The goal of the educator is to determine the student's functional use of hearing and vision so that a program can be developed to increase skills. The basic visual and auditory skills are awareness, attending/fixating, localizing, tracking, scanning, discrimination, recognition, and comprehension. Specific visual skills also include shifting gaze and looking while moving toward a target. As mentioned above, functional assessment of sensory skills must also take into consideration the student's other disabilities. If the student has severe motor disabilities, it is important to determine a position that normalizes muscle tone and facilitates whatever voluntary movement the student may have. The position choice should also allow for the presentation of the visual or auditory stimulus in a variety of positions, to the side, back, and above, just as they would occur in the natural environment. It is also necessary that the educator have a clear view of the student's response. When a student is positioned in sidelying, for example, eye movement as a response to an auditory stimulus would be difficult to detect. Also, if the student has a persistent primitive reflex such as an ATNR (asymmetrical tonic neck reflex), when the head is turned, the arm and leg on the same side as the chin extend while the opposite arm and leg flex. A localization response—turning to the stimulus—could trigger this reflex. Consequently, one would position the student so that the reflex does not inhibit responding. Additionally, the knowledge that the introduction of a visual or auditory stimulus causes a reflex to occur when the student is positioned in a particular manner provides good information about appropriate seating during instructional periods in the classroom.

Goetz and Gee (1987) state that teaching visual behaviors is presumed to involve more than just visual stimulation or providing opportunities for the student to receive information visually. They contend that effective teaching strategies for visual behaviors involve arranging the instructional environment so that the student's use of vision results in specific desirable and functional consequences. Thus, visual assessment and skill instruction should occur not in isolation but as an integral part of an activity and must be assessed within a context.

To identify an appropriate vision objective, the educator must first compare an individual's current visual behaviors within the broader task or activity. Then a decision is made whether to teach the specific skill or adapt the environment. According to Goetz and Gee (1987) this means that one must first analyze the task for its necessary "looking behaviors" prior to assessing whether the student can use vision effectively. It is also helpful for the educator to attempt to accomplish the task himself or herself with and without sight to determine whether vision is critical to the activity. This will help determine if or how an intervention would be beneficial.

Analyze with the vision specialist what adaptations or accommodations might be made to facilitate performing a specific task (e.g., personal assistance, adapted devices, enhanced materials, a change in the sequence of steps) (see Box 9.1, p. 172). Determine the actual need to intervene. A student who is unable to fixate or identify the on/off button may be perfectly capable of activating the computer using a tactile indicator. Moreover, for some students, the visual information they receive is so vague or unreliable that performing a task without using their vision may be more efficient. Thus, it is important to assess whether teaching a specific visual skill will actually improve the student's ability to function.

Training Residual and Alternative Senses

Senses are the way we perceive what is occurring in our environment. We use our senses in coordination with one another to interpret our world. Sensation is simply the ability of a specific organ (eye, ear) to gather information from our environment. What we do with this information, the integration of what is heard or seen, for example, is how we actually are able to form concepts about what we have received. Our ability to effectively use and understand the information our senses gather affects our ability to perform. For individuals with intact vision and hearing, 99 percent of learning occurs through vision and hearing, with 80 percent a result of the visual sense. When a student has reduced ability to see or hear, the other senses must take over as information gatherers (Gee, Atwell, Graham, & Goetz, 1994).

Gee and colleagues (1994) described our senses using two parameters—*distance* senses and *impact* senses (see Figure 9.1, p. 173). Vision, hearing, and smell are distance senses. We use these senses to gather information from a distance, prior to encountering things physically. Taste, touch, and kinesthetic feedback (a sense mediated by end organs located in muscles, tendons, and joints and stimulated by body movement and tensions) are

BOX **9.1**

Making the Preschool Classroom Louder and More Colorful

Here comes Jack. It's his first day of preschool. Jack hears nothing and sees nothing. The bulletin board outside the classroom has Styrofoam apples tacked to it with the children's names written below them. The writing is done with straws. As Jack's hand runs across the apples, he feels the rough Styrofoam, then the long, smooth straw. J-A-C-K . . . he smiles. And the teacher smiles; she has just become a part of Jack's world, Jack's team. She "speaks" his language.

A young student with vision and hearing impairment is a foreigner in a regular education classroom. The brightly colored red apples with each child's name written in a glittery gold paint pen cannot be seen. The laughter and giggling of toddlers cannot be heard, nor can their toothy grins or shy eyes be seen. This child enters a world of silence and darkness that holds no more possibilities than the car ride to school, the dentist's office, or the grocery store. Until someone opens their door—a door that is slightly different in color, has a different feel, and creaks at a slightly higher pitch than the one into the classroom. Opening that door requires a few extra things, a few added keys, one more lock, but all within reach.

Ms. Passman knows that the most critical aspect of communication is flexibility, both in thoughts and actions. The ability to alter methods and means in order to match those of another is essential to open the door between the two. Jack's smile at the recognition of his name on the bulletin board is his way of saying "Wow! That's me!" in the perfect number of words—none.

At the preschool level, exploration is key. The hands are the sensory input systems for the child with multiple disabilities including vision and hearing loss. Ms. Passman provides three-dimensional communication books that allow him to thumb through his choices, reading with his fingers until his want or need is identified. She provides a toothbrush to indicate time to brush teeth, sandpaper for the tactile table, Legos for the building area, a paintbrush for the art table.

Ms. Passman knows that assistive technology devices can help Jack understand cause and effect. She programs a big red switch with appropriate responses allowing one of Jack's peers to record his voice. Snack time proves to be the ideal time and place to use the switch. "I want a cookie, please." "Apple juice for me." All of Jack's classmates want to take a turn recording their voice and helping Jack activate his switch. Jack opens his eyes wide in fear when the fire alarm goes off. He hears that loud sound. He wrinkles his nose in disgust when they cook cabbage. He doesn't like that smell. His favorite place to sit is near the window on a sunny day. He sees bright light or certainly can feel heat and locate the window. His hand reaches out to his neighbor. He wants help.

---

impact senses. We are only able to use them to gather information when we come into physical contact with a person, object, or environmental event. When either or both of the primary distance senses of vision and hearing are impaired, students have difficulty discriminating, recognizing, or interpreting what is happening until they actually make physical contact with the stimulus. For example, when a student with visual and hearing disabilities enters the lunch line, she will be unable to see the food or hear a description of what is being offered. She might be able to smell the various odors emanating from the food, but lacking additional visual or auditory cues, be unable to identify the entrée as hamburger or hamburger pizza. It is only when she is able to physically touch or taste the food that she is able to discriminate her choices. Thus, students with multiple disabilities including vision and

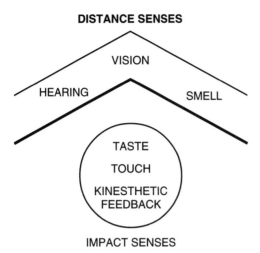

FIGURE 9.1   Distance and impact senses in relationship to the individual.

hearing loss are at a distinct disadvantage in interacting with their environment. Our goal as educators is to determine the student's best means for receiving information, how we will adapt our instructional techniques to take into consideration his or her unique needs and capabilities, and how the student will be allowed to demonstrate his or her knowledge and participate in the environment.

Gee and colleagues (1994) described several strategies that can assist students with visual and hearing disabilities to use their senses more optimally. They suggest it is the educator's responsibility to determine which distance and impact senses will be naturally available to the learner, and what additional information could be enhanced or added to facilitate understanding and interpretation of what is occurring around the student. As information gathering is facilitated, the natural order of delivery—distance to impact senses—should be followed. This means, for example, that if a particular stimulus is traditionally encountered visually, the educator should help the student access the information using residual vision if possible. Perhaps an enhancement such as increasing the light source or providing for greater visual contrast (set the slice of pizza on a solid gray background) will increase the chance for visual access. Educators may also need to allow time for processing sensory information. Finally, we must determine a way of measuring whether the student is, in fact, gaining the information desired and is able to anticipate and interpret individual objects, persons, and environments appropriately.

Educators use the information provided from assessment and interaction with the other individuals on the educational team to augment instruction for students with multiple disabilities (see Box 9.2, p. 174). This is why it is so critical to communicate with all disciplines and to take into consideration all of the student's various disabilities. Knowing what a student sees and hears or how the individual moves and communicates will enable us to plan our instructional strategies and be consistent across those who come into contact and interact with the student. For example, can he see better in low light, can he respond to environmental

BOX **9.2**

Who's on Matt's Team?

Thirteen-year-old Matt has a moderate-severe sensorineural hearing loss and is also blind. Although he is ambulatory, he has hemiplegia cerebral palsy with his left side affected and is often pushed from one place to another in a wheelchair. He wears bilateral hearing aids but is able to use headphones to listen to music if the tape player is turned up to full volume. Matt is in the general education classroom and also participates in physical education, art, and music. He has a full-time paraprofessional who is with him throughout the day. His team has scheduled a meeting to update his instructional program.

Who is on Matt's team? Cindy, Matt's mom; the special education teacher, Mr. Jackson; the physical therapist, Tammy; the occupational therapist, Trish; the orientation and mobility specialist, Mark; Matt's paraprofessional, Jamie; the speech-language pathologist, Carla; the deaf-blind specialist, Jenna; the homeroom general education teacher, Mrs. Kane; and the technology specialist, Kelly. Is anyone missing? Perhaps the school psychologist, since he or she often serves as IEP coordinator in districts. Certainly it would be nice if the building principal attended the meetings.

Matt also has some extended team members. They include Dan, the bus driver, who is with Matt twice a day. It is extremely important for him to be aware of Matt's behavior, communication, and sensory needs. It's his job to keep Matt and his peers safely in check every day. His art, music, and PE teachers are also a part of Matt's extended team. They can provide good information on his performance in their classes, especially since he attends PE without Jamie, his paraprofessional. Ruth, who works the food line in the cafeteria, is also a part of Matt's extended team. She is in contact with him every day at lunch and provides support in the lunchroom. Ruth makes sure that Matt makes it through lunch in the middle school cafeteria unscathed.

Not everyone who plays a part in Matt's educational day will attend the team meeting, but input will be solicited from all of them around a specific agenda. The principal has agreed to free up anyone who wants to attend and who might need to have personal face-to-face input around a need or concern. The agenda has been set and circulated to all interested parties via e-mail. Matt's portfolio, including a videotape of him at home and participating in a variety of activities at school has been made available. The team is well versed in the four Fs of teaming: (1) forming (building trust), (2) functioning (they have a means to communicate and a leader who will make sure they accomplish their task in a timely manner), (3) formulating (they will problem solve the issues that are brought to the meeting and formulate a plan), and (4) fermenting—because they have a mutual trust among the members and a method for resolving conflict, a strong and effective program will be developed for Matt.

---

sounds when they are loud enough, can he participate in an art activity if he is positioned in such a way that he can extend his arm? If everyone has knowledge of the student's best way for gathering information and interacting with the environment, it will aid us in facilitating learning.

Concepts must be introduced through more than one sensory avenue. Common ways in which typically developing peers gain information (e.g., observation, listening, oral explanation, visual modeling) may not be effective for students with multiple disabilities. Gee and colleagues (1994) suggested that educators introduce new concepts via more than one informational source. It is also helpful to organize opportunities to explore persons, objects, and environments using the alternative senses of taste, touch, and kinesthetic feedback. Manipulation and direct contact with the "real thing" is very important for students with multiple disabilities. Moreover, a student's motivation to interact may be reduced because of the lack of feedback from the natural environment and the lack of distance cues. The educator may be able to analyze the characteristics of a concept, situation, or activity, for example, and determine alternative ways in which the student can gain information and participate. Peers can and should be included in this process on an ongoing basis. For instance, if the students in a preschool classroom are learning about spring using the more traditional instructional methods of looking at pictures and reading stories, include all of the children in determining what makes them think of spring (e.g., flowers, warm days, wearing fewer clothes when playing outside). Then encourage everyone to come up with ways to illustrate these things using just the tactile sense, or the sense of smell. In that way, everyone can be a part of designing activities that allow the student with disabilities to both participate and learn the concept of "springness."

Cortical Visual Impairment

As described earlier, cortical visual impairment refers to damage to the ocular area or to lesions of the posterior visual pathway (from the lateral geniculate body to the visual cortex) and is often referred to as cortical blindness (Jan & Groenveld, 1993). This implies no sensory visual responsiveness but most children with a lesion in the visual cortex have some residual vision, hence the term "cortical visual impairment" or CVI. According to Good and colleagues (1994), given the high incidence that residual vision will be present, CVI is a more appropriate term. Some professionals say that CVI is "nothing more than a fancy term for brain damage"; however, the majority of children with documented brain damage are not visually impaired (Groenveld, Jan, & Leader, 1990, p. 13). According to Jan and Wong (1991), approximately 50 percent of all students with congenital ocular abnormalities have additional disabilities, whereas all students with CVI have associated neurological problems. It follows, then, that a number of students with multiple disabilities will have accompanying CVI. Given this probability, it is important to look at the difference between ocular impairments and CVI, and the implications for assessment and intervention.

Baker-Nobles and Rutherford (1995) described both physical and behavioral differences between the two conditions. Students with ocular impairment and some residual vision display the following characteristics. The eyes may look abnormal, visual behavior is generally consistent, and they are able to maintain visual fixation. There is often the presence of sensory nystagmus (drifting or jerky eye oscillations) and an inability to use the eyes to scan the environment. Visual attention span is often normal in students with ocular problems, and if they have peripheral-vision problems, they turn their heads to compensate. Conversely, students with CVI will have eyes that appear normal, and rather than sensory nystagmus they may have motor nystagmus, an unsteady, tremulous fixation of gaze that is due to impaired control from the brain. Students with CVI often exhibit short visual attention spans and use their peripheral vision for looking. They will make a characteristic head turn when looking at or reaching for an object. They do not appear to be actually looking at the object, but are, in fact, using their peripheral vision to locate the visual stimulus. Students with ocular disorders that include peripheral field loss are able to use their heads to scan the environment while students with CVI are often unable to do this.

While it is common for both students with ocular problems and with CVI to lean toward or bring objects closer to their eyes, those with ocular impairment do so for magnification (closer is bigger); students with CVI do so to reduce "crowding" the visual field with background information (Jan & Groenveld, 1993). In this manner, they fill their visual field with a single object, reducing the amount of nonessential visual information from the background. Students with CVI often are compulsive light gazers while those with ocular problems are not. Conversely, eye pressing is prevalent in individuals with ocular disorder where there is retinal involvement and it is almost never evident in students with CVI (Jan, Groenveld, & Sykanda, 1990). Color perception in both groups depends on the amount of residual vision as well as the specific diagnosis. It was noted, however, that students with CVI generally had intact color perception since it has bilateral hemisphere representation and requires fewer functioning neurons than does form perception. Moreover, students with CVI seem particularly attracted to bright colors such as red and yellow. Light sensitivity is also present in about one-third of the students with CVI and can be present also when there is ocular impairment (Jan & Groenveld, 1993).

What does this mean to educators of students with multiple disabilities? Certainly, the characteristics of each type of visual impairment can provide valuable information that can be used for student assessment. Additionally, it has programming implications for the student suspected of having CVI. Techniques that involve environmental modification and adaptation to optimize visual responding will be helpful. Simplify the visual field, provide high contrast and low glare when placing objects for identification, and use color (particularly reds and yellows). For example, at mealtime students might use red silverware that is placed on a gray background with no pattern. Also, students with CVI usually have an easier time processing two-dimensional information rather than three-dimensional. Consequently, they often respond better to information presented on a computer screen than to an actual physical object (Baker-Nobles & Rutherford, 1995). Teach visual scanning when moving since students with CVI may be unable to scan by simply moving their heads. Hang simple pictures without a lot of visual clutter down the school hallway (e.g., a red ball or a green tree). In this way, visual scan can occur without the student having to move the head. He or she simply moves or is moved along the hallway, and the movement does the visual scanning for the student. In addition, the scanning occurs peripherally, often the preferred visual field for students with CVI.

Orientation and Mobility for Students with Multiple Disabilities Including Visual Impairment

As discussed earlier, students with multiple disabilities may have an orientation and mobility (O & M) specialist as a part of their educational team. O & M specialists are trained and certified to teach individuals with vision impairment to use their compensatory senses to achieve safe and efficient travel in the environment. Traditionally, O & M instruction has been part of a medical model of service delivery, a model that typically addresses a specific need or problem area (Bailey & Head, 1993). In the medical model, the disability defines the approach used, and often isolated therapy is provided that builds on a hierarchy of progression through a series of skills, each dependent on the mastering of the previous one. Students with multiple disabilities, however, may be unable to master skills in a developmental sequence. They may also have difficulty generalizing skills learned in one environment to another (York et al., 1985). The result is that training for one specific area may not take into consideration the other disabilities found in this population, including communication, motor, and sensory needs. Professionals trained in the medical model may also be uncomfortable or feel inadequate providing training to students with additional disabilities (Erin, Daugherty, Dignan, & Pearson, 1990).

In a true transdisciplinary approach, orientation and mobility instruction would be provided within meaningful sequences of skill instruction in combination with addressing the student's other disabilities. Also, the determination of the specific skills to be taught and the appropriate instructional strategies will be based on what is functional for the student. Bailey and Head (1993) contend that "learning to trail along a wall that is never traveled is of no value" (p. 45). It is much more appropriate to choose environments for training that will be used frequently by the student. For example, while a student is delivering the lunch count, he is taught to trail the wall to reach the office. If the student also has motor impairment, he can trail the wall while being transported in his wheelchair and indicate anticipation of direction change by leaning the appropriate way when the next hallway is reached.

Bailey and Head (1993) view the role of the O & M specialist in a transdisciplinary model as a collaborative team effort. This involves consultation with all members of the team including teachers, paraprofessionals, parents, and other educators providing direct or consultative services to the student with multiple disabilities. Once the team has determined the necessary skills to be learned, integrated O & M training occurs in combination with the communication, motor, and sensory instructional goals and builds on the student's existing skill repertoire. Assessment and training occurs in the natural environment where the skill will be used. The O & M specialist makes programming recommendations based on the travel and participation needs of the student.

While it is evident that a student's cognitive, motor, communication, and sensory abilities will directly influence the acquisition of orientation and mobility skills, a number of professionals believe that the development of even semi-independent travel skills are important for students with multiple disabilities (Bailey & Head, 1993; Gee et al., 1995). This includes the need for O & M instruction and practice distributed across the day and in various settings. Pogrund and colleagues (1993) recommend that the O & M specialist choose skills to be taught by "skipping around" and beginning lower on the skill hierarchy.

Another development in orientation and mobility training involves training toddlers and preschoolers using both adapted equipment and methods (Pogrund, Fazzi, & Lampert, 1992). One of the first modifications occurred with a long cane that was adapted for use with a young child with multiple disabilities (Kronick, 1987). Push toys and the variety of stand-behind walkers available for infants learning to walk can be used by young children with multiple disabilities including visual impairments. Not only do these devices allow the child access to the environment and promote self-movement and self-confidence, but they are normalizing and age appropriate.

The choice of skills and travel routes are dependent on both the capabilities of the student and travel needs related to age. For example, a kindergartner may need to travel from the play area to the front of the room for show-and-tell, a middle school student may travel between classrooms, and a high school student may want to get from the swimming pool to the locker room or to a job in the community. Given these individual needs, the O & M specialist along with the teacher should conduct a structured observation of the critical activity and environment, analyze the travel components, identify skills to be targeted for instruction, and build training times into the context of the student's day. Finally, consideration must be made for the student's other disabilities. If hearing is limited, alternatives to auditory cues and signals must be determined. For the student with motor impairment or limited range of motion, curb detectors can be attached to the wheelchair to aid in the identification of barriers and obstacles (Gee et al., 1995). Tactile maps are used for route delineation as well as to assist students who are nonverbal and/or have cognitive disabilities.

For students with multiple disabilities, problems with balance and coordination often occur when there is a hearing loss present. Students with motor impairments can have limited range of motion of limbs and body. Individuals with visual impairments often have difficulty orienting their bodies in space. While viewed as an underlying or pre-skill for mobility training, specific orientation training can be appropriate even when mobility is not the ultimate goal. These orientation skills include balance, trunk control, being able to identify one's location within space in relation to the walls and ceiling, and knowing whether one is in an enclosed space or outside. Teach awareness of space using tactile cues such as the feel of air currents within enclosed versus open space, the difference in heat or light when seated near a window, and the use of residual hearing to orient one's location in a room. Placing a young child on his or her back in a "small room" made of cardboard, with toys hanging within reach of his or her random movements and various tactile coverings such as foam or furry fabric, will provide a means for orienting the body in space as well as encourage tactile exploration.

Motor Skills

Cerebral palsy is not a static disability. As the child grows and changes in size and development, his or her motor disability will change as well. According to Pellegrino and Meyer (1998), the implications of a motor disability impact students differently based on their stage of life. For example, the inability to walk is very different for a toddler than it is for an adolescent. While the toddler may desire independence, the adolescent could be more concerned about drooling and speech difficulties associated with oral-motor dysfunction. Thus, it is important for the educational team to take into consideration the motor needs of the student in relationship to each life stage, as well as the impact of the growing student on families and educators when it comes to lifting and positioning.

Issues surrounding the positioning and handling of the student with motor disabilities related to assessment of vision and hearing use have been discussed above. There are many excellent resources that deal with the physiological aspects of motor disabilities including cerebral palsy (Batshaw, 1997; Bobath, 1980; Dormans, 1993; Dormans & Pellegrino, 1998; Glenn & Whyte, 1990; Miller et al., 1995). For the purposes of this chapter, emphasis will be placed on motor issues related to programming for students with multiple disabilities.

The rationale for proper positioning of students with motor disabilities is based on the following: (a) maintaining proper body alignment to prevent scoliosis, skull deformities, and hip subluxation or dislocation; (b) normalizing muscle tone; (c) diminishing primitive reflexes; (d) maintaining passive and active range of motion; (e) preventing skin breakdown; and (f) facilitating acquisition of perceptual, cognitive, and motor skills. Proper positioning can aid in the acquisition of skills by allowing the student to interact with the environment, be involved in social interaction, and facilitate play. Pellegrino and Meyer (1998) state that proper positioning geared to age and functioning level is a key intervention for handling the tone and movement abnormalities associated with cerebral palsy. Table 9.1 provides a list of recommendations for positioning students with motor disabilities. Attention to functional seating with the use of a variety of positioning and mobility devices available may have long-term benefits in the prevention of contractures and joint deformities related to spasticity. Seating and mobility devices also provide independence

TABLE 9.1   Positioning Guidelines and Recommendations for Students with Motor Disabilities

A. Prone position
   1. Prone position stimulates head and trunk control.
   2. It aids in upper extremity weight bearing.
   3. Position the student over wedge or bolster to bring arms forward in position for manipulating objects.

B. Supine position
   1. In general, supine is a position to avoid unless recommended by a therapist who states a clearly defined purpose.
   2. This position, used in conjunction with a firm bolster under the base of the neck, inhibits total extension and prevents the back of the head from receiving stimulation that might result in total extension.
   3. Use head rests when the student is in this position to maintain midline position.
   4. Shoulders should be positioned forward and hips and knees flexed.

C. Sidelying
   1. Sidelying offers a stable position for students with athetosis and helps promote flexion on the "up" side and extension on the "down" side.
   2. Sidelying allows the student to use his or her upper extremities.

D. Sitting
   1. Discourage frog or "W" sitting position.
   2. Encourage long sitting—legs extended.
   3. Encourage side sitting, alternating sides to foster symmetrical muscle development.
   4. The use of a corner seating device provides stability for students who display athetosis or others who lack independent sitting skills but have sufficient trunk extension.
   5. Encourage trunk and hip rotation as many ways as possible.

E. Standing
   1. This position is important because it provides weight-bearing experience.
   2. The lower extremities should be symmetrical.
   3. Kneeling is the transition position prior to standing.

and increase opportunities for play, learning, and socialization. For example, a student can be placed in a prone standing device allowing her to be upright at a level with her peers and capable of using her hands to interact with classroom materials. Table 9.2 provides directions for handling students with multiple disabilities to encourage appropriate motor development and control.

Educators also advocate the use of assistive technology with students with multiple disabilities. Assistive devices can provide access to a variety of environments, enhance communication and mobility, supplement instruction and maintain health (Turnbull et al., 2002). While these devices can range from very simple (Velcro or molded plastic) to extremely "high tech" (computerized communication devices), the overall goal for their use is to provide the student with motor disabilities with greater independence, access, and ultimately, a better quality of life.

There are several issues surrounding the use of assistive technology with students who have multiple disabilities. First, there is the issue of funding. While low-tech devices can be constructed from inexpensive materials, the need to purchase high-tech equipment can make administrators cringe. The Technology-Related Assistance to Individuals with Disabilities Act of 1988 (Bryant & Seay, 1998) provides for federal funds that are granted to states to help create statewide programs for acquisition and delivery of assistive technology devices and services to individuals with disabilities. This includes students in educational settings and can be a resource for educational teams seeking both consultation regarding the appropriateness of a particular device, as well as assistance in acquiring it.

TABLE 9.2   Directions for Handling Students with Motor Disabilities

A. Tell the student what you are going to do before you handle him or her.
  1. Attempt to elicit a response indicating awareness that he or she is about to be moved.
  2. Lifting the student is the first step in assisted transfer.
  3. Moving the student gives him or her opportunities to practice movement patterns.

B. Do not pick the student up under the arms.

C. Handle the student slowly.

D. Give as little support as is necessary for safety. Allow the student to provide as much postural stability as necessary.

E. If the student has a total extension pattern, flex the neck, use rotation to bring the student to a sitting position, and carry him or her in a seated position if possible.
  1. Avoid contact with the back of the head and the balls of the feet because stimulation to these areas can trigger extensions.
  2. Carry the student with knees flexed and legs abducted.

F. When in supine, a student with spasticity should be moved to a sitting position before lifting.
  1. The student can be brought to a sitting position by flexing the neck, bringing the shoulders forward, and bending forward at the hips.
  2. Carry a student with athetosis in a sitting position, controlling the arms and leg movements. If the student lacks head control, carry him or her in the prone position.

A second issue concerns the choice of an appropriate assistive communication device for students with multiple disabilities. Assistive technology can provide a means for individuals who have little or no communication abilities to "augment" their verbal expression. The American Speech-Language-Hearing Association (ASHA, 1989) provides the following definition for augmentative communication services:

> *An area of clinical practice that attempts to compensate (either temporarily or permanently) for the impairment and disability patterns of individuals with severe expressive communication disorders (i.e., the severely speech-language and writing impaired). (p. 107)*

Many of the assistive devices are based on a symbolic language system and can involve very simple picture boards as well as high-tech computers with synthesized voice output. Often these symbol-based devices are prescribed for students who are at a non-symbolic communication level. In other words, the symbols and what they represent are meaningless for the student. When they have difficulty learning to use the device, families and educators may become extremely frustrated.

Burnstein, Wright-Drechsel, and Wood (1998) suggest that educators conduct a needs assessment when deciding on the purchase of an augmentative communication device for students with multiple disabilities. The initial assessment would involve four phases. First, gather information about the student's capabilities and needs. This should include information about the processing of auditory, visual, tactile, vestibular, proprioceptive, and kinesthetic input. The status of the student's sensory and motor capabilities will influence both whether a device is appropriate and the type of input and output desired. Second, cognition level should be determined. The authors state that an understanding of cause and effect (e.g., touching a switch activates this toy) is critical for the child to benefit from assistive technology. Third, a speech-language pathologist can provide information about the student's functional communication status (i.e., whether he or she has a formal comprehension of language both expressive and receptive). Finally, a student's musculoskeletal/neuromotor status should be assessed including range of motion, postural alignment, muscle tone, balance, and postural responses. Since children with cerebral palsy often have significant motor dysfunction, their individual motor capabilities will shape both the appropriateness of a device and the type of equipment that is chosen.

Conclusion

Serving students with multiple disabilities including significant sensory and motor needs appropriately in inclusive educational settings can be a daunting endeavor for families and educators. A successful outcome requires collaboration and planning among large numbers of individuals. While communication among everyone involved with these students remains critical, the philosophy that was stated initially is still the most important basis for our efforts. While the multiplicity of disabilities can have a definite impact on the way in which we serve these students, all students despite the extent of their disabilities have a right to be treated as a whole person. They all have value and the potential to learn.

References

American Speech-Language-Hearing Association. (1989). Competencies for speech-language pathologists providing services in augmentative communication. *Journal of the American Speech-Language-Hearing Association, 31,* 107–110.

Bailey, B. R., & Head, D. N. (1993). Orientation and mobility services to children and youth with multiple disabilities. *RE:view, 25*(2), 57–66.

Baker-Nobles, L., & Rutherford, A. (1995). Understanding cortical visual impairments in children. *American Journal of Occupational Therapy, 49,* 899–903.

Batshaw, M. L. (2002). *Children with disabilities* (5th ed.). Baltimore: Paul H. Brookes.

Bobath, K. (1980). A neurophysical basis for the treatment of cerebral palsy. *Clinics in Developmental Medicine, 75,* 77–87.

Bryant, B., & Seay, P. C. (1998). The Technology-Related Assistance to Individuals with Disabilities Act: Relevance to individuals with learning disabilities and their advocates. *Journal of Learning Disabilities, 31,* 4–15.

Burstein, J. R., Wright-Drechsel, M. L., & Wood, L. (1998). Assistive technology. In J. P. Dormans & L. Pellegrino (Eds.), *Caring for children with cerebral palsy: A team approach.* Baltimore: Paul H. Brookes.

Campbell, P. H. (1987). The integrated programming team: An approach for coordinating professionals of various disciplines in programs for students with severe and multiple handicaps. *Journal of the Association for Persons with Severe Handicaps, 12,* 107–116.

Dormans, J. P. (1993). Orthopedic management of children with cerebral palsy. *Pediatric Clinics of North America, 3,* 645–652.

Dormans, J. P., & Pellegrino, L. (1998). *Caring for children with cerebral palsy.* Baltimore: Paul H. Brookes.

Erin, J., Daugherty, W., Dignan, K., & Pearson, R. (1990). Teaching visually handicapped students with multiple disabilities: Perceptions of adequacy. *Journal of Visual Impairment and Blindness, 84,* 16–20.

Gee, K., Atwell, M., Graham, N., & Goetz, L. (1994). *Inclusive instructional design: Facilitating informed and active learning for individuals who are deaf-blind.* San Francisco: California Research Institute, San Francisco State University.

Gee, K., Houghton, J., Pogrund, R. L., & Rosenberg, R. (1995). Orientation and mobility: Access, information, and travel. In N. G. Haring & L. T. Romer (Eds.), *Welcoming students who are deaf-blind into typical classrooms: Facilitating school participation, learning, and friendships.* Baltimore: Paul H. Brookes.

Glenn, M. B., & Whyte, J. (1990). *The practical management of spasticity in children and adults.* Philadelphia: Lea and Febiger.

Goetz, L., & Gee, K. (1987). Teaching visual attention in functional contexts: Acquisition and generalization of complex visual motor skills. *Journal of Visual Impairment and Blindness, 81,* 115–118.

Good, W. V., Jan, J. E., DeSa, L., Barkovich, A. J., Groenveld, M., & Hoyt, C. S. (1994). Cortical visual impairment in children. *Survey of Ophthalmology, 38,* 351–361.

Groenveld, M., Jan, J. E., & Leader, P. (1990, January). Observations on the habilitation of children with cortical visual impairment. *Journal of Visual Impairment and Blindness,* 11–15.

Haring, N. G. (Ed.) (1988). *Generalization for students with severe handicaps: Strategies and solutions.* Seattle: University of Washington Press.

Hill, J. L. (1999). *Meeting the needs of students with special physical and health needs.* Upper Saddle River, NJ: Merrill/Prentice-Hall.

Hord, S. M., Rutherford, W. L., Huling-Austin, L., & Hall, G. E. (1987). *Taking charge of change.* Alexandria, VA: Association for Supervision and Curriculum Development.

Jan, J. E., & Groenveld, M. (1993). Visual behaviors and adaptations associated with cortical and ocular impairment in children. *Journal of Visual Impairment and Blindness, 87,* 101–105.

Jan, J. E., & Groenveld, M., & Sykanda, A. M. (1990). Light gazing by visually impaired children. *Developmental Medicine and Child Neurology, 32,* 755–759.

Jan, J. E., & Wong, P. K. (1991). The child with cortical visual impairment. *Seminars in Ophthalmology, 6,* 194–200.

Johnson, D., & Johnson, F. (1987). *Joining together: Group theory and group skills.* Englewood Cliffs, NJ: Prentice-Hall.

Kronick, M. K. (1987). Children and canes: An adaptive approach. *Journal of Visual Impairment and Blindness, 81,* 61–62.

Lipsky, D. K., & Gartner, A. (1997). *Inclusion and school reform: Transforming America's classrooms.* Baltimore: Paul H. Brookes.

Menacker, S. J. (1993). Visual function in children with developmental disabilities. *Pediatric Clinics of North America, 40,* 659–675.

Miller, F., Bacharach, S. J., Boos, M. L., et al. (1995). *Cerebral palsy: A complete guide for caregiving.* Baltimore: Johns Hopkins University Press.

Orelove, F. P., & Sobsey, D. (1991). *Educating children with multiple disabilities: A transdisciplinary approach* (2nd ed.). Baltimore: Paul H. Brookes.

Pellegrino, L., & Meyer, G. (1998). Interdisciplinary care of the child with cerebral palsy. In J. P. Dormans & L. Pellegrino (Eds.), *Caring for children with cerebral palsy.* Baltimore: Paul H. Brookes.

Pogrund, R. L., Fazzi, D. L., & Lampert, J. S. (1992). *Early focus: Working with young blind and visually impaired children and their families.* New York: American Foundation for the Blind.

Pogrund, R., Healy, G., Jones, K., Levack, N., Martin-Curry, S., Martinez, C., Marz, J., Roberson-Smith, B., & Vrba, A. (1993). *Teaching age-appropriate purposeful skills (TAPS): An orientation and mobility curriculum for students with visual impairments.* Austin: Texas School for the Blind and Visually Impaired.

Rainforth, B. (2000). Preparing teachers to educate students with severe disabilities in inclusive settings despite contextual constraints. *Journal of the Association for Persons with Severe Handicaps, 25,* 83–91.

Rainforth, B., York, J., & Macdonald, C. (1992). *Collaborative teams for students with severe disabilities: Integrating therapy and educational services.* Baltimore: Paul H. Brookes.

Sacks, S. Z., & Silberman, R. K. (1998). *Educating students who have visual impairments with other disabilities.* Baltimore: Paul H. Brookes.

Schwartz, I. S. (1995). Using social-validity assessments to identify meaningful outcomes for students with deaf-blindness. In N. G. Haring & L. T. Romer (Eds.), *Welcoming students who are deaf-blind into typical classrooms: Facilitating school participation, learning, and friendships.* Baltimore: Paul H. Brookes.

Siegel-Causey, E., & Bashinski, S. (1997). Enhancing initial communication and responsiveness of learners with multiple disabilities: A tri-focus framework for partners. *Focus on Autism and Other Developmental Disabilities, 12,* 105–120.

Soto, G., & Goetz, L. (1998). Self-efficacy beliefs and the education of students with severe disabilities. *Journal of the Association for Persons with Severe Handicaps, 23,* 134–143.

Thousand, J., & Villa, R. (1992). Collaborative teams: A powerful tool in school restructuring. In W. Stainback & S. Stainback (Eds.), *Support networks for inclusive schools.* Baltimore: Paul H. Brookes.

Turnbull, R., Turnbull, A., Shank, M., Smith, S., & Leal, D. (2002). *Exceptional lives: Special education in today's schools* (3rd ed.). Upper Saddle River, NJ: Merrill/Prentice-Hall.

Villa, R. A., Thousand, J. S., Meyers, H., & Nevin, A. I. (1996). Teacher and administrator perceptions of heterogeneous education. *Exceptional Children, 63,* 29–45.

Whiting, S., Jan, J. E., Wong, P. K., Ferrell, K. A., & McCormick, A. Q. (1985). Permanent cortical visual impairment in children. *Developmental Medicine and Child Neurology, 27,* 730–739.

York, J., Long, E., Caldwell, N., Brown, L., Zanella-Albright, K., Rogan, P., Shiraga, B., & Marks, J. (1985). Teamwork strategies for school and community instruction. In L. Brown, B. Shiraga, J. York, A. Udvari-Solner, K. Zanella-Albright, P. Rogan, E. McCarthy, & R. Loomis (Eds.), *Education program for students with severe intellectual disabilities* (vol. 15, pp. 229–276). Madison: University of Wisconsin-Madison and the Madison Metropolitan School District.

10 Directing Paraprofessional Work

MICHAEL F. GIANGRECO
University of Vermont

MARY BETH DOYLE
St. Michael's College

As a general or special educator there is no doubt that you will encounter paraprofessionals in the classrooms where you serve students with and without disabilities. Although paraprofessionals have been working in American schools for decades, particularly within remedial and special education programs, their presence in general education classrooms has increased dramatically over the past decade in response to a variety of factors. Some of these factors include shortages of certified educators, increasing requests for support services, and the increasing severity of needs presented by students with disabilities being included in general education classrooms. After reading this chapter you should be able to:

- Define the similarities and differences between teachers and paraprofessionals
- Describe different ways in which paraprofessionals can be effectively utilized in general education settings
- Suggest specific strategies that paraprofessionals can be taught to use to improve the quality of inclusive education
- Describe ways in which teachers can effectively monitor and provide feedback to paraprofessionals

Partial support for the preparation of this chapter was provided by the United States Department of Education, Office of Special Education and Rehabilitative Services, under the funding categories *Model Demonstration Projects for Children with Disabilities,* CFDA 84.324M (H324M980229), and *Personnel Preparation to Improve Services and Results for Children with Disabilities,* CFDA 84.325N (H325N98022), awarded to the Center on Disability and Community Inclusion at the University of Vermont. The contents of this paper reflect the ideas and positions of the authors and do not necessarily reflect the ideas or positions of the U.S. Department of Education; therefore, no official endorsement should be inferred.

The increase in paraprofessional support for students with disabilities and their changing roles within general education classrooms represents a significant change for many general educators who have been accustomed to working in relative isolation as the only adult in the classroom. It is also a change for special educators who may be used to having paraprofessionals work alongside them in special classes or resource rooms. Yet, for the most part, personnel preparation of both general and special educators at our colleges and universities has not accounted for this very significant change in service delivery that has accompanied the expansion of inclusive opportunities for students with severe disabilities (French & Pickett, 1997).

Given the scope and volume of new information, ideas, and skills that educators are asked to learn and apply, those related to directing the work of paraprofessionals often have taken a back seat. Only recently has there been an increased emphasis on this topic (Pickett & Gerlach, 1997; Salzberg & Morgan, 1995; Wallace, Shin, Bartholomay, & Stahl, 2001). In this chapter we begin by offering a brief overview explaining why it is important for educators to assume a leadership role to direct the work of paraprofessionals. Next, the majority of the chapter is devoted to describing four foundational aspects of directing the work of paraprofessionals: (1) welcoming and acknowledging the work of paraprofessionals, (2) orienting paraprofessionals to their roles in the school, classroom, and with assigned students; (3) planning for paraprofessionals, and (4) communicating with and providing feedback to paraprofessionals. Next we offer suggestions of where to look for online resources about paraprofessionals. The chapter concludes by considering criteria to determine whether your efforts to direct the work of paraprofessionals have been successful.

Why Is It Important to Learn about Directing the Work of Paraprofessionals?

The overarching reasons are quite straightforward. First, as a certified educator it is your professional responsibility to provide leadership in your classroom, which includes directing the work of paraprofessionals who will be working with the students for whom you share accountability. The Individuals with Disabilities Education Act Amendments of 1997 allow for paraprofessionals to assist in the provision of special education and related services, but require that they be appropriately trained and supervised. Second, what you do (or don't do) to direct the work of paraprofessionals *will* have an impact on your students with and without disabilities. Consider the following information from the professional literature about the utilization of paraprofessionals in inclusive schools.

When educators are asked what supports they need to successfully include a student with a severe disability in a general education classroom, invariably access to paraprofessional supports is high on the list (Werts, Wolery, Snyder, Caldwell, & Salisbury, 1996). In many schools, having a one-on-one paraprofessional accompany a student with a severe disability to class has become the primary mechanism to operationalize inclusive education (Giangreco, Broer, & Edelman, 1999). Paraprofessionals in inclusive classrooms are playing an increasingly prominent role in providing instruction for students with severe disabilities (Downing, Ryndak, & Clark, 2000; Giangreco, Broer, & Edelman, 2002; Minondo, Meyer, & Xin, 2001).

Recent literature has challenged the heavy reliance on the use of one-on-one paraprofessionals because it relegates to the least qualified staff the tasks of making decisions and implementing instruction for students with the most complex needs (Brown, Farrington, Ziegler, Knight, & Ross, 1999). Ironically, despite the proliferation of paraprofessional supports and a shift in their roles toward instruction, two comprehensive reviews of the literature indicate that there is no body of research data attesting to the efficacy of providing paraprofessional supports (Jones & Bender, 1993; Giangreco, Edelman, Broer, & Doyle, 2001).

Although many paraprofessionals obviously perform vital functions in schools and do valued work, it remains questionable whether what they *should* be doing is different than what they have been *asked* to do. The National Joint Committee on Learning Disabilities (1999) made their position on this issue clear when they stated, "The intent of using paraprofessionals is to supplement, not supplant, the work of the teacher/service provider" (p. 37). It is vital to remember that *you* are the trained professional educator. It is your responsibility to be the teacher of all the students in your classroom. Therefore, with your team, you should closely scrutinize the tasks you are asking paraprofessionals to perform to ensure that they are supplementing, not supplanting, roles that are appropriately those of qualified educators, special educators, or related services providers. Once appropriate roles are identified, paraprofessionals must be appropriately trained to carry out their roles given professionally prepared plans, sufficiently supported and supervised.

When paraprofessionals are left to fend for themselves without strong teacher leadership, as the literature suggests they frequently are, it can result in detrimental albeit unintended effects (Giangreco, Edelman, Luiselli, & MacFarland, 1997; Marks, Shrader, & Levine, 1999; Young, Simpson, Myles, & Kamps, 1997). Paraprofessional supports that are not well designed can interfere with peer relationships, gender identity, and appropriate personal control. Inappropriate or excessive reliance on paraprofessionals can isolate the student within the classroom, establish insular paraprofessional-student relationships, and create unhealthy dependencies. Most notably, when a paraprofessional's role is allowed to become too prominent or exclusive it can interfere with educators getting directly involved with their students who have disabilities, which in turn can limit a student's access to competent instruction (Giangreco, Broer, & Edelman, 2001). Taken together, the impact of ill-conceived paraprofessional supports potentially can have a detrimental impact on a host of academic, functional, social, and personal student outcomes. The good news is that as a professional educator you can play a critical role in designing paraprofessional supports in such a manner that ensures that all the students in your classroom, including those with severe disabilities, are included meaningfully, socially and instructionally, and supported in appropriate ways. Your efforts can contribute to improving the capacity of paraprofessionals to be of assistance in the classroom while simultaneously contributing to their productivity and job satisfaction.

Directing the Work of Paraprofessionals

The following four sections are offered to assist general and special educators engage in leadership activities to direct the work of paraprofessionals. The categories of content reflected in these four sections—(1) welcoming and acknowledging paraprofessionals, (2) orienting paraprofessionals, (3) planning for paraprofessionals, and (4) communicating with and providing feedback to paraprofessionals—are based on a set of training materials titled, *Teacher Leadership: Working with Paraeducators* (Giangreco, 2001). These training materials, designed for general and special educators, are specifically geared toward directing the work of paraprofessionals in inclusive classrooms. They emphasize the roles of paraprofessionals *assisting* in the provision of special education given professionally prepared plans and under the direction and supervision of a qualified educator. These materials include some overlapping content with other contemporary sources. For example, Wallace, Shin, Bartholomay, and Stahl (2001) recently studied knowledge and skill competencies for teachers directing the work of paraprofessionals across seven areas:

- Communication with paraprofessionals
- Planning and scheduling
- Instructional support
- Modeling for paraprofessionals
- Public relations
- Training
- Management of paraprofessionals

Responses from 569 administrators, educators, and paraprofessionals indicated that competencies within these seven categories were considered important, but that they were not demonstrated at a level commensurate with their reported importance. Teachers who did not demonstrate these important competencies cited lack of preservice preparation or professional staff development opportunities as primary reasons (Wallace et al., 2001). This finding is consistent with an earlier study by French (1998b) that indicated some teachers were reluctant to supervise paraprofessionals and reported that they were not trained to do so.

Perhaps more than any single leadership attribute of an effective professional is the ability to critically self-assess and utilize the insights gained through such reflection to take constructive actions toward personal and programmatic improvement. Toward that end, the *Self-Assessment Preview* (Giangreco, 2001) (see Figure 10.1, pp. 190–191), consisting of a 12-item rubric, provides a simple format for educators to reflect upon some of their own leadership activities in directing the work of paraprofessionals. Before reading the next four subsections, please take a few minutes to consider your own status in reference to the 12 items in the *Self-Assessment Preview*.

Welcoming and Acknowledging Paraprofessionals

As educators, part of our role is to create welcoming environments that are conducive to learning, both for students and adults who are part of the classroom community. You can begin to foster a sense of welcome through simple acts of kindness. Put the paraprofessional's name on the door with yours. Be certain the paraprofessional has a place of his or her own in the classroom (e.g., desk, table). You might even put a coffee cup or a plant on this desk at the beginning of the year. Not only can such gestures go a long way toward establishing and maintaining a positive relationship with the paraprofessional, they can serve as models of genuine thoughtfulness that will be observed by your students.

An initial step to acknowledge the important role of the paraprofessional is to establish routines that communicate to the students that the teachers and paraprofessionals are operating together to support the work of the classroom. For example, at the beginning and end of the day have the paraprofessional join you in greeting students and be included in some aspect of the daily classroom meeting or participate in an end of class routine.

Another way to acknowledge the work, skills, and experiences of the paraprofessional is to create formal or informal opportunities to provide suggestions and input. For example, when planning a new unit you might say, "Here are the goals of this unit. Here are Sarah's goals [a student with severe disabilities] within this unit. Do you have any thoughts about her participation?" Even though it will be the responsibility of the general and special educators to plan the curriculum, instruction, and data collection, often paraprofessionals will bring insights and ideas that can contribute to improving program quality.

Remember to say "Thank you" regularly. Be specific in your thanks so that paraprofessionals can easily see the value of their work and its connection to the overall program. For example, "Thank you for doing hall duty and photocopying today; it allowed me to spend extra time helping Sam with his reading," or "I appreciate how respectful you are when you take care of John's personal needs. It is so important to provide those supports with the level of dignity John deserves. I think he really appreciates it—I know I do." Modeling acknowledgment and value for the full range of instructional and noninstructional classroom tasks, big and small, can help create a classroom culture where acknowledgment is the norm. As a result, you might be surprised at how much of that is observed, and hopefully applied, by your students!

Although symbolic forms of welcome and acknowledgment are appreciated by many paraprofessionals, these gestures are received more favorably when the paraprofessionals' roles are clarified and appropriate, they are adequately oriented to their jobs, and professionals take the time to provide initial and ongoing training (Giangreco et al., 2001). The following sections discuss these and others topics in more detail.

Orienting Paraprofessionals

Part of teacher leadership involves orienting paraprofessionals to the school, the classroom, and the students with whom they will be working (Doyle & Lee, 1997). Recent research suggests that too many paraprofessionals are inadequately oriented and report feeling "thrown into things" (Giangreco et al., 2001, p. 492). Providing multifaceted orientation sends a message of value to paraprofessionals that their work is important. It is also a logical first step toward establishing collaborative relationships with paraprofessionals. The term *orientation* is used broadly in this context to include both initial orientation to the school and classroom (e.g., routines, policies) as well as orientation to the students the paraprofessional will assist in supporting. This includes initial and ongoing training and role clarification.

School and classroom. Start by introducing the paraprofessional to other members of the school community (e.g., office personnel, teachers, school nurse, librarian, other paraprofessionals, maintenance personnel). This could be done in conjunction with a tour of the school building, highlighting places that you or your students use frequently (e.g., library,

FIGURE 10.1 Self-Assessment Preview.

Name: **Job Title:**   **Years of Experience:**

Date: **Course Instructor:**   **Course Site:**

PURPOSE: This Self-Assessment Preview is designed to assist course participants in considering their own work with paraeducators at the outset of the mini-course titled "Teacher Leadership: Working with Paraeducators." The self-assessment helps identify areas of strength and need. It is related directly to course content and practicum activities. At the completion of the mini-course, participants will be asked to self-assess again to reflect on changes that may have occurred as a result of course participation.

DIRECTIONS: For each item circle the number that most closely reflects your status at this time. Respond based on what you do personally. If you work with more than one paraeducator, provide a response considering your overall situation.

#	Content	I don't do this, and I don't know enough about it.	I know it's important, but I just don't get to it.	I'm doing it, but not enough.	I'm doing it and feel it's going well.
1	Paraeducators with whom I work are welcomed in class.	1 2	3 4	5 6	7 8
2	Paraeducators with whom I work are well oriented to the school (e.g., places, people, policies, philosophy, practices, procedures).	1 2	3 4	5 6	7 8
3	Paraeducators with whom I work are well oriented to the classroom (e.g., routines, practices, instructional programs).	1 2	3 4	5 6	7 8
4	Paraeducators with whom I work are well oriented to the students with whom they work (e.g., knowledgeable about: IEP goals, participation in general education curriculum, supports needed, aspects of disability that affect learning, motivations, interests).	1 2	3 4	5 6	7 8

		1	2	3	4	5	6	7	8
5	The roles of the paraeducators with whom I work are explicitly stated and match their knowledge and skills.	1	2	3	4	5	6	7	8
6	My role and the roles of the other professional staff in relation to the paraeducators are clear and well understood by all team members.	1	2	3	4	5	6	7	8
7	Paraeducators with whom I work have a daily written schedule of duties to follow.	1	2	3	4	5	6	7	8
8	Paraeducators with whom I work have written plans to follow when implementing teacher-planned instruction and other duties.	1	2	3	4	5	6	7	8
9	Paraeducators with whom I work receive initial and ongoing training to carry out their assigned duties.	1	2	3	4	5	6	7	8
10	Paraeducators with whom I work have mechanisms to communicate with me on an ongoing basis.	1	2	3	4	5	6	7	8
11	Paraeducators with whom I work receive ongoing feedback on their job performance, both formally and informally.	1	2	3	4	5	6	7	8
12	Paraeducators with whom I work have a thorough understanding of appropriate confidentiality practices and school policies on the topic.	1	2	3	4	5	6	7	8

Source: Reprinted with permission from Giangreco (2002). © M. F. Giangreco.

faculty room, lunchroom, gymnasium). Be certain that the paraprofessional is familiar with any associated policies (e.g., photocopying, media/technology lab, tutoring center). Given the expanding use of technology, it is important to establish clear expectations regarding the use of the Internet and e-mail during school hours.

In the classroom, share things as basic as showing the paraprofessional where the classroom supplies are kept. Provide an orientation regarding the instructional technology that is used in the classroom, paying particular attention to the hardware and software that are used frequently. This time together may highlight additional training needs. Review classroom routines and expectations, classroom management, class rules, and code of conduct for the students. Provide the paraprofessional with the school handbook of schoolwide policies and procedures.

Members of the educational team, including the paraprofessional, will have access to sensitive and confidential information about students (e.g., health information, educational goals, progress reports, family information). So be certain to review the school policy on confidentiality as it applies to students with and without disabilities. Check for understanding by posing several situations for the two of you to discuss using the following questions:

1. Is it okay for several professionals to discuss a student's educational program while they are in the break room?
2. Is it okay for a paraprofessional to discuss a student's educational program with a parent at the grocery store?
3. Do all school personnel have access to student files?
4. Are confidentiality rules applied differently to written versus spoken information?
5. Is it a breech of confidentiality to discuss a student's family situation while in the community?

Maintaining confidentiality is an important aspect of building trusting partnerships with families. Once that trust is compromised, the partnership and subsequent team functioning can be adversely affected. Stress the importance of confidentiality and share the following tips with the paraprofessional:

1. Never discuss a student's educational plans in public places (e.g., faculty room, playground, hallway, community park, grocery store).
2. When meeting to discuss a student's educational plan, only discuss information that is directly relevant to the issues at hand.
3. If someone approaches you and begins to breech the confidentiality of a student provide a kind but clear response. For example, "I'm not on that student's educational team, so I don't think it is appropriate for me to be involved in discussing his educational program."
4. When you or the paraprofessional are no longer on the student's team, you must continue to maintain confidentiality about any the information that you have learned about the student and/or family.
5. When in doubt, put yourself in the shoes of the parents or student and ask yourself: "Would it be okay for people to be talking about me or my family in this manner, in this same location, and for the same purposes?"

As the classroom teacher you have an opportunity to model professionalism and respect for students and their families by adhering to high standards of confidentiality. You may want to utilize other resources designed to assist paraprofessionals in understanding the issues, importance, and intricacies of confidentiality (Doyle, 2002; Pickett & Gerlach, 1997).

Students the paraprofessional will support.   At the heart of the paraprofessional's orientation is learning about students. This means gaining some general knowledge about the population of students to be served as well as information specifically about those students with whom the paraprofessional will be working. This calls for initial and ongoing training that is both generic and student-specific.

Initial generic training may include taking a course or a series of staff development workshops to learn essential information about being a paraprofessional. For example, CichoskiKelly, Backus, Giangreco, and Sherman-Tucker (2000) developed training materials designed to provide entry-level information to prepare paraprofessionals to assist in the provision of special education within inclusive classrooms. These training materials are designed to be taught in six three-hour sessions covering the following topics:

Unit 1: Collaborative Teamwork
Unit 2: Inclusive Education
Unit 3: Families and Cultural Sensitivity
Unit 4: Characteristics of Children and Youth with Various Disabilities
Unit 5: Roles and Responsibilities of Paraeducators and Other Team Members
Unit 6: Paraeducators Implementing Teacher-Planned Instruction

Similarly, the Institute on Community Integration (1999) at the University of Minnesota has developed training materials and approaches for paraprofessionals, as have others (French, 1998a; Parsons & Reid, 1999; Salzberg, Morgan, Gassman, Pickett, & Merrill, 1993; Steckelberg & Vasa, 1998). All training tools have their pros and cons. Some are specifically geared toward inclusive settings, while others were designed for use across general and special class settings. Each has its own emphasis in terms of what is considered important and appropriate. Therefore, as a teacher leader who is considering using existing training materials, be sure to review them closely to ensure that you are selecting materials that are consistent with your school and classroom philosophy, needs, and practices.

It is preferable, though still uncommon, for paraprofessionals to receive this sort of initial, generic training prior to beginning their employment. Since most paraprofessionals typically are offered training after they begin working, it is vital to provide it as soon as possible. It can go a long way toward demonstrating respect for paraprofessionals to offer the training during their scheduled work hours or to pay them for time they spend outside their contracted work day.

After initial entry-level training is completed, it is part of your job to develop a training plan with the paraprofessional to identify future courses, workshops, or other training opportunities that will support their professional development and meet needs identified in the classroom. For example, Backus and CichoskiKelly (2001) developed training materials to assist paraprofessionals in supporting students with challenging behaviors (see Box

---

BOX **10.1**

Paraprofessional Training to Support a Student with Challenging Behaviors in a High School

John has been a paraprofessional for one year at Kennedy High School. During his first year he took a six-week entry-level paraprofessional training course that covered a variety of units (e.g., collaborative teamwork, inclusive education, characteristics of students with disabilities, implementing teacher-planned instruction). Although this generic training was helpful, John found himself being asked to support students with severe disabilities who also exhibited challenging behaviors. It was clear to him that he needed more training in this area, both in general and specifically related to the students he was supporting. At a meeting he and Ms. Brennan, his special educator colleague, planned out a series of training activities. From a generic perspective the plan called for John to attend a four-session mini-course designed for paraprofessionals who were supporting students with challenging behaviors. This mini-course would extend what he learned in the entry-level course and would address such considerations as: (a) understanding student behavior (e.g., communicative intent of behaviors), (b) gathering information about challenging behaviors, (c) preventing challenging behaviors and teaching replacement behaviors, and (d) responding to challenging behaviors. This mini-course included a series of practicum requirements that would give John an opportunity to apply what he was learning under Ms. Brennan's supervision. From a student-specific perspective, John was especially concerned about a series of behaviors that were regularly exhibited by Terry, a 16-year-old with severe disabilities. When walking through halls between class changes, Terry would often grab or pinch other students. In health class, Terry would frequently make loud vocalizations that led to his removal from the class. Finally, in a series of other classes (e.g., science, English, social studies), if Terry was asked to sit for more than five minutes he would start body rocking. If left unchecked for more than a couple of minutes, this often escalated to head banging on nearby people or furniture. The combination of these behaviors was interfering with Terry's school experience, academically, functionally, and socially. In an effort to understand Terry's behaviors, Ms. Brennan taught John how to collect data that was used to help conduct an A-B-C (antecedent-behavior-consequence) analysis in each of the settings where Terry was exhibiting challenging behaviors. The data and the input of other team members were used to develop a positive behavior support plan for Terry. Ms. Brennan then provided ongoing training for John on how to implement Terry's plan. She observed John and Terry together at least weekly to give John feedback on his implementation and ongoing data collection. Terry's behaviors haven't been eliminated, but they have improved noticeably, and John is feeling good about his paraprofessional role supporting Terry's behavior needs in positive ways.

10.1). These materials are designed to be used after paraprofessionals have completed generic entry-level training.

The challenge with any generic training materials for paraprofessionals is that while they can offer valuable information, they not specific to the students with whom the paraprofessional will be working. Therefore, generic forms of staff development must be augmented with training that is student-specific. The level of specificity may range from training on a commercial reading program being used in the classroom to learning about instructional strategies that are unique to an individual student.

Orientation and training pertaining to individual students includes information such as student characteristics (e.g., physical, sensory, cognitive), interests, and needs. The paraprofessional should become familiar with the student's communication skills, educational goals, special equipment, and support needs and with instructional strategies that are known to be effective with the student. For students with severe disabilities the IEP (Individual Education Program) is usually a primary source of such information. Unfortunately, not all IEPs are written with sufficient specificity to be helpful to paraprofessionals. Sometimes IEPs are quite long and contain educational or medical jargon that is unknown to the paraprofessional. Therefore, while providing paraprofessionals access to the information contained in the IEP, it may be more helpful to provide it in a more friendly and concise format, such as a Program-at-a-Glance (Giangreco, Cloninger, & Iverson, 1998). This is a one- or two-page summary that includes vital information about a student's goals and supports and can be readily adapted to include whatever information the team finds most helpful. You might also have a meeting and ask the parents or other faculty members to supply some student-specific information. Consider developing a personal photo-essay booklet about the student's interests, friends, family, characteristics, supports, and educational goals. The photo-essay booklet can be shared by the student with the new paraprofessional or others (Doyle, 2000). This highly personalized and interactive approach can be an excellent first step in having the paraprofessional learn about the student and assist in developing a positive student–paraprofessional rapport.

Role clarification is a critical aspect of orientation. This includes both identifying appropriate roles for paraprofessionals and differentiating between the paraprofessional's roles and yours. For example, paraprofessionals are increasingly involved in providing instruction to students with disabilities. There is general consensus in the field that any such instruction provided by paraprofessionals should be based on professionally prepared plans given appropriate training and supervision. That is nice rhetoric, but too often it does not match reality. This highlights some important areas of differentiation between the roles of educators and paraprofessionals. It is the responsibility of the teacher and special educator to assess students' educational needs and progress; make decisions about curriculum; develop lesson plans that reflect individually determined adaptations, instructional methods, and data collection systems; and be the primary liaison with the family. These are responsibilities that many paraprofessionals are not trained in or qualified to undertake. In cases where they are qualified (e.g., a certified teacher hired in a paraprofessional role), they are not compensated to do teacher-level work and as a paraprofessional are not accountable for the educational program in the same way you are as an educator.

When considering the paraprofessional's role in implementing teacher-planned instruction, it can be helpful to establish parameters around the teaching of new concepts and skills versus reviewing or practicing concepts and skills that have already been introduced. For example, many teachers find it beneficial to introduce new concepts and skills themselves before asking a paraprofessional to provide ongoing teaching and practice with the student. This teacher-first approach allows an opportunity for the educator to model instructional approaches for the paraprofessional and gain firsthand assessment information that will be used to adjust future lessons.

When the paraprofessional begins his or her instructional involvement, the teacher's instructional role should continue (see Box 10.2, p. 196). Be sure to schedule times when

---

B O X **10.2**

**Helping a Paraprofessional Understand Individualized
Curriculum in an Elementary Classroom**

Sandy, a paraprofessional in Ms. Kegan's second-grade classroom, has been accustomed to supporting a few students with mild disabilities as well as their classmates without disability labels who needed some extra help in reading, spelling, writing, and math. Sandy expressed concerns that she felt unprepared for an incoming student, Joey, who has severe disabilities. According to his first-grade teacher and parents, Joey likes active environments but tires easily. He enjoys music, being around other kids, and playing with his dog. Joey uses a wheelchair for mobility and has limited use of legs, arms, and hands. Although Joey communicates with vocalizations and facial expressions, he currently does not have a consistent way to express himself more formally. Joey functions at a severe level of intellectual impairment, but no one wants such labeling to limit his possibilities. As his mom said, "Given his physical and communication challenges, we really don't know for sure how much he is understanding. Because of this we think he should have access to all the same things as other kids his age." Sandy doesn't understand what she will be expected to help him learn because it sounds to her like he has different learning needs than the rest of the class. To address Sandy's concerns, Ms. Kegan arranged a meeting with Sandy, Ms. Phillips (the special educator), and Joey's parents. Ms. Kegan and Ms. Phillips facilitated a team discussion to review Joey's IEP goals and compare them to the typical class activities (e.g., morning circle, journal writing, reading group, math group). For each curriculum area or activity period they reached consensus about whether Joey would pursue the same learning outcomes as his peers, different learning outcomes within the same curriculum, or different learning outcomes from different curriculum areas than those being pursued by his classmates. By the end of the meeting they had decided what Joey would be trying to learn during different parts of the day. For example, during art class he would have the same learning outcomes as his classmates, but would need assistance and adaptations to participate. During morning circle the initial focus would be on greeting others and answering "Yes/No" questions using eye gaze (both IEP goals). During journal writing he would be trying to develop a consistent response mode using an adapted switch to operate a page-turning device and single-response software on a computer. During science, he would be part of a four-student group. His goals within those activities would not be geared toward science; rather the science activities would be used as a vehicle for him to practice his "Yes/No" responding, making choices when presented with options, and practicing his switch use (to help record work being completed by the team). By clarifying the learning expectations for Joey his parents felt comfortable that the IEP goals were being addressed, and the paraprofessional had a way to think about her instructional role with Joey that made sense to her.

---

you are providing instruction for the student with a disability in large groups, small groups, and individually. This way you can ensure that you are the teacher for all of the students in your classroom and are highly knowledgeable about each of your students. In doing so you can avoid the trap of establishing a double standard whereby students with disabilities receive most of their instruction from paraprofessionals while those without disabilities have more regular access to certified educators. Equally as important, recent research has suggested that the level of teacher engagement, which is critical to successful inclusive education, can be significantly affected by the manner in which paraprofessional supports are utilized (Giangreco et al., 2001).

In addition to assisting in the implementation of teacher-planned instruction, paraprofessionals can also provide vital supports by supervising students (e.g., playground, cafeteria), engaging in clerical and general duties, providing social/behavior supports, and providing personal care needs to students (e.g., eating support, dressing, personal hygiene). By engaging in this range of roles, paraprofessionals assist students directly and create opportunities for general and special educators to work directly with students. That is why it is key to acknowledge the value of the noninstructional tasks as well as the instructional tasks. Lastly, part of your leadership role with paraprofessionals is to establish congruence between the paraprofessional's expectations, roles, training, support, and supervision.

Planning for Paraprofessionals

One of the keys to good teaching is good planning. Start with something as simple as providing the paraprofessional with a daily and weekly schedule of activities indicating basic information (e.g., what, when, who, where). The paraprofessional's schedule should be linked to the classroom schedule. For example, it should be clear to the paraprofessional what to do when you are teaching a whole-class lesson. Sometimes paraprofessional support to individual students is not required during those times when the teacher is interacting with all students or when peers might reasonably provide natural supports. When paraprofessionals are unsure what to do during such times of the day, they may unnecessarily be in close proximity to students with disabilities and inadvertently interfere with their participation. At such times you may plan some alternative tasks for paraprofessionals (e.g., materials preparation) or they may need to simply listen to the lesson so that they are in a better position to provide support to students during follow-up small group or individual activities.

Typically educators develop plans for their own use. This allows most educators to have written plans that are brief and provide set of reminders about a lesson's purpose, materials, sequence, and main points. A plan that may work well for experienced educators to use for themselves may not provide the level of specificity required for another person, such as a paraprofessional or substitute, to implement the plan. This is why it is so important to develop plans that provide the content and level of information required for paraprofessionals to effectively carry out a plan devised by a general or special educator.

Since general and special educators utilize a wide range and combination of teaching philosophies and strategies, our purpose here is not to suggest any one particular instructional approach over another. Rather, given whatever approach you use, we encourage you to address some generic planning issues for paraprofessionals. Additionally, your own organizational and management style, as well as the experience and previous training of the paraprofessional, will have an impact on the level of specificity your plans for paraprofessionals include. Consider the following questions:

1. How much information does the paraprofessional need to implement the teacher-planned lesson or activity?
2. What is the essential information?

3. What makes the most sense?
4. How can planned information be provided in ways that do not create unnecessary paperwork?

When considering these questions, paraprofessionals will need to know about, understand, and apply this basic set of components of an instructional plan:

- Purpose of the lesson/activity
- Objectives within the lesson/activity that may differ by student
- Materials needed for the lesson/activity
- How to arrange the learning environment (e.g., how students are positioned)
- How to get and sustain student attention
- How to introduce the lesson/activity (e.g., explanation, demonstration)
- How to encourage student participation
- How to relate the lesson/activity to previous learning
- What desired responses look or sound like (e.g., operational definitions)
- How and what feedback to provide when students give desired responses
- What to do when students are nonresponsive
- What to do when students give incorrect responses
- What data to collect and how it should be recorded
- How to end the lesson/activity
- What to do if the plan does not seem to be working

In addition to instructional plans for lessons and activities, paraprofessionals will also need plans for noninstructional aspects of their work. For example, some students with severe disabilities require knowledge of specialized support procedures or personal care supports such as how they are tube fed, properly positioned in their wheelchair, or transferred between specialized equipment. Some of these noninstructional tasks lend themselves well to being presented through a series of photographs in addition to brief written instructions.

Whether your plan for a paraprofessional is instructional or noninstructional, merely handing over a paper plan (even one with photos) is not enough. Part of your teacher leadership should include how and when you will review your plans with the paraprofessional, provide demonstration, observe the paraprofessional's implementation, review collected data, provide feedback, and provide opportunities for the paraprofessional to offer input to plan adjustments. Although it may seem like a lot of paperwork, planning of this sort can help you think through important aspects of a student's program, provide a starting point to direct the work of the paraprofessional, and have utility when substitute teachers or paraprofessionals are in the classroom. Look for formats that work for you!

Communicating with and Providing Feedback to Paraprofessionals

An ongoing and key aspect of teacher leadership with paraprofessionals is to communicate with them effectively and provide constructive feedback (Doyle, 2002). As the general or special educator, you are responsible for the immediate supervision of the paraprofessional, even though formal evaluation may be the responsibility of an administrator. Develop a system and schedule to provide the paraprofessional with feedback on instructional and noninstructional responsibilities based on your direct observations of his or her work. This system and schedule should be one that works for you and your team and results in action planning for continuous program improvement.

Communicating your feedback to paraprofessionals is something most educators are not trained to do and may even find uncomfortable. Lee (1999) highlights six important aspects of effective communication that can facilitate teacher leadership as you develop and extend your collaborative working relationships with paraprofessionals: (1) developing expectations, (2) preparing ahead, (3) understanding perspectives, (4) asking questions, (5) listening, and (6) speaking clearly. As you read through the following subsections you will notice the interrelationships among these various aspects of communication. These connections point out the reciprocal nature of communication and highlight its power to enhance our work with students and one another.

Developing expectations.   First, as a team, create mechanisms for communication. Decide when, where, and how often you will engage in formal communication (e.g., team meetings, daily check-in, team logbook) and identify informal opportunities for communication. Establish ground rules and expectations for formal meetings (e.g., read reports in advance, follow an agenda, rotate roles, maintain timelines, speak to each other respectfully, ensure opportunities for all members to participate, keep records of team discussions and decisions).

It is also advisable to establish a "chain of command" so that the paraprofessional knows who to approach when concerns arise. For example, if an issue arises in the cafeteria or library, who should the paraprofessional go to first? Developing expectations pertaining to communication and teamwork are foundational to your leadership role with paraprofessionals.

Preparing ahead.   Preparing ahead refers to both class work (e.g., lessons, activities, supports) as well as formal communication (e.g., team meetings). Through your own example, model for the paraprofessional the value and importance of preparation. Explain that lack of preparation wastes valuable instructional time for students as well as for colleagues. In terms of class work prepare your plan, materials, equipment, and physical setup. Be sure you and the paraprofessional are familiar with the lesson or activity in advance.

In preparation for meetings, be certain that team members are aware of the date, time, and location of the meeting. Make sure that members are aware of agenda items in advance so they can arrive prepared and that the necessary tools are available to facilitate the meeting (e.g., markers, chart paper, laptop computer, snacks). Preparation is a sign of mutual respect among members of a team.

Understanding perspectives.   It is not only common for individuals to bring different perspectives to the team, it is desirable. Let the paraprofessional know that different perspectives are welcomed. As a team, seek to understand each other's perspectives—even if you do not always agree with one another. This will require team members to express themselves, listen, accept different communication styles, be observant, defer judgment, and occasionally be silent. Be certain to adopt or develop constructive approaches to resolve differences (e.g., applying a specific problem-solving approach).

Asking questions.   One of the best ways to understand the perspectives of others is to ask questions. Asking questions actively demonstrates an interest in understanding and conveys open-mindedness. Posing questions rather than immediately offering a counter perspective can assist teams in generating creative ideas that join together two or more divergent perspectives. As Lee (1999) stated, "People feel empowered when others show their interest by asking questions." So ask questions, and encourage the paraprofessional to ask questions about curriculum, instruction, student characteristics, and classroom functioning.

Listening.   As a teacher leader you probably have a lot to say, but do not underestimate the power of listening. Active listening calls for concentration and attentiveness, and requires that you seek to understand what the paraprofessional is saying before you think about what your response might be; it is more difficult than it sounds. This means that as a listener you will not be conjuring up a response until after you are certain that you understand what the paraprofessional has said and he has finished speaking. Good listeners may ask for clarification or try to extend their understanding by asking questions like, "I'm not certain that I understood what you meant. Can you say it another way?" Or "Will you tell me more about that idea?" Or "Can you give me a few examples?" When we listen well we are more likely to understand one another's perspectives and ideas. Listening affords each of us with an opportunity to grow and learn. So be a listener and encourage listening.

Speaking clearly.   As the educator it is your responsibility to ensure that effective communication has occurred with the paraprofessional. This means being as explicit and unambiguous as possible about what you are communicating. It may mean communicating using multiple modes (e.g., oral and written). Do not expect that your meaning will always be received in the manner in which you intended. What may seem obvious to you may not be so clear to the paraprofessional, or to any other team member for that matter. In an effort to ensure that you have delivered your communication clearly, ask for feedback that your message was understood. Be aware of your use of jargon and acronyms that may be unfamiliar to the paraprofessional. When we speak clearly we enhance the effectiveness of our communication and increase the likelihood that our message will be understood. Lee (1999) summarized many of the communication issues discussed in this chapter as "Ten Tips for Collaborating Effectively with Paraprofessionals" (see Table 10.1).

Finding Paraprofessional Resources Online

New information about paraprofessional support of students with disabilities in general education classrooms is growing constantly. If you are using a search engine on the Internet such as Altavista (http://www.altavista.com) or Google (http://www.google.com) to locate information about paraprofessionals, be aware of the differing terminology used around the country. Search under a variety of terms or phrases such as *paraprofessional, paraeducator,*

TABLE 10.1 Ten Tips for Collaborating Effectively with Paraprofessionals

- Start and end each day with the paraprofessional.
- Provide the paraprofessional with constructive feedback ASAP.
- Say thank you frequently for specific acts.
- Ask the paraprofessional how *you* can help.
- Demonstrate what you mean.
- Recognize the individual and unique contributions of each paraprofessional.
- Occasionally meet together away from the school or work area.
- Encourage the paraprofessional to keep a daily journal of activities, thoughts, and feelings.
- Ask the paraprofessional what he or she would like to learn.
- Advocate for the paraprofessional's professional growth.

Source: Adapted from Lee (1999).

teacher assistant, teacher aide, instructional assistant, or other variations you are aware of. Another free source to search the professional literature is Ask ERIC, which provides online access to the ERIC database. We suggest using the advanced search option (http://www.ericir.syr.edu/Eric/adv_search.shtml).

With the full recognition that websites come and go, here is a list of a few noncommercial websites devoted to paraprofessional issues:

> *Minnesota Paraprofessional Consortium*
> http://www.ici2.coled.umn.edu/para/default.html
> *National Resource Center for Paraprofessionals in Education and Related Services*
> http://www.nrcpara.org/
> *National Clearinghouse of Paraeducator Resources: Paraeducator Pathways into Teaching*
> http://www.usc.edu/dept/education/CMMR/Clearinghouse.html
> *Northwest Regional Educational Laboratory: Paraeducator Resources*
> http://www.nwrac.org/links/paraed.html
> *Paraeducator Issues: Paraeducators Helping Kids Shine—The Washington Education Association*
> http://www.wa.nea.org/Prf_Dv/PARA_ED/PARA.HTM
> *Paraeducator Support of Students with Disabilities in General Education Classrooms*
> http://www.uvm.edu/~cdci/parasupport/
> *Paraeducator and Supervisor Training Designed to Meet the Needs of Students with Disabilities in General Education Classrooms*
> http://www.uvm.edu/~cdci/paraprep/
> *Project PARA: University of Nebraska, Lincoln*
> http://www.para.unl.edu/

Conclusion

How will you know if you have been successful as an educator directing the work of a paraprofessional? There are four primary indicators of your success in this arena. First, gauge the job satisfaction of the paraprofessional. If the paraprofessional's job satisfaction is high, it is likely that your leadership is a positive contributing factor. Not only is job satisfaction positively correlated with work productivity, it can assist the school in retaining qualified paraprofessionals, who are increasingly in short supply. This maximizes the training and supervision resources that are dedicated to paraprofessionals and builds a school's capacity.

Second, as the educator, do you feel satisfied with the work of the paraprofessional? Is he or she assisting you in ways that are vital to the functioning of your classroom and allow you to do a better job with your students? When the paraprofessional is providing supports that allow you to devote more energy to other aspects of your teaching responsibilities it is a sign that your teacher leadership is being effective. The work of the paraprofessional should allow you to know as much or more about the student with a disability as the paraprofessional and should afford you time to be directly involved with teaching that student. If you sense that under your direction the paraprofessional is helping you in these areas, he or she probably is—so trust your instincts.

Third, you will know that you have been effective in directing the work of the paraprofessional when you can link it to positive student outcomes. These may include academic and functional outcomes such as acquiring a new skill, as well as personal and social outcomes such as developing confidence and new friends. Making the connection between the support provided by paraprofessionals and student outcomes will require an analysis of student data, direct observation, and reports of team members.

Finally, consider the perspectives of your students with disabilities regarding paraprofessional supports. If possible, ask the student's opinion directly. If the student has expressive language difficulties, you will need to look for nonsymbolic forms of communication by observing the student's reactions and considering how classmates are reacting to the presence of the paraprofessional. Every effort should be made to provide paraprofessional supports in a manner that is respectful toward the student with a disability and is as normalized as possible.

As an educator you can improve your own teaching effectiveness and student outcomes by exhibiting leadership in directing the work of paraprofessionals. By welcoming, acknowledging, orienting, and training paraprofessionals within a team context that relies on effective communication and feedback, you can establish productive and collaborative relationships. These relationships are the bedrock upon which exemplary educational programs and services are built.

References

Backus, L., & CichoskiKelly, E. (2001). *Supporting students with challenging behaviors: A paraeducator curriculum (Instructor and participant manuals)*. Stillwater: National Clearinghouse of Rehabilitation Training Materials, Oklahoma State University.

Brown, L., Farrington, K., Ziegler, M., Knight, T., & Ross, C. (1999). Fewer paraprofessionals and more teachers and therapists in educational programs for students with significant disabilities. *Journal of the Association for Persons with Severe Handicaps, 24,* 249–252.

CichoskiKelly, E., Backus, L., Giangreco, M. F., & Sherman-Tucker, J. (2000). *Paraeducator entry-level training for supporting students with disabilities (Instructor and participant manuals).* Stillwater: National Clearinghouse of Rehabilitation Training Materials, Oklahoma State University.

Downing, J., Ryndak, D., & Clark, D. (2000). Paraeducators in inclusive classrooms: Their own perspective. *Remedial and Special Education, 21,* 171–181.

Doyle, M. B. (2000). Transition plans for students with disabilities. *Educational Leadership, 58*(1), 46–48.

Doyle, M. B. (2002). *The paraprofessional's guide to the inclusive classroom: Working as a team* (2nd ed.). Baltimore: Paul H. Brookes.

Doyle, M. B., & Lee, P. A. (1997). Creating partnerships with paraprofessionals. In M. F. Giangreco (Ed.), *Quick-guides to inclusion: Ideas for educating students with disabilities* (pp. 57–84). Baltimore: Paul H. Brookes.

French, N. K. (1998a). *Paraprofessional Academy.* Denver: Center for Collaborative Educational Leadership, University of Colorado at Denver.

French, N. K. (1998b). Working together: Resource teachers and paraeducators. *Remedial and Special Education, 19,* 357–368.

French, N., & Pickett, A. L. (1997). Paraprofessionals in special education: Issues for teacher educators. *Teacher Education and Special Education, 20,* 61–73.

Giangreco, M. F. (2001). *Teacher leadership: Working with paraeducators (Instructor and participant manuals).* Stillwater: National Clearinghouse of Rehabilitation Training Materials, Oklahoma State University.

Giangreco, M. F., Broer, S. M., & Edelman, S. W. (1999). The tip of the iceberg: Determining whether paraprofessional support is needed for students with disabilities in general education settings. *Journal of the Association for Persons with Severe Handicaps, 24,* 280–290.

Giangreco, M. F., Broer, S. M., & Edelman, S. W. (2001). Teacher engagement with students with disabilities: Differences between paraprofessional service delivery models. *Journal of the Association for Persons with Severe Handicaps, 26,* 75–86.

Giangreco, M. F., Broer, S. M., & Edelman, S. W. (2002). "That was then, this is now!" Paraprofessional supports for students with disabilities in general education classrooms. *Exceptionality, 10*(1), 47–64.

Giangreco, M. F., Cloninger, C. J., & Iverson, V. S. (1998). *Choosing outcomes and accommodations for children: A guide to educational planning for students with disabilities* (2nd ed.). Baltimore: Paul H. Brookes.

Giangreco, M. F., Edelman, S. W., & Broer, S. M. (2001). Respect, appreciation, and acknowledgment of paraprofessionals who support students with disabilities. *Exceptional Children, 67,* 485–498.

Giangreco, M. F., Edelman, S. W., Broer, S. M., & Doyle, M. B. (2001). Paraprofessional support of students with disabilities: Literature from the past decade. *Exceptional Children, 68,* 45–64.

Giangreco, M. F., Edelman, S., Luiselli, T. E., & MacFarland, S. Z. C. (1997). Helping or hovering? Effects of instructional assistant proximity on students with disabilities. *Exceptional Children, 64,* 7–18.

Institute on Community Integration. (1999). *Strategies for paraprofessionals who support individuals with disabilities (5 module series)*. Minneapolis: Institute on Community Integration, University of Minnesota.

Jones, K. H., & Bender, W. N. (1993). Utilization of paraprofessionals in special education: A review of the literature. *Remedial and Special Education, 14,* 7–14.

Lee, P. (1999). *Collaborative practices for educators? Strategies for effective communication.* Minnetonka, MN: Peytral.

Marks, S. U., Schrader, C., & Levine, M. (1999). Paraeducator experiences in inclusive settings: Helping, hovering, or holding their own? *Exceptional Children, 65,* 315–328.

Minondo, S., Meyer, L., & Xin, J. (2001). The roles and responsibilities of teaching assistants in inclusive education: What's appropriate? *Journal of the Association for Persons with Severe Handicaps, 26,* 114–119.

National Joint Committee on Learning Disabilities. (1999, March). Learning disabilities: Use of paraprofessionals. *ASHA, 41*(Suppl. 19), 37–46.

Parsons, M. B., & Reid, D. H. (1999). Training basic teaching skills to paraprofessionals of students with severe disabilities: A one-day program. *Teaching Exceptional Children, 31,* 48–55.

Pickett, A. L., & Gerlach, K. (1997). *Supervising paraeducators in school settings: A team approach.* Austin, TX: Pro-Ed.

Salzberg, C. L., & Morgan, J. (1995). Preparing teachers to work with paraeducators. *Teacher Education and Special Education, 18,* 49–55.

Salzberg, C. L., Morgan, J., Gassman, G., Pickett, A. L., & Merrill, Z. (1993). *Enhancing skills of paraeducators: A video-assisted training program.* Logan: Utah State University, Department of Special Education and Rehabilitation.

Steckelberg, A. L., & Vasa, S. F. (1998). How paraeducators learn on the web. *Teaching Exceptional Children, 30,* 54–59.

Wallace, T., Shin, J., Bartholomay, T., & Stahl, B. J. (2001). Knowledge and skills for teachers supervising the work of paraprofessionals. *Exceptional Children, 67,* 520–533.

Werts, M. G., Wolery, M., Snyder, E. D., Caldwell, N. K., & Salisbury, C. L. (1996). Supports and resources associated with inclusive schooling: Perceptions of elementary school teachers about need and availability. *Journal of Special Education, 30,* 187–203.

Young, B., Simpson, R., Myles, B. S., & Kamps, D. M. (1997). An examination of paraprofessional involvement in supporting students with autism. *Focus on Autism and Other Developmental Disabilities, 12,* 31–38, 48.

PART TWO

Inclusive Education
at Different Ages

11 Preschool

**EVA HORN, BARBARA THOMPSON,
SUSAN PALMER, RONDA JENSON,
AND VICKI TURBIVILLE**

University of Kansas

There is a clear link between program quality and child outcomes. A high-quality early childhood program is a necessary foundation of preschool inclusion. To be sufficient, however, the program must ensure that the developmental needs of all young children are met. Thus, when a child with severe disabilities is placed in an inclusive program, an additional bar is added—quality of inclusion to ensure meaningful access to the learning environment for the child with a severe disability. To ensure positive impacts on both child and family outcomes, a range of supports must be in place.

The recommended practices discussed in the previous ten chapters are very much at the heart of these critical supports needed for preschool children with severe disabilities. There are, of course, some unique issues that arise in implementation for preschool children and their families. This chapter will focus on describing some of these unique aspects, but first a few definitions are necessary. Preschool children are those children 3 through 5 years of age typically participating in community-based preschools, child care and other types of group care, and learning settings that are not part of more traditional school-based (K–12) educational system. Services and supports for preschool children with severe disabilities include a range of educational, developmental, and therapeutic activities. Finally, preschool inclusion is not about a place, an instructional strategy, or a curriculum; inclusion is about belonging, being valued, and having choices. Just as is the case across the age continuum, preschool inclusion is about accepting and valuing diversity, and providing the necessary support so that all children and their families can participate in the programs of their choice.

Inclusion at the preschool level is unique from inclusive programs and practices at the elementary, middle school, and high school levels. A number of researchers and authors have noted factors that create a context for preschool children that differs substantially from inclusion for older children (Odom, Wolery, Lieber, & Horn, 2001); for example:

- Since public school systems provide programs for typically developing school-age children, the possibility for inclusion exists at the elementary, middle, and high school levels but not always at the preschool level. As a result, administrators and families have to look outside public school buildings (i.e., into Head Start or community-based programs) to find inclusive settings for preschool children with disabilities. In looking for these inclusive opportunities, they sometimes run into substantial barriers.

- Preschool classrooms differ from typical public school classes for older children on a range of dimensions including class size, teacher–child ratio, and physical characteristics. A major difference is often the formal educational training of the staff and their compensation. Many community preschools require minimal educational backgrounds and do not have certification or licensure requirements. Furthermore, they frequently provide salaries significantly below those obtained by public school teachers. Again, this can result in substantial barriers to high-quality inclusion.

- The nature of the curriculum is different in early childhood programs and in elementary/middle/high school programs. Early childhood programs take a more "developmentally appropriate" approach to curriculum planning (Bredekamp & Copple, 1997), while general education programs for older children are more academically oriented. Further, the pressures of "high stakes" achievement testing have not extended down to the preschool level (Nolet & McLaughlin, 2000). For older students, the impact of testing has had implications for curriculum planning (i.e., curriculum may be directed more narrowly toward the form and content of the achievement tests). This difference allows for greater flexibility in individually defining curriculum content to match an individual child's learning needs and abilities. The lack of standards, however, may make it difficult for preschool special educators to ensure that every child has meaningful access to the general curriculum and receives instruction in the same challenging content as required by IDEA.

- The developmental skills of young children obviously differ from those of older children. For preschool children, there may be less developmental difference between children with disabilities and their same-age peers than occurs in classes for older children. Also, social relationships with peers appear to be less firmly fixed for young children than for older children. Thus, it is possible that less significant modifications and potentially isolating accommodations need to be made for young children with severe disabilities, allowing for more "natural" participation, engagement, and interaction.

Although some common issues exist, these points highlight the differences between inclusive programs for preschool and school-age children. In preschool, there are unique aspects that support successful inclusive opportunities for young children with severe disabilities, but there are also unique barriers.

In the remainder of this chapter we will discuss the unique aspects of implementation of preschool inclusion and illustrate strategies for ensuring high-quality services for young children with severe disabilities. However, before we begin a discussion of how to develop and implement an appropriate program, we must introduce the reader to Lindy (see Box 11.1).

BOX 11.1

Lindy

We first met Lindy when she was 2 years old and was referred to the Part C—infant and toddler early intervention program. We knew right away that if an inclusive program were to be available for Lindy when she turned 3 (in just ten months), we would need to begin the transition process immediately. A transition outcome was written into her Individualized Family Service Plan (IFSP) to help the team prepare to meet Lindy's unique needs and to overcome barriers to an inclusive education for her.

Lindy lived in a trailer on the edge of a small rural community with her grandmother. Transportation was always a problem. Her grandmother didn't drive due to her poor health and transportation resources were not available in the local community. A church member helped when possible. Lindy's family physician was reported to comment at each checkup that she was living proof that he could be wrong. He had never believed she would survive more than a few weeks, and yet here she was gaining new skills slowly but steadily. While the physician was supportive, he consistently urged the grandmother not to plan ahead or get her hopes up.

Lindy had multiple disabilities including mental retardation, cerebral palsy, and serious health impairments. She was tube fed, needed regular suctioning, and was frequently aspirated. There were few choices for programs for any child in this rural community. They did not have a preschool or even a child-care program. The local school district participated in a special education cooperative program, which at that time housed all ECSE programs, 35 miles away in a larger town. Lindy's grandmother did not feel comfortable with any program that would not be close by in case of an emergency. Head Start offered home-based programs in the area and was in the process of establishing a site for a center in the community. The Head Start personnel, however, were unsure of their ability to meet Lindy's needs even when the site was opened.

The early intervention team continued to serve Lindy and began a carefully planned transition to a home-based Head Start program, with special education and related services provided within the home, as Lindy turned 3. All team members (infant, toddler, and preschool) were frequently found at Saturday night bingo in the local community hall to raise money for equipment that Lindy needed and to help her grandmother cover expenses. It was during these kinds of events that Lindy's team was beginning to know one another as people and not just teachers, physical therapists, and nurses.

At $3\frac{1}{2}$ years, Lindy began to attend a Head Start center one afternoon a week. Her time at the center was slowly increased, but she missed frequently due to illness. She was alert to the children around her and they always looked forward to her arrival. The staff grew more comfortable with her special health-care needs and was able to use her equipment in ways that helped her to be a part of the group and not just an observer. Related service providers and the early childhood special educators visited both at home and at Head Start to assure everyone was participating in Lindy's program.

Lindy's challenges were many—the severity of her disabilities, the family's limited resources, her poor prognosis, the limited access to community resources, and the remoteness of her home. Yet Lindy proved more than her physician wrong by living; she showed many of the educators in the area that inclusion could (and should) be available anywhere for anyone if it is the best program for the child. It wasn't easy and it didn't occur immediately, but it did happen. Everyone on her team overcame both personal and agency barriers by working with Lindy, and Lindy went to school like everyone else (adapted from Circle of Inclusion, n.d.)

Contexts for Preschool Inclusion

As was done for Lindy, we must first look for a context in which to provide preschool inclusion. If we think of preschool inclusion broadly, that is, as preschool children who are typically developing and those with disabilities playing and learning together in early education programs, then there are many ways in which inclusion can occur. For preschool children, inclusion is a way of providing services that fit a child's individual needs, correspond with the wishes of a child's family, and reflect the unique opportunities that exist within a child and family's community. As Lindy's team assessed opportunities for Lindy in the community, the lack of organized access to typical group learning settings was evident. Further, Lindy's grandmother expressed a clear preference for services close to home. Armed with this information, the team identified the Head Start program as an appropriate future setting for Lindy.

Just as we see in Lindy's case, because of the challenge of not always having same-age peers within the schools of the district or even within the broader community, school districts have established inclusive options in a variety of contexts. Odom and colleagues (1999) identified three common organizational contexts implemented by school districts to achieve preschool inclusion: community-based programs, public school programs, and Head Start programs. The administrative issues that arise with the implementation within each of these contexts are unique. The issues, as well as innovative solutions to them, are described in detail in Wolery and Odom (2000) and are summarized briefly below.

Community-Based Programs

In this approach, school districts provide services to preschool children with disabilities, including those with more severe disabilities in privately owned or nonprofit childcare settings. The advantage of community-based programs, in addition to access to same-age peers, is that they may be located in the child's and family's own community, and they may reflect greater opportunity for family choice. School districts, however, must adopt policies to allow services to be provided outside of the public school building. Decisions about who pays tuition to the community-based programs must be made. That is, does the district "buy" a certain number of slots or do the parents absorb the cost because of a policy prohibiting payment to private programs? Odom and colleagues (1999) reported that sometimes policies have been established by which districts pay tuition for the educationally relevant portion of the day as specified on the IEP (e.g., 2.5 to 3 hours). A critical issue with this approach can be transportation. Odom and colleagues found that some programs transported children to and from their home to the child-care program, and in other programs parents provided the transportation and absorbed all costs.

Public School Programs

Some public schools do provide classes for typically developing preschool children and also use them as inclusive options for preschoolers with disabilities. This approach typically avoids logistical problems such as paying child-care tuition, providing transportation, and dealing with different regulations from different licensing agencies. In addition, teachers are employed by the school system. In many districts, teachers are required to have certification/licensure and training that exceeds what is required within community-based programs. Furthermore, school district administrators have more control over the quality of public school–based early education programs than in the community or Head Start programs (e.g., number of children, teacher-to-child ratio, curriculum, materials, and equipment).

Administrative challenges also arise from this approach. One such challenge occurs when the early education program is administratively housed in a division of the school district other than special education (which is often the case). Administrative resistance within the system for accommodating children with disabilities and other communication breakdowns between the divisions can occur. Another challenge presented by public school–based programs is finding acceptable inclusive placements. Many of these programs serve only 4- and 5-year-old children, thus not addressing the need for placements for 3-year-old children with disabilities. Further, many of these programs are established for at-risk populations and therefore are not available equally in all areas of the community.

Another challenge to note is when the school district develops a fee-for-service or tuition-based program. This type of arrangement may present challenges in both funding and public perception. In many school districts, the financial structure is not equipped to receive payment from parents for their typically developing children's participation in programs, so new policies and procedures must be established. In addition, public school–based child-care programs may be perceived by some early education programs in the community as being in competition. Their concern is that school-based programs have an unfair advantage when the school's program is supplemented by the school district. Tuition-based public school early education programs sometimes lead to an inadvertent segregation by income level (Odom et al., 1999). That is, parents of children who are typically developing who pay tuition are more likely to be of higher-income families who can afford the tuition. Most children in Head Start and publicly funded preschools for at-risk children come from lower-income families. Thus, middle-income parents of a child with a disability may more likely select the tuition-based program for their child because of the class makeup. A final challenge is space. In some school districts, finding even minimally adequate classroom space presents a significant challenge.

Head Start Programs

For many communities, Head Start represents a well-established early education resource, as it did for Lindy. National Head Start policy dictates that at least 10 percent of the children receiving Head Start services be children with disabilities, and in recent years the push has been toward providing services to children with substantial disabilities. Issues also arise with this approach (Odom et al., 1999). The schedules and regulations for Head Start programs and school districts are different, which requires some flexibility on the part of both agencies. Head Start has an income criterion that families must meet. For children with disabilities whose family incomes are above the criterion, Head Start programs have a limited number of income waivers that can be used to allow families to participate. Further Head Start programs and school districts may have different teaching philosophies and preparation requirements. As can be seen from Lindy's story, active collaboration between the school district and the Head Start agency, and in her case the early intervention agency, can lead to a positive outcome. In Lindy's case, such collaboration was fostered by open communication, sharing of resources, and joint planning and input from respective staffs, administrators, and Lindy's family.

Summary

The context for providing high-quality preschool inclusion for children with severe disabilities will differ from community to community. Most school districts create inclusive options for preschool children with disabilities that fit the unique factors of the community and district. Challenges exist for all approaches, and teams must find alternatives to overcome them.

Preparing and Supporting Adults to Work and Play Together Well

Change is stressful under the best of circumstances (Fullen, 2001). When children with severe disabilities are included in preschool programs, new adults also appear. These program personnel must adapt to new models of working and modify their current roles to meet the children's needs in the inclusive preschool. Thus preschool inclusive programs must develop strategies for preparing staff—such as the Head Start staff in Lindy's case—and supporting all members of the team to work together and form a functional team.

Preparation

Staff preparation activities are critical to ensuring that each individual approaches the inclusion of young children in an optimal way (Hargreaves, 1997). The basic goal of staff development activities should be for participants to acquire new knowledge and apply it to their practice in such a way that services for children with disabilities are improved. Thompson and colleagues (2002) provided a set of suggestions for an effective approach to inservice education for participants in preschool inclusion:

- Involve participants in planning by assessing their past experiences, prior training, and anticipated needs for inservice as it relates to the child and program. Regularly reassess their needs across time.

- Ensure that inservice begins before the child with disabilities starts in the program if at all feasible. In Lindy's case, because of a well-developed transition plan during her last six months of Part C services, preparation and training were provided in advance of her initial home services with the Head Start program and continued as she transitioned into the center-based program.

- Provide jointly delivered inservice for the entire team. Many of the topics and skills that need to be addressed will be beneficial to all team members.

- Provide incentives for participation such as release time from job responsibilities, additional pay, and college or continuing education credit. In Lindy's case the Head Start program was able to count the in-service time of the school district staff as an in-kind contribution for the purpose demonstrating community matching funds.

- Involve participants in delivering the content and encourage collaboration by recognizing and using each individual's expertise in the plan.

- Encourage family members to attend and participate in the in-service program as both receivers and presenters of information. For example, Lindy's grandmother provided the team with initial information on her nonverbal communicative responses. As the speech therapist and the grandmother worked together to shape Lindy's nonconventional responses into use of "eye-gaze choice making," together they shared Lindy's progress with the team as she moved to the Head Start classroom.

- Identify times and places to hold in-service sessions that will be convenient for the participants. Consider rotating places to introduce team members to various programs and facilities. Pay attention to the comfort of the participants during the inservice.

- Provide individualized training related to specific skills and for supporting specific unique needs that a child might present. For example, all of Lindy's direct support staff needed specific training to understand and address her positioning and handling needs.

- Evaluate in-service programs and sessions to ensure that the content and approach is meeting the perceived need of all team members. For Lindy this was particularly important given that her services changed quite significantly over the year and included new team members.

Collaboration

No matter what type of service delivery model or context used (see Odom et al., 1999), early childhood special educators, early childhood general educators, related services professionals, and families must work together to meet the needs of the child. Teamwork becomes a necessity (Lieber et al., 2001). According to one service provider, "The whole attitude that the preschool [special education] office is trying to put forth . . . is the collaborative model. . . . None of us has any magic. It's in our collective work that we can get things done" (Lieber, Beckman, & Horn, 1999, p. 7).

In Chapter 2 of this volume, collaboration as the cornerstone for effective inclusive education for learners with severe disabilities is discussed. While the same principles apply for preschool inclusion, the critical importance of effective collaboration warrants briefly discussing some ideas that can be used by teaching staff and others who work directly with young children (Lieber et al., 2001).

- Have a positive attitude toward change. While the teachers in Lindy's Head Start program were unsure of their ability to support Lindy, and her grandmother was nervous about letting others care for Lindy, the opportunity to work together more closely for the benefit of Lindy was a chance to "grow and stretch."

- Take the initiative. The early intervention staff together with the school district's early childhood special education teachers took the initiative to begin working together with the Head Start program for Lindy and her grandmother.
- Be flexible. Flexibility is crucial when groups of adults work together, because change and compromise are necessities.
- Develop communication strategies both formal and informal. Formal communication strategies such as regular face-to-face interaction with members of the team, providing written "visit" notes for all other team members, and monthly team meetings were used effectively by Lindy's team. Informal strategies such as the incidental interaction within the community resulted in strong team bonds.

Through these strategies Lindy's team grew into a group of adults who worked and played well together to provide a high-quality inclusive program for Lindy.

Access and Progress in the General Curriculum

For young children with disabilities in inclusive settings, a high-quality early childhood classroom is the necessary foundation (Bailey, McWilliams, Buysee, & Wesley, 1998; Wolery & Bredekamp, 1994). However, placement and participation in a high-quality early childhood classroom alone will not provide a sufficient level of instruction for addressing the individual learning needs of children with disabilities (Carta, Schwartz, Atwater, & McConnell, 1991). An important function of an educational team for children with disabilities should be to develop goals and objectives that (a) meet the unique needs of the child, (b) are meaningful for the child, and (c) are functional in a variety of contexts (Notari-Syverson & Schuster, 1995). However, these goals and objectives must not become the child's curriculum. Developing appropriate goals and objectives and supporting the individual needs of young children with severe disabilities requires early childhood special educators to anchor their child program planning in the expectation of the general education curriculum. Meeting the mandate of access and progress in the general curriculum requires educators not only to help the child access the environment and participate in the activities, but also to provide opportunities for the child to learn the important content reflected in the curriculum offered to all children in the early education program (Nolet & McLaughlin, 2000). The general curriculum should be viewed as the cornerstone to which all instruction is anchored.

Identifying the General Curriculum

The first step is to identify the general curriculum. A curriculum is not simply the array of activities that occur within the preschool classroom. Rather, a curriculum is an interrelated set of plans and activities that are intended to result in identifiable outcomes that pertain to student learning (Marsh & Willis, 1995). Sometimes preschool teachers will find that these outcomes are stated very directly, as is the case in the performance standards established in some states. At other times, curricular outcomes are simply implied by the program's choice of activities and materials. Curriculum is the "what" of early education; it is the content that the educators provide and that the children learn (Nolet & McLaughlin, 2000). It is separate from the strategies or procedures used to teach children the content, although the line between curriculum and instruction often is difficult to separate in day-to-day practice.

Because preschool teachers working with young children with severe disabilities, as noted earlier, will find themselves working in a range of contexts, identification of the preschool general curriculum is not always a simple task. For example, the preschool teacher working with Lindy found at least four curriculums across the programs in which children on her roster were participating. The Head Start program used the Creative Curriculum (Trister-Dodge & Colker, 1992), another program implemented a Montessori curriculum, another Developmentally Appropriate Practices (Bredekamp & Copple, 1997), and yet another used a behavior analytic approach. Each of these curriculum or curricula approaches represent different levels of specificity, scope, and sequence of the content that is to be taught. Further, these curriculums represent different levels of specificity related to the instructional/teaching strategies to be used. Ultimately all high-quality preschool programs have at the heart of their curriculum the outcome that children will make progress across the developmental domains of communication, social competence, fine and gross motor skills, cognitive abilities, and adaptive behaviors. The method used and emphasis placed on each developmental domain can vary greatly.

The primary task in identifying the preschool curriculum for young children with severe disabilities actually becomes identifying the most critical knowledge across developmental domains that all children will be expected to learn as a result of participating in the program and the approximate time frame in which the children would need to have acquired the knowledge. This list does not need to be exhaustive, but it should represent the most enduring, salient knowledge all the children need to learn. This "knowledge" then becomes the top priority in developing the individualized child outcomes and planning for their access and progress within this curriculum. For Lindy and the other children in her Head Start program, some of these "top priority" outcomes were: (a) communication skills to satisfy basic needs and to have access and control of their environment; (b) social competence within group contexts with their peers and adults; (c) physical skills that allow for active participation with the various aspects of the environment and independent mobility to move safely and freely around the environment; and (d) problem-solving skills to address dilemmas that arise within context of everyday activities. Each of these priority outcomes were seen as necessary for the children to be successful in the next environment they would enter in one to two years—kindergarten.

Supporting Access and Progress

Children with severe disabilities must have opportunities to participate as fully as typically developing children in all activities and routines. Teachers ensure the child's access to the preschool curriculum by making appropriate adaptations and modifications. Preschool teachers must also know how to embed individualized instruction into the ongoing activities and routines.

Let's examine modifications that teachers may make to support the child. A curriculum modification or adaptation is a change in a classroom activity of material that allows a child to participate (Horn, Lieber, Sandall, Schwartz, & Wolery, 2001). Increased participation creates more opportunities for children to develop and learn. Teachers should use a curriculum modification strategy when the child is interested in the ongoing activities but is not able to fully participate or may not stay with the activity long enough. The key is to help the child participate. Preschool teachers can implement a range of adaptations, and several authors have identified and classified these strategies (e.g., Cavallaro & Haney, 1999; Thompson et al., 2002). Researchers from the Early Childhood Research Institute on Inclusion (ECRII) identified and described eight types of curriculum modifications and adaptations: environment support, material adaptations, special equipment, use of children's preferences, simplification of the activity, adult support, peer support, and invisible support (Horn, Lieber, Sandall, & Schwartz, 2001; Lieber, Schwartz, Sandall, Horn, & Wolery, 1999; Sandall et al., 2002). Let's look at each of these and see how Lindy's team utilized them to facilitate her participation.

Three of the modification strategies address changing or adding materials or events within the classroom; that is, those things that are external to the child. *Environmental support* refers to altering the physical, social, and temporal environment to promote participation, engagement, and learning. For example, Lindy's teacher changed the layout of the various areas of the classroom slightly to allow her wheelchair to be moved easily from one area of the classroom to another even when one of her peers with less experience and skill was "driving." *Material adaptations* occur when teachers modify materials so that the child can participate as independently as possible. Examples of material adaptations for Lindy included stabilizing materials, such as taping the paper for painting to the table, using Velcro straps to hold the paintbrush in Lindy's hand to compensate for her weak grasp, using nonskid backing under the paint cup, and using contact paper as backing for collages because gluing was too difficult for her. *Special equipment* was another modification that was frequently used for Lindy. This included homemade as well as commercially available therapeutic equipment. For example, Lindy had a special switch positioned on the tray of her adapted wheelchair that she could press to "call" for assistance. A beanbag chair on the floor was used to provide her with supportive positioning during group activities in which everyone sat on the floor.

Two of the modification strategies focus on matching activities with the child's abilities and preferences: *use of children's preferences* and *simplification of the activity*. If the child is not taking advantage of the available opportunities, the adults identify child preferences and integrate them into the activity to make it more motivating. Lindy's physical therapist indicated that Lindy needed to actively participate in moving her limbs, particularly her legs. Her preschool teachers noted how well she attended during the large group circle time, particularly during fingerplay songs. They added some songs that required "peddling" and stepping movements of the children's legs and were pleased with the efforts Lindy produced in moving her legs "like" her friends. Simplifying a complicated activity by breaking it into smaller parts or changing or reducing the steps involved is the second strategy in this group. Here, for example, when Lindy was completing puzzles with the other children, she was provided with a puzzle in which only two, and later three, pieces were out of place. She could use a sliding movement to slide them into their correct "slots."

The final set of three modification strategies focuses on providing either *adult, peer, or invisible support* to the child. In adult support, a teacher may model an appropriate behavior, join the child in play, praise the child, and/or provide encouragement. For example, with her paintbrush in hand and everything set up to paint, Lindy was just watching the other children as they painted. The teacher joined in, commenting to Lindy that she too really enjoys seeing what the other children are painting. She then turned to Lindy and said, "Let's see what you can paint," assisted Lindy in getting paint on her brush, and praised Lindy's brushstrokes on the paper, noting that she had the same color as another child. Peers can also help children with severe disabilities reach learning objectives. For example, Lindy's teachers had her peers provide her with the picture choices of the next center she would like to participate in and then "drive" her chair to the area once she had indicated her choice. Finally, invisible supports occur when teachers rearrange aspects of naturally occurring activities to support the child's success in participating. For example, Lindy's class was making a card with a heart shape created by red paint fingerprints of each child as a farewell gift to a volunteer. The teacher made sure that Lindy was first in line for placing her fingerprint since her accuracy of hitting a "target" was limited and thus she would not be in danger of placing her fingerprint on top of another child's.

Curriculum modifications, used well, can help achieve one goal of inclusion, that is the active participation of young children with severe disabilities and typically developing children in the same classroom. However, modifications may not be sufficient to ensure that the child has learning opportunities to meet her individually defined needs in relation to the top priority outcomes of the general curriculum. To address this, early childhood special education professionals have recommended embedding instruction into existing classroom activities and routines (Bricker & Cripe, 1992; Davis, Kilgro, & Gamel-McCormick, 1998; Horn, Lieber, Sandall, Schwartz, & Li, 2000; Noonan & McCormick, 1995; Wolery & Wilburs, 1994). Embedding is "a procedure in which children are given opportunities to practice goals and objectives that are included within an activity or event in a manner that expands, modifies, or adapts the activity/event while remaining meaningful and interesting to children" (Bricker, Pretti-Frontczak, & McComas, 1998, p. 13).

Embedding learning opportunities is based on the premise that for many child-learning objectives, providing access to the general early childhood curriculum is insufficient (Horn, Lieber, Sandall, & Schwartz, 2001). We need to provide instruction through modeling, verbal prompting, and physical guidance in order for children with special needs to learn new or more complex skills within the context of the general curriculum and preschool environment. Teachers should identify the opportunities that are most salient to individualized learning objectives and embed short, systematic instructional interactions that support children's achievement of goals within existing routines and activities. For example, rather than setting up special sessions to have Lindy learn to indicate choice with an eye gaze, the task was embedded into the ongoing activities: choosing between two peers' photographs to indicate by whom she wanted to sit in opening circle, choosing between a drawing of a cup or spoon to indicate whether she was ready for a drink or bit of food during her snack, choosing between two symbols for center options to indicate to which center she would like to move next, and so on.

With embedded learning opportunities the activities and routines become the structure for supporting children's learning. Many of the activities are child initiated, so we know they are motivating (Bricker & Cripe, 1992). By embedding effective instruction into fun and motivating activities, learning often occurs more quickly (Losardo & Bricker, 1994). More important, since the children have learned the skill in a more natural setting, they are able to use the skill when they need it to obtain an item or participate in an activity. Teachable moments are created, recognized, and used to enhance a child's developmental progress. As with all good instruction, progress toward achieving learning objectives is monitored. Instructional decisions, such as progressing to more complex or next-level skills or changing the instructional procedures, are made through careful analysis of data collected. The focus is on access to and participation in fun, enjoyable, and interesting activities for young children while making learning progress.

Facilitating Family-Centered Inclusion

As noted in Chapter 5 of this book, proving services in a family-centered way has become a highly valued practice in special education, and particularly so in early childhood special education (Sandall, McLean, & Smith, 2000). Part of our role as preschool teachers involves listening to families' concerns and desires for their children, providing them with the necessary information to make decisions about services, and recognizing the diversity that exists across families. When planning services and placements for children, keeping the family at the center of the process is essential. One of the major components of a family-centered approach to service provision is the notion that families are the primary decision makers for their child and that they have a right to participate actively in making decisions for their child (Winton, 1993). However, to be active and informed decision makers, families need to have easy and complete access to information.

When families learn that they have a child with disabilities, they usually want as much information as they can possibly get about the disability. They will want to know how their child's health and development are affected and what to expect for the child's future. With a child with severe disability, the focus initially may be on stabilizing the child's health and basic survival. Preschool teachers must understand that the family's need to know may be more pressing than making placement decisions or learning about IEPs. Lindy's grandmother did not begin to think about "services" for supporting Lindy's learning until well into her second year of life, when she had already defied the doctor's dim predictions.

Preschool teachers need to recognize the important link between communication and access to information, and decision making. For families to make well-informed decisions about their child and their child's program, they need access to good information. Providing real access to information, however, is not simply a matter of delivering a packet of information about the program that has been prepared by school officials. Information must be provided in ways that are consistent with family members' language, culture, experience, educational background, and current expressed focus of need. Providers need to encourage families to ask questions and explore options in order to determine the best match for the needs of the child and family.

As preschool teachers and other members of the team develop relationships with a family, they frequently learn more about the family's frame of reference. Learning about how the family views the child and the child's disability and what goals the family has for the child can help us understand their view on service options presented. In many cases, such knowledge can help the team better match the program plan to the needs of the family.

Because of Lindy's health issues and her grandmother's concerns about keeping her healthy, the team developed a plan for service that allowed Lindy to build her physical stamina slowly over time, and let her grandmother closely monitor her progress along this dimension.

Preschool team members must remember the basics. One of the needs expressed most by families is that their child receive services that match his or her needs (Beckman, 1996). If the parents feel their child is not benefiting from the program, they are unlikely to be satisfied, even if it is a program that meets indicators of a high-quality inclusive preschool. An essential component of a program is that the families believe the child is benefiting and the teacher communicates effectively with families, provides useful information, and builds families' trust (Hanson, Beckman, & Horn, 2001).

Conclusion

A cornerstone of early education is the establishment of educational goals that result in children learning and developing (Bredekamp & Copple, 1997; Sandall, McLean, & Smith, 2000). High-quality individualized instruction within high-quality programs is the early educators' means to ensuring that all young children learn and develop. Individualization—or, put another way, ensuring a match between what is offered and what is needed—is the critical component. This match is unique to each child and family and changes across time. Through collaborative partnerships across all team members, families and professionals can ensure that children with severe disabilities thrive, learn, and develop in high-quality inclusive preschool programs. Success in the preschool years can lay a solid foundation for the school years to follow.

References

Bailey, D. B., McWilliams, R. A., Buysee, V., & Wesley, P. W. (1998). Inclusion in the context of competing values in early childhood education. *Early Childhood Research Quarterly, 13,* 27–48.

Beckman, P. (1996). *Strategies for working with families of young children with disabilities.* Baltimore: Paul H. Brookes.

Bredekamp, S., & Copple, C. (1997). *Developmentally appropriate practice in early childhood programs* (rev. ed.). Washington, DC: National Association for the Education of Young Children.

Bricker, D., & Cripe, J. J. (1992). *An activity-based approach to early intervention.* Baltimore: Paul H. Brookes.

Bricker, D., Pretti-Frontczak, K., & McComas, N. R. (1998). *An activity-based approach to early intervention* (2nd ed.). Baltimore: Paul H. Brookes.

Carta, J., Schwartz, I., Atwater, J., & McConnell, S. (1991). Developmentally appropriate early practice: Appraising its usefulness for young children with disabilities. *Topics in Early Childhood Special Education, 11,* 1–20.

Cavallaro, C., & Haney, M. (1999). *Preschool inclusion.* Baltimore: Paul H. Brookes.

Davis, M. D., Kilgro, J. L., & Gamel-McCormick, M. (1998). *Young children with special needs.* Boston: Allyn and Bacon.

Fullen, M. G. (2001). *The new meaning of educational change* (3rd ed.). New York: Teachers College Press.

Hanson, M. J., Beckman, P. J., & Horn, E. (2001). Family perceptions of inclusion. In S. L. Odom (Ed.), *Widening the circle: Including children with disabilities in preschool programs* (pp. 98–107). New York: Teachers College Press.

Hargreaves, A. (1997). *Rethinking educational change with heart and mind.* Alexandria, VA: Association for Supervision and Curriculum Development.

Horn, E., Lieber, J., Sandall, S., & Schwartz, I. (2001). Embedded learning opportunities as an instructional strategy for supporting children's learning in inclusive programs. In M. Ostrosky & S. Sandall (Eds.), *Young exceptional children monograph series: Teaching strategies—what to do to support young children's development* (vol. 3, pp. 59–70). Longmont, CO: Sopris West.

Horn, E., Lieber, J., Sandall, S., Schwartz, I., & Li, S. (2000). Supporting young children's IEP goals in inclusive settings through embedded learning opportunities. *Topics in Early Childhood Special Education, 20,* 208–223.

Horn, E., Lieber, J., Sandall, S., Schwartz, I., & Wolery, R. (2001). Classroom models of individualized instruction. In S. L. Odom (Ed.), *Widening the circle: Including children with disabilities in preschool programs* (pp. 46–60). New York: Teachers College Press.

Lieber, J., Beckman, P., & Horn, E. (1999). Working together to provide services for young children with disabilities: Lessons from inclusive preschool programs. In S. Graham & K. R. Harris (Eds.), *Teachers working together: Enhancing the performance of students with special needs* (pp. 1–29). Cambridge, MA: Brookline Books.

Lieber, J., Schwartz, I., Sandall, S., Horn, E., & Wolery, R. (1999). Curricular considerations for young children in inclusive settings. In C. Seefeldt (Ed.), *The early childhood curriculum: Current findings in theory and practice* (3rd ed., pp. 243–265). New York: Teachers College Press.

Lieber, J., Wolery, R., Horn, E., Tschantz, J., Beckman, P., & Hanson, M. (2001). Collaborative relationships among adults in inclusive preschool programs. In S. L. Odom (Ed.), *Widening the circle: Including children with disabilities in preschool programs* (pp. 81–97). New York: Teachers College Press.

Losardo, A., & Bricker, D. (1994). Activity-based and direct instruction: A comparison study. *American Journal of Mental Retardation, 98,* 744–765.

Marsh, C., & Willis, G. (1995). *Curriculum: Alternative approaches, ongoing issues.* Englewood Cliffs, NJ: Merrill/Prentice-Hall.

Nolet, V., & McLaughlin, M. J. (2000). *Accessing the general curriculum: Including students with disabilities in standards-based reform.* Thousand Oaks, CA: Sage.

Noonan, M. J., & McCormick, L. (1995). "Mission impossible"? Developing meaningful IEPs for children in inclusive preschool settings. *Frontline, 2,* 1–3.

Notari-Syverson, A., & Schuster, S. (1995). Putting real-life skills into IEP/IFSPs for infants and young children. *Teaching Exceptional Children, 27,* 29–32.

Odom, S. L., Horn, E., Marquart, J., Hanson, M., Wolfberg, P., Beckman, P., Lieber, J., Li, S., Schwartz, I., Janko, S., & Sandall, S. (1999). On the forms of inclusion: Organizational context and service delivery models. *Journal of Early Intervention, 22,* 185–199.

Odom, S., Wolery, R., Lieber, J., & Horn, E. (2001). Social policy and preschool inclusion. In S. L. Odom (Ed.), *Widening the circle: Including children with disabilities in preschool programs* (pp. 120–136). New York: Teachers College Press.

Sandall, S., McLean, M., & Smith, B. J. (2000). *DEC recommended practices in early intervention/early childhood special education.* Longmont, CO: Sopris West.

Sandall, S., Schwartz, I., Joseph, G., Chou, H., Horn, E., Lieber, J., Odom, S., & Wolery, R. (2002). *Building blocks for successful early childhood programs: Strategies for including all children.* Baltimore: Paul H. Brookes.

Thompson, B., Wickham, D., Wegner, J., Mulligan Ault, M., Shanks, P., & Reinertson, B. (2002). *Handbook for the inclusion of young children with severe disabilities.* Lawrence, KS: Learner Managed Designs.

Trister-Dodge, D., & Colker, L. J. (1992). *Creative Curriculum for Early Childhood.* Washington, DC: Teaching Strategies.

Winton, P. (1993). Providing family support in integrated settings: Research and recommendations. In C. Peck, S. Odom, & D. Bricker (Eds.), *Integrating young children with disabilities into community programs: Ecological perspectives on research and implementation* (pp. 65–80). Baltimore: Paul H. Brookes.

Wolery, M., & Bredekamp, S. (1994). Developmentally appropriate practice and young children with disabilities: Contextual issues in the discussion. *Journal of Early Intervention, 18,* 331–341.

Wolery, M., & Wilburs, J. (1994). *Including children with special needs in early childhood programs.* Washington, DC: National Association for the Education of Young Children.

Wolery, R. A., & Odom, S. L. (2000). *An administrator's guide to preschool inclusion.* Chapel Hill: University of North Carolina, Frank Porter Graham Child Development Center and the Early Childhood Research Institute on Inclusion.

12 Elementary School

CHRISTINE SALISBURY

University of Illinois-Chicago

TONI STRIEKER

Kennesaw State University

Elementary schools provide an important initial environment within which young children begin their formal education. The early elementary years in particular provide a range of experiences that affect the young child's physical, social, emotional, and intellectual development. While core curriculum and instructional practices influence the young child's development of content knowledge and learning skills, other elements play an equally important role in shaping the child's understandings about school as a learning community. Embedded within the ecology of the school is a culture that reflects the underlying values, activities, and meanings of its participants. The diversity of the classroom and school context contributes in a meaningful way to the culture of the school.

The composition of today's classrooms mirrors the diversity of the communities in which young children live. These classrooms and their inherent diversity create opportunities for young children to learn about and appreciate perspectives other than their own (Bowman & Stott, 1994). Currently comprising over 10 percent of the school population (U.S. Department of Education, 1999), students with disabilities and those considered "at risk" represent one source of the increasing diversity in today's elementary classrooms.

As schools and classrooms have become more diverse, teachers have been challenged to provide instruction that is responsive to the needs of all students, including those with disabilities. Responsive instructional practices address the diversity within and among students, and connect curriculum to what is known about how students learn. According to McGregor and Vogelsberg (2000), teaching practices that are responsive to the ways in which students learn include: (a) integrated approaches to curricular content; (b) instruction designed to capitalize on different ways of learning; (c) teaching for thinking, problem solving, and understanding to optimize student achievement; and (d) assessment connected to teaching and learning. Clear parallels exist between these strategies and prevailing practices in the field of general education (Carr & Harris, 2001; Tomlinson, 1999).

Inclusive practices represent a perspective about how we educate children and structure learning environments to support them. Recognizing that there is limited consensus in the field regarding a definition of inclusion, we draw upon the work of colleagues to characterize our frame of reference:

> *Inclusion is not just a place or a method of delivering instruction, but is a philosophy that undergirds the entire educational system. Inclusion is part of the culture of a school, defining how students, teachers, administrators, parents and others view the potential of children. (National Association of State Boards of Education, 1990)*

Inclusive schooling practices are therefore responsive to the needs of individual students. Effective practices at the elementary level take into account structures, strategies, and supports in the design and implementation of quality instruction.

Focusing Points

Four points serve as unifying themes for the information presented in this chapter. While shared across the grade levels in many ways, their utility is particularly well suited to the elementary level.

Responsive Instruction

Elementary classrooms that are responsive to the diverse needs of all learners ensure that accommodations and modifications are made to enable students with disabilities, including those with significant needs, to participate in and benefit from general education classroom instruction. By addressing specific barriers to learning, schools meet the individual needs of all students and demonstrate commitment to diversity and inclusion. Responsive practices also involve the promotion of caring and supportive learning communities. Such efforts create an emotionally and socially supportive culture within the classroom in which all students feel safe, welcome, and integral as members of the learning community.

Classrooms in Context

Classrooms exist within the larger context of the elementary school and its local community. Roach, Salisbury, Strieker, and McGregor (2001) describe the importance of context and the interdependencies among structures, policies, and practices in inclusive schools and systems. It is important to understand how what transpires in classrooms can be influenced by factors within and outside the classroom. Such insight can help teachers and support personnel make decisions that are responsive to the needs of all children. General education, whether at the building or classroom level, should be considered the referent context for developing and implementing inclusive teaching and learning practices (Salisbury, Strieker, Roach, & McGregor, 2001).

It is also important to make visible the implicit or less understood elements of structure and policy that affect the capacity of schools to serve all learners (Salisbury et al.,

2001). Structures such as schedules, teams, location of classrooms, school calendars, and classroom norms influence the teaching and learning environment in schools. Policies are the written and unwritten rules that drive how schools operate. For example, policies influence what curriculum gets taught, how resources are deployed, which students are assigned to which teachers and schools, and how testing and assessment will be done. Practices are the instructional and noninstructional activities that create learning opportunities for children within and outside of the classroom. As aspiring or practicing classroom teachers, you should find this information helpful in understanding and leveraging the factors that affect your instructional practices and ultimately your students' performance.

Learning Opportunities

Elementary classrooms have a culture of their own, and within that culture are activity settings and routines that create learning opportunities for students (Gallimore, 1996). Classroom and school routines anchor the daily work of teachers and provide the context into which IEP goals and objectives can be embedded. Analysis of current and future context requirements has been a prevailing recommended practice in the field of special education for many years (see Salisbury & Vincent, 1990; Vincent et al., 1980) and helps to inform the development of curriculum and responsive instructional practices.

Collaborative Practices

A collaborative culture is inherent in an inclusive elementary school (Salisbury, Palombaro, & Hollowood, 1993). Inclusive schools have structures that support teaming, planning, and problem solving among students, parents, and professional staff. At the foundation of these collaborative practices are attitudes and beliefs regarding the value of diversity and the importance that all students, including those with disabilities, be included in classroom and school activities. When practices are collaboratively designed and implemented, staff and students alike are viewed as integral members of classrooms. Each contributes in ways that are meaningful (see Horn et al., Chapter 2).

Elementary Context: Classroom Activities and Structures

To understand how to create responsive classroom-level supports, it is first important to situate what we do on behalf of students with disabilities in the larger context of the elementary school curriculum. This information provides an important framework for understanding the changes that occur in elementary classrooms when students with disabilities, including those with significant needs, are included.

Since 1990, professionals in research, policy, curriculum development, and school reform have called for changes in instructional practices in America's schools (Zemelman, Daniels, & Hyde, 1993). Despite the fact that these groups represent different subject specialties, the reforms called for in teaching and learning are strikingly similar. Table 12.1 summarizes the key instructional reforms that relate to elementary classrooms. These

TABLE 12.1 Educational Reforms Applicable at the Elementary Level

Reform Characteristic	Implications for Classroom Practices
Student-centered	Opportunities for students to select their reading and writing topics, research partners
Authentic	Using real-life events and issues as focus of instruction; using performance descriptions as an adjunct to grades and tests
Challenging	High expectations for all students to learn complex information and skills as directed by the local and state standards
Constructivist	Opportunities for deep study on fewer topics
Developmental	Attention to varying cognitive, affective, and learning styles of individual students
Cognitive	Emphasis on higher-order thinking to learn key concepts, principles, and skills
Democratic	Heterogeneous groups that include students with disabilities
Collaborative	Using cooperative learning to develop the classroom into an interdependent unit
Reflective	Students engage in self-regulation and management of their own learning
Holistic	Subject matter taught in integrated units
Social, active learning	Active, noisy classrooms

reforms create a context in the classroom within which all students, including those with severe disabilities, can be taught.

Daniels (1994) suggests that all of these reforms can be met through the implementation of six teacher methods/structures: integrative units, cooperative learning, representing-to-learn, classroom workshop, authentic learning experiences, and reflective assessment. These six teaching methods/structures provide the foundation for all instruction and are applicable to all grade levels and subject areas. Importantly, these practices develop classrooms that are inclusive and responsive to the learning needs of a diverse student population because they foster choice, responsibility, expression, and an overall sense of community. Each method is briefly described below.

Integrated Units

Integrated units employ interdisciplinary inquiry and are often co-planned with students (Beane, 1995). Integrated curriculum design embeds mandated content and skills (and IEP goals and objectives) within units of instruction that are complex and holistic. Among the most common models are whole-language approaches, problem-based learning, and reading across the disciplines. Integrated units are particularly responsive to the needs of students with disabilities because they assist students in understanding the connections between the disciplines and make the abstract concrete.

Cooperative Learning

Over the past two decades, classroom researchers have demonstrated the effectiveness of cooperative learning structures in improving the academic achievement and social development of students with (Cullen & Pratt, 1992) and without disabilities (Cohen, 1986; Sharan & Sharan, 1992). Four common instructional structures that support cooperative learning in an elementary classroom are:

- *Partner reading.* Students read in pairs to one another, each holding a copy of the same book. Whether reading or listening, students are required to ask questions. Same-age or cross-age partners can use this strategy.
- *Literature circles.* Literature circles are classroom book clubs where students select books and reading partners, set their own schedules, and find ways to share their reading with others. Older elementary students use note taking or journaling strategies to record their responses to the reading.
- *Peer response and editing groups.* Heterogeneous groups of three to five students meet on an ongoing basis to assist peers in developing written assignments. Some teachers prefer for students to meet on a regular basis; however, students are free to ask for support from their groups during undesignated free time.
- *Group investigations.* This strategy uses multiple student research teams to investigate complex topics or current events. Initially, the classroom teacher facilitates a whole-class discussion around the topic or event. The class then divides into the research teams that study various components of the larger topic. By definition, cooperative learning requires heterogeneous grouping of students; therefore, it naturally lends itself to including students with disabilities in the instructional process. Students with disabilities can be paired with more-able readers and they can also serve as cross-age tutors for younger students who are less-able readers. LaPlant and Zane (1994) described adaptations to partner learning that were successful in assisting students with disabilities to meet social and academic goals. Peer-mediated models of support, such as classwide peer tutoring, also have proven successful in increasing the engagement and outcomes of students with mild and moderate disabilities (Greenwood, 1996).

Representing-to-Learn

Constructivist learning theory suggests that for students to remember new information and skills, they must act upon them. Representing-to-learn facilitates students' construction of meaning and provides a means for students to share what they have learned by writing, drawing, sketching, mapping, moving, singing, and so on. These opportunities are different from traditional tasks in that they are embedded throughout the instructional day and are not always graded. Rather, teachers and students use them during class to share understandings. Three popular strategies are: (a) journals (i.e., ungraded, written work designed to stimulate discussion) and genres (i.e., more detailed types of written work such as mystery writing, poetry, editorials and/or laboratory reports; (b) two-minute videos (i.e., a production assignment that involves researching, developing, and recording a presentation using a written script); and (c) hypermedia stacks (i.e., use of software packages like *Wiggleworks* and *Hyperstudio* to allow students to author multimedia presentations to express their understanding of complex ideas). Because representing-to-learn activities are flexible and creative, they facilitate the inclusion of students with disabilities by increasing their rate of interaction with nondisabled peers.

Classroom Workshop

Workshop approaches are also consistent with constructivist theory and provide time for students to engage real-life learning tasks. In the context of classroom workshop, the learners observe teacher demonstrations and then engage in the same task with feedback and close supervision. The classroom workshop is a powerful strategy in an inclusive classroom because of the individualized nature of the student–teacher conferences. The dialogue progresses around the product the student has produced, and when the child's need for support is recognized by the teacher, he or she has the opportunity to address the student's needs as the product is developed. One example, writer's workshop, has gained popularity in the area of language arts over the past 15 years. Graves (1983) and Calkins (1986) have developed cooperative learning roles and responsibilities to organize the activities conducted during writer's workshop. Similar models have been offered in math (Halter, 1998), history (Jorgensen, 1993), and science (Saul et al., 1993).

Authentic Learning Experiences

According to Daniels (1994), authentic learning is couched in real-life experiences and brings together the child's natural curiosity with his or her intellect and emotions. Authentic curriculum addresses real issues and helps children understand the world in which they live. For example, students can learn about equity in the classroom by practicing principles of democracy. Authentic learning experiences in schools take many forms, from writing a personal letter to planting a garden, and often provide opportunities for children to engage in service-related activities in their communities. These strategies can be very successful in inclusive classrooms because they provide opportunities for students to engage in functional, real-life activities.

Reflective Assessment

Reflective assessment requires children to think critically about their own performance and daily work. Reflective assessment is different from traditional assessment practice in that it is directly linked to focusing instruction and developing responsive practices. Reflective assessment focuses upon how students use information, not just on what students know or can remember. Reflective assessment is collaborative, and often involves the teacher and student examining information so that students self-monitor and evaluate their own progress. To be competent in implementing this type of assessment, the teacher needs a rich repertoire of strategies including portfolios, conference checklists, anecdotal records, rubrics, and curriculum-based tests.

Inclusive Classroom Structures and Practices

The overview of general education reforms provides a framework for understanding the context of elementary classrooms. With this information as our backdrop, let's meet Sara (see Box 12.1), who attends fourth grade in an inclusive elementary school.

Table 12.2 provides a sample of Sara's individualized goals and objectives from her IEP. Remember that classrooms exist within a larger organizational arena, and so it is important to understand the visible and less visible structures that make it possible for Sara and her teachers to be successful. Although schools vary in their curricular and instructional practices, there are common factors that affect the delivery of instruction that should be taken into account in developing instructional supports for all learners. These factors are correlated with effective instruction and tend to be prominent in schools that are building capacity to think and act inclusively: (1) assignment to age-appropriate, grade-level classroom; (2) adequate time for planning; (3) embedding instruction in classroom routines and activities; (4) creative scheduling; and (5) collaboration and co-teaching.

Assignment to Age-Appropriate, Grade-Level Classroom

Inclusive elementary schools assign students with disabilities, including those with significant needs, to the grade-level classroom they would attend if they did not have a disability. For Sara, this meant that at age 5 she entered kindergarten along with her neighborhood friends. Each year, Sara either moved to the next grade level or, like her peers, stayed within a looped team (grades K–2).

Planning

Inclusive elementary schools provide ample time, on an ongoing basis, for the instructional team to plan for the instructional needs of their students. Planning, preparing, teaching, and

---

B O X 12.1

Sara

Sara attends her neighborhood school in an urban community and has a ready smile. At six months of age Sara was diagnosed with severe cognitive and physical impairments. She has limited visual tracking and scanning ability. Sara loves music and "lights up" when she hears it come on. She has trouble holding her head in position, but can reach, grasp, and release with both arms when in her prone stander. She appears to enjoy textures and is able to acknowledge and attend to her peers with smiles and eye contact. Sara can anticipate events, choose between objects, and communicate through movements and sounds. She can eat, drink, and swallow, but does not know how to use utensils at this time. While Sara appears to enjoy interactions with classmates at school, out-of-school recreation and social life is limited. Sara lives at home with her mom, dad, and older brother.

TABLE 12.2 **Sample Goals and Objectives from Sara's IEP**

Annual Goal	Sample Objective
Sara will increase choice and control within her environment. (cognitive/social)	Sara will select the classmate to assist her each day by visually scanning two enlarged photographs of her peers.
Sara will increase receptive and expressive communication through the use of movement. (communication)	Sara will request object/action by signaling with movement cues.
Sara will increase her social participation during mealtime. (social/self-help)	Sara will use a cup and straw with minimal spilling. Sara will initiate social interactions during cooperative group lessons by orienting or gazing to peers.
Sara will anticipate events or changes in classroom routines. (cognitive/social/visual sensory/motor)	Sara will anticipate changes in the events and demonstrate understanding by shifting her gaze or smiling.
Sara will improve motor function.	Sara will use a switch to signal changes in class activities.

student-conferencing time can be obtained through a number of strategies (Jorgensen, Fisher, Sax, & Skaglund, 1998):

- *Block scheduling* (create fewer classes and more opportunities to meet)
- *Restructuring or rescheduling time* (teach more minutes four days per week; stagger schedules; create a common lunch period for teachers followed by a planning period)
- *Changing staffing patterns* (bring in regular substitute teachers; use other adults to create release time; create a hobby period once a week, staffed with parents and community leaders; have older students work with minimal supervision with younger students; group two smaller classes together)
- *Adding time to the school day or year* (shorten classroom time each day, but add more days to the school year; extend the school day; move to a year-round schedule; add meeting days to school year)

In addition to ongoing planning, transition planning must be conducted as students move from one grade level to the next or from one school to the next. Transition planning provides the opportunities for parents and professionals to share information, coordinate services and supports, and orient the child to his or her new classroom space, teachers, and peers (Rosenkoetter, Hains, & Fowler, 1994).

Transition planning was conducted for Sara as she moved from second to third grade. Persons who attended her transition planning session included the sending and receiving (general and special education) teachers, her mother, and her speech pathologist, vision specialist, occupational therapist, and inclusion facilitator. The transition planning team emphasized the importance of maintaining Sara's time in general education to maximize her exposure to verbal 8-year-olds and discussed the importance of implementing class activities, structures, and routines to ensure Sara's safety. The instructional team that was *sending* Sara recommended: (a) instructional practices that provided opportunities for Sara to learn self-help skills and maximize her residual vision; (b) appropriate reinforcers such as music, manipulatives, switch toys, choice of activities, and peers; and (c) strategies for promoting the inclusion of Sara in everyday school activities. Sara's *receiving* teachers requested: (a) training in lifting and positioning, (b) a tilt chair and head strap, (c) assistance with developing a germ-control plan, and (d) information about the ways that Sara learns best. The transition team recommended that a teacher assistant, rather than a personal assistant, serve as the paraeducator for Sara's new class. Sharing information and including key personnel in the transition process helped ensure that Sara's transition was smooth and that she was successful.

Embedding Instruction in Classroom Routines and Activities

Classroom routines and activity settings provide natural opportunities for teaching students important knowledge and skills. At the elementary level, students learn procedural skills that help them regulate their own behavior. For example, students learn to keep work materials organized, manage free time, make decisions about how to spend their time, respond to timelines, and plan within groups. Each day, Sara's teacher updates an interactive bulletin board that acts as an organizer and assists all students in developing important skills and habits. The board includes "Activities for Today," brief descriptions of the assignments, and important due dates and folders for students to use to submit their completed work. Sara needs additional support to understand and organize her day. Each day, her speech therapist and teachers create a picture schedule for Sara. Staff create opportunities for Sara to be independent and help her coordinate her preferences with the activities of her peers.

For Sara, the general education classroom and related arts classes in her school provide rich settings in which IEP and non-IEP skills can be taught. Sara's teachers and therapists use an "IEP at a Glance" tool to determine where Sara's goals and objectives can best be met during the course of the school day. For example, her physical therapists decided to teach posturing supported by a head strap during lunchtime. Sara's general and special education teachers decided that writer's workshop provided opportunities for Sara to select preferences using eye gaze and/or request objects with movement cues. Her teachers also identified cooperative learning games as opportunities for Sara to use her switch to indicate changes in student activities. Finally, her teachers created opportunities for Sara to select peers to assist her during class transitions through use of Sara's gaze at enlarged photographs of her peers. Figure 12.1 provides a sample of Sara's "IEP at a Glance" and Figure 12.2 (pp. 232–233) provides an example of Sara's instructional day.

FIGURE 12.1 Sara's IEP at a glance.

IEP Objectives	7:30 Arrive	8:00 DOL	8:15 Spanish	8:40 Read	9:15 Free Play	10:15 Writer's Workshop	10:30 Lunch / Toilet	11:00 Math	12:00 Special	12:50 Recess / Toilet	1:15 Snack	1:30 Science or Social Studies	2:00 Lit Circles	2:35 Depart
Eat	I						I				I			
"More"			O		O		I				I			
Pincer					I		I		I		I	I		
Palmar			I	I	I	I			I	I		I	I	
Request			I	O	I	O		O	O	I	O			
Switch			I		I			I				I	I	
Choice: Gaze	I	I		I	I	I	I	I	I	I		I	I	
Sit Posture	O	O	O	O	O	O	O	O	O	O	O	O	O	O
Accept/Reject	O	O	O	O	O	O	O	O	O	O	O	O	O	O
Scan			I				I	I	I	I			I	
Extend Arm	G		I	I				I				I	I	G
Lift Hips							G			G				

KEY: I = instruction; O = as opportunities arise; G = generalization

231

FIGURE 12.2 Example of Sara's day.

Time & Class Activities	Class Activity IEP Objectives	Accommodation/ Modification	Person Responsible or Person Supporting Sara
7:30–8:00 ■ Review Sheets ■ Accelerated Reading ■ Book Bags ■ Notes from Home	■ Lift arms to assist in undressing ■ Use eye gaze to select peer	■ Peer pushes Sara to bus ■ Home/school communication notebook indicates family activities, concerns & questions	Paraeducator checks notebook & assists with undressing
8:00–8:15 ■ Daily Oral Math or Language ■ Partner Reading	■ Sit erect in chair ■ Use eye gaze to select peer	Sara's wheelchair is fitted with a head strap for her to use during partner reading	Classroom teacher positions Sara in her chair
8:15–8:40 ■ Spanish Games ■ Spanish Songs	■ Activate sound using switch ■ Use Palmar grasp	Horn is activated with a Big Mac switch for Sara to hit at appropriate times during Spanish Vocabulary Game	Peer assembles and positions switch for Sara to use
8:40–9:15 Reading (station teaching with 2 teachers & independent work)	■ Use pincer grasp ■ Activate sound using switch to indicate time to change groups	Sara is seated next to her teacher. As the students read, Sara grasps the pages (using a pincer grasp)	Classroom teacher
9:15–10:15 ■ Free Play ■ Bathroom (Transition Time)	■ Visually scan to select peers to assist ■ Lift hips during changing	Enlarged photographs of class-mates for Sara to visually scan	Parent volunteers take individual pictures of all of the students in the class and laminate them
10:15–10:30 ■ Writer's Workshop	■ Focus to indicate choice ■ Uses smile to accept & or frown to reject	Toys to represent the characters and objects in the story. Sara selects a toy to hold (Palmar grasp) by smiling when it is offered	Paraprofessional and teachers collect toys and objects to coincide with story starters
10:30–11:00 Lunch	■ Use eating utensil ■ Use gesture to indicate "more" ■ Use pincer grasp	Adapted eating utensils	Occupational therapist orders adapted materials

232

Time/Activity	Sara's Objectives	Adaptations	Personnel
11:00–12:00 Math (station teaching with 2 teachers, parents & independent work)	▪ Request objects/actions by shifting & focusing her gaze ▪ Activate sound using switch to indicate time to change groups	Large objects or manipulatives used to teach the math lesson. Sara requests one object from field of two	Paraeducator and teachers collect toys, objects & other manipulatives to teach math concepts
12:00–12:50 Specials: ▪ Art ▪ Music ▪ PE	▪ Use pincer or Palmar grasp ▪ Focus gaze to indicate choice ▪ Accept or reject task	Sara is given a picture response card on a Popsicle stick for her to hold (using Palmar grasp) above her head to answer questions	▪ Occupational therapists order Popsicle sticks ▪ Paraprofessional creates picture response cards
12:50–1:15 Recess (Transition Time)	▪ Visually scan to select peers to assist	Enlarged photographs of classmates for Sara to visually scan	Parent volunteers take individual pictures of all of the students in the class and laminate them
1:15–1:30 Snack	▪ Use gesture to indicate "more" ▪ Use pincer grasp	Sara will use pincer grasp to pick up snack with her fingers	Paraprofessional to assist during eating times to ensure that Sara doesn't choke on food
1:30–2:00 Science or Social Studies (2-minute video)	▪ Use gestures or smile to indicate anticipation of event ▪ Use Palmar or pincer grasp	Like her peers, Sara wears a costume to portray historical event in the 2-minute video. Sara smiles to indicate anticipation of going "on-stage"	Classroom teacher and parent volunteers create costumes for video presentation
2:00–2:35 Literature Circles	▪ Use Palmar or pincer grasp ▪ Extend arm above head ▪ Visually scan to select peers to assist	Create picture response card to illustrate story & glue on Popsicle sticks. Answers to teacher questions are written on the back. Sara holds the picture (extending her arm) as peer reads answers from card	Paraprofessional creates picture response cards
2:35 Depart from School	▪ Lift arms to assist in dressing	▪ Home/school communication log completed and returned to parents ▪ Peer of Sara's choice pushes her to bus	Classroom teacher and paraprofessional write to parents regarding the events of the day

233

Creative Scheduling

Block scheduling.   Block scheduling provides related services providers, special education, and other support teachers with the time and opportunity to work with students for longer periods of time and/or on a less frequent basis (Snell, Lowman, & Canady, 1996). For example, rather than scheduling students for speech therapy in separate thirty-minute sessions two days a week, students are scheduled for one classroom-based session, one day per week. The longer session allows the therapist to observe the student in his or her natural setting and more fully understand the functional requirements of daily classroom activities. Many times, related service providers also co-teach lessons in the general education classroom, using one of the models described earlier. Block scheduling also creates opportunities for therapists and teachers to plan and develop unit materials in ways that include all students.

Flexible schedules.   Flexible schedules are designed to provide general education teachers with classroom-based support during key instructional times and/or to allow for support to students with challenging needs. For example, to receive adequate support, the general education teachers may have to stagger their classes across the day such that language arts is taught in the morning and the afternoon, rather than in the morning only. With this model, students with disabilities are scheduled into age-appropriate general education classrooms according to natural proportions. Therefore, students with disabilities are scheduled across all sections, rather than in one or two general education classrooms per grade level. Support staff is then assigned to each teacher based upon the needs of the students and state certification guidelines. Initially, support teachers and related service professionals are often unfamiliar with the general education curriculum. To ensure sufficient opportunity to become familiar with the curriculum and establish relationships with core teaching staff, it is recommended that support teachers and related services personnel work with no more than three classroom teachers at different grade levels, and that they provide a minimum of one hour of daily service to each class (see Giangreco & Doyle, Chapter 10).

Collaborative Teams and Co-Teaching

As previously noted, inclusive schools often reflect collaborative cultures that support the education of all students, including those with severe disabilities. Classroom-based instructional teams are one of several types of collaborative teams in inclusive elementary schools.

Collaborative classroom teams.   Sara's core instructional team consists of her parents and those professionals who are responsible for implementing her IEP (see Figure 12.1). For students with severe disabilities, the core team typically comprises general and special education teachers, speech pathologists, paraprofessionals, occupational and physical therapists, parents, and peers. These individuals work together to ensure that the materials, equipment, lessons, and supports around Sara are appropriately meeting her needs. When this happens, Sara is able to learn and contribute, as are others in her class.

Sara also has a support team that assists the core team in implementing service and supports delineated in her IEP. Her support team includes specialists who have periodic but regular contact with Sara—the vision specialist and social worker. Other support team professionals that could be included are nutritionists, hearing specialists, or mobility specialists. The composition of the team is based upon the needs of the student and typically changes year to year. All members are expected to: (a) participate in consensus-based decision-making about how to implement the IEP; (b) contribute their expertise in problem-solving across all aspects of the student's program; (c) share their discipline-specific knowledge, skills, and resources; (d) support the efforts of other team members; and (e) continue to learn new practices to support students with disabilities in general education (Rainforth & York, 2000).

Classroom teachers have a particular challenge in scheduling the flow of professionals into their classroom. To address this challenge, teachers often rely on asset maps, schedules, and other tools to help manage who is in the classroom and the students they are working with. The essence of these tools is that they help the teacher leverage personnel in the classroom so that students receive needed support, resources are used flexibly, and staff know clearly what is expected of them.

Students with significant needs often have therapy services as a part of their instructional support plan. As a classroom teacher, the challenge becomes how to connect these supports to the general education curriculum and how to deliver the services in workable, meaningful ways throughout the school day. To do this, Sara's teachers and therapists need to communicate effectively with each other and design supports that are integrated within the context of ongoing classroom routines. If therapy were provided for Sara in a separate classroom, she would have great difficulty maintaining eye contact and understanding when and how to apply the skills she is being taught. However, when therapy is provided in her classroom, Sara is far more likely not only to maintain eye contact, but also to shift her gaze when her favorite peers move from one place in the classroom to another.

In addition to these general roles, team members also conduct specific tasks related to their discipline. For example, related services professionals are typically responsible for: (a) developing adaptations and equipment to encourage functional participation; (b) facilitating functional activities; (c) engaging in reciprocal consultation; (d) removing barriers to participation; (e) preventing regression, deformity or pain; and (f) providing resources to families (Giangreco, 1990). Regardless of their discipline, all team members are encouraged to be creative in embedding IEP objectives into classroom routines. In so doing, students are able to physically and instructionally access all areas of the classroom, and become involved in class activities across the entire day.

Co-teaching.   Co-teaching is a collaborative approach where general and special education teachers share responsibility for educating a heterogeneous group of students. This approach is prevalent in elementary school settings. Co-teaching implies equal status of two teachers as they plan and deliver the instruction, as well as assess student performance (Cook & Friend, 1993). There are seven models of co-teaching: (1) station teaching, (2) parallel teaching, (3) one teach/one observe or assist students, (4) duet teaching, (5) tag teaching, (6) alternate teaching, and (7) support teaching (Sands, Kozleski, & French, 2000):

   1. *Station teaching.* Stations or centers are established for individual seatwork or computer work as well as teacher- or peer-led small groups. At approximately twenty-

minute intervals, students move from one station to another and the teachers provide the same instruction to another group of students.

2. *Parallel teaching.* The class is divided in half and both teachers teach the same content. This model requires careful planning to assure that students in both groups receive the same information.

3. *One teach/one observe or assist.* One instructor teaches the lesson, while the other assesses information about the student, the teacher, or the class. The second teacher may also quietly assist students. Either person may assume either role. While this model of co-teaching requires the least amount of planning, it is very important that both teachers equally contribute to the lesson and that one person does not just "float."

4. *Duet teaching.* Teachers co-present to the whole group. One leads the discussion, the other adds information or creates charts or outlines for the students to follow. Both presenters speak alternately, and use proximity, visual cues and gestures, voice tempo and intonation, and humor to keep the class focused throughout the presentation.

5. *Tag teaching.* Content is divided and teachers take turns presenting the information to the whole class. This provides the least benefit to the class, but provides teachers with the flexibility to attend team meetings, consult with staff, and so on.

6. *Alternate teaching.* One teacher instructs students on nonessential information, while the other preteaches or reteaches material to students who will need additional support. For this model to be most effective, the groups of students selected for pre- or reteaching need to be flexible.

7. *Support teaching.* One teacher presents the information and another creates the materials to be used in the lessons, curriculum accommodations, modifications, study guides, and so on.

Strategies to Support Sara's Learning and Achievement

Several strategies were used by Sara's core and support teams to ensure that she benefited from the learning opportunities available in her fourth-grade class.

Collaborative Problem Solving

This strategy has proven particularly useful as a way of mobilizing the creativity of classmates to address issues related to the physical, social, and instructional inclusion of students with mild to profound disabilities in elementary classrooms (Salisbury, Evans, & Palombaro, 1997). The process requires students or teachers to (a) identify the issue; (b) generate all possible solutions; (c) choose a solution to implement; and (d) evaluate the solution. Criteria for judging potential solutions require that teachers consider the participation of all students in each lesson, making adaptations whenever possible; the implications for the student with severe disabilities if adaptations could not be made; and the perspective of the student in considering their choices and decisions; and that they evaluate their efforts in terms of enhanced levels of participation and inclusion. Sara's teachers used the problem-solving process with their team to develop adaptations for the end-of-year field day events so that Sara could participate with her classmates.

Teacher Inquiry

Teachers use inquiry as a way of making decisions about their teaching and about student learning. The knowledge generated from inquiry about what is happening during instruction enables teachers to identify discrepancies between what they want and what exists in classroom practice (Lytle & Cochran-Smith, 1997). A key element in this strategy is that decisions are made from data sources developed and used by practitioners. Salisbury, Wilson, and Palombaro (1998) described how this strategy was applied to the physical, social, and instructional inclusion of students with mild to profound disabilities in elementary schools. Data were gathered and used by teachers to change practices and improve learning outcomes for students. As a form of evidence-based practice, this strategy can be useful to both general and special education teachers in helping them understand what the barriers to inclusion are and how to address them.

Curricular Approaches

Instructional goals and objectives for students with severe disabilities are often represented in areas of: (a) functional academics, (b) choice-making, (c) self-care, (d) communication, (e) social skills, (f) self-advocacy, (g) motor skills, and (h) cognitive skills. In inclusive classrooms, these goals and objectives are embedded in classroom routines and instruction. Often, changes must be made in classroom routines to ensure that students have sufficient opportunities to practice skills in each of these areas. For students with severe disabilities, three approaches are often used to individualize instruction: (1) multilevel curriculum, (2) curriculum overlap, and (3) alternate curriculum (Sands et al., 2000). These three approaches can be used alone or in combination with one another.

Multilevel approach.   With the multilevel approach, all of the students are focused upon the same content, but at various levels of difficulty. For example, during a cooperative learning activity, students are asked to read books about their favorite animals, at their reading ability level or, in Sara's case, using an appropriate communication strategy. Upon finishing the reading, they all return to their group and discuss what they have learned, complete a Venn diagram comparing and contrasting the basic features of their animals, and share their results with the class. For Sara, adaptations would be needed at each point in the lesson process to ensure that she could participate and that the types of participation reinforce the attainment of IEP and non-IEP objectives.

Curriculum overlap approach.   With the curriculum overlap approach, the students address more than one curriculum area within the lesson. For example, with the cooperative learning lesson described above, students with mild and moderate disabilities might well engage in the lesson through the multilevel approach. However, students with significant reading and/or cognitive disabilities could not. To successfully participate in this activity, these students would have to address different educational goals, such as following directions, grasping, and tracking. When Sara participates in cooperative learning activities, she is working on motor goals and objectives that address her ability to use a Palmar grasp and extend her arm above her head. To assist her in accomplishing these goals, her teachers prepare picture response cards with answers to teacher questions printed on the back (the picture response cards are glued to a Popsicle stick). As students share their results with the class, Sara uses a Palmar grasp to hold the stick and extend it above her head. When asked, a student who is a nonreader answers teacher questions by describing the picture. A student who reads at a lower grade level reads a response from the back of the card.

Alternate curriculum.   The alternate curriculum approach is used *only* when the student's participation in school is increased through learning skills or information separately or in small groups. Sara's curriculum is modified such that she spends nearly 100 percent of her instructional day in general education. Alternate instruction occurs when her teachers give her additional instruction on self-help skills that her peers have already mastered (e.g., toileting in a separate bathroom).

Curricular Adaptations

Throughout the instructional day, there are times when lessons must be tailored or individualized to ensure that students experience success and benefit from their participation in the general education curriculum. This planning is often referred to as curriculum adaptation. For our purposes, we define adaptations as the umbrella under which accommodations and modifications are organized. Accommodations are changes that are made to the instruction that "level the playing field," thereby increasing the student's participation in instruction without significantly altering the complexity or difficulty of the content. Accommodations are generally grouped into the following categories: (a) presentation, (b) response, (c) setting, and (d) timing/scheduling. *Accommodations* typically provide greater access to the general education classroom and course of instruction, but do not significantly alter the content of the instruction. *Modifications* are different from accommodations in that they *do* significantly alter the content of the instructional task. Modifications are generally grouped into two categories: (1) parallel (off-grade level) instruction, and (2) embedded skills. Modifications also ensure that students with disabilities have the opportunity to learn in the general education classroom, but their participation does not connote that they work on the same goals and objectives as their nondisabled peers.

With curricular adaptation, the instructional team plans lessons that are flexible and allow students some degree of choice in what they learn, how they learn it, and how they demonstrate mastery of key content and skills. We recommend that curricular adaptations be embedded in all lesson planning, rather than added on after the lesson is planned for typically achieving students.

Curriculum adaptation guidelines.   Udvari-Solner (1995) recommended an eight-step decision-making framework to assist teachers in adjusting curriculum for all students with unique learning needs. To illustrate, we offer the following example. It is important to remember that these categories are not mutually exclusive, and that as you adjust your curriculum you may combine the steps in the framework.

- *Change the structure of the instruction.* Teachers who currently work in classrooms where whole-class discussions and activities dominate the instructional day may find advantages in cooperative and/or authentic learning experiences. However, once reforms occur in general education structures, the instructional team must analyze student mastery and alter the instructional format as necessary to create greater student choice, and differentiate instruction to address diverse teaching and learning styles. For Sara, her teachers may develop authentic learning experiences that involve service learning, or other community-based experiences that provide her with opportunities to work on functional goals.

- *Change the demands of the tasks and criteria for success.* Many times, teachers can increase the participation of students by adjusting the performance standards, and/or altering the pace at which the content is taught. For example, if one group of students is having difficulty with a particular content, co-teaching can be used to preteach or reteach students in flexible small group arrangements. Different types of assessments (e.g., performance, portfolio, interviews, observation, teacher-designed tests and protocols) may also increase participation. In Sara's case, assessment of her goals and objectives should occur daily using classroom observation and performance-based measures to ensure that instruction is responsive to her needs and is producing the desired results.

- *Change the elements of the learning environment.* Because Sara needs adaptive equipment (prone stander, corner chair, lap tray) to address her physical needs and ensure her participation in general education activities, adjustments needed to be made in classroom organization. The classroom does not use desks, but round tables. Sara is seated in a specially adapted chair next to one friend and across the table from another. Bookcases and tables are strategically positioned in the classroom so that Sara can move along furniture to several areas in the room (e.g., reading corner, cubbies, carpeted area).

- *Change the way the task is done.* Teachers in inclusive elementary classrooms employ *natural* verbal, visual, or tactile prompts and cues to support student learning throughout the instructional day. Instruction for students with severe disabilities is most appropriate and effective when it is intentional, when goals and objectives are embedded within age-appropriate meaningful activities, and when assistance is provided only as needed. Assistive technology supports (e.g., adapted equipment, augmentative communication, switches to activate sounds, movement and lights, and/or reaching devices) are often required to ensure that students can access and benefit from instructional activities with their classmates. For example, during station teaching and other cooperative learning activities, Sara was often responsible for using a switch to activate a sound to inform students when they needed to change groups.

- *Change the support structure.* In elementary classrooms where cooperative learning is conducted regularly, peer support for students like Sara is easily provided. However, there may be times when cooperative learning is not used. During those times, Sara may need support from other adults (parent volunteers, paraprofessionals, special education teachers, student teachers) or cross-age tutors from the middle or high school.

Evaluating the adaptations.   We recommend that teachers apply the RSVP method (Sands et al., 2000) to determine whether the adaptations created for students with severe disabilities are effective and useful. The acronym is a mnemonic device to help teachers remember:

R   Is the adaptation reasonable?
S   Is the adaptation sound?
V   Is the adaptation valid?
P   Does it have power?

Adaptations should be made to ensure educational benefit and access to the general education curriculum when needed. Data should be collected regularly and used to determine whether the adaptations and instruction are having their intended effect. Data-based decisions about the effectiveness and impact of instruction are central to quality practices at the elementary level.

Classroom Assessment: The Cornerstone of Instruction

Assessment is a recursive process that helps ensure that teaching is effectively addressing student needs and that students are learning what it is we need for them to learn. The response limitations of many students, like Sara, interfere with performance on norm-referenced tests and make it difficult to accurately estimate abilities (Keogh & Sheehan, 1981). A valid option is to employ a cross-disciplinary, multidimensional approach that brings together various instruments, sources, and perspectives. This convergent assessment approach should include norm-referenced, criterion-referenced, judgment-based, and ecological measures from multiple sources across multiple settings, domains, and occasions (Bagnato, Neisworth, & Munson, 1989). The result will be a more complete and accurate picture of what the student is capable of doing and the conditions under which performance is optimized.

Formal assessment.   Sara's teachers used formal assessments to paint a comprehensive picture of her strengths and needs across settings and people. Standardized tests were used to determine eligibility for related services, while clinical evaluations and criterion-referenced measures were used to establish instructional and support targets. However, most of the assessment used in Sara's classroom is informal. Informal assessments are those created by teachers and other school professionals to measure student success in the classroom and school context. Each day Sara's paraeducator takes data on the number of verbal and physical prompts that are necessary for Sara to eat, as well as the amount of time that it takes Sara to complete her meal. The benefit of informal assessment is that it is *authentic* and mirrors what the child is required to do outside the classroom. Several types of informal assessment are relevant for students with severe disabilities and are easily incorporated into the elementary classroom environment.

Ecological assessment.   In general, ecological assessments occur in the natural environment, and compare an individual's performance on functional activities to that of their peers or to expectations required of any participant in the setting. Ecological assessments are designed collaboratively by teachers, school psychologists, and (often) parents and depend upon careful observation by all involved. Rainforth and York (2000) suggest a four-step assessment process: (1) collaborative planning; (2) conducting the assessment in the natural environment; (3) analyzing the performance discrepancies between the student and nondisabled peers; and (4) conducting diagnostic, discipline-referenced assessments.

Classroom observation. Classroom observations may be done by a variety of personnel and are generally used to inform current and future practice. Each day Sara's teachers and parents use a home/school communication log to relay information about Sara's day, her health, her successes, and her needs, as well as important events that happen at home and school. Other forms of classroom observation are quantitative and provide frequency counts and a time sampling of student behavior that can be used in planning instruction, behavioral supports, or determining how to alter existing instructional practices (Wolery, Bailey, & Sugai, 1988).

Portfolios. Typically, portfolios are viewed as a collection of student work that demonstrates progress on a variety of activities. To develop the portfolio, students select their own work for inclusion in the portfolio and provide a rationale for its selection. For students with severe disabilities, the portfolio process is somewhat different in that the students' teachers and parents select work, videos, charts, and so on as evidence of growth on prioritized goals and objectives. With the advent of greater accountability in education, some states are requiring portfolios as a means of alternate assessment for students with severe disabilities. Sara's teachers are required to develop a portfolio that provides evidence of her learning in all developmental areas. That evidence is scored on a state rubric and submitted to the state for public reporting.

Strategies to Support a Sense of Belonging

During the primary grades, children begin to understand and adopt the core values of their culture, and they develop the social skills needed to act effectively on those values (Solomon, Watson, Delucchi, Schaps, & Battistich, 1988). Because of this, inclusive elementary classrooms hold particular importance as a context for the development of social relationships between groups of children with and without disabilities. Young children develop more equitable, positive social relationships when educators create opportunities for collaboration among students with and without severe disabilities (Eichinger, 1990). There are a number of strategies that general educators in inclusive elementary classrooms employ naturally and embed within typical instructional practices to promote social relations among students with diverse needs and abilities (see Kennedy, Chapter 6). Sara's teachers used many of these practices to help promote her social inclusion in the class.

Active Facilitation of Social Interactions

Practices in this area reflect ways in which teachers use classroom structures and processes to promote equity and concern for others.

Cooperative grouping.   Considered an essential strategy, these instructional arrangements enable students with severe disabilities to be physically, socially, and instructionally included in content subject activities. In Sara's class, she was included in round table learning activities and paired with a peer partner in an assigned role (e.g., recorder, leader, and time keeper). Cooperative learning groups were used for language arts, math, and science activities.

Collaborative problem solving.   Explicit instruction is used to teach students how to raise troublesome issues, identify potential solutions, implement, and evaluate. In Sara's class, teachers taught students steps in the problem-solving process that were then used to resolve barriers to the academic, social, and physical inclusion of Sara and other students in their class. Other examples were provided in an earlier section of this chapter.

Peer tutoring and classroom roles.   Peer tutoring was used to reinforce skills, provide practice, and promote equity and concern for others. Classroom jobs were created to provide physical assistance to Sara and other students who needed help, and to give Sara a visible role with responsibility. For example, Sara was designated as collector of lunch count one week, line leader for another, and feeder of the fish on yet another week. Some of these jobs required a partnering with a peer, others required only minimal assistance from the classroom teacher. All jobs in Sara's class were available to all students, a point that was key to preserving equity and dignity among all students in the class.

Structuring time and opportunity.   Simply creating time and the opportunity in the daily schedule for students to "connect" and just be together is important. Sara's teacher created flexibility for social interaction during DIRT (Developing Individual Reading Time) and around other common times (e.g., recess, lunch, transitions).

"Turning It Over to Kids"

Teachers see students as resources in promoting the social inclusion of students with disabilities in the class are willing to release control of decision making to students and to value their insights about classroom issues. A correlate of the collaborative problem-solving practice described above, this practice draws upon the creativity and knowledge of peers in helping all students feel welcome and included in the classroom. Sara's teachers involved the class in setting classroom norms and rules, and in resolving issues that affected individuals, groups, and/or the entire class. For example, students voiced concern that Sara would miss class time if she had to leave early to make it to gym class on time. Students caucused with Sara and the teacher and decided to modify the class schedule and assign a buddy to help Sara negotiate stairs and ramps so that she could depart and return from class with her peers.

Building Community in the Classroom

Teachers mediate the development of attitudes and values about how the class can function together as a group. Teachers intentionally build a climate of concern for others using activities, classroom rules, care-and-share sessions, and class meetings. The emphasis here is to create practices that peers and adults can use to develop a responsive, caring learning environment. Among the rules adopted by Sara's class were "No put-downs," "Everybody plays," and "We all go." Such rules embody the values of this class and school that no one should be excluded. Teachers used class meetings to help develop the rules and process breakdowns in their implementation.

Modeling Acceptance

Despite Sara's visible physical and intellectual challenges, Sara's teachers were clear about the need to model for their students not only acceptance of Sara as an equal member of the class, but an accepting attitude about the challenges she presented. Students are able to sense acceptance and learn incidentally from adults how to interact with and value those who are different from themselves. When adaptations and accommodations are embedded as naturally occurring events and applied to all students within the classroom, children presume that every classmate should be included. They learn that inclusion is an expectation and not something special.

Conclusion

The development of inclusive practices at the elementary level is a realistic expectation. To be successful, practitioners will need a solid understanding of the general education curriculum and the collaborative support of parents, administrators, and teaching partners. The strategies and concepts described in this chapter can help weave together a responsive, coherent, and workable system of supports for students, including those with severe disabilities, and the staff who support them. Student and staff success will need to be judged along many dimensions. The ultimate evidence of our success will be apparent when we see how we have influenced the performance, potential, and acceptance of all children.

References

Bagnato, S. J., Neisworth, J. T., & Munson, S. M. (1989). *Linking developmental assessment and early intervention: Curriculum-based prescriptions.* Rockville, MD: Aspen.

Beane, J. A. (1995). Curriculum integrations and the disciplines of knowledge. *Phi Delta Kappan, 4,* 100–106.

Bowman, B. T., & Stott, F. M. (1994). Understanding development in a cultural context: The challenge for teachers. In B. L. Mallory & R. S. New (Eds.), *Diversity and developmentally appropriate practices* (pp. 119–134). New York: Teachers College Press.

Calkins, L. (1986). *The art of teaching writing.* Portsmouth, NH: Heinemann.

Carr, J. F., & Harris, D. E. (2001). *Succeeding with standards: Linking curriculum, assessment, and action planning.* Alexandria, VA: ASCD.

Cohen, E. (1986). *Designing groupwork: Strategies for the heterogeneous classroom.* New York: Teachers College Press.

Cook, L., & Friend, M. (1993). Educational leadership for teacher collaboration. In B. Billingsley (Ed.), *Program leadership for serving students with disabilities.* (pp. 421–444). Richmond: Virginia Department of Education.

Cullen, B., & Pratt, T. (1992). Measuring and reporting student progress. In S. Stainback & W. Stainback (Eds.), *Curriculum considerations in inclusive classrooms: Facilitating learning for all students* (pp. 175–196). Baltimore: Paul H. Brookes.

Daniels, H. (1994). *Literature circles: Voice and choice in the student-centered classroom.* York, ME: Stenhouse.

Eichinger, J. (1990). Goal structure effects on social interaction: Nondisabled and disabled elementary students. *Exceptional Children, 56,* 408–417.

Gallimore, R. (1996). Classrooms are just another cultural activity. In D. L. Speece & B. K. Keogh (Eds.), *Research on classroom ecologies* (pp. 229–250). Mahwah, NJ: Lawrence Erlbaum Associates.

Giangreco, M. (1990). Making related services decisions for students with severe disabilities: Roles criteria and authority. *Journal for Persons with Severe Handicaps, 15,* 22–31.

Graves, D. (1983). *Writing: Teachers and children at work.* Portsmouth, NH: Heinemann.

Greenwood, C. (1996). Research on the practices and behavior of effective teachers at the Juniper Garden Children's Project: Implications for education of diverse learners. In D. Speece & B. Keogh (Eds.), *Research on classroom ecologies: Implications for inclusion of children with learning disabilities.* Mahwah, NJ: Lawrence Erlbaum Associates.

Halter, D. (1998). A community of mathematicians. In H. Daniels & M. Bizar (Eds.), *Methods that matter: Six structures for best practice classrooms.* York, ME: Stenhouse.

Jorgensen, C. M., Fisher, D., Sax, C., & Skaglund, K. L. (1998). Innovative scheduling, new roles for teachers, and heterogeneous grouping. In C. Jorgenson (Ed.), *Restructuring high schools for all students* (pp. 49–70). Baltimore: Paul H. Brookes.

Jorgensen, K. (1993). *History workshop: Reconstructing the past with elementary students.* Portsmouth, NH: Heinemann.

Keogh, B. K., & Sheehan, R. (1981). The use of developmental test data for documenting handicapped children's progress: Problems and recommendations. *Journal of the Division for Early Childhood.*

LaPlant, L., & Zane, N. (1994). Partner learning systems. In J. Thousand, R. Villa, & A. Nevin (Eds.), *Creativity and collaborative learning: A practical guide to empowering students and teachers.* Baltimore: Paul H. Brookes.

Lytle, S. L., & Cochran-Smith, M. (1997). Teacher research as ways of knowing. In I. Hall, C. H. Campbell, & E. J. Meich (Eds.), *Class Acts: Teachers reflect on their own classroom practice* (pp. 1–32). Cambridge, MA: Harvard Educational Review.

McGregor, G., & Vogelsberg, R. T. (2000). *Inclusive schooling practices: Pedagogical and research foundations.* Baltimore: Paul H. Brookes.

National Association of State Boards of Education. (1990). *Winning ways.* Washington, DC: Author.

Rainforth, B., & York, J. (2000). *Collaborative teams for students with severe disabilities: Integrating therapy and educational services.* Baltimore: Paul H. Brookes.

Roach, V., Salisbury, C., Strieker, T., & McGregor, G. (2001). *Utility of a policy framework to evaluate and promote large scale change.* Manuscript submitted for publication.

Rosenkoetter, S. E., Hains, A. H., Fowler, S. A. (1994). *Bridging early services for children with special needs and their families.* Baltimore: Paul H. Brookes.

Salisbury, C., Evans, I., & Palombaro, M. (1997). Collaborative problem-solving to promote the inclusion of young children with significant disabilities in primary grades. *Exceptional Children, 63,* 195–209.

Salisbury, C. L., Palombaro, M. M., & Hollowood, T. M. (1993). On the nature and change of an inclusive elementary school. *Journal of the Association for Persons with Severe Handicaps, 18,* 75–84.

Salisbury, C., Strieker, T., Roach, V., & McGregor, G. M. (2001). *Pathways to inclusive practices: Systems oriented, policy-linked, and research-based strategies that work.* Chicago: University of Illinois-Chicago, Child and Family Development Center.

Salisbury, C. L., Wilson, L. L., & Palombaro, M. M. (1998). Promoting inclusive schooling practices through practitioner directed inquiry. *Journal of the Association for Persons with Severe Handicaps, 23,* 223–237.

Salisbury, C. L., & Vincent, L. J. (1990). Criterion of the next environment and best practices: Mainstreaming and integration 10 years later. *Topics in Early Childhood Special Education, 10,* 78–89.

Sands, D., Kozleski, E., & French, N. (2000). *Inclusive education for the 21st century.* New York: Wadsworth Thomas Learning.

Saul, W., & Reardon, J., Schmidt, C., Pearce, K., Blackwood, D., & Bird, M. (1993). *Beyond the science kit: Inquiry in action.* Portsmouth, NH: Heinemann.

Sharan, Y., & Sharan, S. (1992). *Expanding cooperative learning through group investigation.* New York: Teachers College Press.

Snell, M., Lowman, D. K., & Canady, R. L. (1996). Parallel block scheduling: Accommodating students' diverse needs in elementary schools. *Journal of Early Intervention, 20,* 265–278.

Solomon, D., Watson, M. S., Delucchi, K. L., Schaps, E., & Battistich, V. (1988). Enhancing children's prosocial behavior in the classroom. *American Educational Research Journal, 25,* 527–554.

Tomlinson, C. A. (1999). *The differentiated curriculum: Responding to the needs of all learners.* Alexandria, VA: ASCD.

Udvari-Solner, A. (1995). A process for adapting curriculum in inclusive classrooms. In R. A. Villa & J. S. Thousand (Eds.), *Creating an inclusive school.* Alexandria, VA: ASCD.

U.S. Department of Education. (1999). *To assure the free appropriate public education of all children with disabilities. Annual report to Congress on the implementation of the Individuals with Disabilities Education Act.* Washington, DC: Office of Special Education Programs.

Vincent, L. J., Salisbury, C., Walter, G., Brown, P., Gruenewald, L., & Powers, M. (1980). Program evaluation and curricular development in early childhood special education: Criterion of the next environment. In W. Sailor, B. Wilcox, & L. Brown (Eds.), *Methods of instruction for severely handicapped students* (pp. 303–328). Baltimore: Paul H. Brookes.

Wolery, M., Bailey, D., & Sugai, G. (1988). *Effective teaching: Principles and procedures of applied behavior analysis with exceptional children.* Boston: Allyn and Bacon.

Zemelman, S., Daniels, H., & Hyde, A. (1993). *Best practices: New standards for teaching and learning in America's schools.* Portsmouth, NH: Heinemann.

13 Middle School

**DOUGLAS FISHER AND
NANCY FREY**
San Diego State University

CRAIG H. KENNEDY
Vanderbilt University

Middle school is an important point of transition for students. There are, of course, the physiological changes associated with the onset of puberty, but there are other important changes. One is a shift from a student's family as the primary source of social interaction and support to a greater reliance on peer groups. In addition, students are required to become increasingly independent in completing their school workload and coping with more complex school schedules. It is within this context that middle school educators help shape the development of this group of students.

There are a range of definitions regarding what constitutes a "middle school," but we will opt for the most commonly used description (Clark & Clark, 1994; Irvin, 1992, 1997; Kennedy & Fisher, 2001), which states that a middle school comprises three to four grade levels between fifth and ninth grades. For example, some middle schools are configured to educate students from fifth through eighth grades, others provide support from grades seven through nine. What these various configurations share is an attempt to provide students with continuity as they experience a range of significant life changes and provide a bridge from elementary to high school.

This chapter seeks to provide an overview of how educational programs in middle schools effectively include students with severe disabilities in general education settings. Our goal is to review support needs, instructional strategies, and contexts of middle school education. However, before we begin a discussion of how to provide supports to middle school–age students with severe disabilities, we should introduce the reader to Roosevelt Middle School, which will serve to illustrate how to implement inclusive supports for this age group.

Welcome to Roosevelt Middle School

Upon entering the school to sign in, you notice one of the office staff members wearing a shirt that says, "Roosevelt Middle School: More than a School, It's an Attitude!" As you enter the courtyard on the way to the school office, you realize that this school has been remodeled—there are ramps where most of the stairs used to be. The hallways are filled with students talking to one another. You notice a group of students who seem to be engaged in a very serious conversation and note that one of them has a severe disability. Once you arrive at the office, you ask your host if you can follow this group of students to their classroom and see what you can find out about inclusive education from this group of 12- and 13-year-olds.

Ms. Noriega's seventh-grade social studies class is in the midst of an investigation of the volcanic eruption in ancient Pompeii. All the seventh-grade students are busy exploring an "essential question" (Jorgensen, 1998): "How should we prepare for a natural disaster?" The team of teachers with whom Ms. Noriega teaches decided to respond to this question with an in-depth look at Pompeii. Roosevelt Middle School is organized into six teacher teams with 125 students and five teachers in each team. The teacher teams begin working with students in sixth grade and stay with them throughout their middle school experience. Thus the teachers move up each year from sixth to seventh to eighth grade, then start over again. They have found this personalization to be very beneficial for students, in terms of both academic development (not having to start over again at the beginning of the year with new students) and social development (developing strong relationships with fewer numbers of students).

In the science class earlier this morning, the students had discussed the destructive force of volcanoes. Previously they had examined earthquakes, tidal waves, hurricanes, and tornadoes. The science teacher, Ms. Ramos, likes to supplement her textbook with daily read alouds and independent reading materials that are appropriate for a diverse group of students. For example, she had read the book *Disaster Science* (Klutz, 1998) to stimulate a conversation about this type of natural disaster. She knows that her colleagues have used books such as *Disaster* (Bonson, 1997) and *Hurricane* (Wiesner, 1990). The students are also attending Mr. Johnson's English studies class, where they have been reading about people who have lived through disasters and studying the genre of realistic fiction. Mr. Johnson selected *The Cay* (Taylor, 1969) for his daily read-aloud and invited his students to select a personal book to read from the collection of appropriate titles identified by the librarian.

The culminating group project is a report of information on preparing for natural disasters. Students are expected to produce a brochure that can be used by people in the community to prepare for a disaster. Students have been previously organized into a "village" (whole class), "clans" (groups of 12), and "lodges" (groups of 4). Ms. Noriega has used heterogeneous groupings to maximize participation and community building (Lapp, Fisher, & Flood, 1999). Today, each lodge is working on their report. They will use resources from the classroom and school media center to determine the characteristics of their assignment, the geographic areas in which a particular type of disaster occurs, and the available safety information. Tomorrow, the "lodges" will meet as "clans" to share their findings and begin to design informational brochures.

The seventh-grade team led by Ms. Noriega often designs interdisciplinary units of instruction because it produces a deeper understanding of concepts for their students (Jacobs, 1989). At a previous team meeting, Mr. Johnson noted, "These thematic lessons we've been using have really made a difference in the quality of accommodations and modifications. They just seem more sensible." Ms. Vieu, the special educator assigned to the team, nods in agreement. The team's focus on problem-based learning and an interdisciplinary approach has made her instructional and assessment duties more meaningful. She now has time to supervise and train paraprofessionals working with the seventh-grade teams. Because Roosevelt Middle School has redefined roles and responsibilities for all staff, Ms. Vieu now works with paraprofessionals for both special education and Title 1 supports. The team has been pleasantly surprised at the impact this has had in their classes. Because adults are no longer exclusively assigned to students with particular disabilities, assistance is available for all members of a classroom.

Two students in Ms. Noriega's second-period class illustrate the range of supports available to students at Roosevelt Middle School. Jamal is an active 12-year-old, interested in videogames, soccer, and socializing with friends. He was identified as having a learning disability that impacts his ability to comprehend text. Arelyn turned 13 last month. She enjoys sharing her music collection with her friends. Arelyn has a severe disability, and uses a power wheelchair and a Talk Back® augmentative communication device.

Today, Jamal's group (i.e., "lodge"), which also includes two students without disabilities, is studying hurricanes. After the village receives instruction on what to investigate, his group heads for the media center. Mr. Rawlings, a paraprofessional, will be accompanying the group. Ms. Vieu previously provided Jamal with a blank graphic organizer featuring the questions Ms. Noriega had posed in class. Mr. Rawlings will assist Jamal in completing the organizer by first modeling the note taking, then fading the time-delay prompts. Ms. Vieu trained the paraprofessional staff in this instructional strategy last month. Along with supporting Jamal, Mr. Rawlings is also assisting other students in the classroom. This *part-time support* is scheduled each Tuesday, when Ms. Noriega's class does research (see Table 13.1).

Arelyn's group is studying volcanoes. Because Mrs. Vieu collaborates with Ms. Noriega using the Unit Planning Guide (see Achievement section below), she knows in advance the group's assigned topic. Because Arelyn's family speaks Spanish at home, the special education teacher also collaborates with the English Language Development teacher for assistance in programming her communication device with both Spanish and English phrases. For this assignment, Ms. Vieu created a graphic organizer with BoardMaker® picture symbols that contains text from both languages. Her group has enjoyed learning vocabulary words in two languages. Arelyn's support for the day's activity comes primarily from her peers without disabilities, who are learning to prompt her to spontaneously use her communication device. Her orientation and mobility specialist uses the Tuesday trips to the media center to instruct Arelyn on navigating the school. Russell, an eighth grader who is a peer support in the class, accompanies Arelyn to the media center to assist in using her Talk Back®. Russell is a technology whiz, and has become proficient at programming

TABLE 13.1   Levels of Support for Students with Severe Disabilities

Full-Time Supports
The staff person (teacher or assistant) remains seated in close proximity to student. Support staff may need to assist student with materials/supplies needed to complete class assignments and group work. The staff provides a role model for cooperation, collaboration, acceptance, and respect for all.

Part-Time Supports
The support staff provides assistance to a student at a predetermined time, or on a rotating basis. The staff person maintains an awareness of curriculum and assignments to encourage student productivity, completion of assignments, tutorial or organizational support.

Intermittent Supports
The support staff provide assistance in the classrooms on a daily or every other day basis, to troubleshoot immediate challenges and/or to assist with surprise assignments or projects.

Peer Supports
This type of support is provided by students who are enrolled in the class. This student usually volunteers to provide support by taking notes, recording homework assignments, and so on. In addition, they may assist in mobility to and from class, carrying or remembering materials, taking notes, assisting with completing assignments, and facilitated communication, as well as being a role model for social/friendship interactions. The peer supports may also participate in the development of support strategies.

Supplemental Supports
This type of support is provided by speech and language specialists, orientation/mobility specialists, and physical/occupational therapists, and counselors. They provide services to the student within the context of the general education classroom. If this is not possible, services are provided at a time that is least disruptive to instruction, such as during breaks or silent reading.

her communication device to keep up with the demands of the conversation. Today, Arelyn is accessing *peer supports* (her classmates) and *supplemental supports* (Orientation and Mobility specialist).

A general education student, Bernardo, gathers information for his group on floods (of which Arelyn is a member). They are surprised to learn that floods are one of the most common natural disasters in their hometown. However, the group is having a difficult time locating appropriate references for their report. The special educator, Ms. Vieu, is circulating in the media center to assist various students and observes the students struggling to find information. She is able to intervene immediately and help the group locate the Internet, thereby reducing the likelihood of their group going off-task. Today Bernardo and the other students benefited from the incidental support available in the media center by being taught how to access web pages showing flood zones in his community.

The seventh-grade team takes pride in its multilevel instructional practices and their connection to curriculum-based assessment. Using the Unit Planning Guide, Ms. Vieu knows how the students will be assessed on various projects. Students have kept a reflective log, and Mr. Johnson, Ms. Ramos, and Ms. Noriega have read and responded to the entries throughout the unit. Jamal uses a word-processing program on the computer to take advantage of the editing, spell check, and word prediction features. Arelyn uses magazine pictures to create a pictorial response to the written prompts, and is assisted in the placement of the pictures by Mr. Rawlings *(intermittent support)*. These accommodations and modifications were featured in their Student Profiles (see Table 13.2) and were designed by the special education teacher *(specialized support)*. Although Bernardo required no accommodations for this assessment, he took advantage of the graphic organizer used by Jamal to plan some of his compositions.

When the team met to debrief regarding implementation of the unit "Disasters," they agreed it was a success. Students enjoyed the unit, were highly engaged, learned to work together, and gained new knowledge and insights. Ms. Ramos made some suggestions for how she might refine the rubric creation process, and Mr. Johnson shared documents showing specifically what progress students made in their writing skills. Ms. Vieu made notes on the success of the accommodations and modifications created for students with individualized education programs (IEPs). Mr. Rawlings, the paraprofessional, had been an important informant for this. The seventh-grade team agreed on a major point—the curriculum design of the unit allowed for a wide range of diverse learners to participate in a meaningful way. Ms. Noriega said, "I was really hesitant about whether weekly research sessions would work. After all, it means I've got students spread out all over the school. But it really works, because we can put adults where we need them, when we need them."

Achievement

Schools are about achievement—achievement for all students, not just those without disabilities. To ensure that all students achieve, the curriculum must be designed with a diverse student group in mind. The lesson planning process used by the teachers at Roosevelt Middle School involves several steps, including:

1. Developing a core theme or question based on grade-level standards.
2. Identifying assessments that document student understanding of the standards and expectations.
3. Designing daily lesson plans and other activities that link together and provide students with knowledge and experiences about the unit of study.
4. Identifying rich source material about the topic that is available on many different instructional levels.
5. Ensuring that culminating projects require that students demonstrate their knowledge of the topic.

Although the careful design of curriculum and instructional activities will ensure the academic success of many students, some students will require additional support to be successful. In this case, curriculum accommodations and modifications must be considered.

TABLE 13.2 Student Profile of Arelyn

STUDENT PROFILE

School Name: Roosevelt Middle School
Student Name: Arelyn Sablan
Age: 12   Grade: 7   Phone #: 555-1234
Classroom Teacher: Ms. Noriega
Advocate Teacher: Ms. Vieu

Skills addressed in this class: Request assistance when needed, arrive on time, use speech output device to communicate, answer yes/no questions, locate classrooms, use switch for cause/effect activities, and improve use of Picture Communication Symbols (PCS).

Areas of strengths/interests: Arelyn is very helpful and has developed a good rapport with her teacher and classmates. She often involves herself in social situations. Arelyn enjoys listening to music and socializing.

Successful learning strategies/modifications/adaptations needed: Arelyn needs taped recordings of readings. She can make her needs and wants known through the use of a speech output device or yes/no questions, but must be asked. She works well with peer supports in cooperative learning structures when paired with clearly defined group roles. Make pictures available to support her writing and reading.

Communication strategies: Arelyn utilizes picture schedules to manage her time and anticipate transitions. She needs complicated tasks broken down into 1–2 step directions. Directions are better understood when verbal and visual cues are paired. When frustrated, she may begin hitting her lap tray. This is usually an indicator that too many directions have been given at one time.

Positive behavior support strategies: Arelyn uses a visual schedule for her daily activities. She needs advance notice when changes in the environment or schedule occur. She experiences frustration when there is a prolonged wait in line, when the area is overcrowded, and/or when she is not around classmates. Arelyn needs peer supports when entering new environments and activities. She prefers to be called by name (affix her name to the chair in classes).

Grading accommodations: Arelyn maintains a literacy portfolio. This work is evaluated by both the special education and general education teachers, who each provide 50% of the grade. Grading rubrics for projects may need to be modified to reflect her goals. She may require extra time to complete some assignments and tests.

Important family/health information: Arelyn is hypersensitive to noise, smell, and sometimes to touch. She responds well to light pressure on her shoulders, fingers, and elbows. Her intellectual disability impacts her communication, but not her socialization. Arelyn has asthma and uses an inhaler when needed.

As noted by Ryndak and Billingsley (Chapter 3), an *accommodation* is a change made to the teaching or testing procedures in order to provide a student with access to information and create an equal opportunity to demonstrate knowledge and skills. Accommodations do not change the instructional level, content, or performance criteria for meeting curriculum standards. Examples of accommodations include enlarged print, providing oral versions of tests, and using calculators.

A *modification* is a change in what a student is expected to learn and/or demonstrate as evidence of meeting curriculum standards. Although a student may be working on modified course content, the subject area remains the same as the rest of the class. If the decision is made to modify the curriculum, it is done in a variety of ways, for a variety of reasons, with a variety of outcomes. Again, modifications vary according to the situation. Listed below are four modification techniques often used in middle schools.

Same (only less): The assignment remains the same except the number of items that need to be completed is reduced. The items selected should be representative of the curriculum. For example, a social studies test consisting of 25 multiple-choice questions may be given to the class. However, this test could be modified for Jamal and the number of possible answers reduced to 10.

Streamline the curriculum: The assignment could be reduced in size, breadth, or focus to emphasize key points. For example, in English class, most students would be required to produce a final essay on the theme "Justice." This assignment could be modified for Arelyn to involve a paper on the main points of the unit, one example from a book about the theme, and a list of books that address the theme.

Same activity with infused objectives: The assignment could remain the same, but additional components such as IEP objectives or skills identified on the Infused Skills Grid are incorporated. This is often done in conjunction with other adaptations and/or modifications to ensure that all IEP objectives are addressed. For example, Arelyn has an IEP objective to answer yes/no questions using her eyes to locate the words on a lap tray. In her science class, the teacher and the students in the class are phrasing questions in a yes/no format so she can practice this skill in multiple general education settings, and providing her with gestural prompts as an error correction procedure.

Curriculum overlapping: The assignment for one class may be completed in another class. Students may experience difficulty grasping the connections between the different classes. In addition, some students work slowly and need additional time to complete assignments. Curriculum overlapping as a strategy is especially helpful for these situations. For example, in a word-processing class, students can type assignments for other classes and submit them to the word-processing teacher for a typing grade and to the English teacher for an essay grade.

Deciding which technique to use depends on the type of assignment and a student's support needs. One assignment may need only to be reduced in size in order for the student to be successful, while another may incorporate infused objectives. All four techniques, as well as appropriate additional supports, should be considered for each situation. However, it is important to remember that the *curriculum does not always need to be modified*—even when considering students with more severe disabilities. When general education teachers provide multilevel instruction, adapting a lesson may not be necessary. Differentiating instruction allows the students a variety of ways to demonstrate knowledge while continuing to meet the requirements of the class. At other times, the curriculum can be made more accessible through accommodations. When students do need curriculum accommodations and modifications, the Lesson Planning Guide is a useful tool. Table 13.3 provides an example of the Lesson Planning Guide that was used for Arelyn.

TABLE 13.3   Lesson Planning Guide Used for Arelyn

SCIENCE

Title of Course: Science—Natural Disasters

Major Unit Objectives
1. Students will understand the causes of earthquakes, volcanoes, tidal waves, tornadoes, and hurricanes.
2. Students will create a "report of information" that is factually accurate about one of these natural disasters.

Materials
1. Book: *Earth Science*
2. Educational videotapes related to natural disasters
3. Websites that track natural disasters
4. Chapter worksheets
5. Primary source: *Disaster Science*
6. University professor to discuss current research on natural disasters

Using the Same Content/Processes or Modifications Required?
Modifications:
1. Book chapters read and recorded on audiotape
2. Modify worksheets to emphasize key points of chapters
3. Peer assistance with *Disaster Science* activities

Instructional Arrangements
1. Large group instruction with overheads to introduce the unit
2. Small groups to complete labs, worksheets, and report of information
3. Two cell labs will be completed in partners (volcanoes and tidal waves)
4. Individual time to complete illustrated vocabulary

Using the Same Content/Processes or Modifications Required?
Modifications:
1. Copy of teacher's overhead transparencies given to student
2. Peer takes notes in class; student types notes on computer for both
3. Use of "read, write, pair, share" strategy as chapter review
4. Part-time staff support during labs
5. Peer support to complete illustrated vocabulary

Projects
1. Homework: Complete vocabulary
2. Group projects and presentations on report of information
3. Write-up for each completed lab with illustrations

Using the Same Content/Processes or Modifications Required?
Modifications:
1. Magazine pictures to illustrate key points
2. Speech output device programmed accordingly
3. Lab write-up sheet completed with peer using computer; illustrations supplement write-up

(continued)

TABLE 13.3 Lesson Planning Guide Used for Arelyn (*Continued*)

Assessments
1. Add illustrated vocabulary words to class portfolio
2. Culminating activity: Group-developed brochure: How should we prepare for a natural disaster?
3. Chapter test

Using the Same Content/Processes or Modifications Required?
Modifications:
1. Specific instructions for group members
2. Chapter test read orally with additional time given, reducing the number of options for multiple-choice questions, and providing options for short-answer questions.

Belonging

The issue of belonging is addressed in several ways at Roosevelt Middle School. First, the teachers have examined their beliefs and feelings about students and have agreed that all students should be in general education classrooms. That is, they share a common vision about the importance of belonging. While it is not always easy or comfortable, it is important for teachers to spend time reflecting on their own values, and understanding how those values impact their students. Bringing teachers together to share their values and belief systems is risky, but necessary for creating a common vision for how a school implements inclusive education. The following core values are upheld at Roosevelt Middle School:

1. All students can think and learn.
2. All students have value and unique gifts to offer their school.
3. Diversity within a school community should be embraced and celebrated.
4. All students differ in the ways they most effectively learn and express their understandings.
5. All students learn best when they are actively and collaboratively building knowledge with their classmates and their teacher.
6. All students learn best when studying interesting and challenging topics that they find personally meaningful.
7. Effective teaching for students with disabilities is substantively the same as effective teaching for all students.

Students know when they are valued and respected by adults, and the beliefs listed above help create a strong sense of community and belonging at a school. However, although strong values are necessary, they are not sufficient. One of the challenges for a middle school is to create a sense of belonging for students as they learn how to transition between different academic subjects and classrooms throughout the day. To facilitate these outcomes the teachers at Roosevelt Middle School work on developing strong relationships with their students. The fact that students and teachers remain together for their three-year middle school experience within teams helps with relationship development.

Again, these relationships are necessary, but not sufficient. An inclusive middle school cannot be dependent on adults to create a sense of belonging. Students must be taught to value their peers. One additional way that the teachers at Roosevelt Middle School address belonging is through a series of classroom activities that allow students to examine their beliefs and values about individual differences. Most importantly, these are connected to the core curriculum that the class is studying. For example, Mr. Johnson recently selected the book *Petey* (Mikaelsen, 1998) for his daily read-aloud. This book focuses on the life of a young man with a severe disability who lives in a nursing home. Through class discussions, Mr. Johnson allowed students to talk about their experiences with their peers with disabilities and to ask questions that they had been afraid to ask. As one student without disabilities said, "None of the adults talked about kids like Arelyn for the first few weeks of sixth grade. We didn't know if it was okay to ask questions. When Mr. Johnson read us *Petey,* we realized it was okay to ask questions about disabilities."

In science, Ms. Ramos asked her students to identify something about each of them that was unique. Her students were each proud of their unique qualities as they shared them aloud. She talked about biodiversity and how life is enriched when there is a greater diversity of things in the environment. Ms. Ramos then related this theme back to how inclusive schools are richer learning environments because of the different perspectives that students bring to learning. She then introduced her uniqueness—a prosthetic foot. Her students were amazed and wanted to ask all kinds of questions about how it worked and why she had it. The teachers at Roosevelt Middle School believe that asking questions is important and that they should not shy away from conversations about individual differences, including disabilities.

Another means of facilitating belonging is to encourage students with and without disabilities to work and interact with each other. Because a great deal of classroom time in middle schools is devoted to academic work that is completed individually, this can be a challenge. Along with teachers using a range of cooperative learning strategies in their classrooms, the use of peer supports can help increase appropriate interactions between pairs of students. An important but often overlooked goal for teachers is to teach students to have the skills and opportunities to interact with one another under adult supervision. Establishing classroom environments in which this can occur simultaneously with academic learning helps establish a culture of belonging in a classroom and school.

Collaboration

A key factor in the success of providing educational services to students is the ability to communicate effectively with general education teachers about students' academic and personal support needs, lesson planning, and input into the IEP. Several processes have been developed to increase communication among teachers. The Academic Unit Lesson Plan has previously been discussed. We will review two additional tools that teachers find very helpful in facilitating the communication process, the *Student Profile* and *Infused Skills Grid.*

Student Profile

The development of a complete profile of a student serves as another important tool (see Table 13.2). The information in a student profile is collected from the student, family interviews, previous teachers, peers, and others who know the student well. General education teachers often find this one of the most useful pieces of information they receive from special educators. This profile contains critical information they can use to make instructional decisions for students. The profile contains the following sections:

Specific objectives for the student. These are often taken from the IEP and Infused Skills Grid and written in accessible language for teachers. This section of the profile often changes with each class in order to address the specific course requirements. General education teachers should keep the student's IEP goals clearly in mind when modifying or accommodating assignments.

Areas of strength and interest. This is critical information for engaging and tailoring successful learning activities for a student. This is highly useful information when designing projects or class activities. In addition, teachers often use the information in this section to make decisions about cooperative groups and partner activities.

Successful learning strategies, modifications, and adaptations. This list is useful for describing a student's learning style, as well as successful curriculum modifications. This critical information can become a roadmap for teachers to follow in designing individual class assignments as well as group activities.

Communication strategies. This section describes any type communication supports that a student is receiving, including augmentative and alternative strategies. In addition to specific modes or methods of communication, such as Picture Communication Symbols or sign language, this section can include information about ways to engage the student in conversation and how the student initiates interactions.

Positive behavior support strategies. Behavioral problems sometimes pose challenges to inclusion. Positive behavioral support techniques are critical for teachers to identify so the student is treated with respect and maximizes his or her likelihood for success. In effect, this section should provide answers to two questions: What does the student need to be successful at school? How can supports be provided to the student to prevent challenging behaviors from happening?

Grading and assessment accommodations. To be successful, students may require additional time on tests, large print, oral versions of tests, or preferential seating. These strategies, often agreed upon during an IEP meeting, should be recorded here. In addition, specific grading requirements should be identified. These include collaborative grading (an average of the special and general education teachers' grades), notations to the transcripts regarding accommodations or modifications (if this is done), and competency tests that may be required.

Important health or family information. Health histories or other information from the family that is important for teachers to know can be recorded here. Especially important is information about seizures, assistance required for eating or using the restroom, and positioning for comfort.

Overall, the student profile is a useful tool to assist teachers in deciding how assignments and activities can be modified for a particular student and how that student can build upon personal experiences to learn new material.

Infused Skills Grid

Teachers use this planning matrix to determine what, when, and where to teach specific skills. This form is a grid that shows how functional skills can be infused into a student's daily routine as he or she participates in the general education curriculum and school activities (see Table 13.4). Priority skills that the student needs to work on are listed at the top of the grid. These skills are generated by the student profile and the family. Along the left-hand column are listed the general education activities of the student's day. A check mark is then placed in each box that indicates a time period in which the skill can naturally be addressed. For example, if the family interview revealed that the student needed to learn how to dress himself, then a check mark would be placed in the activity of PE, since this is a time period when the student will have a natural opportunity to work on this skill.

The point of this grid is to identify times throughout the day when the student can functionally apply the skills that were determined to be important by the IEP team. Because students with disabilities commonly have a difficult time generalizing concepts and skills, it is more likely that they will learn skills when they are able to practice them in multiple settings. In addition, it is important to note that skills can be taught and used several times during the day. For example, answering yes/no questions can be infused into many activities during the day, such as English class, lunch, PE, and social studies.

In addition, to ensure that all skill needs are addressed during the school day, the Infused Skills Grid provides general education teachers information that is useful to them as they plan instruction. The Infused Skills Grid may help the classroom teachers realize that they do not need to change the flow of their general education classrooms to meet IEP

TABLE 13.4   Infused Skills Grid Used for Arelyn

Skills from IEP Identified to Be Infused at School:

1. Request assistance when needed
2. Arrive on time
3. Use speech output device to communicate
4. "Yes/No" questions
5. Locate classrooms
6. Use switch for cause/effect
7. Improve use of Picture Communication Symbols
8. Learn to dress self

Time/Location	Infused Skill
Arrival	1, 2, 3, 4
English	1, 2, 3, 4, 5, 6, 7
Math	1, 2, 3, 4, 5, 6, 7
Lunch	1, 3, 4, 7
Science	1, 2, 3, 4, 5, 6, 7
Social Studies	1, 2, 3, 4, 5, 6, 7
P.E.	All
Dismissal	1, 2, 3, 4

objectives for students with disabilities. Instead, many of these specific skills can be addressed within the flow of the regular classroom activities throughout the day.

Conclusion

Of all grade levels, middle schools occupy an interesting niche. Middle schools serve as a transition point between elementary and high school. Traditionally, the importance of middle schools has been minimized. However, in the last decade the important roles that middle schools serve has received increased visibility and appreciation among educators, researchers, and community members. Because of the vulnerability of preadolescents due to the multiple changes that are occurring in their lives, success in middle school is often predictive of successful high school performance and success as a young adult.

To facilitate success in middle school a number of best practices have emerged. School teams help create a sense of belonging and continuity for students and staff. A shared vision of an inclusive school that strives for individual excellence has also proven important. Other critical issues reviewed in this chapter have included: (a) multilevel instructional practices, (b) matching supports to student strengths and needs, (c) facilitating access to the general education curriculum, (d) creating a sense of belonging, and (e) interdisciplinary collaboration. Although many of these characteristics of an effective middle school are shared with other grade levels, they have proven essential for establishing an effective and inclusive learning environment for students with severe disabilities. A hallmark of a successful middle school education is a student who has made advances toward becoming more independent, has continued to make academic advances, feels a sense of belonging with peers and adults, and is prepared for the challenges of high school.

References

Bonson, R. (1997). *Disaster.* New York: DK Publishing.

Clark, S. N., & Clark, D. C. (1994). *Restructuring the middle level school: Implications for school leaders.* Albany: State University of New York Press.

Editors of Klutz. (1998). *Disaster science.* New York: Klutz.

Irvin, J. L. (1992). *Transforming middle level education: Perspectives and possibilities.* New York: Allyn and Bacon.

Irvin, J. L. (1997). *What current research says to the middle level practitioner.* Columbus, OH: National Middle School Association.

Jacobs, H. H. (1989). *Interdisciplinary curriculum: Design and implementation.* Alexandria, VA: ASCD.

Jorgensen, C. M. (Ed.). (1998). *Restructuring high schools for all students: Taking inclusion to the next level.* Baltimore: Paul H. Brookes.

Kennedy, C. H., & Fisher, D. (2001). *Inclusive middle schools.* Baltimore: Paul H. Brookes.

Lapp, D., Fisher, D., & Flood, J. (1999). Does it matter how you're grouped for instruction? Yes! Flexible grouping patterns promote student learning. *California Reader, 33*(1), 28–32.

Mikaelsen, B. (1998). *Petey.* New York: Hyperion.

Taylor, T. (1969). *The cay.* New York: Avon.

Wiesner, D. (1990). *Hurricane.* New York: Clarion.

14   High School

MICHAEL WEHMEYER AND WAYNE SAILOR
University of Kansas

The high school period, generally referring to grades nine through twelve, is a time of significant change in the lives of students with and without disabilities. Preadolescence and adolescence are periods of biological, physical, social, and psychological changes for all young people, and the complex mixture of physical maturation, changing peer and family relationships, emerging sexuality, increased responsibility and expectations, demands to prepare for adulthood, and other variables lead to complex and sometimes difficult circumstances. The presence of a disability is one more variable to consider, although only one among many.

It is too often the case, however, that the presence of a severe disability in the lives of adolescents overshadows the other variables impacting that student's life and educational program. Consequently, students with severe disabilities are not supported or expected to strive toward typical adolescent pursuits such as individuation, autonomy, self-determination, or independence. As a result, the educational programs of students with severe disabilities too often reflect limited expectations and outcomes that vary, qualitatively, from those of most same-age peers. This chapter focuses instead on ways to raise such expectations and to ensure that students with severe disabilities are provided educational supports during high school that better enable them to lead self-determined lives by focusing on ways in which excellence in high school programs for *all* students can benefit students with severe disabilities.

There are about 18,000 high schools in the United States, the majority of which are comprehensive high schools (including both academic college preparation courses and vocational courses) (Kimmel & Weiner, 1995). High schools vary across a number of features and factors, including grade levels of students served (traditionally grades ten through twelve, but increasingly more high schools cover grades nine through twelve), size, demographic characteristics, and curricular scope and content. Nonetheless, there is an emerging understanding of what constitutes an excellent high school, and this chapter examines the high school experience of students with severe disabilities from this perspective—that is, the perspective of high-quality high school experiences for all students, including students with severe disabilities.

Martin Luther King, Jr., High School

It is 7:55 A.M. and the first bell has rung, indicating that classes at Martin Luther King, Jr., High School, located in a large, urban area, are about to begin. In the hallway clusters of students wrap up conversations about the varsity basketball team's overtime win from the night before or about their plans for the evening, stuffing coats into overly full lockers. MLK is a comprehensive high school with more than 1,200 students, many of whom are from ethnic minority populations, particularly students who are African American, Hispanic, and Asian American. MLK is located in an area that has experienced difficult economic circumstances in the past decade. Once a focal point for a proud community, the buildings surrounding the school have deteriorated and many sit abandoned and unused.

This morning, one group of students, all girls and primarily African American students, make their final arrangements to meet for lunch before heading to their first class of the morning. This cadre of students is unremarkable, compared to other students in the school, except that one member, LaTricia, experiences multiple physical and cognitive disabilities. Through much of her educational career, LaTricia had been served in separate campus buildings or self-contained classrooms. However, when her family enrolled her at MLK, her segregated experiences came to an end. LaTricia navigates her electric wheelchair along with the rest of the girls in the small group as they head toward their first class. Occasionally one of the other students will reach down to adjust the books that LaTricia carries precipitously on her lap or will take a half step to avoid being run over by one of the tires on her chair. All of the girls include LaTricia in their conversation, though she cannot answer them verbally. One student in particular, Shondra, stays near LaTricia. Shondra first met LaTricia in a peer-buddy program in junior high. Shondra discovered that LaTricia lived only two blocks away and gradually began to invite LaTricia over to her house or to drop by LaTricia's home to see if she wanted to go with her to some school event. Eventually, they became friends, and Shondra, one of the most popular girls in the school, became LaTricia's ticket to a rich social network.

The first stop in the morning for all five girls is Ms. Crossland's room. MLK has assigned each student to an adult mentor who serves as an advisor for a small group of students. Every adult in the high school, from the principal to the facilities support staff, meet daily with five to seven students. Mentors do more than counsel students, however; their task is to advise but also to enable students to solve their own problems. Each adult mentor received training in promoting problem solving and decision making and meets regularly with a group of other mentors to discuss what did and did not work. This morning Ms. Crossland spends most of her time helping the girls solve a problem concerning making sure that LaTricia can accompany her peers on a field trip in two weeks. The girls identify ways to ensure that LaTricia's chair can be transported, and discuss who will assist her during lunchtime and how to ensure that LaTricia receives her medicine. At each juncture, Ms. Crossland or one of the students checks with LaTricia to make sure she agrees with the decisions being made. Other mornings, the group discusses any number of issues, from what courses group members should take to how to deal with social or relationship problems. When the bell sounded indicating their 20 minutes with Ms. Crossland was over, the girls each moved on, but to very different activities. Two of the group, Sandra and Kathy, will spend most of their day in the Computer Academy, located on the second floor in the opposite wing of the building. Shondra heads toward the Business Academy. Both Jennifer and LaTricia head toward the front of the school, where they will spend the majority of the school day in community-based learning. Jennifer is involved with a project on ecology and conservation and has been meeting with a small group of peers at the Keystone hydroelectric dam outside of town as they work on a plan to balance the growing need for power in the city with the impact of the lowered water levels of Lake Keystone on the ecology around the lake. Jennifer's group spent several weeks in the biology classroom preparing for their project before engaging in community-based learning. LaTricia's first stop is the community college, where she has been taking a course offered to all students concerning effective planning for the transition to adulthood. LaTricia is working her way through a self-directed transition planning process with the support of a community-learning aide who accompanies her to learning sites. LaTricia's activities will lead to her identifying potential goals to include on her IEP with regard to her final year at the high school campus. Afterward, LaTricia and a peer, who needs instructional experiences to become more independent at the local burger hangout joint, meet for their lunch and instruction on ordering and paying for their meals. LaTricia returns to MLK for an afternoon science class, where she is reunited with Shondra. At any given time, up to one-third of the students at MLK are involved in community-based learning, and all students have a community-learning component.

Back on the MLK campus, LaTricia and Shondra move through the halls toward science class, observing the schoolwide rules for conduct. Shondra had served on a student-led planning team to establish these rules. Adults throughout MLK habitually commend students for observing school behavioral rules. Before MLK structured the school day around schools-within-schools, or smaller learning communities, they had to address many of the same challenges experienced by other urban high schools. However, once MLK structured learning in smaller communities and instituted schoolwide positive behavior supports, problems decreased, including fewer discipline problems and office referrals and reductions in instances of violence and drug and alcohol use. Conflicts still arose, of course, but in most cases they were handled through a peer-mediated conflict-resolution council.

Shondra and LaTricia's biology class is a hum of activity, with students grouped in small, cooperative learning groups each engaged in a seemingly different activity. Shondra and LaTricia are in the same small group, which is examining the third generation of their *Drosophila melanogaster,* the ubiquitous fruit fly found in biology classes nationwide, for genetic mutations. Shondra and most other team members are working on a lesson developed to meet the school's science standard with regard to understanding issues pertaining to genetic inheritance and heritability. LaTricia's IEP team examined the benchmarks related to that standard and decided that it was not appropriate for her to work toward the same benchmarks. Instead, the biology teacher, Ms. Goddard, considered the types of activities in which all students would be engaged, and identified a goal related to social interactions that could form the basis for LaTricia's involvement. In another class a teacher has purchased CD-ROM–based learning materials to present information to LaTricia that otherwise would have been only in text format, and has LaTricia respond by pointing to graphic indicators of the correct response.

MLK is organized around a block-schedule, so the science class lasts 90 minutes, after which Shondra goes to business calculus and LaTricia heads toward the physical education wing. LaTricia is an avid swimmer, surprising even her parents with her agility and capacity to swim through the water. It's not yet the season for the swim team to compete, but LaTricia works out with them each afternoon. When the season begins, LaTricia participates as a member of the "B" squad, which swims local competitions against other high schools. LaTricia has never actually won a race, but she revels in the companionship that accompanies her membership on the team.

After the swim workout, as LaTricia dresses with assistance from a paraeducator, she yawns. On her way out to the bus, she finds Shondra, who makes plans to pick LaTricia up at 7 P.M. for the school play at the auditorium that night. Shondra's father is a community leader, and he has a meeting at the school building that night and can give the girls a ride.

Excellent High Schools for All Students

Nationwide school reform efforts have begun to identify the characteristics of high-quality high schools and strategies to ensure that all students achieve to high standards. To better understand these efforts and strategies, we briefly review two national initiatives that speak to the issue of high-quality high schools, like Martin Luther King, Jr., High School that LaTricia attends—the *New American High School* initiative and the *High Schools of the Millennium* initiative—and use the principles and strategies introduced by those initiatives to discuss high-quality high schools for all students, including students with severe disabilities.

New American High Schools

Since 1995, the U.S. Department of Education has identified and documented the activities of innovative high schools whose whole-school reform efforts focused on ensuring that all students were: (a) challenged by rigorous academics and high expectations, (b) benefiting from a small, safe, personalized learning environment, and (c) well prepared for college and careers. The New American High Schools initiative has identified common strategies in place in these schools. Table 14.1 lists those strategies.

High Schools of the Millennium Initiative

A second effort, similar to that of the New American High Schools program is the High Schools of the Millennium initiative. This initiative focuses primarily on policy issues pertaining to high school, but has identified a set of key elements of high-quality high schools. Those key elements are depicted in Figure 14.1 (p. 264).

Strategies for Including All Students in High-Quality High Schools

These two initiatives illustrate the types of activities that constitute a high-quality high school. The following section takes, as its starting point, the common dimensions of these initiatives to examine how students with severe disabilities can be included in and benefit from high-quality high schools designed to meet the needs of all students.

TABLE 14.1 Strategies Used by New American High Schools

All students are expected to master the same rigorous academic material.

All the core activities focus on student learning and achievement.

The curricula are challenging and relevant, and cover material in depth.

Schools create small, personalized, safe learning environments.

Staff development and planning emphasize student learning and achievement.

Periods of instruction are longer and more flexible.

Technology is integrated into the classroom to provide high-quality instruction.

Students learn about careers and college opportunities through real-life experiences.

Students get extra support from adults.

Schools use new forms of assessment.

Strong partnerships are forged with middle schools and colleges.

Schools form active alliances with parents, employers, community members, and policy makers to promote student learning and ensure accountability for results.

1. *High-quality high schools establish a vision, set high standards, and ensure access to a challenging curriculum.* The prevalent school reform method in the U.S. has been standards-based reform. The process of setting standards as a means of facilitating change in the educational system involves the establishment of content standards that "define the curriculum" and performance standards that "define what students should learn," both of which serve as exemplars of high-quality outcomes of the educational process. The establishment of such standards, the development and implementation of curricula to enable students to attain these standards, the implementation of instructional activities to deliver the curriculum, and the alignment of standards and curriculum with testing to determine student progress toward the standards form the essential components standards-based reform (Sykes & Plastrik, 1993). As discussed in a previous chapter, the 1997 amendments to the IDEA required that the IEP of students with disabilities document how students will participate and progress in the general curriculum. The intent of these mandates was to ensure that students with disabilities are held to high expectations, receive a challenging curriculum, and are not excluded from schoolwide and districtwide measures of accountability. How students with severe disabilities can gain access to and progress in the general curriculum, and thus be included in standards-based reform efforts, are discussed subsequently.

2. *High-quality high schools establish small, personalized, and safe learning communities.* A second general theme in high-quality high schools is the establishment of small learning communities within the context of the larger school. High schools typically enroll literally thousands of students and often become unwieldy in their structure and organization and confusing for students and teachers alike. One successful strategy adopted to improve student performance in such large settings is to group teachers and students together in smaller learning communities. There are multiple benefits to this strategy: students and teachers more easily get acquainted, teachers can more effectively individualize

VISION, STANDARDS, AND EXPECTATIONS—Communities create High Schools of the Millennium when they have a clear vision of the standards, expectations, and educational experience they want for ALL their youth. A High School of the Millennium sets high academic standards that are challenging and that reflect the community's expectation of the knowledge and skills needed for full and meaningful adult lives and participation in a civic society.

PRINCIPLES OF YOUTH DEVELOPMENT—A High School of the Millennium recognizes the needs, beyond the academic needs, of high school–age youth and embraces a youth development approach to create engaging learning opportunities. It helps prepare youth for lifelong learning, civic involvement, leadership, and careers and engages young people in learning, work, and service throughout their community. High Schools of the Millennium surround youth with caring and competent adults to help them navigate not only the challenges of high school and preparation for college and further learning, but also the stages of adolescence.

NEW FORMS OF ASSESSMENT—Assessments are used on an ongoing basis to determine how well students are learning the course work and to provide information to teachers about how to alter or modify their practice to better meet their students' needs. High Schools of the Millennium use multiple assessments for demonstrating learning in recognition that no one test can truly measure a student's knowledge, understanding, and skills.

IMMERSION IN THE ADULT WORLD—High Schools of the Millennium recognize the importance of an advocate in a child's life and ensure that each student has a relationship with at least one caring adult and, hopefully, many of them in various settings. Students have opportunities to experience authentic learning situations with adults—at work, in the community, and through volunteer activities, sports, clubs, band, or other youth groups.

ACCOUNTABILITY—High Schools of the Millennium are accountable to the community (both the learning community and the broader community) and provide information on their performance on a regular basis. The wider community measures its performance in the development of healthy and successful youth by looking at a variety of youth indicators.

USING THE COMMUNITY FOR LEARNING—Underlying a High School of the Millennium is its connection and relationship to the community and its resources that support learning. The community and the educational system partner to ensure that all students have access to the supportive networks to allow them to pass through adolescence safely and with high levels of achievement. The High School of the Millennium is a critical piece of the system of lifelong learning that exists in the community.

STRUCTURE AND ORGANIZATION—A High School of the Millennium is designed to provide small, personalized, and caring learning communities for students, with a clear focus on a career, academic, or thematic topic.

TEACHING AND LEARNING—Learning occurs in a wide variety of settings and contexts, in teams and independently. Learning occurs anytime, anywhere: at home, in the community, and in work settings. Students have many opportunities to engage in authentic learning, which involves them in the creation of knowledge, disciplined inquiry, and engagement in real-world issues. The general and vocational tracks do not exist; all students are expected to pursue a course of studies that leads to high academic achievement with the goal of postsecondary education leading to careers. Teaching and learning is competency based, not time based or credit based. All students have the opportunity to experience learning in the community. Teachers are highly competent, have access to ongoing professional development and externships in the community, and are given authority for determining the curriculum. Principals provide instructional leadership for the high school.

Key Elements of a High School of the Millennium

FIGURE 14.1 Key elements of High Schools of the Millennium. Adapted from High Schools of the Millennium Report, 2000.

instruction, students benefit from the sense of community formed in smaller groups, and it is easier to arrange instructional time and settings to meet the needs of students. The U.S. Department of Education (1999a) identified two common strategies for creating smaller learning communities. The first is a "schools-within-schools" model in which teachers and students are grouped according to some overarching theme, typically something like career or discipline interests or curriculum content. The smaller units operate as autonomous entities and students take most of their courses within that smaller group. The second approach is to keep cohorts of students together for as long as possible, usually by assigning students to a particular teacher who serves as an advisor or mentor.

School reformers focus on establishing smaller learning communities because research has shown that smaller school sizes lead to improvements in students' grades and test scores, as well as a more positive school climate with fewer problems (U.S. Department of Education, 1999b). Similarly, however, the creation of learning communities and smaller student groups provides greater opportunity for supporting students with severe disabilities. Creating learning communities is a first step toward ensuring success for students with severe disabilities in inclusive classrooms (Snell & Janney, 2000; Wehmeyer, Sands, Knowlton, & Kozleski, 2002). Such communities support and value diversity, including linguistic and cultural diversity, and recognize that students come to learning environments with differing levels of capacity and readiness to learn. As such, it is expected that teachers in small learning communities will differentiate instruction, provide personalized supports, promote cooperative and peer-mediated learning, and engage in classroom-level activities that enable all students to succeed, including students with severe disabilities.

3. *High-quality high schools promote community-referenced planning and community-based learning.* High schools are, by their very nature, centers for transition, and whether they serve the transition needs of all students depends on how such transitions are managed. To the extent that high schools offer transition preparation functions that take into account the needs of all students and foster self-determination by offering choices among options for career planning, they provide a natural framework for a shared educational agenda between special and general educators, at least to the extent that they pursue inclusive (as opposed to segregated, or "exclusive") educational opportunities (Sailor, 1991).

Historically, best practice in the education of students with severe disabilities has been that as students grow older they receive proportionally more of their instruction in ecologically valid, community-based settings such that by the time they reach high school, they are receiving instruction in the community for much of their school day. More recently, however, there has been a growing conflict between the best practices established in community-based instruction for youth with more intense support needs and the widely held value for their inclusion. School reform efforts have shown, however, that issues of inclusion and community-based learning need not be mutually exclusive. Indeed, the High Schools of the Millennium initiative identified *immersion in the adult world* and *using the community for learning* as strategies employed by effective schools for all students, as is the case in LaTricia's school. Such schools provide students with experiences to work and learn in the community (often side by side with adults who serve as mentors or facilitators), establish career counseling programs to expose students to careers and workplace expectations, utilize internships and apprenticeships in the community, and as discussed subsequently, utilize service learning projects and activities. Nor is this movement the only example of school reform efforts that emphasize community-referenced planning and community-based instruction. Gardner (1993) differentiated such learning experiences as different from the typical field trip because students return to the same location many times over the course of a school year to complete projects (working on sculpture at a local art museum, studying the life cycle of butterflies at the zoological park). Gardner's emphasis on community-referenced planning and community-based learning is based on his theory of how knowledge about cognitive development and learning must drive instructional activities.

If there is a schoolwide commitment to community-referenced and community-based learning, a larger number of resources will potentially be available for students with severe disabilities to learn in the community, and that experience becomes the typical experience for all students, not the exception only for students with severe disabilities. The typical classroom is expanded to include the community. Decisions about the amount of time students receive instruction in the community are then made based on student proximity to graduation or school departure and on future plans for education or employment, as well as issues of generalization. A senior without a disability whose career objective relates to a specific vocational area may spend much of his or her school day in the community learning the knowledge and skills he or she needs to become gainfully employed upon graduation. A student who is entering college the following year may spend more learning time in library settings that not only provide resources for completing high school courses but also enable them to learn important study and writing skills. In such a circumstance, a student with severe disabilities receiving his or her education in the community would not create the inclusion/community-dichotomy problem.

4. *High-quality high schools focus on lifelong learning and multiple adult outcomes and structure learning around careers and students' interests.* Just as community-based learning has been best practice in the education of adolescents with severe disabilities, so too has been a focus on providing functional, adult-outcomes-oriented instructional and learning activities. Federal law mandates that the IEPs of students with disabilities from the ages of 14 onward consider transition-related services and supports. There are concerns on the part of many, however, that for a variety of reasons the 1997 IDEA focus on access to the general curriculum will limit the degree to which these adult-oriented and functional curricular activities occur. While there are legitimate reasons to consider the unintended consequences of certain components of standards-based reform—particularly high-stakes testing—on the ongoing delivery of transition and adult-focused instructional activities (Wehmeyer et al., 2002), this should not be a concern in high schools implementing reforms consistent with those discussed here. Indeed, a primary feature of such schools is that they focus on all students as lifelong learners, target multiple adult outcomes, and structure learning around careers and students' interests.

An important component of the educational experiences of students with severe disabilities over the last decade has been a focus on promoting and enhancing self-determination (Wehmeyer, Agran, & Hughes, 1998). One component of this focus has been promoting active student involvement in educational planning and decision making, with particular focus on fulfilling IDEA requirements for student involvement in transition planning. While the movement toward promoting self-determination has too often excluded students with severe disabilities (see Wehmeyer, 1998, for extensive discussion), there are multiple activities and efforts that can enhance the involvement of students with severe disabilities in their educational planning, decision making, and program implementation (Wehmeyer & Sands, 1998) and that are consistent with school reform efforts to focus on students' interests. Of particular mention with relation to high school students with severe disabilities are the IDEA age-of-majority requirements. *Age of majority* is a legal term referring to the age at which an individual is no longer considered a minor and, as such, becomes legally able to exercise rights accorded to adults in their state or province. The actual age at which individuals reach the age of majority differs from state to state according to local law. Most governments, however, recognize the age of majority as 18 or 19, or when he or she is married or convicted of a criminal offense as an adult.

The 1997 amendments to IDEA require that schools notify students and their families one year in advance that at the age of 18 rights accorded to the parent under IDEA will transfer to the student. The age of majority requirements in the IDEA were added for the simple reason that state statutes regarding the age of majority pertain to all citizens *unless* they have been determined to be incompetent through the appointment of a guardian. If the state's statute places the age of majority at a time during which the student is entitled to receive education services, school districts cannot legally deny students the rights accorded by the law that, up until the age of majority, are exercised by the parent on behalf of the student. To do so is, in essence, discriminating on the basis of disability under other statutes like Section 504 of the Rehabilitation Act.

Such rights include the right to provide informed consent about one's educational program. While for all practical purposes students with severe disabilities, particularly severe cognitive impairments, will need extensive supports throughout their lives and may not be able to independently provide informed consent, the age-of-majority decision by the IEP team should provide an impetus for considering ways in which students can be provided instructional and other experiences that enable them to become more independent, participate more fully in educational planning, and, in general, become more self-determined (Lindsey, Wehmeyer, Guy, & Martin, 2001).

5. *High-quality high schools form alliances with parents, employers, community members, and policy-makers.* A final feature of reformed high schools is the formation of partnerships with a wide array of stakeholders in the educational process. Such an emphasis has, indeed, been a feature of special education services or, more accurately perhaps, a goal of such services. There has been considerable work in creating school/home/community partnerships, and thus a broader discussion is warranted and forms the basis for the next section.

Inclusive, Collaborative High Schools for Students with Severe Disabilities

Evidenced-based models for inclusive, collaborative educational programs in high schools are rare in the research literature. Much of the early outcomes work on inclusion of students with extensive support needs was conducted at the early childhood and elementary age levels, and more recently at the middle and junior high levels. High school, however, presents a very different configuration of resources and educational practices and therefore presents a wholly different set of challenges for inclusively oriented educators.

Some of the key issues confronting students with severe disabilities that need to be addressed at the high school include: (a) collaborative assistance and partnership development in planning career and future living circumstances (i.e., person-centered planning) and how those choices are reflected in the high school curriculum; (b) collaborative assessment and problem solving at the team level to determine needed access modifications, supports, and/or services to maximize student opportunities for a successful educational experience; (c) collaborative problem-solving assessment and interventions needed to assure healthy social development, including positive measures to address problem behavior associated with disability; (d) collaborative problem solving to develop partnerships and mechanisms to accomplish a reasonable balance of on-campus and off-campus instruction, as needed; and (e) collaborative processes to foster friendships and social connectedness to peers at school who may or may not require special supports and assistance.

Wehmeyer and colleagues (Wehmeyer, Lattin, & Agran, 2001; Wehmeyer, Lance, & Bashinski, in press; Wehmeyer, Sands, Knowlton, & Kozleski, 2002) have reported models to ensure access to the general curriculum for students with severe disabilities and an inclusive high school framework to address the issues highlighted in the previous paragraph. These models are focused on (a) access to the general curriculum, (b) community-based instruction, (c) systematic classroom instruction, (d) positive behavioral support, (e) scheduling, and (f) accessing peer support.

Promoting Access to the General Curriculum

Wehmeyer, Sands, Knowlton, and Kozleski (2002) identified steps, summarized in Table 14.2, to ensure that students with severe disabilities gain access to and progress in the general curriculum. Figure 14.2 (p. 270) summarizes the key elements of this approach, which involves three levels of action (planning, curriculum, and instruction), three levels of the scope of instruction (whole school, partial school, and individualized), and three levels of curriculum modifications (adaptation, augmentation, and alteration). A brief description of each of the five steps to access follows.

Step 1: Standards setting and curriculum design. Schools are challenged to establish standards that maintain high expectations and lead to a challenging curriculum while not excluding students with differing language and/or cognitive abilities or from nontraditional backgrounds by the way such standards are written. Standards and benchmarks vary in their specificity and the flexibility building- and campus-level educational personnel have in creating the general curriculum, and these factors impact student access and progress. Close-ended standards or benchmarks are those written to be highly specific as to the content, action, or student product and which are often narrowly defined (e.g., students will *orally* recite their multiplication tables using numbers 0 to 10; students will *write* a five-page paper on the history of the United States) (Wehmeyer et al., 2002). Such standards are typically grade- or age-normed, and students who cannot comply with the very specific activity or requirement (e.g., *write* a five-page paper, *orally* recite tables) will not succeed on such

TABLE 14.2   Steps to Gaining Access to the General Curriculum for Students with Severe Disabilities

Action Step	Description
Standard setting and curriculum design	Standards are written as open-ended and the curriculum is planned and designed using principles of universal design that ensure that all students can show progress.
Individualized Educational Planning	The individualized planning process ensures that a student's educational program is designed based on the general curriculum, taking into account unique student learning needs.
Schoolwide materials and instruction	There is school-wide use of universally designed curricular materials and high-quality instructional methods and strategies that challenge all students.
Partial school and group instruction	Groups of students who need more intensive instruction are targeted and building and classroom instructional decision-making activities focus at the lesson, unit, and classroom level to ensure students can progress in the curriculum.
Individualized interventions	Additional curricular content and instructional strategies are designed and implemented to ensure progress for students with learning needs not met by school-wide efforts or partial school efforts.

standards. Alternatively, open-ended standards provide greater flexibility in content delivery and student response, as illustrated by statements such as those that expect all students to have knowledge about themselves as a learner; to ask questions, manipulate materials, make observations, and analyze data; or to have basic tools of literacy and numeracy. Research suggests that open-ended designs allow for greater flexibility as to what, when, and how topics will be addressed in the classroom (Stainback, Stainback, Stefanich, & Alper, 1996) and are more consistent with universally designed curricula, ensuring that a wider range of students, including students with severe disabilities, can show progress in the curriculum (Bingham, 1995).

At the campus level, administrators and faculty need to have the latitude to decide how they will implement instruction so as to achieve the standards. This often begins with a visioning process that: (a) determines a shared vision for all students in the school; (b) sets goals that involve all students; (c) ensures a fit among vision, goals, and standards/curriculum; (d) identifies targeted outcomes; (e) sets standards for professional practice and identifies needed inservice and training; and (f) identifies how the organizational structure of campus facilitates or hinders goal achievement and implementation of the plan.

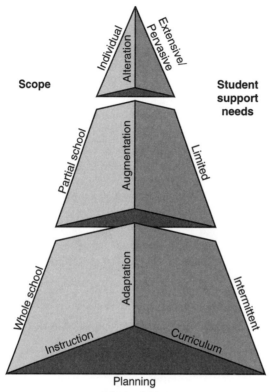

FIGURE 14.2   Multilevel focus for gaining access to the general curriculum.

Source: Adapted from Wehmeyer, Sands, Knowlton, & Kozleski (2002).

Many schools use a curriculum-mapping process to address these issues. This process involves the collection of information about each teacher's curriculum, including descriptions of the content to be taught during the year, processes and skills emphasized, and student assessments used, utilizing the school calendar as an organizer. Through a variety of review steps involving all school personnel, a curriculum map for the school is developed. Through this process, schools can find gaps or repetition in the curriculum content. Schools can then be sure they are teaching all parts of the curriculum framework, performance objectives, and other standards at the appropriate grade/course (Jacobs, 1997). This information in turn can be used to identify where in the curriculum students with severe disabilities can receive instruction on content both from the general curriculum and based on the student's unique learning needs.

Step 2: Individualized educational planning.   The education of students with disabilities has always emphasized the importance of individualized planning, a value that should not be abandoned when focusing on the general curriculum, particularly for students in high school. Figure 14.3 (Wehmeyer, Lattin, & Agran, 2001) depicts a decision-making process to ensure that IEP teams begin educational planning with both knowledge of the general

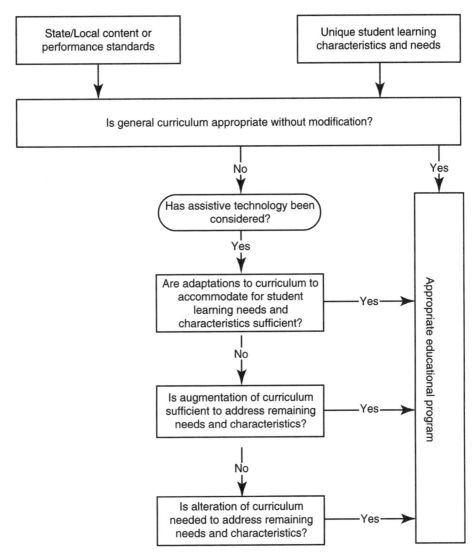

FIGURE 14.3   IEP team decision-making process to promote access to the general curriculum.

Source: Adapted from Wehmeyer, Lattin, & Agran (2001).

curriculum (standards and curriculum) for students who are the same age and grade level as the student for whom the IEP is being designed, as well as with information about unique student learning needs (based on input from multiple stakeholders and assessment sources). When considering a student's formal curriculum, the IEP team is first encouraged to consider how assistive technology can accommodate for student limitations and can enable the student to progress without curriculum modifications. Once AT has been considered, teams consider three levels of curriculum modifications. The first is *curriculum adaptation,* which refers to efforts to adapt the curriculum's *presentation* and *representation* or the student's *engagement* with the curriculum (as discussed subsequently). A second level of modification is *curriculum augmentation,* where additional content is added to the curriculum to enable students to progress. Such efforts typically include teaching students additional "learning-to-learn" or self-regulation strategies that in turn enable students to progress more effectively in the curriculum. Neither of these levels of curriculum modification changes the general curriculum content.

The third level, *curriculum alteration,* does change the general curriculum to add content specific to students' needs, which might include traditional functional skills or other needed skills not in the general curriculum. As all students age, the general curriculum becomes increasingly complex and difficult to master. For students with severe disabilities one outcome of such increased complexity is greater difficulty meeting age- or grade-referenced standards, and thus progressing in the curriculum. Concurrently, as students with severe disabilities get older there is greater need for them to be involved in instructional activities that focus on functional, transition-related content. Thus, it may be necessary to identify alternative curricular content areas for students with severe disabilities. However, the latter should only occur after the IEP team has considered the role of the general curriculum in the formal education program in light of student accommodations and curriculum adaptations and augmentations.

Step 3: Schoolwide materials and instruction.   The 1997 IDEA also emphasized the importance of schoolwide interventions to provide greater access for all students. Schoolwide interventions are those that are implemented throughout the school campus. Such interventions have the effect of minimizing the need for more individualized interventions. There are several schoolwide efforts that warrant consideration. First, instructional materials need to be designed with principals of universal design in mind. Researchers at the Center for Applied Special Technology (CAST) noted:

> The basic premise of universal design for learning is that a curriculum should include alternatives to make it accessible and applicable to students, teachers, and parents with different backgrounds, learning styles, abilities, and disabilities in widely varied learning contexts. The "universal" in universal design does not imply one optimal solution for everyone, but rather it underscores the need for inherently flexible, customizable content, assignments, and activities. (CAST, 1998–1999)

Orkwis and McLane (1998) defined "universal design for learning" as "the design of instructional materials and activities that allows the learning goals to be achievable by individuals with wide differences in their abilities to see, hear, speak, move, read, write, understand English, attend, organize, engage, and remember" (p. 9). The onus is on curriculum planners to employ principles of universal design to ensure that students with a wide range of capacities can access, advance, and succeed in the curriculum.

Researchers at CAST suggested the following three essential *qualities* of universal design: (a) provide *multiple representations* of content; (b) provide *multiple options for expression* and control; and (c) provide *multiple options for engagement.* These qualities reflect the activities that constitute curriculum adaptation and each is briefly discussed below.

Curriculum provides multiple means of representation. Researchers at CAST suggested that "universally designed materials accommodate diversity through alternative representations of key information. Students with different preferences and needs can either select the representational medium most suitable for them, or gather information from a variety of representational media simultaneously." World Wide Web pages designed to be accessible present one example of using multiple means of representation. One of the benefits of the web over traditional mediums is the capacity to use graphic images in a variety of ways, from icons to hyperlinked pictures to streamed video. Similarly, the design of curricular materials should include multiple representations of important topics, features, or points. Such multiple representations include a variety of methods of presentation of the material based on learner needs and characteristics. Students with cognitive disabilities, for example, may need print-based information presented with graphic depictions, free from unnecessary clutter, and with key information repeated or highlighted.

Curriculum provides multiple means of expression. CAST researchers noted that the dominant means of expression used in schools has been written expression. However, there are a variety of ways of student responding that could indicate progress, including "artwork, photography, drama, music, animation, and video" (CAST, 1998–1999), that would enable students to express their ideas and their knowledge. Once again, technology promises to provide avenues for expression that have heretofore been unavailable.

Curriculum provides multiple means of engagement. Student engagement in learning has long been an indicator of motivation in the classroom. By the utilization of multiple representation and presentation modes, particularly those involving digital representation of knowledge that are graphically based and incorporate video, audio, and other multimedia components, student engagement and, as such, student motivation can be enhanced. Universally designed curriculum takes into account individual student interests and preferences and individualizes representation, presentation, and response aspects of the curriculum delivery accordingly. Current technologies allow that level of individualization and, thus, provide greater flexibility in ways for the student to engage in learning (CAST, 1998–1999).

Based on Bowe's (2000) examination of the principles of universal design as applied to education, Lance and Wehmeyer (2001) developed a list of principles (Table 14.3, p. 274) for use in evaluating the degree to which instructional materials incorporate principles of universal design.

A second schoolwide emphasis is the implementation of positive behavior supports. Carr and colleagues (2000) overviewed the literature pertaining to positive behavior interventions and supports. Noting that problem behaviors like aggression, self-injury, or tantrums have been barriers to the successful integration and inclusion of some students with cognitive and developmental disabilities, these authors stated that the "goal of positive behavior support is to apply behavioral principles in the community to reduce problem behaviors and build appropriate behaviors that result in durable change and a rich lifestyle" (p. 3). Positive behavior supports focus on two primary modes of intervention, altering the environment before a problem behavior occurs and teaching appropriate behaviors as a strategy for eliminating the need for problem behaviors to be exhibited (Carr et al., 2000).

TABLE 14.3   **Principles of Universal Design Applied to Education**

Principle	Explanation
Equitable use	Materials can be used by students who speak various languages, address a variety of levels in cognitive taxonomies, provide alternatives that appear equivalent, and thus do not stigmatize students.
Flexible use	Materials provide multiple means of representation, presentation, and student expression.
Simple and intuitive use	Materials are easy to use and avoid unnecessary complexity; directions are clear and concise; examples are provided.
Perceptible information	Materials communicate needed information to user independent of ambient conditions or user's sensory abilities; essential information highlighted and redundancy included.
Tolerance for error	Students have ample time to respond, are provided feedback, can undue previous responses, can monitor progress, and are provided adequate practice time.
Low physical and cognitive effort	Materials present information in chunks that can be completed in a reasonable time frame.

Source: Adapted from Lance & Wehmeyer (2001).

Significantly for educators, researchers in positive behavior supports have focused considerable attention on addressing problem behaviors in school settings (Horner, Albin, Sprague, & Todd, 2000; Sugai & Horner, 1994; Turnbull & Turnbull, 2001; Warren et al., 2000). Positive behavior support has been demonstrated to reduce office referrals in schools, create classroom environments more conducive to learning, and assist students with behavior problems to improve their behavior. Positive behavior supports involve the application of behaviorally based approaches to enhance the capacity of schools, families, and communities to *design environments* that improve the fit or link between students and the environments in which teaching and learning occurs. Attention is focused on creating and sustaining school environments that improve lifestyle results (personal, health, social, family, work, recreation) for all students by making problem behavior less effective, efficient, and relevant, and desired behavior more functional (Wehmeyer, Wickham, & Sailor, 2000).

Finally, the implementation of high-quality, empirically validated instructional strategies campuswide is a critical feature of providing access for students with severe disabilities. Too often, instructional strategies that benefit other students are not attempted with students who have severe disabilities, either inadvertently or based on the assumption that because of the cognitive demands inherent in a particular strategy that strategy is not "appropriate" for students with severe disabilities. Thus, important practices such as aligning curriculum, instruction, and assessment; nurturing the development of problem-solving and critical-thinking skills, creative instructional groupings or arrangements, differentiated instruction, multilevel curriculum, and curriculum overlap in unit and lesson design; scaffolding key concepts to be learned; using strategies like advance organizers; getting students more actively involved in the learning process; and adapting the environment to the physical context in which learning is to take place are not used with students with severe disabilities (Wehmeyer, Lance, & Bashinski, in press).

Step 4: Partial school and group instruction.   Even when schoolwide efforts are in place, there will be students who do not progress without additional supports. The next level of intervention is at the group level, where more targeted interventions are designed and implemented for smaller groups of students. This includes classroom-level instructional decisions that focus on lesson and unit design so that all students in the class will progress, as well as specific learning experiences for groups of students. In order to adhere to school behavior rules, for example, ninth-grade students who recently transitioned to high school might need specific opportunities to learn what is expected of them when going from class to class, whereas tenth or eleventh graders would not require such learning opportunities.

Step 5: Individualized instruction.   Once schoolwide and partial-school practices are in place, there will likely continue to be a need to design individualized and more intensive interventions to enable students with severe disabilities to succeed, including some functional activities driven by alternative curricula. However, these students should also be involved in schoolwide interventions and engaged in learning activities driven by the general curriculum.

Collaborative Schools Model.   Gee's (2002) process model is ideally suited to be implemented in a context that reflects at least some of the structural assumptions of the rubric for community schools and for the reformed high school movements discussed earlier. These assumptions include a division of the school into smaller teaming communities with coordinated staff and professional supports within these smaller "houses" or units; team processes within houses that budget teacher planning and collaboration time and operate efficiently and productively; multidisciplinary perspectives including families (Lawson & Sailor, 2002); empowerment to implement the fruits of collaborative problem-solving efforts; and use of systematic data to make ongoing decisions.

Against this structural background, the place to begin, especially for students with high needs for assistance and support, is with team processes directed to curriculum planning. General education high school teachers, according to Gee, Akin, and Levin (2001), tend to be accepting of students with severe disabilities in their subject-area classrooms, but depend upon special educators to assist with curricular adaptations, evaluation, and grading issues. It becomes important not to burden subject teachers with extra or prolonged meetings when there is a goal of enlisting their support and enthusiasm for inclusive educational practices.

Secondly, the curriculum planning process should include techniques for embedding instruction on day-to-day living skills in the context of instruction in literacy, math, science, and so forth. The process described by Wehmeyer, Lattin, and Agran (2001) and depicted in Figure 14.3 captures the basic steps in such a decision-making process. Beginning this process with a focus on the curriculum planning process for the general education population helps to introduce the special needs considerations in a context that is meaningful to the general education teacher. Table 14.4 (p. 276) presents a prototype for introducing the

TABLE 14.4   Team Planning Tool for Systematic Instruction and Embedded Objectives for Joseph within the Unit on the Wizard of Earthsea

Typical Class Activities and Routines	Typical Teaching Strategies	Expectations for General Ed Students	Expectations for Joseph	How Will Joseph Receive Information	How Will Joseph Provide Information	Further Integration and Support Ideas
			Object calendar	Object board	Object board	Circle of friends
▪ Reading aloud	▪ Large group, vary readers, discuss in between passages	▪ Follow reading, reading aloud, participate in discussion	▪ Response to name and tactile signal; use of microswitch to activate tape	▪ Peers sitting next to him, will prompt, general ed teacher will provide cues	▪ Microswitch attached to tape recorder with pre-recorded passages	▪ Set aside five minutes on a regular basis to train the peers in his support circle how to support him during particular activities and tasks. Make sure they know how to read his eye-gaze shifts and can provide consistent ways of interacting. Provide the peers with feedback so that they know when J. is looking at them and what he likes/dislikes, etc.
▪ Journal and homework written assignments in Thoughtful Ed model with four styles	▪ Independent work or with partner	▪ Complete assignments after every two chapters. Grammar, spelling, reading for comprehension and understanding, critical thinking	▪ Computer use with microswitch; with partners select fantasy pictures for coloring album for class	▪ Peer partners will set context by their assignment; support person provides instructional assistance	▪ Print out pages for class coloring book	At support circle meetings, discuss upcoming projects and look at possibilities for J. Arrange for homework discussions and projects.
▪ Debate	▪ Room divides in half on a position; students who change their mind physically move, etc.	▪ State arguments clearly, determine agree or disagree, share thoughts, articulate positions	▪ Contingency awareness: When J. moves his eyebrows or eyes, partners move him quickly to the other side	▪ Peers will move him in his chair and will make it known when he has made a movement that is relevant	▪ Changing expression and moving eyebrows or large "sign"	
▪ Mandalas	▪ Students design mandalas based on the themes from the book	▪ Critical thinking, creative approaches to themes, understanding story themes	▪ Computer selection of colors and background designs using new program; social interactions	▪ Support staff and peers will provide choices on computer program Kid Pix	▪ Shift of gaze; microswitch for output of choice	
▪ Sociograms	▪ Students work in groups on sociograms of the characters over the course of the book	▪ Understanding the relationships between the characters in the book	▪ Peer interactions; use computer program set up to make sociogram; choice making	▪ Support staff and peers will provide cues and assistance	▪ Shift gaze, use of microswitch, sigh, facial expression	
▪ Play: fantasy	▪ Four groups of students: Students design a play which is a fantasy also, in one act, and perform it for the class	▪ Writing, articulating story plots and themes, understanding fantasy as a literary form, work skills, etc.	▪ Use microswitch to activate lines in play; social interactions; name recognition; object calendar	▪ Peers	▪ Tape recorded lines by peers	

needs of a special education student in the context of a collaborative curriculum planning team. The table displays a team planning heuristic illustrating how teaching objectives and instructional techniques for Joseph, a freshman with severe cognitive delays and other special support needs, can be embedded into a general education unit on literacy. In a team context, the planning heuristic asks the general education teacher to provide information on outcome expectations for her students on this unit; the range of these expectancies; expectations of social behavior; and typical teaching activities and routines that she will be using to engage students in the learning process.

Against this backdrop, the special education teacher presents information about the student with severe disabilities; outcomes and expectations that are reasonable for him or her in this unit; any modifications that may be needed if agreeable; any accommodations, adaptations, or augmentations that may be required to deliver information to this student; any modifications in the manner that the student will need to be able to present information to the teacher or class; and suggestions for enlisting the understanding and support of the class to foster a welcoming environment for participation by the student with special needs.

Issues of Scheduling.   One of the more challenging aspects of planning for inclusive educational programs for students with extensive support needs at the high school level is creating a schedule that accommodates community-based instruction. The team planning process, then, for a student with extensive special needs, will need to consider the scope and variety of the block schedule for students who choose (perhaps with their families, advocates, special educators) a supported vocational and community-living track in the high school program. Decisions will need to be made, with input from subject-area teachers, on the selection of classes for on-campus participation; personnel required for scheduled off-campus instruction, including general education peers; issues of timing between the two sets of environments; transportation issues; insurance considerations; securing community instructional environments (securing vocational instruction sites); and supervision and safety issues. Many high schools have course credit opportunities for general education students in peer tutorial participation, instructional aide training, and so forth. With school and parental permission, these scheduled opportunities afford a method to gain additional support for off-campus instruction with students with severe disabilities. For example, a student with extensive needs for support may be enrolled in "consumer math," offered through off-campus instruction, as an alternative to enrollment in a school-based math class. Students enrolled in an elective called "instructional assistants" might go off campus to assist in making purchases, counting change, or managing time for public transportation. In this case, valuable peer-mediated instructional objectives can be met for both populations.

Positive Behavior Support (PBS).   As discussed previously, one of the more recent innovations to emerge from special education research that is facilitative of inclusive educational programs at the high school level is represented by schoolwide positive behavior support (Warren et al., 2000). Schoolwide PBS is proving to be a major source of support for urban schools, for example, that are seeking solutions to high incidences of antisocial behavior from large segments of the entire school population (Warren et al., 2000). High school applications of PBS offer the potential for an embedded curriculum for social development (i.e., "character education") in a context of classroom as well as nonclassroom environments. Schoolwide PBS can thus serve as the discipline model for the school, and approach social development proactively, with an inclusionary philosophy.

Typical high school discipline models and procedures are geared to an exclusionary focus. Students who step out of line are invited to leave the classroom, and valuable classroom instructional time is lost. Under schoolwide PBS models, students are taught schoolwide expectations for social behavior and are acknowledged for incremental progress. School staff are taught methods to embed social instruction into the curriculum.

In urban high schools, approximately 65 percent of students may need individual support to successfully complete high school. This level of support will usually require team planning and monitoring; participation by teaching staff, family members, and perhaps community personnel; a comprehensive functional behavioral assessment; a written PBS plan; and an ongoing evaluation system with which to monitor progress and make adjustments. While this level of support is extensive, it provides a good fit with comprehensive school improvement model team structures (Lawson & Sailor, 2000), and the process of developing the PBS plans can provide a useful staff and professional development method for building school capacity to deliver schoolwide PBS.

The provision of schoolwide PBS can provide a catalyst for the formation of "community school" models (Lawson & Sailor, 2000). As Cuban (2001) recently pointed out, comprehensive school reform templates have not performed well in urban settings. According to Cuban, linkages to standards-based reform require schools to reference student progress to standardized tests of achievement, in addition to providing evidence for the satisfactory fulfillment of requirements for graduation. Test scores, particularly in math and literacy, are not sensitive to the efforts to restructure education when myriad variables outside of the reach of schools significantly interact with test scores, such as health problems, drug and/or physical abuse, social problems including homelessness, community and home violence, and so forth.

Cuban (2001) and others have suggested mechanisms for the formation of school, community, and family partnerships for the purpose of linking and integrating a broader array of resources with which to address social as well as academic outcomes for students. Lawson and Sailor (2000) have reviewed these developments associated with the community school movement, including the important roles to be played by special educators in the process and by universities and colleges in supporting these efforts through the provision of interprofessional training programs linked to community schools.

The processes required to implement schoolwide PBS are a good fit with the processes required to assist a high school to evolve into a community school. These processes afford a wide range of opportunities for university/college-based teacher training programs to form practicum- and course-level cohorts with other human services professional preparation programs. When student cohorts are infused into the structural web of "houses" and teams at the school, everyone benefits. Professional trainees learn collaborative processes and team-building activities, and participate in joint problem-solving efforts. Trainees learn to value and appreciate the perspective brought to these processes by family members. Additional levels of support are afforded through the cohort field experience requirement. Schoolwide PBS may supply at least one of the "missing links" identified by Cuban (2001) in analyzing why comprehensive school reform is failing in urban schools.

Conclusion

The challenges to providing an appropriate education for high school students with severe disabilities that is inclusive, meets functional needs, and provides access to the general curriculum is, under the best circumstances, a challenge. The growing gap between the cognitive and academic abilities of students with severe disabilities and their nondisabled peers is, too often, the excuse for involving students in an alternative curriculum. As illustrated by examples from the New American High Schools and the High Schools for the Millennium movements, however, what constitutes a good educational experience for all students can in fact constitute a good educational experience for students with severe disabilities.

The access to the general curriculum mandates in the 1997 amendments to the IDEA present both a challenge and an opportunity to educators focused on the education of students with severe disabilities. The challenge is to examine the demands of the school reform movement toward accountability and high standards in the context of what is best for students with severe disabilities. The opportunity presented is to raise expectations for students with severe disabilities and to move beyond just where a student receives his or her educational program to include discussions of what is in that educational program and how it is implemented.

References

Bingham, A. A. (1995). *Exploring the multi-age classroom.* York, ME: Stenhouse.

Bowe, F. G. (2000). *Universal design in education: Teaching nontraditional students.* Westport, CT: Bergin & Garvey.

Carr, E. G., Horner, R. H., Turnbull, A. P., Marquis, J. G., McLaughlin, D. M., McAtee, M. L., Smith, C. E., Ryan, K. A., Ruef, M. B., & Doolabh, A. (2000). *Positive behavior support for people with developmental disabilities: A research synthesis.* Washington, DC: American Association on Mental Retardation.

Center for Applied Special Technology (CAST). (1998–1999). The National Center on Accessing the General Curriculum [On-line]. Available: *http://www.cast.org/initiatives /national_center .html*

Cuban, L. (2001). Managing the dilemmas of high school reform. *Curriculum Inquiry, 30,* 105–118.

Gardner, H. (1993). *Multiple intelligences: The theory in practice.* New York: Basic Books.

Gee, K. (2002). Looking closely at instructional approaches: Honoring and challenging all children and youth in inclusive schools. In W. Sailor (Ed.), *Whole-school success and inclusive education* (pp. 123–141). New York: Teachers College Press.

Gee, K., Akin, J., & Levin, E. (2001, November). *Collaboration with special and general education teachers in middle and high school.* Paper presented to National TASH Conference, Anaheim, California.

High Schools of the Millennium Report. (2000, August). Washington, DC: American Youth Policy Forum.

Horner, R. H., Albin, R. W., Sprague, J. R., & Todd, A. W. (2000). Positive behavior support. In M. E. Snell & F. Brown (Eds.), *Instruction of students with severe disabilities.* (5th ed., pp. 207–244). Upper Saddle River, NJ: Merrill.

Jacobs, H. H. (1997). *Mapping the big picture: Integrating curriculum and assessment K–12.* Washington, DC: Association for Supervision and Curriculum Development.

Kimmel, D. C., & Weiner, I. B. (1995). *Adolescence: A developmental transition* (2nd ed.). New York: John Wiley & Sons.

Lance, G. D., & Wehmeyer, M. L. (2001). *Universal design checklist.* Lawrence: Beach Center on Disability, University of Kansas.

Lawson, H., & Sailor, W. (2000). Integrating services, collaborating, and developing connections with schools. *Focus on Exceptional Children, 33,* 123–139.

Lindsey, P., Wehmeyer, M. L., Guy, B., & Martin, J. (2001). Age of majority and mental retardation: A position statement of the Division on Mental Retardation and Developmental Disabilities. *Education and Training in Mental Retardation and Developmental Disabilities, 36,* 3–15.

Orkwis, R., & McLane, K. (1998, Fall). *A curriculum every student can use: Design principles for student access.* ERIC/OSEP Topical Brief. Reston, VA: Council for Exceptional Children.

Sailor, W. (1991). Special education in the restructured school. *Remedial and Special Education, 12,* 8–22.

Snell, M., & Janney, R. (2000). *Collaborative teaming: Teachers' guides to inclusive practice.* Baltimore: Paul H. Brookes.

Stainback, W., Stainback, S., Stefanich, G., & Alper, S. (1996). Learning in inclusive classrooms: What about the curriculum? In S. Stainback & W. Stainback (Eds.), *Inclusion: A guide for educators* (pp. 209–219). Baltimore: Paul H. Brookes.

Sugai, G., & Horner, R. H. (1994). Including students with severe behavior problems in general education settings: Assumptions, challenges, and solutions. In J. Marr, G. Sugai, & G. Tindal (Eds.), *The Oregon conference monograph 6* (pp. 102–120). Eugene: University of Oregon.

Sykes, G., & Plastrik, P. (1993). *Standards setting as educational reform.* Eric Clearinghouse on Teacher Education, Trends and Issues Paper, No. 8. Washington, DC: American Association of Colleges for Teacher Education.

Turnbull, A. P., & Turnbull, H. R. (2001). Extending a school-wide approach of positive behavior interventions and support to families and the community. *Families, professionals, and exceptionality: Collaborating for empowerment* (4th ed.) Upper Saddle River, NJ: Merrill/Prentice-Hall.

U.S. Department of Education, Office of Vocational and Adult Education, New American High Schools Program (1999a). *Aiming high: Strategies to promote high standards in high schools.* Washington, DC: Author.

U.S. Department of Education, Office of Vocational and Adult Education, New American High Schools Program (1999b). *Key high school reform strategies: An overview of research findings.* Washington, DC: Author.

Warren, J. S., Edmonson, H. M., Turnbull, A. P., Sailor, W., Wickham, D., & Griggs, P. (2000). *School-wide application of positive behavioral supports: Implementation and preliminary evaluation of PBS in an urban middle school.* A manuscript submitted for publication.

Wehmeyer, M. L. (1998). Self-determination and individuals with significant disabilities: Examining meanings and misinterpretations. *Journal of the Association for Persons with Severe Handicaps, 23,* 5–16.

Wehmeyer, M. L., Agran, M., & Hughes, C. (1998). *Teaching self-determination to students with disabilities: Basic skills for successful transition.* Baltimore: Paul H. Brookes.

Wehmeyer, M. L., Lance, G. D., & Bashinski, S. M. (in press). Promoting access to the general curriculum for students with mental retardation: A multi-level model. *Education and Training in Mental Retardation and Developmental Disabilities.*

Wehmeyer, M. L., Lattin, D., & Agran, M. (2001). Promoting access to the general curriculum for students with mental retardation: A decision-making model. *Education and Training in Mental Retardation and Developmental Disabilities, 36,* 329–344.

Wehmeyer, M. L., & Sands, D. J. (Eds.). (1998). *Making it happen: Student involvement in educational planning, decision-making and program implementation.* Baltimore: Paul H. Brookes.

Wehmeyer, M. L., Sands, D. J., Knowlton, E., & Kozleski, E. B. (2002). *Teaching students with mental retardation: Promoting access to the general curriculum.* Baltimore: Paul H. Brookes.

Wehmeyer, M. L., Wickham, D., & Sailor, W. (2000). *A whole school model of positive behavior interventions and supports to access the general curriculum.* Unpublished grant proposal.

15 Transition to Adulthood

MARY E. MORNINGSTAR AND DANA L. LATTIN
University of Kansas

The term "transition" in its most basic context means change, or "a passing from one condition or place to another" *(Webster's New World Dictionary)*. Transitions from one life stage to another are often characterized as times of stress, conflict, redefinition, growth, and sometimes dysfunction. In special education, the term is associated with the passage from school to adult life for students with disabilities. Transition in this sense is seen as a bridge between the security of school and home and the risks and opportunities of adult life (Will, 1984). All adolescents experience stresses and adjustments related to the transition to adulthood; however, families and youth with severe disabilities often experience high levels of distress (Hanley-Maxwell, Whitney-Thomas, & Pogoloff, 1995). The transition to adulthood for youth with severe disabilities is most often described by families as being marked by confusion and uncertainty. These young adults and their families are moving from a familiar system of educational services to which they are entitled by law to an adult system based upon eligibility, with conflicting policies, and most often characterized by agency-controlled services (Gallivan-Fenlon, 1994).

This chapter focuses on the transition from school to the community for youth with severe disabilities. However, rather than focusing narrowly on settings into which these young adults will move, this chapter presents the challenges, innovations, research, and practices that lead to quality adult life outcomes.

Redefining Adulthood

Transition to adulthood is typically marked by the high school graduation ceremony, a ritual that takes place for tens of thousands of youth across the country each spring. These young adults leave high school and go onto postsecondary educational settings, straight to work, or perhaps take some time off before they decide which direction their life will take. For youth with severe disabilities the transition from school to adult life looks very different from their peers without disabilities. Among other students with disabilities, youth with severe disabilities continue to be identified as experiencing the least successful adult outcomes (Blackorby & Wagner, 1996). This is especially disconcerting when we realize that it is all too often considered appropriate for young adults with severe disabilities to transition to segregated work and residential settings devoid of real opportunities for inclusion in the community. Given the difficulties in obtaining even the most segregated services, the trend toward innovative ways to support adults with disabilities in attaining a quality adult life is still mostly unobtainable for the majority (Braddock, Hemp, & Parish, 2000).

Barriers to Adulthood

Such ongoing poor adult outcomes for students with severe disabilities prompt us to consider what it means to be an adult with severe disabilities. This question resonates throughout research and practice related to the transition to adulthood for students with severe disabilities. Supporting such inquiry, Ferguson and Ferguson (2000) have described how young adults with severe disabilities are denied the status of adulthood by society's view of such individuals as *eternal children*. Being viewed this way leads to few opportunities to take on adult roles such as having a job, living in the community, or developing relationships. Because they are viewed as incapable of making decisions, individuals with severe disabilities are then placed in the role of *client*. Such a role creates dependency, anonymity, and lack of potential for growth or change. It stands to reason then that individuals with severe disabilities are most often isolated from their communities because of this bureaucratic control over their lives.

A third barrier described by Ferguson and Ferguson (2000) occurs when the transition is *stalled or unfinished*. Under such circumstances, families and educators of students with severe disabilities often do not experience the age-linked cues leading to the shift in responsibilities from parents to the young adults (e.g., getting ready for school, making a meal, babysitting, spending the night out, going on a date). Because families cannot rely on the natural process of change and growth, they must instead work with professionals to deliberately plan for their child's movement into adulthood, oftentimes requiring families to become more overtly involved in their teenager's life (Stineman, Morningstar, Bishop, & Turnbull, 1993). Most likely, this added burden is a direct result of the lack of appropriate adult options (Hanley-Maxwell, Pogoloff, & Whitney-Thomas, 1998).

What It Means to Be an Adult

In a discussion of their son's transition from school to adult life, Ferguson and Ferguson (2000) described a framework for considering adulthood that combines theories of chronological development and societal perceptions of adulthood (a summary is found in Table 15.1, p. 284). However, this notion of adulthood, as we shall describe later in this chapter, must be redefined to meet the specific life circumstances of youth with severe disabilities.

How do young adults with severe disabilities fare along the three dimensions of adult life? Unfortunately, almost two decades of research regarding postschool outcomes offers a distressing picture. Using the three elements of adulthood—autonomy, membership, and change—we will describe the current status of adult outcomes for youth with severe disabilities.

TABLE 15.1   Dimensions of Adulthood

Autonomy	Being your own person, expressed through the attainment of symbols such as:
	■ *Economic self-sufficiency*—having a job, living on your own, being independent).
	■ *Emotional self-sufficiency*—coping with crisis, emotional competence.
	■ *Self-determination*—individuality, independence, maturity, personal freedom to make life choices, responsibility for one's actions
	■ *Completeness*—possessing confidence about capabilities and how to act in a variety of situations
Membership	Community connections, collaboration, and sacrifice expressed through:
	■ *Affiliation*—voluntary associations and fellowships in both organized groups (e.g., service organizations, church membership) and individual interpersonal relationships
	■ *Citizenship*—responsibilities to one's community and to others; most directly played out in activities of collective governance (e.g., voting, signing up for the draft, volunteering for a political candidate, recycling)
Change	■ Adulthood as a continual process of growth with change occurring across all aspects of adult life (e.g., employment, living, friendships and relationships)
	■ Realization of accomplishments and place in life
	■ Leads to a sense of wholeness and striving for order and meaning

Source: Adapted from Ferguson & Ferguson (2000).

Autonomy.   Looking at the outcomes data on employment and living for young adults with severe disabilities, it would appear that irrespective of more than fifteen years of federal and state initiatives and mandates, the economic self-sufficiency of young adults with severe disabilities remains well behind those of their nondisabled peers, indeed behind their peers with disabilities.

The typical employment pattern for young adults with severe disabilities is a cycle of unemployment, low pay, and low-status jobs. For young adults with mental retardation who have graduated or exited high school at age 21, the employment rate remains at less than 50 percent. If, however, these students dropped out of school, then employment rates remain around 16 percent (Peraino, 1993). For students with severe disabilities, the rate of employment is only 20 percent; and in most cases, research has included segregated settings such as sheltered workshops as a successful employment outcome (Benz, Yavonoff, & Doren, 1997). Therefore, we can ascertain that youth with severe disabilities continue to achieve some of the lowest rates of adult employment outcomes in the most restrictive settings.

By the same token, living on their own is not a readily achievable or common occurrence for young adults with severe disabilities. According to the National Transition Longitudinal Study (NTLS; Blackorby & Wagner, 1996), the rate of community living for youth with mental retardation is only 11 percent for those who have graduated within two years (compared to 36 percent for nondisabled youth). From the more recent National

Health Institute Survey Disability supplement (NHIS-D), it is clear that adults with more severe disabilities continue to fall far behind their peers without disabilities. For example, 60 percent of adults labeled MR/DD live with family and relatives, as compared to 20 percent of nondisabled adults. More recent research does indicate a substantial and positive increase in the number of individuals with severe disabilities living in small residential settings of three or fewer or in homes of their own (Prouty, Smith, & Lakin, 2001).

Membership. In terms of the social engagement and adjustment of young adults with severe disabilities, research data show that most are not actively involved in either affiliation or citizenship relationships. Young adults with mental retardation and severe disabilities spend the majority of their time at home in passive activities; few participate in group memberships; and most spend their time with professionals and with others with disabilities, particularly those identified as having severe and profound disabilities ("Postschool Outcomes"). Others have reported similar results indicating that social networks are comprised primarily of family and staff and that recreational activities are more likely to take place at home.

Change. In terms of continual personal growth and development, finding appropriate outcomes data related to youth with severe disabilities is difficult. Lakin and Larson (1992) describe change as ongoing learning that combines internal processes with interactions and involvement of the individual with severe disabilities with his or her environment. However, very few postschool outcomes studies have examined anything other than postsecondary educational opportunities as they relate to growth and change. Again, students with severe disabilities do not fare well. In fact, one postschool outcomes study of young adults with severe disabilities found that almost half (48 percent) were not involved in *any form* of postsecondary education or training. Of the remaining half, only 10 percent participated in a formal education or training program. The most frequently identified forms of postschool programs were segregated day activity or training centers (Johnson, McGrew, Boomberg, Bruininks, & Lin, 1996).

Clearly, opportunities for fulfilling the dimensions of adulthood are extremely limited for young adults with severe disabilities. Indeed, the poor postschool outcomes as described above have been a catalyst for the development of federal mandates for transition planning and services, workforce incentives, and high performance standards for young adults with disabilities prior to exiting high school (Morningstar & Mutua, in press). The postschool outcomes research indicates that federal mandates are not enough for youth with severe disabilities to attain quality adult outcomes.

It is critical for secondary educators and adult providers to embrace cutting-edge research and practice that refocuses how we prepare and support young adults with severe disabilities to attain meaningful, valued, and inclusive adult roles after school. Fortunately, innovative professionals, family members, and self-advocates have begun to examine a "new paradigm" for considering adulthood for individuals with disabilities (Hagner, 2000). While models of inclusive supported adult life have developed and taken root in many communities, there are still severe gaps in disseminating and replicating these services and systems of support. Such new and innovative means for supporting young adults with severe disabilities will be described in the remaining sections of this chapter.

Preparing for the Transition to Supported
Adulthood for Youth with Severe Disabilities

The emergent model of supported adulthood focuses on the duality of independence and belonging, converging into a posture of interdependence (Ferguson & Ferguson, 2000). The dimensions of supported adulthood, then, are: (a) supported autonomy, (b) supported membership, and (c) supported change. Professionals and families who use this approach are committed to facilitating community participation and affiliation. At the core of the supported adulthood model are the values essential when taking a community inclusive stance:

1. Community inclusion is not a place or goal, but the purpose of services and supports.
2. The level and types of supports are based upon the individual's autonomy, needs, and self-determination.
3. A combination of supports from a variety of services, agencies, and natural supports (i.e., generic and disability-specific) are provided.
4. Personal life plans are developed and services and supports are arranged to meet these plans. Life plans are not limited by the services available in a community.
5. Community membership hinges upon friendships and social connections with others. (Hagner, 2000, p. 21)

The transition to supported adulthood for students with severe disabilities requires new ways to plan and prepare for quality adult outcomes. In this section, we will review innovative research, policies, and practices for school- and community-based programs. We will offer examples of recommended practices grounded in research (e.g., supported employment, commencement models, supported living, and community membership). In addition, innovative policies, funding mechanisms, and practices will be described in order to fully explore current recommended practices.

Commencement Models for the Transition
to Supported Adulthood

The traditional high school experience for students with severe disabilities ages 18 to 21 has been community-based instruction and vocational programs in which students spend more and more time in the community rather than the high school setting. While there are tremendous benefits to participating in a curriculum of this nature, it often means that these students do not have time in their day to fully participate in typical educational settings with peers without disabilities. This service orientation is especially difficult to reconcile for advocates of inclusive educational experiences in general education classrooms, but who also recognize the importance of a functional curriculum focusing on adult outcomes (Bauer, 2001).

An emergent alternative is to differentiate secondary educational opportunities according to the age of the student (Fisher & Sax, 1999), in other words, to offer inclusive educational programs during the high school years (ages 14 to 18) and a transition-focused community-based program for students aged 18 to 21. This alternative has been described as a deferred graduation or commencement program (Schuh, Tashie, Lamb, Bang, & Jorgensen, 1998). Because IDEA allows students with disabilities to receive special education services until the age of 21 (in some states, even older), commencement programs are becoming a viable alternative.

Commencement programs provide an opportunity for students to receive the best of both worlds—inclusive education during the high school years until they participate in graduation ceremonies with their peers, and a comprehensive community-based program after graduation (Izzo, Johnson, Levitz, & Aaron, 1998). Students participating in these programs continue to be enrolled by the school district until they complete their transition and community-focused goals and objectives as delineated in their IEPs. Some students may complete their transition-specific IEP goals and objectives prior to age 21, and these students then receive their diploma and exit from special education services, while others will continue until they age out of special education. Although originally developed for students who typically stayed in high school until 21 (e.g., students with severe disabilities and mental retardation), commencement programs have expanded to meet the needs of students with all disabilities, including learning disabilities, behavior disorders, physical disabilities, and mild mental retardation (Grigal, Neubert, & Moon, 2001).

The most unique aspect of commencement programs is that they are entirely community based. Programs are located on a postsecondary campus (e.g., community college, vocational-technical schools, or university), in an apartment or house in the community, or in an office or storefront space in a commercial district (Morningstar, Kleinhammer-Tramill, & Lattin, 1999). Students are completely immersed in community activities outside of school and gain experiences and learn skills that directly impact their desired adult living outcomes and inclusion in the community.

Commencement programs are designed to be very flexible and person centered. Programs are tailored to meet each student's transitional needs and goals. For example, one student may learn to do laundry and cook at his or her own apartment or home; another student may be learning to use the community transportation system to get to and from work; and yet another student may be supported to enroll in courses at a college or university. If the program uses an apartment or house, students may also have an opportunity to experience overnight stays for periods of up to two weeks (Kranich & Erstling, 1996). Program participants also learn how to handle issues related to getting along with roommates, such as making decisions together about meals, budgets, and bill paying (McKenzie & Wildgen, 1999).

Some commencement programs also use strategies to create community connections while the student is still receiving support from school staff (see Box 15.1, p. 288). "Third Places" is a part of the Community Transition (C-Tran) Program in Lawrence, Kansas. Supported by a staff person, students may spend time in one or two community settings getting to know people, hanging out, and socializing. Many of the C-Tran graduates are seen around town in these familiar spots socializing and relaxing.

In summary, commencement programs are school-sponsored services developed out of the recognition that students with disabilities should spend time in typical high school settings until they graduate. Students with disabilities then experience the rite of passage

BOX **15.1**

Third Places: Making Community Connections

Sam has severe disabilities, and although he can't talk and doesn't use sign language, he is very expressive. Sam is in his first year in the 18–21 community-based transition program offered by his school district. One of the things Sam's family is particularly interested in focusing on are his friendships with peers without disabilities. The friends Sam had while in high school have graduated and most have gone off to college. Sam's family is afraid he will end up spending his free time at home or with his family, with few opportunities to meet new people in the community.

Mrs. Dominguez, the lead teacher with the 18–21 transition program, understands this concern of most of the families in her program. She and her staff have decided to create a new aspect of the program that will help Sam and the other students meet new people in the community. Every Friday afternoon, two students and one staff person will go to a coffee shop in town. Sam, his classmate Regina, and Barbara, a staff person, start going to The Mug, located in a popular shopping center. Barbara introduced Sam and Regina to The Mug's owners, Ed and Marguerite, and encourages them to talk and interact with Sam and Regina. Each time they go, Barbara makes a point of telling Ed and Marguerite something unique about Sam and encourages a conversation among them. Sometimes after dinner or on a weekend, Sam's sister or parents go to The Mug with him.

This approach has helped Sam to get to know the people who work at The Mug, and they have gotten to know him. In fact, they can always anticipate what he's going to order. Because Sam has become friends with Ed and Marguerite, he has also gotten to know clerks from the other stores in the shopping center when they come to The Mug to get an afternoon "pick-me-up." Many of them stop to chat with Sam, and he has gone to visit them at their stores. Sam and his family plan to find an apartment located near The Mug so that he can continue the connections he has made there. They hope that with support and guidance from the 18–21 program staff, these friendships will take on a life of their own outside of The Mug and the shopping center.

---

that comes with the commencement ceremonies, and then move into a community setting to gain postschool adult living experiences and skills. While little empirical research is available regarding adult outcomes for community-based commencement programs, it would appear that postsecondary programs targeting specific transition goals positively impact adult life outcomes such as employment, living, and community participation (Izzo, Cartledge, Miller, Growick, & Rutkowski, 2000).

Further studies are needed to examine the impact of program components on adult outcomes for students with severe disabilities. In addition, critical issues to be explored include increasing the direct involvement of outside agencies responsible for providing or paying for transition services. Currently, most programs rely heavily on school-funded services and staff rather than collaborating with agencies and funding streams outside of the school. Models of effective interagency collaboration—including the sharing of resources, funding, and services—are needed. It is critical that by the time students with severe disabilities are enrolled in school-sponsored commencement models, they are also actively involved with and receiving services from an array of community agencies.

The Transition to Supported Employment for Young Adults with Severe Disabilities

Prior to the 1980s, employment options for adults with severe disabilities and their families were limited to segregated environments such as sheltered workshops and day activity centers (often called prevocational programs). During the 1970s and 1980s, research and demonstration programs emerged but were primarily implemented within university research centers (Wehman, Bricout, & Kregel, 2000). Today, however, supported employment is a service option for individuals with severe disabilities who receive services from vocational rehabilitation. With the 1984 reauthorization of the Rehabilitation Act, and in all subsequent reauthorizations, federal policies and funding streams have specifically emphasized this employment option.

Supported employment is based on the philosophy that individuals with severe disabilities have the right to work in the community with the support needed to be productive and contributing members of society. Over the past decade, it is estimated that well over 200,000 people have gained employment in regular work settings with the support that they need (Kiernan, 2000). However, the enthusiasm for supported employment must be tempered by the fact that out of those adults with disabilities receiving such services, individuals with the most severe disabilities (for which this model was specifically developed) continue to be least likely to have access (Dreilinger, Gilmore, & Butterworth, 2001).

Barriers to supported employment for individuals with severe disabilities. Researchers and practitioners involved with supported employment have additional concerns regarding this approach. First, these services continue to remain predominantly agency-controlled, often by agencies that also run segregated workshops, resulting in conflicting self-interests, values, and services (Sowers, McAllister, & Cotton, 1996). Second, while innovative, consumer-directed and natural support models have emerged over the past decade, these approaches continue to be the exception rather than the norm (Sowers et al., 2000).

Third, supported employment services continue to expand, but so too do the number of sheltered work settings (McGaughey, Kiernan, McNally, Gilmore, & Keith 1995). The percentage of individuals with severe disabilities in integrated employment has remained relatively unchanged since 1993 (22 percent), versus the 77 percent who continue to receive facility-based and nonwork services (Dreilinger, Gilmore, & Butterworth, 2001). Indeed, large-scale efforts to increase consumer-directed services and to convert segregated programs to the supported employment model remain a severe challenge (Fesko & Butterworth, 2001). In large part, conflicting reimbursement mechanisms and federal and state disability policies are disincentives to ensuring that individuals with severe disabilities are a part of an integrated workforce ("Community Integration," 2002). Finally, for too great a percentage of young adults with severe disabilities, the "hand-off" in services between school and community employment agencies is often poor, leaving large numbers of families and young adults with long periods of unemployment, underemployment, and in unsatisfying segregated settings.

Preparing youth with severe disabilities for supported employment. School-sponsored work experiences for students with disabilities has been in place in some form or another since the turn of the century. Halpern (1992) has traced several vocational and work-study models from the 1920s to present time. He noted that it was not until the 1960s, however, that educational and vocational models were systematically developed to comprehensively address employment and career education for students with disabilities, and even later for students with the most severe disabilities. In fact, prior to the mid-1980s, the typical vocational program for students with severe disabilities was based on the assumption that these students would move from school into sheltered workshops and prevocational centers. Therefore, typical vocational preparation programs consisted of teaching a variety of vocational skills considered appropriate for the workshop setting, such as sorting, assembling, and packaging (Westling & Fox, 2000).

Today, the most appropriate vocational program for students with severe disabilities is to prepare students for the transition to supported employment. Work experience models for students with disabilities are typically based on research promoting the model of supporting students to move through three stages of career development: (a) career awareness, (b) career exploration, and (c) career experiences. A combination of in-school learning and community-based work experiences is most often recommended for students with severe disabilities (Hagner & Vander Sande, 1998). Continual assessment of work preferences, interests, and skills is also important so that a work portfolio or career path is established (Moon & Inge, 2000).

Research has demonstrated that one of the most critical indicators for successful postschool employment outcomes is opportunities for students with severe disabilities to participate in job training across a variety of real employment settings (Luecking & Fabian, 2000). Therefore, during the secondary school years, students with severe disabilities should be involved in both paid and unpaid vocational experiences. If such experiences are unpaid training sites, it is critical that school vocational programs follow the regulations within the Fair Labor Standards Act Training Agreement (cf. Simon, Cobb, Halloran, Norman, & Bourexis, 1994). Moon and Inge (2000) stress that work experiences must include systematic instruction emphasizing natural supports among coworkers. In addition, assistive technology devices, worksite modifications, and job-related accommodations are critical. Finally, Moon and Inge assert that paid work should be the goal for students exiting school, along with appropriate support services and funding structures.

In summary, supported employment is now an established and effective postschool option for students with severe disabilities and should be the goal for school-based vocational preparation programs. While barriers and challenges to successful supported employment programs still exist, emergent best practices, such as relying on community and workplace supports, using assistive technologies, and new policies for workforce incentives are critical to the success of supported employment outcomes, particularly as they relate to youth with severe disabilities. School-based programs can and should emulate new approaches currently utilized by innovative community-supported employment agencies (Griffin & Targett, 2001).

The Transition to Supported Community Living for Youth with Severe Disabilities

Providing the supports necessary to successfully live in the community continues to fall outside of the prevailing model of congregate care offered by state and local agencies. In the traditional model, the individual with disabilities and his or her family either accept such services (e.g., living in a group home of three or more individuals) or they are not served by the agency. In some cases, group home providers won't admit individuals with significant medical and cognitive disabilities, because they require too intensive a level of support and care (Morningstar et al., 2001). Ironically, it is often those families rejected from the traditional service system who create comprehensive and alternative lifestyles for their adult children with severe disabilities (Turnbull & Turnbull, 1999).

The traditional model is predicated on the idea that people have to prove themselves in order to be allowed to move on (e.g., achieve success in a group home before going on to independent living). At each point along this continuum a different set of rules and regulations are often enforced. The consequences for success or failure typically fall on the individual and not upon the program's inability to meet his or her support needs (Nisbet, 1992). The traditional model requires a certain level of individual autonomy and independence as a prerequisite that in effect holds back individuals with significant support needs from ever making it out of the established continuum (Taylor, 2001).

In contrast, supported living is a concept that has emerged over the past decade to mean living in a home chosen by the individual with disabilities, shared with roommates at the individual's discretion, and not owned by an agency (Klein, Wilson, & Nelson, 2000). Supported community living requires agencies and services to hold a new set of values, such as those summarized in Table 15.2.

The supports provided in community living settings are tailored to the preferences and needs of the individual and might include: (a) services on demand—only when the person wants it; (b) scheduled supports—performed at an agreed-upon level/hour; and (c) emergency backup systems—supports that are immediately available (e.g., a neighbor who can come in an emergency) (Klein, 1992). Personal assistance service (PAS) is the method most often used in supported living settings. This type of self-directed assistance supports the individual with severe disabilities in a dignified and personalized way.

Supported living advocates insist that the most successful forms of PAS are those that are self-directed and independent of traditional agency services. This is not to say that professional assistance will not be necessary, but the process for deciding types and levels of support shift from the agency to the individual and family (Klein & Strully, 2000). Several limitations continue to exist that stand in the way of allowing PAS to reach it's full potential including: (a) a lack of real control of the individual to hire personal assistances because funds flow to agencies; (b) the lack of appropriate funding levels for PAS resulting in underpaid staff with a high rate of turnover; and (c) policies that tie PAS only to those individuals or families who can show they can self-direct, thereby limiting the types of individuals able to access PAS (Snow, 2001). Addressing these barriers is critical to ensure that a greater diversity of people with disabilities, including those with severe disabilities, are able to live and work in their community.

A home of your own (HOYO): An innovative approach to community living.   The notion of home ownership for individuals with disabilities has only recently gained acceptance primarily as a result of the efforts of a handful of people with disabilities, their families, and advocates. Over the past decade, the HOYO initiative has emerged as a national model for home ownership for individuals with disabilities. Klein, Wilson, and Nelson (2000) have reported early results from this project and are able to demonstrate that homeownership is

TABLE 15.2   Nine Principles of Community Living for All

Nine Principles of Community Living for All

1. People will have a voice	Every person with a disability must have an effective means of communicating his or her desires, needs, feelings and thoughts. People with disabilities and those who assist them need to learn to use all available means to increase the ability to communicate and understand one another.
2. People will have control over their personal assistance	People with disabilities must receive the assistance they need and have control over this support. This means helping people to design and plan for supports based on their needs and desires; recruit, interview, hire, train, manage, compensate fairly, and schedule the assistance; and solicit support from unpaid individuals in their communities and neighborhoods.
3. Personal relationships will be promoted and supported	Friendships need to be encouraged to develop and grow based on common interests and mutual fondness. People with disabilities need to be supported to spend time in places and engage in activities offering chances for relationships to begin. Deciding to live with roommates must be based on relationships rather than on disabilities.
4. Resources will be flexible	People with disabilities and their families must have access to and control over funding, benefits, and financing options. Then people can purchase services they need. Services should be offered "à la carte" rather than as "package deals" that force people to live in certain locations in order to receive assistance.
5. Housing will be affordable	Communities have a responsibility to provide safe, accessible, desirable, and affordable housing. Home ownership for individuals with disabilities must be promoted so that people will become empowered by contributing to their local economy. Federal subsidies need to be flexible enough to be used for rent or mortgages.
6. Services will meet the needs of individuals	Health care and long-term supports must promote opportunities for people with disabilities to live in a home they control and receive the assistance they need, regardless of the type or severity of their disability. The majority of funding streams must be devoted to people rather than service systems.
7. Learning will occur naturally	Education and training must focus on gaining skills, building capacity, and developing and broadening interests. People with disabilities must be included in everyday life and have greater opportunities to learn in

TABLE 15.2 Nine Principles of Community Living for All *(Continued)*

	typical ways. The focus should be on what people can and want to do, supporting them with what they cannot do, and creating opportunities for learning in natural settings.
8. Assistive technology will be available and affordable	Technology is a necessary form of assistance for people with disabilities. The increasing affordability and availability of assistive technology will make it possible for people with disabilities to communicate, live on their own, maintain jobs, and participate in their communities.
9. Communities will be strengthened to support the needs of all citizens	All people in a community must be valued equally for their unique talents and contributions, and supported in overcoming their struggles. No single member must be viewed as more or less valuable than the next. Communities must organize, choose leaders, identify common goals, and use resources to build the capacity of all citizens.

Source: Adapted from Klein & Strully (2000).

obtainable for individuals with disabilities who might never have qualified for a mortgage under traditional criteria (due to, e.g., annual income, employment history, credit history). In a national survey of 26 HOYO programs, these researchers identified four common features shared by successful programs:

1. Collaborating with key partners including lending authorities, banks, state agencies, and housing organizations, as well as families, individuals with disabilities, neighborhood organizations, and advocacy groups.
2. Creativity in arranging financing in that many programs blended funds from a variety of sources such as state housing finance authorities, private lenders, and the borrowers themselves. Many programs were successful in creating policy changes to ease the barriers that prevented homeownership.
3. Using a team approach to generate an individualized plan for the home buying process and to ensure support, planning, and financing throughout the process. This included support during all phases of purchasing a home (applying for loans, arranging down payment and closing costs, developing budgets, establishing credit worthiness, and viewing homes).
4. Offering education for homebuyers and key partners such as housing professionals.

Individualized funding and self-directed services: Self-determination in action.   Along with the shift in how community living services are offered is the movement to give control over funding to the consumer (i.e., the individual with disabilities and his or her family and support network). In the mid-1980s, with the advent of the Medicaid Home

Community-Based Services (HCBS) waivers, individuals with disabilities began to experience a different funding approach allowing for services in the community. By the early 1990s, federal and state agencies were trying to curb the expansive growth of Medicaid health-care costs, including the HCBS program. At the same time, disability advocates were becoming increasingly dissatisfied with HCBS services due to the lack of flexibility and personalized supports offered by these programs (Nerney & Shumway, 1996). Chief among their concerns was the lack of family and individual choice or control over which agencies provided HCBS services. It was clear that state and federal regulations for HCBS services were too restrictive, resulting in highly regulated programs offering few choices except for the established service system. These policies all but eliminated any form of financial support for more natural and informal community supports.

Community living advocates received a tremendous boost in 1996 when the Robert Wood Johnson Foundation (RWJF) offered over $5 million in grants to support state efforts to develop individualized funding structures and policies. Since this time, the RWJF Self-Determination Project has directly assisted 19 states, as well as spawned flexible funding initiatives in other states. Key to this model is the development of individualized budgets that delineate the lifestyle preferences and support needs of the individual with severe disabilities. The dollars associated with these budgets are separate from the pool of funds that traditionally flow to congregate care agencies. Thus, the individual and his or her family, along with a circle of support from professionals and community members, have real control over the budget (see Box 15.2).

Rather than the money coming directly to the individual, however, most states have developed a system of autonomous *fiscal intermediary agencies* to direct the flow of HCBS funds from the state to the individual. The fiscal intermediaries manage all paperwork, including tax filings and payments to support staff. The individual and his or her family hire and supervise staff. A second feature of individualized funding is the use of *independent support brokers*. This replaces the case manager in a traditional service delivery system. Support brokers are unique in that they do not provide services, but instead become an agent of the individual with disabilities and facilitate the person-centered life plan, identify and arrange for formal services and informal networks to provide the support needed, and

---

B O X **15.2**

Individualized Funding: Making a Difference for Ryan

Ryan Banning, a young man born with Down syndrome, exited public school without having to face the traditional and limited options of moving into a group home or working in a sheltered workshop. Instead, Ryan graduated from his school-sponsored 18–21 transition program with a true vision for his future, one that involves his family and friends, living on his own, working and making money, and someday getting married. His vision for the future is being translated into reality by Ryan and his family with support from the Kansas Self-Determination Program, a state program that promotes individualized funding for individuals with severe disabilities. Now, Ryan lives in his own home and works two jobs in his community—one at a fast-food restaurant and the other operating his own vending machine business.

How did all of this take place? For Ryan and his family, the vision for a future of full community involvement has always been central in their lives. Accessing the funding streams to support the vision was the key that unlocked the doors. His mom, Martha, expresses the importance of individualized funding in this way, "Self-determination has made an incredible world of difference in terms of service delivery and has decreased dramatically the level of stress. It has also brought wonderful people into Ryan's life." The Bannings worked to set up funding streams that support Ryan. As his dad explains, "It's all tied up in funding. Ryan has help from SSI [Supplemental Security Income], from Social Security Disability Income [SSDI], and from the Lawrence Housing Authority. It's a collage of support systems . . . from the state's perspective, it doesn't cost any more for Ryan to live in the community in his own home than it would be if he lived in an institutional setting."

His parents found out about the self-determination program through their advocacy efforts within their school district, community, and state. Ryan and his family had to first go to the local Community Developmental Disabilities Organization (CDDO) that serves as the single point of entry into services for individuals with developmental disabilities in Kansas. Ryan was required to go through a screening process to determine his level of support needs. Once this was completed, he was able to access the Home and Community-Based Services (HCBS) Medicaid waiver for a specified level of funding to support his needs. However, unlike the typical HCBS program in Kansas, Ryan and his family, the service coordinator, and others in the Banning's support network developed an individualized budget focusing on a plan to support their vision for Ryan's adult life. Then the HCBS funds that traditionally have gone to agencies to provide day and residential services instead flow to an independent fiscal intermediary so that all taxes and other fiscal issues can be taken care of and Ryan and his family don't have to worry about these details. The funds are used to pay for the services and supports that Ryan and his family want and need. They are the ones who decide how his money will be spent. They decide who will be hired or fired.

In this way, working with his parents and service coordinator, Ryan moved into his own home, at first living with his older sister and her husband. Now he lives with roommates who provide daily support for Ryan. He has kept the fast-food job he had while he was in school but has also started his own business, "Ryan's Vending Service." He was able to start up his small business with a grant from the Kansas Council on Developmental Disabilities. Ryan uses some of his individualized funds to hire his job coach, Tommy, who works with Ryan at Arby's as well as with the vending service. Because Ryan and his family were able to hire his job coach directly, it ensures a greater level of success. As for Ryan, he really connects with Tommy: "Tommy's funny. He takes me in his car. I'm Tommy's best guy."

This network of support is key to individualized funding. His father understands the importance of having a safety net of support surrounding Ryan. But Bob also thinks that the individualized funding program does a lot more. "It provides Ryan with a safety net but also opportunities to do things he wouldn't have been able to do. For example, in a group home, he wouldn't have personal choices like he does now. He wouldn't get out in the community as much. He goes out to eat and to the movies with support people and friends. He goes out to dinner. . . . There's a continual flow in his life. He's like a lot of 23-year-olds."

Success for Ryan comes from the people in his life, and this is key. "What we strive for are people who will support Ryan but also provide respect and friendship . . . kind of like formal and informal support from the same person. Ryan needs the support for a good quality of life, yet we don't want people who are just paid. These are people who see past the behavior problems, and see the good things about [Ryan]."

Source: Adapted from T. Malone. (n.d.). Ryan Banning. *Stories from the Free State.* Topeka, KS: Lawson Phillips Associates.

assist with ongoing evaluation and consultation (Mosely & Nerney, 2000). They serve as an advocate and mediator for the individual with disabilities and his or her family.

Preparing youth with severe disabilities for supported living.   In describing how educators can support students with severe disabilities to gain skills that will prepare them for living at home and in the community, Browder and Bambara (2000) adhere to a specific set of values. First, deciding what to teach must be made in partnership with students and families. Second, student self-determination must be considered as a critical curricular domain of the instructional process. Third, a variety of settings should be considered in which home and community skills are taught (e.g., general educational environments, school, home, and community). Finally, home and community skills gain importance as the students become older. Table 15.3 offers a range of examples of how these four values can be actualized as part of the day-to-day teaching and learning process for students, families, and educators.

Typically, educators and school support staff tend to focus on how they can enhance the skills necessary for adult life for students with severe disabilities. Of course, skill-building should be a critical aspect of all educational programs. However, for students with severe disabilities, a new paradigm of educator responsibilities must also be considered. With the increasing awareness of effective strategies for inclusion in the general educational environment, self-determination, interdependence and support networks from peers and community members, and the vision for a supported adulthood, "it becomes clear that there are no prerequisites for having a home of one's own and having full access to the community" (Browder & Bambara, 2000, p. 584).

This means that educators must also consider themselves to be part of the systems change network. They will need to partner with adult service providers who are interested in a new way of supporting adults with severe disabilities in the community. *Pathfinders,* based out of New York City, is just such a model. This program has brought together schools and adult providers to support young adults with severe disabilities as they make the transition from school to a supported and inclusive adult life. The focus of this program becomes one of "capacity thinking, the art of discovering the qualities a person can contribute to community life and then discovering people and places that value that contribution" (O'Brien, Mount, O'Brien, & Rosen, 2001, p. 5). Figure 15.1 (p. 300) offers an illustration of how Pathfinders has operationalized capacity thinking.

In summary, planning for the transition to community supported living for young adults with severe disabilities involves more than finding an agency that provides residential services. Rather, supported living holds community inclusion and presence as basic values. Developing a system of support that puts into practice this set of values requires a reorganization of both the policies and practices associated with traditional services. It requires a new way of living, such as HOYO, and innovative funding steams such as those created by the Self-Determination projects.

Despite the remarkable outcomes of model projects focusing on home ownership and individualized and consumer-directed funding, there remains real concern about the opportunities for individuals with severe disabilities to live on their own with the supports they want and need. Indeed, in a recent survey of state agencies serving individuals with mental retardation and developmental disabilities, fewer than half of the states responding indicated

TABLE 15.3 Critical Values and Instructional Strategies for Teaching Home and Community Skills to Students with Severe Disabilities

Values	Instructional Strategy	Description
Value One: **Plan Instruction in Partnership with Students and Families**	1. Use person-centered planning strategies	1. Personal futures planning, McGill Action Planning (MAPs), and Planning Alternative Tomorrows with Hope (PATH) can all be used to collaboratively plan with students and families to ensure that plans for instruction fit within the context and preferences of current and adult life outcomes.
	2. Organize collaborative planning meetings	2. Teams come together informally to solve problems around a specific issue, focusing on the goals and preferences of the student and family, such as how students can participate in family routines and activities, decreasing challenging behaviors, being more involved with peers at school and home, and increasing community access and participation, and ways teachers and family members can work together to support students' needs at home.
Value Two: **Encourage Student's Self-Determination**	1. Develop choice-making skills	1. Developing instructional goals based on student preferences is a first level of instruction focusing on choice. Teachers can also embed multiple choice opportunities into instruction: (a) The *choice diversity model* allows teachers to analyze steps and component parts of a routine and identify types of options that can be made available during each step (e.g., "Connie, which do you want to make first, your drink or your sandwich?"). (b) Teachers must *match the student's communication mode* with choice-making skills (e.g., using actual objects to choose from, using pictures rather than words, pointing, labeling, or grimacing).
	2. Utilize self-prompting skills	2. Teaching students to respond to naturally occurring cues and prompts by: (a) identifying and teaching the salient features of a natural cue (e.g., wrinkles on the bed) (b) delaying correction (e.g., letting the student realize he didn't get out the ham for his sandwich) (c) using nonspecific prompts (e.g., "What's next?") Students who continue to have difficulty in responding to natural cues can be taught to use permanent prompts to guide learning (e.g., color-coded labels, picture recipe lists, audio and visual job task lists)

(continued)

TABLE 15.3 Critical Values and Instructional Strategies for Teaching Home and Community Skills to Students with Severe Disabilities (*Continued*)

Values	Instructional Strategy	Description
	3. Develop self-management skills	3. Teaching students to self-manage behaviors involves teaching multiple skills (e.g., setting personal goals, recording progress toward goals, and self-evaluating and reinforcing accomplishments). Two instructional strategies include: (a) *Self-instruction*—students self-talk a series of steps in a task (e.g., teaching a "did-next-now" verbal sequence) or teaching students verbal problem-solving sequence: (1) identify problem, (2) state possible response, (3) evaluate response, and (4) self-reinforce. (b) *Self-scheduling* allows the student to determine and control multiple tasks within a day, and the order in which they are accomplished. Students are taught to select enjoyable and necessary activities, plan in advance when they will be completed during a day or week, and use the schedule to initiate activities.
Value Three: **Choose Instruction that Blends with General Education Contexts and Encourages Peer Interaction**	1. Choose inclusive instructional settings	1. Consider the following questions: (a) What settings will be used for instruction and do they contain other students without disabilities (e.g., school, home, community)? (b) Can the skills be embedded in typical school activities (e.g., learning cooking skills in a home economics class)? (c) If not, will a simulated activity be feasible or effective (e.g., teaching critical skills for ordering in a restaurant in a school setting)? (d) Or, is it best to schedule instruction in the settings where the skills typically are used (e.g., going out to lunch with high school peers without disabilities)?
	2. Plan for generalization of skills	2. Teachers can maximize instructional time by carefully planning for the generalization of skills. *General case instruction* is one effective way to plan. This approach requires teachers to: (a) *Identify* an instructional universe (e.g., grocery shopping at the neighborhood store, all grocery stores on a certain bus line, or all grocery stores in a community). (b) *Write* a generic task analysis for purchasing groceries. (c) *Select* which stores will be used to train the skills. Consider how each store samples the range of stimulus and response variation among grocery stores (e.g., electric doors, push doors, pull doors). (d) *Teach* the skills in the variety of store settings selected. (e) *Test* for generalization at new stores not used for training.

3. Use effective and efficient instruction

3. Maximizing instruction involves effective instructional methods such as: (a) *observational learning*—direct instruction, prompting and feedback to one student at the same time prompting and reinforcing other students to observe and follow instructions using picture recipe books, and (b) *instructive feedback*, which allows teachers to include additional information by adding it to teacher prompts (e.g., "Use a mitt . . . the food may be hot and could burn you") or to supplement feedback upon completing a task (e.g., "A baked potato is good because it is low-fat and won't make you gain weight, unless you add too much butter or sour cream!").

Value Four:
Home and Community Skills Gain Importance as Students Become Older

1. Use transition planning to focus community-based instruction

1. The age of the student is a critical consideration. For example, younger students may complete small household chores, pick up their clothes, and make snacks, but they go shopping and to restaurants with family members. Adolescents and young adults, however, are starting to complete complex household tasks (e.g., laundry) and prepare full meals. They are going places in the community on their own (e.g., getting dropped off at the movies).

2. Community-referenced skills and activities should be selected using a person-centered approach to enhance dignity and inclusion in community settings. For example, prompting and collecting data can be done discretely. Intensive instruction and repeated practice may be needed, but this can be done in a private setting rather than in the community.

3. A student's IEP should reflect the increasing importance of home and community skills, including job skills, as the student gets older. The specific IEP goals and objectives should reflect the student and family's interests and preferences, and teachers should consider how these skills will enhance student self-determination, community participation, and involvement with nondisabled peers.

Source: Adapted from Browder & Bambara (2000).

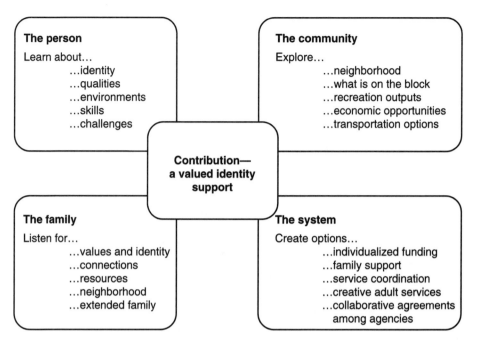

FIGURE 15.1   Pathfinders approach to capacity thinking to achieve community inclusion.
Source: Adapted from O'Brien, Mount, O'Brien, & Rosen (2001).

that they had individualized funding policies in place (Metzel, 2001). Of great concern are young adults with severe disabilities who remain in the minority of those living outside of their families' homes, receiving supported community living services, and moving toward home ownership (Klein, Wilson, & Nelson, 2000).

When considering the potential for high quality-of-life outcomes as can be supported under a system of individualized funding, independent support brokers, and living in homes of one's own, it becomes even more imperative that educators and transition specialists prepare youth and families for this option. We should no longer be thinking from a continuum mindset, but instead focus on supported living, supported adulthood, and the funding structures to support this model. Educators must be preparing students and families to develop a vision of supported adulthood and to inform them of the new and innovative resources, funding structures, and policies that go along with these values.

The Transition to Supported Membership, Friendships, and Community Inclusion

As indicated earlier, families and many service providers are now considering the importance of offering individual supports for sustained community inclusion (Hagner, 2000). However, the traditional service structure continues to support sheltered and segregated settings. Social isolation is often a top concern of families with young adults with severe disabilities in that they recognize the importance of having friends and a social network outside of the family (Sowers, Glang, Voss, & Cooley, 1996). Ferguson and Ferguson (2000) describe the importance of supported membership for their son, Ian, in this way:

> The more hands that are there to catch him when he falls the better. We firmly believe that the more deeply embedded Ian is in the life of his neighborhood, workplace, and the city in general, the more people there will be who will notice if he is not there and who will work to keep him there as a member of his community. (p. 650)

Barriers to inclusion in the community. A critical goal for students with severe disabilities making the transition to adulthood is to develop connections in their communities to enrich their lives. Few individuals with severe disabilities have developed social relationships from the traditional approach of community participation. Often the lack of a social network outside of the family is due in part to inadequate supports (Walker, 1999). Under such circumstances, individuals have few opportunities to meet and develop one-on-one relationships with others. Therefore, professionals need to reconceptualize how they offer services, in a way similar to the agency administrator who stated, "I used to think that community integration meant doing things in the community, now I know it means helping people to have friends" (Amado, 1993, p. 301). Rather than being a mere presence in the community, people with severe disabilities should experience a *sense of community*.

Supporting and sustaining membership in school and the broader community. When using a community-inclusive approach, school and support staff focus on building *individual* social relationships (i.e., personal friends) as well as *public* social relationships (e.g., through participation in clubs and activities). A variety of strategies for enhancing the social relationships of students with severe disabilities have emerged through research and practice including: (a) personalized planning (Cipriano, 1998); (b) using inclusion facilitators (Lutfiyya, 2001); (c) creating intentional communities (Forest & Pearpoint, 1992); and (d) making connections to community groups and associations (O'Brien & O'Brien, 1992). There is no doubt that a first step is to develop a plan that focuses on increasing social networks and community memberships. Table 15.4 (p. 302) describes four steps that can be used by school and community staff to begin the development of social networks and community memberships.

As indicated above, inclusion facilitators are one way to ensure an appropriate level of support and expertise. Their role is to support the individual as he or she gets to know and be known by many different people, to expand the individual's social network and maximize the variety of relationships possible, and to support the development of positive and emergent relationships. Schools that are committed to fully including students with severe disabilities in classrooms and settings throughout the school often have inclusion facilitator positions. These educators typically facilitate many aspects of social inclusion, including the planning process described in Table 15.4. They are also responsible for developing *circles of friends* for each student. Inclusion facilitators spend considerable time with teachers and other school staff to ensure that the overall climate within the school is supportive of school and community inclusion. For older students, such specialists may start the process to support the student to develop relationships with members of the community at large, both on an individual level and by introducing the student to community clubs and social groups.

TABLE 15.4   Planning for Community Membership

Step	Explanation	Example
1. Assess	Identify the interests, gifts, strengths, and contributions of the individual.	Using a MAPS meeting with school-age peers as a way to identify strengths and interests and develop a circle of friends.
2. Explore and plan	Identify possible connections based upon these interests—don't limit them, include *everything*. This step may involve exploring the community and identifying local leaders and community associations.	Spending time visiting different places in the community; meeting people in public places and at organizations. Reviewing school clubs and organization directories to see what kinds of clubs and activities are available in the school.
3. Implement	Provide personal introductions that include shared interests.	"Nancy, this is Carol. I know you love to watch KU basketball, and Carol is a huge fan, too." Not, "Nancy, would you like to be Carol's friend?"
4. Evaluate and maintain	This may involve providing assistance and tips for communication. Identify when to step out so that the friendship progresses naturally.	Problem solving when transportation inhibits activities between friends.

Source: Adapted from Amado (1993), Cipriano (1998), and M. E. Morningstar (1993), unpublished manuscript, University of Kansas, Lawrence.

Schools often use a person-centered planning process (e.g., MAPS, Personal Futures Planning) not only for planning the transition to adult settings (Furney, 1999), but also to emphasize and coordinate the development of social relationships for students with severe disabilities. For maximum results, this type of planning is conducted either prior to or as a part of the traditional IEP meeting in order for the information gathered from the person-centered planning process to best inform the development of IEP goals and activities.

A second effective strategy involves building intentional communities, sometimes called circle of friends or circles of support (Forest & Pearpoint, 1992). This approach brings together a group of people around a student with severe disabilities. Those in a circle of support plan act to achieve the group's vision of full community participation for the individual with severe disabilities. In fact, the MAPS process was designed with this approach in mind. MAPS were first introduced with school-age children to promote full inclusion and had the circle of friends as a core strategy for implementing and supporting inclusion. Circles of friends are often a part of elementary school inclusion for students with severe disabilities, but are less common in secondary schools. Secondary schools that use the circles approach often do so in conjunction with extracurricular clubs and sports teams as a way to better meet the structure and climate of the secondary school setting.

A third method for achieving community connections for students with severe disabilities is to create connections to community associations, described by O'Brien and O'Brien (1992) as "bridging to community." This involves introducing a person to new places, connecting them to valued citizens and organizations in the community, and supporting them in sustaining these new connections. Participating in community associations is one way that allows students with severe disabilities to contribute new perspectives, energy, and meaning into an organization. In fact, volunteer and service opportunities are becoming more and more prevalent as a method for connecting individuals with disabilities. The contributions they make to their community bring a sense of belonging, opportunities to learn, and respect from others (Shoultz & Lakin, 2001).

For secondary schools, service learning (for both students with and without disabilities) is often viewed as one important way to enhance student growth and learning. As students with disabilities experience being of service to others, they will learn not only that their individual efforts matter, but will better understand themselves within the context of the larger community (Smith, Mavis, & Washenberger, 2001). Regardless of size, every community has volunteering opportunities; often it is just a matter of matching the potential contributions and interests of the student with a particular setting or community need (Amado, 2001).

To summarize, if community inclusion is to be successful, then families, educators, school support staff, and service providers must consider the development of social support networks as part of their primary responsibilities. Supporting social relationships and social networks is considered to be a critical element of inclusive education; therefore, students must have the same variety of social experiences as their peers without disabilities, and when needed, families and educators should facilitate such social networks (Jorgenson, 2002).

In other words, we must all make the shift from viewing students with severe disabilities as merely participating in activities in school and the community to one in which they are actively involved in community groups and associations. In addition, students with severe disabilities must be provided with numerous opportunities to meet people with whom they can develop lasting and meaningful friendships and personal relationships. Students with severe disabilities must also be supported with opportunities to volunteer, provide assistance to others, and make contributions to their community at large. Friendships do not pop up overnight, they require opportunities, support, and ongoing nurture—the way transition services are provided should not hinder this vital part of the human experience.

Conclusion

What does the transition to community mean for students with severe disabilities? To a large extent, a supported adult life mirrors the complexities, challenges, contributions, and fulfillment of any adult life. The added burdens for individuals with severe disabilities, family members, and educators supporting the transition to adulthood are the wide disparity of services, agencies, and funding sources. The maze that must be negotiated is often intense, requiring a new level of knowledge about adult options and often the tenacity to advocate for a new vision of a supported adult life. We need to ask ourselves, "What is the ultimate outcome?" While far from the norm in many communities, the answer to this question lies in the values inherent in a supported adult life. It becomes less about independence and productivity and more about supporting a complex pattern of interwoven perspectives, ideas, and values that shift over time depending upon the ebb and flow of issues, supports, and people present (Ferguson & Ferguson, 2000).

If the transition to a supported adult life is to be successful, educators and families must begin early to plan for a new vision for the future. Using a person-centered planning approach that focuses on transition is a critical first step (cf. Furney, 1999). This process supports families, students, and educators to think about a vision for the future that looks beyond segregated services. A second important piece is to ensure that students have appropriate experiences that directly relate to the vision for supported adulthood. For educators, this means ensuring that the skills being taught are related directly to quality adult outcomes. As we have discussed in this chapter, teaching community-referenced skills can and should occur in a variety of settings, and during the high school years, the majority of these should happen in school with peers without disabilities. In fact, Fisher and Sax (1999) stress that high schools offer opportunities for membership, social interactions, problem solving, communication, interesting curriculum, literacy, work habits, and expectations for high standards; all of which are important aspects of the transition to adult life. Removing students from secondary settings takes away both essential learning opportunities and their circle of friends and support network. Indeed the secondary school years should be the time when educators and families devote considerable attention to supporting community memberships and social networks among peers without disabilities for the student with severe disabilities.

Third, students with severe disabilities must have the opportunities and experiences that lead to the achievement of the outcomes of supported employment, supported living, and community participation and membership. Particularly from the ages of 18 to 21, these experiences should be occurring in a community setting. The commencement model of services described in this chapter offers a new way of actualizing such a vision for the future. Research supports the importance of educational programs in integrated settings that combine high standards with effective, individualized programs and services combined with *extended* school and agency-supported experiences into the post–high school years (Izzo et al., 2000).

The transition to supported adulthood for students with severe disabilities requires educators to reconsider their roles and responsibilities. In essence, educators and family members must learn a new set of skills that promote a new way of thinking about adulthood. It requires developing an understanding of new and innovative programs and practices that facilitate the transition to supported adulthood. It means that educators and families alike must consider their role in supporting and facilitating social networks and community memberships. In essence, educators and families must take on the role of *systems change agent,* which requires:

1. Developing a vision for the future that promotes the transition to supported adulthood.
2. Planning and implementing a systematic curriculum focusing on the skills and experiences that students require to be fully involved in their adult lives.
3. Facilitating social interactions and community membership during the secondary school years and into early adulthood.
4. Developing effective post–high school commencement programs implemented exclusively in the community.
5. Collaborating with agencies and services that are willing to take on new approaches inherent in a supported adult life.
6. Ensuring that families have current and accurate information about new models, programs, funding sources, and services that will support the transition to a quality adult life.

References

Amado, A. N. (1993). Steps for supporting community connections. In A. N. Amado (Ed.), *Friendships and community connections between people with and without developmental disabilities* (pp. 299–326). Baltimore: Paul H. Brookes.

Amado, A. N. (2001). Why bother? People with disabilities benefit as volunteers. *IMPACT, 14*(2), 4–5.

Benz, M. R., Yavonoff, P., & Doren, B. (1997). School-to-work components that predict postschool success for students with and without disabilities. *Exceptional Children, 63,* 151–165.

Blackorby, J., & Wagner, M. (1996). Longitudinal postschool outcomes of youth with disabilities: Findings from the National Longitudinal Transition Study. *Exceptional Children, 62,* 339–413.

Braddock, B., Hemp, R., & Parish, S. (2000). Transforming service delivery systems in the states. In M. L. Wehmeyer & J. R. Patton (Eds.), *Mental retardation in the 21st century* (pp. 359–378). Austin, TX: Pro-Ed.

Browder, D. M., & Bambara, L. M. (2000). Home and community. In M. Snell & F. Brown (Eds.), *Instruction of students with severe disabilities* (5th ed., pp. 543–589). Upper Saddle River, NJ: Merrill/Prentice-Hall.

Cipriano, R. E. (1998, April). Individualized Person-Centered Approach to Therapeutic Recreation Services. *TASH Newsletter, 24*(4), 6–7.

Community integration, employment of people with disabilities and the Olmstead decision. (2002, February). *InfoLines, 13*(1), 1–6.

Dreilinger, D., Gilmore, D. S., & Butterworth, J. (2001, July). National day and employment service trends in MR/DD agencies. *Research to Practice, 7*(3).

Ferguson, P. M., & Ferguson, D. M. (2000). The promise of adulthood. In M. Snell & F. Brown (Eds.), *Instruction of students with severe disabilities* (5th ed., pp. 629–656). Upper Saddle River, NJ: Merrill/Prentice-Hall.

Fesko, S. L., & Butterworth, J. (2001). *Conversion to integrated employment: Case studies of organizational change* (vol. 3). Boston: Institute for Community Inclusion, Children's Hospital, University of Massachusetts.

Fisher, D., & Sax, C. (1999). Noticing differences between secondary and postsecondary education: Extending Agran, Snow, and Swaner's discussion. *Journal of the Association for Persons with Severe Handicaps, 24,* 303–305.

Forest, M., & Pearpoint, J. (1992). Putting all kids on the MAP. *Educational Leadership, 50*(2), 26–31.

Furney, K. S. (1999). *Making dreams happen: How to facilitate the MAPS process.* University of Vermont: Vermont Transition Systems Change Project.

Gallivan-Fenlon, A. (1994). Their senior year: Family and service provider perspectives on the transition from school to adult life for young adults with disabilities. *Journal of the Association for Persons with Severe Handicaps, 19,* 11–23.

Griffin, C., & Targett, P. S. (2001). Finding jobs for young people with disabilities. In P. Wehman (Ed.), *Life beyond the classroom: Transition strategies for young people with disabilities* (3rd ed., pp. 171–210). Baltimore: Paul H. Brookes.

Grigal, M., Neubert, D. A., & Moon, M. S. (2001). Public school programs for students with significant disabilities in post-secondary settings. *Education and Training in Mental Retardation and Developmental Disabilities, 36,* 244–254.

Hagner, D. (2000). Supporting people as part of the community: Possibilities and prospects for change. In J. Nisbet & D. Hagner (Eds.), *Part of the community: Strategies for including everyone* (pp. 15–42). Baltimore: Paul H. Brookes.

Hagner, D., & Vander Sande, J. (1998). School-sponsored work experience and vocational training. In F. R. Rusch & J. G. Chadsey (Eds.), *Beyond high school: Transition from school to work* (pp. 340–366). Belmont, CA: Wadsworth.

Halpern, A. (1992). Transition: New wine in old bottles. *Exceptional Children, 58*(3), 202–211.

Hanley-Maxwell, C., Pogoloff, S. M., & Whitney-Thomas, J. (1998). Families: The heart of transition. In F. Rusch & J. Chadsey (Eds.). *Beyond high school: Transition from school to work* (pp. 234–264). Belmont, CA: Wadsworth.

Hanley-Maxwell, C., Whitney-Thomas, J., & Pogoloff, S. M. (1995). The second shock: A qualitative study of parents' perspectives and needs during their child's transition from school to adult life. *JASH, 30,* 3–15.

Izzo, M. V., Cartledge, C., Miller, L., Growick, B., & Rutkowski, S. (2000). Increasing employment earnings: Extended transition services that make a difference. *Career Development for Exceptional Individuals, 23*(2), 139–156.

Izzo, M. V., Johnson, J. R., Levitz, M., & Aaron, J. H. (1998). Transition from school to adult life: New roles for educators. In P. Wehman & J. Kregel (Eds.), *More than a job: Securing satisfying careers for people with disabilities* (pp. 249–286). Baltimore: Paul H. Brookes.

Johnson, D. R., McGrew, K., Bloomberg, L., Bruinicks, R. H., & Lin, H. C. (1996). Postschool outcomes and community adjustment of young adults with severe disabilities. *Policy Research Brief, 8,* 1–11.

Jorgenson, C. M. (2002). *Essential elements of inclusive educational practices.* Durham: Institute on Disability, University of New Hampshire.

Kiernan W. E. (2000). Where are we now? Perspectives on employment of people with mental retardation. In M. L. Wehmeyer & J. R. Patton (Eds.), *Mental retardation in the 21st century* (pp. 151–164). Austin, TX: Pro-Ed.

Klein, J. (1992). Get me the hell out of here: Supporting people with disabilities to live in their own homes. In J. Nisbet (Ed.), *Natural supports in school, at work, and in the community for people with severe disabilities* (pp. 277–340). Baltimore: Paul H. Brookes.

Klein, J., & Strully, J. L. (2000). From unit D to the community: A dream to fulfill. In M. L. Wehmeyer & J. R. Patton (Eds.). *Mental retardation in the 21st century* (pp. 165–178). Austin, TX: Pro-Ed.

Klein, J., Wilson, B. B., & Nelson, D. (2000). Postcards on the refrigerator: Changing the power dynamic in housing and assistance. In J. Nisbet & D. Hagner (Eds.), *Part of the community: Strategies for including everyone* (pp. 177–201). Baltimore: Paul H. Brookes.

Kranich, K. (Producer), & Erstling, M. (Director). (1996). *Lifelink: A transition lab* (videotape). Available from Pennsylvania State University, 118 Wagner Building, University Park, PA 16802, 800-770-2111.

Lakin, K. C., & Larson, S. A. (1992). Satisfaction and stability of direct care personnel in community-based residential services. In J. W. Jacobson & S. N. Burchard (Eds.), *Community living for people with developmental and psychiatric disabilities* (pp. 244–262). Baltimore: Johns Hopkins University Press.

Luecking, R. G., & Fabian, E. S. (2000). Paid internships and employment success for youth in transition. *Career Development for Exceptional Individuals, 23,* 205–222.

Lutfiyya, Z. M. (2001, October). Personal relationships between people with and without disabilities. *TASH Newsletter, 27*(10), 25–26.

McGaughey, M., Kiernan, W., McNally, L., Gilmore, D., & Keith, G. (1995). Beyond the workshop: National trends in integrated and segregated day and employment services. *Journal of the Association for Persons with Severe Handicaps, 20,* 270–285.

McKenzie, D., & Wildgen, L. (1999, April). *C-tran: How it got started and where we are now.* Presentation at the 1999 Kansas Transition Council Leadership Conference, Topeka.

Metzel, D. (2001). The extent of consumer-directed funding by MR/DD state agencies in day and employment services. *Research to Practice, 7,* 6.

Moon, M. S., & Inge, K. (2000). Vocational preparation and transition. In M. Snell & F. Brown (Eds.), *Instruction of students with severe disabilities* (5th ed., pp. 591–628). Upper Saddle River, NJ: Merrill/Prentice-Hall.

Morningstar, M. E., Kleinhammer-Tramill, P. J., & Lattin, D. L. (1999, May). Using successful models of student-centered transition planning and services for adolescents with disabilities. *Focus on Exceptional Children, 31,* 1–19.

Morningstar, M. E., & Muta, K. (in press). Transitions to adulthood for youth with disabilities. In F. E. Obiakor, C. A. Utley, & A. Rotatori (Eds.), *Psychology of effective education for learners with exceptionalities. Advances in Special Education* (vol. 15). Stamford, CT: JAI Press.

Morningstar, M. E., Turnbull, H. R., Lattin, D. L., Umbarger, G. T., Reichard, A., & Moberly, R. L. (2001). Students supported by medical technology: Making the transition from school to adult life. *Journal of Developmental and Physical Disabilities, 13,* 229–260.

Moseley, C., & Nerney, T. (2000, July). Emerging best practice in self-determination. *Common Sense, 7.* National Program Office on Self-Determination. Retrieved from *http://www.self-determination.org/newsletter1249/pdf/july2000.pdf*

Nerney, T., & Shumway, D. (1996). *Beyond managed care: Self-determination for people with disabilities.* Concord: Institute on Disability/UAP, University of New Hampshire.

Nisbet, J. (Ed.) (1992). *Natural supports in school, at work, and in the community for people with severe disabilities.* Baltimore: Paul H. Brookes.

O'Brien, C., Mount, B., O'Brien, J., & Rosen, F. (2001). *Pathfinders: Making a way from segregation to community life.* Lithonia, GA: Responsive Systems Associates.

O'Brien, J., & Lyle O'Brien, C. (1992). Members of each other: Perspectives on social support for people with severe disabilities. In J. Nisbet (Ed.), *Natural supports in school, at work, and in the community for people with severe disabilities* (pp. 17–63). Baltimore: Paul H. Brookes.

Peraino, J. M. (1993). Post-21 follow-up studies: How do special education graduates fare? In P. Wehman, *Life beyond the classroom: Transition strategies for youth people with disabilities* (pp. 21–70). Baltimore: Paul H. Brookes.

Prouty, R. W., Smith, J., & Lakin, C. (Eds.). (2001). *Residential services for persons with developmental disabilities: Status and trends through 1998.* Minneapolis: University of Minnesota, Research and Training Center on Community Living, Institute on Community Integration.

Schuh, M. C., Tashie, C., Lamb, P., Bang, M., & Jorgensen, C. M. (1998). Community-based learning for all students. In C. M. Jorgensen (Ed.), *Restructuring high schools for all students: Taking inclusion to the next level* (pp. 209–231). Baltimore: Paul H. Brookes.

Shoultz, B., & Lakin, K. C. (Fall, 2001). Volunteer and service opportunities for people with developmental disabilities. *IMPACT, 14,* 2–3.

Simon, M., Cobb, B., Halloran, W. D., Norman, M., & Bourexis, P. (1994). *Meeting the needs of youth with disabilities: Handbook for implementing community-based vocational educational programs according to the Fair Labor Standards Act.* Minneapolis: University of Minnesota, National Transition Network.

Smith, J. G., Mavis, A. L., & Washenberger, J. (Fall, 2001). Preparing youth with disabilities for volunteer service as adults. *IMPACT, 14,* 10–11.

Snow, J. (2001, June). *Personal assistance: What it is and what it is not.* Retrieved February 13, 2002, from the National Program Office on Self-Determination website: *http://www.self-determination.org/publications1251/personal_assist.html*

Sowers, J., Glang, A. E., Voss, J., & Cooley, E. (1996). Enhancing friendships and leisure involvement of students with traumatic brain injuries and other disabilities. In L. E. Powers, G. H. S. Singer, & J. Sowers (Eds.), *On the road to autonomy: Promoting self-competence in children and youth with disabilities* (pp. 347–371). Baltimore: Paul H. Brookes.

Sowers, J. A., McAllister, R., & Cotton, P. (1996). Strategies to enhance control of the employment process by individuals with severe disabilities. In L. E. Powers, G. H. S. Singer, & J. A. Sowers (Eds.), *On the road to autonomy: Promoting self-competence in children and youth with disabilities* (pp. 325–346). Baltimore: Paul H. Brookes.

Sowers, J., Milliken, K., Cotton, P., Sousa, S., Dwyer, L., & Kouwenhoven, K. (2000). A multi-element approach to creating change in a state employment system. In J. Nisbet & D. Hagner (Eds.), *Part of the community: Strategies for including everyone* (pp. 203–236). Baltimore: Paul H. Brookes.

Stinemen, R. M., Morningstar, M. E., Bishop, B., & Turnbull, H. R. (1993). Role of families in transition planning for young adults with disabilities: Toward a method of person-centered planning. *Journal of Vocational Rehabilitation, 3,* 52–61.

Taylor, S. J. (2001). The continuum and current controversies in the USA. *Journal of Intellectual & Developmental Disabilities, 26,* 15–33.

Turnbull, A. P., & Turnbull, H. R. (1999). Comprehensive lifestyle support for adults with challenging behavior: From rhetoric to reality. *Education and Training in Mental Retardation and Developmental Disabilities, 34,* 373–394.

Walker, P. (1999). From community presence to sense of place: Community experiences of adults with developmental disabilities. *Journal of the Association for Persons with Severe Handicaps, 24,* 23–32.

Wehman, P., Bricout, J., & Kregel, J. (2000). Supported employment in 2000: Changing the locus of control from agency to consumer. In M. L. Wehmeyer & J. R. Patton (Eds.), *Mental retardation in the 21st century* (pp. 115–150). Austin, TX: Pro-Ed.

Westling, D. L., & Fox, L. (2000). Teaching students with severe disabilities (2nd ed.). Upper Saddle River, NJ: Merrill.

Will, M. (1984). *OSERS programming for the transition of youth with disabilities: Bridges from school to working life.* Washington, DC: U.S. Department of Education.

AUTHOR INDEX

SUBJECT INDEX